sexuation

SIC

A
series
edited
by
Slavoj
Žižek
and
Renata
Salecl

SIC stands for psychoanalytic interpretation at its most elementary: no discovery of deep, hidden meaning, just the act of drawing attention to the litterality [*sic!*] of what precedes it. A "*sic*" reminds us that what was said, inclusive of its blunders, was effectively said and cannot be undone. The series SIC thus explores different connections of the Freudian field: each volume provides a bundle of Lacanian interventions into a specific domain of ongoing theoretical, cultural, and ideologico-political battles. It is neither "pluralist" nor "socially sensitive": unabashedly avowing its exclusive Lacanian orientation, it disregards any form of correctness but the inherent correctness of theory itself.

sexuation

Renata Salecl,
editor

sic **3**

DUKE UNIVERSITY PRESS   Durham and London 2000

© 2000 Duke University Press

All rights reserved

Printed in the United States

of America on acid-free paper ∞

Typeset in Sabon by Tseng

Information Systems, Inc.

Library of Congress Cataloging-in-

Publication Data appear on the

last printed page of this book.

Contents

Renata Salecl | **Introduction**

Sexual difference seems today a slightly outdated topic. Is not the lesson of the postmodern political practices and of deconstructionist theory, as well as of modern digital media, that male and female sexual identities in these arenas are socially constructed and/or even performatively enacted? Sexual identity is thus, according to these perspectives, the result of complex discursive practices and of the interplay of power relations: what has been constructed in concrete historical constellations can also be deconstructed and radically changed. The only serious alternative to this notion that we are passing from the patriarchal era of fixed, naturalized identities to a new era in which our sexual identities and orientation are more and more becoming something fluid and dispersed, a matter of playful choices, is the New Age Jungian resexualization of the universe ("men are from Mars, women are from Venus"). According to it, there is an underlying, deeply anchored archetypal identity which provides a kind of safe haven in the flurry of contemporary confusion of roles and identities; from this perspective, the ultimate origin of today's crisis is not the difficulty of overcoming the tradition of fixed sexual roles, but the disturbed balance in modern man, who places excessive emphasis on the male-rational-conscious aspect, neglecting the feminine-compassionate aspect.

But is this choice between social constructivism and New Age obscurantism really all embracing? Does not Lacan's paradoxical statement that "there is no such thing as a sexual relationship" point in a wholly different direction? For Lacan, sexual difference is not a firm set of "static" symbolic oppositions and inclusions or exclusions (heterosexual normativity that relegates homosexuality and other "perversions" to some secondary role), but the name of a deadlock, of a trauma, of an open question, of something that *resists* every attempt at its symbolization. Every translation of sexual difference into a set of symbolic opposition(s) is doomed to fail, and it is this very "impossibility" that opens up the terrain of the hegemonic struggle for what "sexual difference" will mean. The reassertion of sexual difference in Lacanian psychoanalysis is thus not a return to biology but a way to stress that what we call "sexual difference" is first and above all the name for a certain fundamental *deadlock* inherent in the symbolic order. Lacan's "formulas of sexuation" provide the logical matrix of this deadlock.

The four parts of the present volume elaborate different aspects of this deadlock of sexual difference. Part I, "Sexual Difference," renders the fundamentals of Lacan's teaching on sexual difference: Jacques-Alain Miller examines the role of semblances in the relation between the sexes; Geneviève Morel shows how, for psychoanalysis, sexual difference is not a question of anatomy but concerns the impasse of the real; and Colette Soler points out the difference between sexuation and identification. Part II, "Paternal Prohibition," focuses on the role of the symbolic prohibition in the process of the subject's sexual formation: Eric L. Santner's reading of the Freudian myth in *Moses and Monotheism* unravels the transgressive violence constitutive of the order of Law itself; Darian Leader provides a Lacanian account of Freud's essay "A Child Is Being Beaten"; and Paul Verhaeghe examines the changed role of the father in today's society and the impact this change has on the sexual difference. Part III, "Feminine Exception," deals with the specificity of the feminine sexual position: Geneviève Morel takes various literary examples to analyze *jouissance* at work in feminine jealousy: Elisabeth Bronfen discerns in Wagner's *Tristan und Isolde* the contours of the noir universe; and Slavoj Žižek examines the role of the maternal Thing in the science fiction universe, exemplarily in the masterpieces of Andrei Tarkovsky. Part IV, "Love," questions how love supplements the fact that "there is no such thing as a sexual relationship": Alain Badiou offers a philosophical explanation of the difference between love and desire; Alenka Zupančič analyzes the issue of love with regard to the difference between phallic and feminine *jouissance;* and Renata Salecl questions whether women and men who often double their partner into an "official" spouse and an inaccessible lover do this in a different way.

Since all the texts in the present volume refer to a basic set of Lacanian concepts without fully explaining them, it would be helpful to add here a brief attempt at their clarification. Perhaps the best way to begin is with *le grand Autre* (the "big Other"), Lacan's designation for the symbolic order—not only the order of language in the narrow linguistic sense, but the entire cobweb of symbolic relations that form the "substance" of our social being. The Lacanian "big Other" is not confined to the explicit symbolic rules regulating social interaction; it also includes the intricate net of *unwritten* "implicit" rules. Roger Ebert's hilarious *Little Book of Hollywood Cliches*[1] contains hundreds of stereotypes and obligatory scenes, from the famous "Fruit Cart!" rule (during any chase scene involving a foreign or ethnic locale, a fruit cart will be overturned, and an angry peddler will run into the middle of the street to shake a fist at the hero's departing vehicle) to more refined cases of the "Thanks, but No Thanks" rule (when two people have just had a heart-to-heart conversation, as Person A starts to leave room, Person B says tentatively, "Bob? [or whatever A's name is]" A pauses, turns, and says, "Yes?" B then says, "Thanks") or the "Grocery Bag" rule (whenever a scared, cynical woman who does not want to fall in love again is pursued by a suitor who wants to tear down her wall of loneliness, she will go grocery shopping; the bags will then always break and the fruits and vegetables spill out, either to symbolize the mess her life is in or so the suitor can help pick up the pieces of her life, not only her oranges and apples). This is what the "big Other" *qua* the symbolic substance of our lives is: a set of unwritten rules that effectively regulate our actions. In the multitude of meanings the "big Other" has in Lacanian theory, at least one more should be mentioned: the guarantee of Truth, the invisible witness to which we address our speech beyond the face-to-face interlocutors with whom we interact. This witness can also be again embodied in a single person—an example is a strange, apparently "irrational" feature of the majority of James Bond films, in which, after capturing Bond, the Big Criminal, instead of killing him immediately, keeps him alive and even gives him a kind of quick inspection tour of his enterprise, explaining the big coup he is planning to execute in the next hour—it is, of course, this very need for a witness to whom the operation should be explained that costs the Big Criminal dearly: this delay gives Bond the chance to spot a weakness in his enemy and to strike back at the last minute (or sometimes even second).

So why does Lacan sometimes write the big A as barred, crossed out? In order to emphasize that the symbolic order is circular, inconsistent, lacking any ultimate foundation (two of Lacan's further statements make the same point: "there is no Other of Other," and "there is no metalanguage"). For that reason, the so-called Master Signifier, the ultimate point of reference that seems to guarantee the consistency of a given symbolic field, is, as Lacan puts it, a "signifier without signified," a stand-in for the lack in the midst of the big Other. This is why Lacan claims that the meaning of this empty Master Signifier is the "imaginary" number (the square root of -1): the paradox of the square root of -1 is that it is an "impossible" number whose value cannot ever be positive, but which nonetheless "functions"—as when, apropos of some notion, we enthusiastically feel that "this is *it,* the true thing, the true meaning," although we are never able to explicate *what,* precisely, this meaning *is.* In a political discourse, the Master Signifier (Our Nation) is this kind of empty signifier which stands for the impossible fullness of meaning, that is, its meaning is "imaginary" in the sense that its content is impossible to positivize—when you ask a member of the Nation to define in what the identity of his Nation consists, his ultimate answer will always be, "I cannot say it, you must feel it, it is *it,* that's what our lives are really about." This is how Lacan grounds the distinction between the series of "ordinary" signifiers (S_2) and the exceptional Master Signifier (S_1): if a field of signifiers is to retain the semblance of consistency, if this field is to be "totalized," there has to be an additional or extra signifier that as it were gives a positive figure to that which cannot be properly included in this field, somewhat like Spinoza's well-known criticism of the traditional personalized notion of God: at the point at which our positive knowledge of the causal links fails, we supplement this lack with the idea of "God," which, instead of providing a precise idea of a cause, just fills in the lack of this idea.

Strictly correlative to the inconsistency of the big Other (the symbolic order) is the infamous *objet petit a* ("object small a"). The ultimate function of the "small other" is precisely to act as a "filler," to fill in the void or lack in the big Other. In the symbolic order *objet petit a* stands for the mysterious object that sets in motion our desiring capacity precisely insofar as it forever eludes symbolization. In a first approach, one can determine it as that elusive X on account of which we desire a certain thing, but which cannot ever be reduced to a simple, positive property of this thing, like the famous statement of the lover to the beloved: "There is something in you, a certain magic *je ne sais quoi*, that makes you irresistibly attractive to me, that shines through all your real properties, although I do not known what this X effectively is." This elusive X— not the desired object itself, but the feature *on account of which* we desire the desired object—can nonetheless sometimes be materialized in certain features or even persons.[2] Henry Krips[3] evokes the lovely example of the chaperone in seduction: the chaperone is an ugly elderly lady who is officially the obstacle to the direct goal-object (the woman the suitor is courting), but precisely as such, she is the key intermediary moment that effectively makes the beloved woman desirable—without her, the whole economy would collapse. (And does not the same often go for the parents themselves? Recall the proverbial suitor who, in order to impress the future bride's father, engages with him in such intense conversation that, at a certain point, the poor girl explodes: "Where am I in all this? I feel like a disturbing element—why do not the two of you just go along and forget about me?") Or take another example from a different level: the curl of blond hair, this fatal detail of Madeleine's in Hitchcock's *Vertigo*.[4] When, in the love scene in the barn toward the end of the film, Scottie passionately embraces Judy refashioned into the dead Madeleine during their famous 360-degree kiss, he stops kissing her and withdraws just long enough to steal a look at her newly blond hair, as if to reassure himself that the particular feature that makes her the object of desire is still there. It is thus crucial to distinguish between *objet a*, the *cause* of desire, and the *object* of desire.

All we have to do now, in order to get all four elementary Lacanian "mathems," is to add to the triad of S_1, S_2, and *small a* a fourth term, the *subject* itself, written by Lacan as $, the "barred," crossed-out subject— why? The point is not only that the Lacanian subject as the subject of desire is by definition and constitutively "lacking" its object, the object that would bring about full satisfaction and thus suffocate desire; the point is also not only that the subject is "barred" in the sense of being subjected to and determined by the anonymous symbolic order, that all content (his desires, fantasies) are provided by this Other, that the subject is spoken rather than speaking. Lacan's point is here much more radical: the lacking object is ultimately *the subject itself,* that is, the lack is the lack of the subject's *being,* which is why for Lacan, the subject is characterized by a fundamental "lack of being" [*manque-à-être*]. This thesis, according to which the subject is not a firm substantial entity but the pure void of negativity, is to be understood not only in its standard philosophical sense (articulated from the tradition of German idealism up to Sartre), but also in a very palpable *clinical* sense: for Lacan, the question that defines the hysterical stance is precisely, "What kind of an object am I for the Other, for his desire? What, if anything, does he see in me that is worthy of his desire?" And, furthermore, from this example of the hysterical question, we can also see how the three concepts with which we were dealing—the inconsistent big Other, the small other, and the barred subject—interlock: the inconsistency of the big Other, the symbolic order, ultimately means that there is no signifier that would adequately represent the subject, that is, that the subject—the human being whose universe is that of speech, a *parlêtre,* as Lacan puts it—forever lacks a firm hold in the other order of symbolic existence; and the ultimate function of the *objet petit a* as the object of fantasy is precisely to supplement, fill in, this symbolic lack, to provide a fragile, temporary semblance of being for the subject. This is what Lacan's formula of the fantasy ($ \$ \Diamond a $) aims at: a phantasmatic object correlative to the subject's lack of being.

The psychoanalytic name of this lack is (symbolic) castration, the loss incurred by the human animal's entry into the symbolic order. For Lacan, who here follows Freud, the signifier of this lack is *phallus*—not phallus as an organ (penis), but the phallic *signifier.* Here, however, the reproach of Lacan's "phallocentrism" immediately emerges. While this is not the place to elucidate this point, a couple of clarifications may be appropriate here. First, it is crucial to maintain the distinction between phallus as *signified* (the "meaning of phallus") and the phallic *signifier,* or, in Lacan's mathems, the small *phi* (ϕ) from the capital *Phi* (Φ): the phallic signified is, of course, phallus as the symbol of virility, penetrating power, the force of fertility and insemination, and so on, while the phallus as signifier stands for the much more obscure and traumatic reverse of this meaning, for the price the subject has to pay if he is to assume the "meaning of phallus." In this sense, the phallic signifier and symbolic castration are not opposed, but coincide: the phallic signifier *is* the direct signifier or operator of the symbolic castration. That is to say, against the standard notion of phallus as the siege of "natural" male penetration–aggressive potency–power (to which one then opposes the "artificial," playful, prosthetic phallus), the point of Lacan's concept of phallus as a *signifier* is that phallus "as such" *is* a kind of "prosthetic," "artificial" supplement: it designates the point at which the big Other, a decentered agency, supplements the subject's failure. When, in her criticism of Lacan, Judith Butler emphasizes the parallel between the subject's idealized mirror image (ideal ego) and phallic signifier,[5] one should shift the focus to the feature they effectively share: both mirror image and phallus *qua* signifier are "prosthetic" supplements for the subject's foregoing dispersal or failure, for the lack of coordination and unity: in both cases, the status of this prosthesis is "illusory," the difference being that in the first, we are dealing with imaginary illusion (identification with a decentered immobile image), while in the second, the illusion is symbolic—it stands for phallus as pure semblance. The opposition between "true," "natural" phallus and the "artificial," prosthetic supplement ("dildo") is thus false and misleading: phallus *qua* signifier is already "in itself" a prosthetic supplement.

To put it in yet another way, the feature that distinguishes symbolic from the "real" castration is its *virtual* character. That is to say, Freud's notion of castration anxiety has meaning only if we suppose that just *the threat of castration* (the prospect of castration, the "virtual" castration) *produces real "castrating" effects*. This actuality of the virtual, which defines symbolic as opposed to real castration, has to be connected to the basic paradox of power, which is that symbolic power is by definition virtual, the power in reserve, the threat of its full use which never actually occurs (when a father loses his nerve and explodes, this is by definition a sign of his *impotence*, painful as it may be). The consequence of this conflation of actual with virtual is a kind of transubstantiation: every actual activity is a "form of appearance" of another invisible power, whose status is purely virtual—the real penis turns into the form of appearance of (the virtual) phallus, and so on. Therein resides the paradox of castration: whatever a man does in reality, with his real penis, is just redoubling, following as a shadow, another virtual penis whose existence is purely symbolic—that is, phallus as a signifier. Let us recall the example of a judge who in his real life is a weak and corrupt person, but the moment he puts on the insignia of his symbolic mandate, the big Other of the symbolic institution speaks through him: without the prosthesis of his symbolic title, his real power would instantly disintegrate. And Lacan's point apropos of the phallus as a signifier is that the same "institutional" logic is at work even in the most intimate domain of male sexuality: in the same way that a judge needs his symbolic crutches, his insignia, in order to exert his authority, a man needs a reference to the absent or virtual phallus for his penis to exert its potency.

If, then, castration is something that characterizes human subjectivity as such, is it nonetheless "sexed" in the sense that it affects the two sexes in a different way? Lacan's "yes" is elaborated in the so-called formulas of sexuation from his *Seminar* book 20, *Encore*.[6] The idea is that man and woman do not relate in the same way to this symbolic castration, to the lack incurred by the assumption of the phallic signifier: it is "all" of man that is subsumed under this phallic function, while "not-all" of the woman is subsumed under it. And here, again, a key misreading is to be avoided: Lacan's point is not simply that man is wholly, without remainder, integrated into the symbolic order, while woman is integrated only partially, with some part of her resisting the symbolic power. Rather, Lacan reads each of these two positions as the paradoxical connection of two opposite features: it is precisely because "all" of man is integrated into the symbolic order that there is an exception constitutive of this universality, and, on the other hand, it is precisely because woman's relationship to the symbolic order is characterized by a "not-all" that there is no exception, nothing in her which is *not* caught in the symbolic order, no ineffable feminine secret. This very position of the Woman as exception (say, in the guise of the lady in courtly love) is a masculine fantasy par excellence. As the exemplary case of the exception constitutive of the phallic function, one usually mentions the phantasmatic obscene figure of the primordial father-*jouisseur* who was not encumbered by any prohibition and was as such able fully to enjoy all women: all fathers are bearers of symbolic authority, embodiments of the castrative Law, with the exception of the primordial father killed by the united sons in the mytical crime that founded civilization. But does not the figure of the lady in courtly love fully fit these determinations of the primordial father? Is she not a capricious master who "wants it all," that is, who, herself not bound by any law, charges her knight-servant with arbitrary and outrageous ordeals? In this precise sense, Woman is "one of the names of the father," as Lacan put it. The crucial detail not to be missed here is the use of plural and the lack of capital letters: not "Name-of-the-Father," but "one of the names of the father"—one of the nominations of the excess called "primordial father." In the case of Woman—the mythical "She," the Queen from Rider Haggard's novel of the same name, for example—as well as in the case of the primordial father, we are dealing with an agency of power that is presymbolic, unbridled by the law of castration.[7]

Is this account of sexual difference (neither as a biological fact nor as a specific cultural formation, but as the articulation of a certain deadlock that pertains to the most elementary relationship between the human animal and the symbolic order) a tool that effectively enables us to approach in a new and productive way a set of contemporary problems, from the dilemmas of feminism to transformations in the functioning of power in our "postmodern" era? The present volume is an attempt to answer this question in an affirmative way.

Notes

1 See Roger Ebert, *The Little Book of Hollywood Cliches* (London: Virgin, 1995). I owe some of the examples used in this brief clarification to Slavoj Žižek.

2 See Renata Salecl, *(Per)versions of Love and Hate* (London: Verso, 1998).

3 See Henry Krips, *Fetish: An Erotics of Culture* (Ithaca: Cornell University Press, 1999).

4 I thank Mark Cousins for this observation.

5 See chap. 2 of Judith Butler, *Bodies That Matter* (New York: Routledge, 1993).

6 See *The Seminar of Jacques Lacan,* book 20: *Encore,* ed. Jacques-Alain Miller, trans. Bruce Fink (New York: W. W. Norton, 1998).

7 For the best accounts of these formulas of sexuation in English, see Bruce Fink, *The Lacanian Subject: Between Language and Jouissance* (Princeton: Princeton University Press, 1995); and Joan Copjec, *Read My Desire: Lacan Against Historicism* (Cambridge, Mass.: MIT Press, 1994).

PART I **sexual
difference**

1

On Semblances

in the Relation

Jacques-Alain Miller | **Between the Sexes**

Once again, we are back to semblances, this time their role in the relation between the sexes. Where do men stand on this point? Perhaps they are more captivated by semblances than women are, and perhaps women are closer to the real, so that if we speak of "women and semblances," it is men who are in the role of the semblance.

The Race of Women

It appears that Hesiod was the first to speak of "the race of women" [*genos gynaicon*] in his *Theogony,* source of many myths. And after Hesiod, in the literature of Greek antiquity, women are referred to as *ikelon,* which means "semblance" or "copy"; *dolos,* which means "ruse"; and *pema,* which means "calamity." This shows that the calumny against women began a very long time ago.

Semonides, from the aptly named city of Amorgos, had already composed a poem entitled *Iambe,* in which he speaks not of a *genos gynaicon,* but rather of the "tribes of women." In this poem, which was recently reprinted in England, he draws up a list of women. This poem is a catalog—written, of course, without prior knowledge of Mozart's *Don Giovanni*—that lists different types of women, which he calls *phyla* rather than *genos.* The first word of his poem is *koris,* which is translated as "aside," but since Lacan, we realize that it should be understood to connote not unity but diversity. This is the word with which Semonides starts his poem.

Among other things, I want to take the risk of proposing another type of woman for this catalog, a type we shall encounter throughout this essay.

The citations we have mentioned lead us to think that Lacan's statement—Woman does not exist, there are only women—is something that has been known for a while now, at least since the Greeks. Today, Lacan's formula is known well enough for us to use it as our point of departure.

The fact that Woman does not exist does not mean that the place of woman does not exist, but rather that this place remains essentially empty. The fact that this place remains empty does not mean that we cannot find something there. But in it, we find only masks, masks of nothingness, which are sufficient to justify the connection between women and semblances.

Nothingness, Shyness, and Respect

What is a semblance? A semblance is something whose function is to mask nothingness. As such, the veil is the first semblance. As history and anthropology reveal, men have been consistently preoccupied with the veiling or covering of women. We no doubt cover women up because we cannot discover Woman. So, we can only invent her.

In this sense, we call subjects who have an essential relation to nothingness "women." I employ this formulation with some trepidation, because every subject, according to Lacan's definition, has a relation to nothingness; but the relation of female subjects is more essential and more immediate.

Freud theorized women's relation to nothingness on the basis of physical, anatomical nothingness. In a 1932 article, he enumerates some psychical consequences of feminine maturation, like shyness, which he explains as being initially the intention to veil the absence of the genital organ.

There is therefore a paradox in shyness. According to Freud, it simultaneously veils absence and constitutes this absence as something. In other words, the act of veiling creates, gives rise to, brings out.

Historical variations in shyness show that it is an invention which, by its localization, attracts the gaze. One could also say that it phallicizes the body. There is no shortage of assertions by men, both in literature and in psychoanalytical cases, in which shyness appears in its phallic value. The veil of shyness can actually impart the value of the phallus, to use Freud's terminology, to any part of the body; here we see that the use of the veil is phallicizing.

There is very little distance between shyness and respect. Respect means that something must not be seen or touched. Like shyness, it is related to castration. Could it be that respect is always respect for castration, that a demand for respect always involves respect for the distance of the father? What is respected in the father, if not what Lacan called the father's former capacity as a warrior? When there is respect, nothingness is always at stake, and, correlatively, offenses—which makes us understand that being offensive can take on an erotic value.

In analytic circles, we sometimes see what Lacan would call a delirious respect, a stringent demand for respect on the part of older people or of people who have positioned themselves as such. This has something to do with the fact that the analyst does not exist. It is because the analyst does not exist that sensitivities around the issue of respect take on a role that might be considered excessive in the functioning of a psychoanalytical milieu, even if it is a school.

Toward a Clinical Understanding of Femininity

It seems that Freud, unlike Lacan, limited himself to an anatomical conception of the feminine difference and considered women indeed to be marked by a lack; in other words, feminine castration was considered complete. But even if we admit the fact of this lack, the question of its subjectivation remains—that is to say, what significance this not-having acquires for the subject. Freud proposed the concept of penis envy [*Penisneid*], his term for not-having.

This opens the way for what we could call a clinical understanding of femininity, or a "clinic for the feminine." Without claiming to exhaust the subject, we can speak of a clinic for the feminine as a direct conceptualization of this lack. We could speak, for example, of the space taken up by the feeling of injustice, a theme that often takes up entire sessions of analysis. We could even speak of a fundamental fantasy of injustice. We could say—and no doubt this would be amusing—that the origin of the concept of justice is to be found in women's complaints. We could also speak of the extent, frequency, and constancy of a feeling of underappreciation that is linked to something which we could roughly place in the domain of an inferiority complex. The clinical study of inhibition, for example, shows very different characteristics in men and women. This is not only an inhibition in relation to knowledge or intellectual pursuits, but frequently there is also a deep-seated sense of not having the right to knowledge, in other words, a feeling of illegitimacy, which is not found to the same degree among men in analysis.

Freud focuses on the compensations the subject discovers—or invents—for this fundamental lack to which the subject is linked. To do this, he pushes his analytical investigation toward the possessions that can succeed in filling the hole in the lack. He puts the emphasis on obtaining and possessing down to an attempt to achieve this end. And in fact, Lacan loved to point out the appellation *bourgeoise* given to the wife in popular French parlance, as in *ma bourgeoise* (my wife). This indicates that she is the one who is in charge of the family finances.

Freud also placed the child in this series, and to a certain extent maternity itself can be considered part of feminine pathology. To become a mother, to become the Other of demand, is to become "she who has" par excellence.

The question remains open. Is the solution to the feminine position to become a mother? It is a solution on the side of "having," and it is not certain if Freud conceived of any other kind of solution for women.

There is, however, another solution, or another register of solution, which is that of "being." This solution consists not in filling the hole, but rather in metabolizing it, dialectizing it, and in being this hole, that is to say, in making oneself a being with nothingness. This opens up a whole new clinic of the feminine, a clinic of the lack of identity, which is not experienced as intensely in men as in women. And so we must speak of a being of nothingness and of the pain specific to this being of nothingness. In addition to the lack of identity, there is a lack of consistency, which can be observed in testimonies to a feeling of corporeal fragmentation. This can go so far that we label it psychosis and give it a different diagnosis. This is also where we would situate lack of control, the affect that makes the subject feel that control of the body is not available to it. In treating women, we also encounter testimonies to a psychic pain linked to an affect of nonbeing, of being nothing, of moments of absence from oneself. There are also testimonies of a strange relation with the infinite, which can present itself on the level of something unfinished—in other words, of a feeling of radical incompleteness.

Here we encounter the solution that consists of being this hole, but in relation to the Other, as if one solution for escaping from this identity defect were to displace it onto the Other by attacking the Other's completeness. This consists both in a belief that the Other, the virile Other, is missing a hole, and in an attempt to embody this hole. Lacan's expression "being the phallus" corresponds to this variation of being the hole in the Other by giving it a positive form. One must note that the expression "being the phallus" implies a certain depreciation of the virile Other's having, a reduction of the Other's having to a semblance.

The Act of a "True" Woman

Lacan does not only say that Woman does not exist; he also says that there are true women, which is puzzling. It is not that we fail to understand that woman and truth could have something to do with one another, since truth is distinct from knowledge; truth has the structure of fiction and so depends on semblances. We also understand that women can be localized as the truth of a man, inasmuch as they reduce masculine sublimations to lies and embody—because Woman does not exist—the shortcomings of his self-conception.

What is a true woman? There is a simple answer. The truth in a woman, in Lacan's sense, is measured by her subjective distance from the position of motherhood. To be a mother, the mother of one's children, is to choose to exist as Woman. To exist as Mother is to exist as Woman inasmuch as she now has.

Under what conditions does Lacan say "there's a true woman"? On the one hand, one should always use the expression "there is a true woman," because we are not constructing the concept of the True Woman. The True Woman can only be invoked case by case, and only at a particular moment, because it is not certain that a woman can remain in the position of a True Woman. This can only be expressed as *tuché*. One can only say "she is a true woman" in a jolt of surprise, out of either wonder or horror, and perhaps only when one realizes that the mother has not visibly or palpably filled the hole in her. It is linked to the sacrifice of possessions, and perhaps a woman merits being called a "true woman" just when she has consented to the precise modality of her castration. Thus I am afraid that I cannot offer a model of a sufficiently good mother, as Winnicott does, or of a supportive wife.

On the other hand, I would like to follow a remark made by Lacan and say something about a figure who could serve as a model of a true woman, even if the example is somewhat extreme and not one with which to identify. Lacan analyzes her much more discreetly than I do, but so much time has passed since Lacan's death that I feel that now is the time to discuss Medea once more.

Medea has done everything for her man, Jason. She has betrayed her father and her country and convinced Pelias's daughters to kill him, and for that reason she lives in exile in Corinth with her husband and children. This is all made clear at the beginning of Euripides' play, where it is explicitly stated that she has tried hard to consent to Jason's every desire. They have had no disagreements; she has been the perfect wife and mother. She has had some criminal tendencies, she has been a bit of a witch, but as a wife and mother, she has been perfect. And then Jason announces that he wants to marry someone else—Creon's daughter. As Medea says, this is an enormous offense. And she has what we would now call a bout of depression. In her own words, she has lost her love for life, she cries all the time, and we hear her say these beautiful words: "Of all living things which are living and can form a judgment / We women are the most unfortunate creatures."[1]

Jason comes to her with his fine words to explain and to reassure her of his good intentions: he will not neglect his children, and he will pay all her bills. She refuses these offers. As she says explicitly, she is already in a place where "having" has no meaning if Jason is not there.

How does she plan to avenge herself? She does not kill the unfaithful Jason. That would be too simple. Her vengeance consists in killing his most precious possessions: Jason's new bride and her own children by Jason. Euripides underscores the value of this extreme act in that he presents Medea as a mother who deeply loves her children. She speaks lovingly of her children, what they are, what she hopes for them; he describes how she stays with them until they die, and how she accompanies them into what will be their tomb. But now she is prepared to kill them and—in a most horrific piece of theater—does so. She kills her and Jason's children. This is where the woman takes precedence over the mother. She is not to be emulated, but this is a radical example of what it means to be a woman beyond being a mother. Through this act, she emerges from her depression. Her whole self is in the act. After this moment, all words are useless, and she exits once and for all from the register, or the reign, of the signifier.

Here we have to note, even if I will not develop the point, something that is very much present in the play: Medea's knowledge. The word *episteme* fits her well. Lacan refers to some lines in Euripides where Medea appears in the role of sage, of someone who knows things, in a way that echoes the role of the analyst. In fact, the lines that Lacan quotes do not refer to Medea's crime; they are her words to Creon: "If you put new ideas before the eyes of fools / They'll think you foolish and worthless in the bargain; / And if you are thought superior to those who have / Some reputation for learning, you will become hated."[2]

For Lacan, the act of a true woman is not necessarily as extreme as Medea's, but it has the same structure, in that she sacrifices what is most precious to her in order to pierce man with a hole that can never be filled. This is certainly something that surpasses all laws and all human affections, but not because it is played out superficially, as Goethe believed. A true woman explores an unfamiliar zone, oversteps all boundaries, and if Medea offers us an example of what is bewildering about a true woman, it is because she is exploring uncharted territory, beyond all limits.

One must also emphasize that she acts with less rather than more. At the heart of a situation where she appears to be defenseless, she finds a mortal weapon. It is in doing less that she finds her true weapon, one which is stronger and more effective than any other. We must also add that she does so for a man, in the well-defined context of her relationship to a man.

Lacan thought he recognized Medea's act in what Gide's wife did. She is an easy target for ridicule: a virgin bride, Protestant, petit bourgeois, susceptible to the ideas of her social circle, sticking by Gide's side like a stubborn, sacrificial angel. But what draws Lacan's attention is her infamous act of burning Gide's letters, which she herself says were her most precious possessions. They were his love letters, a correspondence that spanned many years, beginning with their first meeting. He also said the letters were his most prized possession, the most beautiful correspondence of his life, and the child he never had. It is in this context that we can see how Lacan's statement "poor Jason, he does not recognize Medea" could refer to Gide. In effect, he does not recognize Medea in his angelic wife. Poor men, who do not know how to recognize the Medea in their wives! That is because there is no middle ground, as a character from Euripides might wish. There is no negotiation here, only the absolute emerging.

These cases, whether involving Medea or Madeleine Gide, are all about reactions to the man's betrayal, a sort of punishment.

Not-Having and Having

There are other modalities, something of which Lacan is also aware when he points out that there is no limit to the concessions that a woman can make to a man with her body, her soul, and her possessions. "Concessions" here means to give up. This means that every woman is capable of going as far as not-having and of being a woman through not-having.

The "Lacanian" man, as he appears through the seminars and the papers, is on the other hand a being who is heavy, encumbered, burdened by having. Having is an encumbrance to him, and as he has something to lose, he is condemned to prudence. The Lacanian man is fundamentally cowardly. And if he goes to war, it is in order to flee women, to escape the hole. Man is therefore not without semblances, but they are semblances that protect his petty "having." This is not the case with the semblance proper, which really is a mask of lack. One could speak of the subjectivation of the genital organ in men and so put them on the side of having—having in the sense of a feeling that gives him a proprietary sense of superiority, a possession which also implies the fear of someone's stealing it from him. Here, masculine cowardice is in strong contrast to the limitless feminine.

Having is clearly linked to masturbation. Phallic *jouissance* is proprietary *jouissance* par excellence, meaning that the subject does not give anyone the keys to the castle and sometimes goes so far as to protect himself through being impotent in a satisfying way. And when he does finally give, it is as if he had been robbed, to the point that he reserves masturbation as the refuge of *jouissance* for himself: *one for her, one for me!*

It seems to me that Lacan thought, not just differently from but contrary to Freud, that there was no solution for woman on the side of having, which could only result in falseness and inauthenticity.

What does it mean to exist beneath the significance of having? I will attempt an answer by introducing a character called the "postiche woman" [*femme à postiche*].

The Postiche Woman

The postiche woman (or the fake woman) is a woman who artificially adds on what she lacks, but only if secretly it comes from a man. In a postiche woman, appearance is everything, in that it must seem to come from herself, to belong to her.

Let me clarify an ambiguity in the concept of the phallic woman. We must distinguish the phallic woman who constructs herself as the woman who has, who is on the side of having and whom I am calling the postiche woman, from the woman who constructs herself as being the phallus. They have nothing to do with one another, even if they can coexist in the same woman.

A woman who constructs herself on the side of being the phallus assumes her lack of having. It is because she recognizes her lack of having that she is able to be the phallus, which is what men lack. The postiche woman, however, hides her lack of having and pretends to be the possessor who lacks nothing and no one. She remains a woman and shows this through her savagery in protecting that which is hers—a savagery marked by hubris, or excess. The other type, on the side of being, displays her lack. A true woman, according to Lacan, allows the man to show himself as the one who desires, because she assumes the lack and also the semblances that constitute their game of lacking. In contrast, the postiche woman denounces men as being castrated and often completes herself in this way with a man, in whose shadow she remains.

When, at the end of Euripides' play, Medea departs on the winged chariot of the sun, she is the postiche woman, the most conservative subject imaginable, the one who does not permit herself to be seen from close up and demands enormous respect, the distance necessary to make the postiche look real. She demands respect as an absolute right. A true woman, in contrast, reveals to man the absurdity of having. To a certain extent, she is man's ruination. It is easier to be with a postiche woman, so that one can put away one's own goods in a safe. The postiche woman, who does not seem castrated, does not threaten men, because she does not demand that he desire, and so she acquires respect and rest from castration.

The word *postiche* appears in the French edition of Lacan's *Écrits* (p. 825), when he speaks about the absence of the penis which constitutes phallic woman and advises that this absence be evoked by making the woman wear a postiche under her costume for a masked ball.[3] This initiative does not come from the woman; rather, she simply submits to the man's desire that she accept his demand by lending herself to his fantasy. And the man is not afraid of castration, of the female not-having, because the Lacanian postiche is not meant to make it seem as though she has something. Quite the opposite. The postiche is the sign of what she does not have, a sign that points out her lack and brings it to the fore. The Lacanian postiche, insofar as it is manipulated by a man, reveals itself as postiche. It is a postiche that says, "I am a postiche." In the same way that the Magritte painting declares, "ceci n'est pas une pipe," the Lacanian postiche is a semblance that admits to being a semblance. By contrast, the postiche of the postiche woman lies. It is a semblance that says, "this is not a semblance." It wants others to believe in it. That is why it puts such an emphasis on respect and considers lack of respect an offense. One could say that the postiche woman loves respect as she loves herself, as in Freud's statement about those who love their madness as they love themselves. Similarly, she respects masculine semblances and adopts them, while the sometimes hidden truth in a woman is that she respects no one and nothing and denounces the phallus as a semblance in relation to *jouissance*.

The Supposed Knowledge of Women

It is only on the basis of feminine sexuality that one can situate sexual *jouissance* in the strict sense of something beyond the phallus and the all-signifier [*tout-signifiant*].

The church had already discovered true women before psychoanalysis did. It saw in them a threat and developed a solution: marry them off to God. And so, even today, there are women who take vows of obedience, poverty, and chastity for life. These vows frame *jouissance* beyond the phallus. They reveal that no man can be at this level of *jouissance*, and that no one less than God himself is needed here. And the feminine lack-of-having comes to terms with the vow of poverty, as outlined by the church.

It is no accident that a Catholic writer such as Léon Bloy could have written *The Poor Woman* [*La femme pauvre*] and defined the fundamental feminine position. One could also, from this starting point, situate the origin of the infinite and the function of secret.

The structural secret of speech, inasmuch as there is something that cannot be said, is a secret among women. This secret can be the condition of *jouissance* for women, and they can also enjoy [*jouir*] the secret as such, constituting the lie itself as *objet a*. Hence the famous question of women's ignorance, of how they should be educated and taught, which is so prevalent throughout history that sometimes women end up believing they are ignorant. The truth is that because of the nature of speech, women embody that which cannot be said—a secret, veiled knowledge—and this is why they are held to be subjects-supposed-to-know. All the fuss about what they should be taught cannot mask the male fear of the supposed knowledge of women.

Of course, women sometimes require analysis to become aware of the knowledge that they are supposed to possess. This is one of the reasons why we can say that psychoanalysis suits women. It suits women because, as Freud asserts, they embody the subjects in culture who are preoccupied with sexuality, love, desire, and *jouissance*. The preoccupations of psychoanalysis are the same as women's. It is only recently that men have appropriated these themes in large numbers. The position of *objet a* also suits them well to the extent that the position requires flexibility in relation to the Other's fantasy.

With respect to this, perhaps we can say something about women in analysis, because analysis offers them, at first, a respite, a rest, from the semblance, a respite from the captivity which is directed at them insofar as they function within male fantasy as *objet a*. Remaining in this position is tiring, and analysis offers a place of rest by allowing the woman to delegate this position to the analyst. It is also good for a woman to occupy the position of the barred subject, the subject which experiences its lack of identity. There are cases that prove that women can be so involved in their role of *objet a* that they cannot cede it to the analyst; they are so used to the role of the subject-supposed-to-know that they cannot tolerate it in another.

Fantasy According to the Sexes

Without developing these themes, perhaps I should mention that it is useful to think through the different function of fantasy in men and in women. In masculine desire, whose character, according to Lacan, only marginally accentuates perverse desires (since for Lacan there is a homology with perverse desire), objects are put in the parentheses of what we write as Φ in order to signify that there is a will to *jouissance* that necessitates fantasy. Lacan writes it like this: $\Phi(a)$. This was his first way of formulating masculine desire, where *objet a* appears as a partial object, or an object of drive.

We can transfer this formula to the formula of fantasy, now understood as masculine fantasy, and we then get $\$ \lozenge \Phi(a)$, inasmuch as masculine desire is maintained by phallicized semblances. It occurs in analysis that by traversing different levels of fantasy, the formula is concentrated and accentuates the function Φ—in other words, that traversing levels of fantasy reduces it to its bare bones and renders the phallic function even more insistent. In exchange, if we refer to Lacan's writing of feminine desire, $\cancel{A}(\phi)$, even if Lacan later said many other things, we can already see the relation of this desire, on the one hand with $\cancel{A}$ and on the other with the phallus. In the different courses of this desire, the object of drive does not appear, except in either passing through $\cancel{A}$ or the other, with the supposed genital object. What these two formulas indicate is that at the moment when a man discovers the course of his desire, the Φ function becomes more insistent, while as the course of his desire for a woman begins to come into action, he is lucky to reach $\cancel{A}$, in other words to realize that the Other does not exist.

Feminine cynicism sometimes gives us a glimpse of this when it (as well as women themselves) reminds men that their sublimations are nothing compared to *jouissance* and that they are fooling themselves with semblances. In this, women are closer to reality than men, and it is their lot to have an easier access to truth than men and to know the phallus is not everything and is a semblance. Obviously, as subjects, they can end up as Φ, which is how we write *postiche*, and they can inscribe themselves as subjects as little *phi*, in other words $\phi(x)$, by playing at the *postiche* and by embodying $\cancel{A}$ in a castrated man.

An analysis of feminine desire taken in this extreme sense can end up canceling $\cancel{A}$, which creates a monster who shouts, "I know everything." It is then that these oracular figures take shape, as in the case of the brilliant Melanie Klein, who doubted nothing. But if we eliminate this possible course, we can say that desire leads woman naturally toward $\cancel{A}$, while in men the Φ function is an obstacle to the reduction of the phallus to a simple semblance.

The Goddess of Psychoanalysis and the Goddess of the School

The situation described above is sometimes revealed in the process of the pass [*la passe*].

The *passant* (one who is passing) may or may not have reached the end of his analysis, in the opinion of the board.[4] Even so, he himself believes that he is well and presents himself to the pass if he thinks that he is ready, finished. He believes to have seen everything that the psychoanalyst can do for him and feels what at least in France is called the feeling of the end of analysis [*sentiment de fin d'analyse*]. The analysand presents himself to the pass at the moment he believes the Goddess of Psychoanalysis has granted his wish, and he goes to present the joy obtained from psychoanalysis to the supposed experts, so that they may judge if this joy is real or not.

In the pass, one does in fact observe that analysands change through the process of analysis: bachelors get married, couples get divorced, women who are crazy about their bodies become normal, obsessives are able to think of other things, and the anxiety stricken are able to relax. Sometimes, it is unclear whether it is due to analysis or simply to age, since often the only thing that one can be sure of is that they age.

The *passant* does not always come to say that the Goddess has granted his wish. Sometimes he wants to say just the opposite, that the Goddess has done nothing, that she has rejected his pleas, and that what he expected from the analyst is still unfulfilled. But if he does the pass, it is because he has learned that the wish itself was a wish for nothing, or that the Goddess who could have fulfilled it does not exist. The *passant* is truly convinced that he will obtain nothing else from the Goddess and that there is nothing more to hope for from her. And he prays to another Goddess, the Goddess of the School, for her to grant his dream of becoming part of the group of this school's analysts. In this manner, it is the incurable patient who presents the most promising case for nomination; he represents the subject's access, and consent, to incurability. Other analysands offer another kind of testimonial, of having realized their wishes and received a gift from the Goddess. Both attest to the fact that psychoanalysis has cured them of their lack of being; but the cure has not always been the one they had in mind.

For some, this occurs through identification with the symptom. They no longer have the hope of ridding themselves of the symptom. Instead, they have turned themselves into a symptom. They are their own symptom, and in this case the feeling of the end of analysis translates the revelation of the *jouissance* of the symptom. It is the revelation of this *jouissance* which eliminates their lack of being.

For the others, the cure is the passage through the fantasy. If, for the first, a feeling of need connotes access to the impossible, for the second it has an affect of liberty, in other words, of possibility, which gives access to contingency. When one ends with identification with the symptom, there is a sense of need and of access to the impossible. When one passes through the fantasy, there is a feeling of liberty and access to contingency. This can be put in Freudian terms: modification becomes an increase in flexibility of the erotic condition which determines the choice of object.

From the jury's point of view, what the pass teaches — at least this is my belief at the moment — is that there is a certain amount of sexual difference in fantasy. There is a pregnancy that is very specific to fantasy in male sexuation. And sometimes the fantasy, far from permitting a traversal through masculine desire, reveals a compression of this desire. I do not know if you are familiar with the work of the French sculptor Cesar, who takes an entire stack of cars and compresses it in order to produce a sculpture in the shape of a cube. It is a cube made of compressed cars. In the same manner, one possible result of analysis is a terrifying compression of fantasy. It is as if one obtained, by the traversal, the unveiled signification of *jouissance*, and the subject remained attached to this last signifier.

I present this as a question. Once all of the semblances are reduced, the last one remains, as a screen for A. This occurs to such an extent that one could think that, after the Proposition of '67 on the pass defined as traversal through the fantasy, Lacan was adding, as the fruit of his experience, the end of analysis as identification with the symptom.

This could perhaps be another end of analysis. Should we recognize this type of end, in which, after all, the phallic function remains untouched? We can easily see that in Lacan's two formulas on the sexuation of masculine and feminine desire, this is finally reduced to the first term. And the question is how analysis is practiced with the Φ function. It is often practiced rigidly, brutally, though not dishonestly. In fact, its stony silence is often not without its positive aspects. Should we recognize identification with the symptom as another mode of the end of analysis?

Freud realized that an obsessional neurosis continues until the illness can no longer be distinguished from the cure. He says that the symptoms end up representing satisfactions and that this significance eventually becomes the most important one. The subject seeks satisfaction in his symptoms.

The most typical, ideal pass is sought on the level of A, but it must be said that it belongs to women. Lacan privileged the end of analysis on the feminine side, in the same way that he identified the position of the analyst with the feminine position.

My last word of advice, then, could be: Men, another effort!

Translated by Sina Najafi and Marina Harss

Notes

1   Euripides, *Medea,* trans. Rex Warner, in *Euripides I,* ed. David Grene and Richmond Lattimore (Chicago: University of Chicago Press, 1955), 66–67.

2   Ibid., 69.

3   Miller is here using the term *postiche* to denote a fake object in general [Translators].

4   *Pass* refers to the moment of transition when the former analysand becomes an analyst. In Lacanian psychoanalysis, there is a requirement that the analysand report his or her own analysis to a specially organized board, which decides if the analysand is ready to become an analyst.

Geneviève Morel | **Anatomy**

For psychoanalysis, sexual difference is not a question of anatomy. Anatomical reality is important, however, if only for its "psychical consequences," as Freud put it in 1925.[1] In the practice of analysis, we can verify the difficulty that every subject, whether psychotic, perverse, or neurotic, experiences in assuming his or her own sex. But what exactly is "his" or "her" sex, if not the anatomical one? For Freud, the process of differentiation between man and woman is an extremely complex one related to the development of the sexual drive, and one that occurs quite late, since at least up to the phallic stage the two sexes are really only one. In any case, the result is never a pure one: "[In] human beings pure masculinity and femininity is not to be found either in a psychological or a biological sense," he wrote in 1915 in *Three Essays*.[2] Freud never gave up the idea of bisexuality, not only in the anatomical but also in the psychic sense, although the origin of this bisexuality remained inexplicable for him.

Anatomy remains essential in the trajectory that runs from the Oedipus complex to the castration complex in boys and the reverse in girls: first the anatomy of the self, then that of the opposite sex. For the boy, with a penis, the perception of its absence in the girl gives full weight to the threat of castration by the adult. For the girl without a penis, it is by seeing it that she will succumb to penis envy [*Penisneid*]. And this is without taking into consideration the decisive role that the mother's anatomy plays in neurotic, perverse, or psychotic structures, on the one hand, and in the process of sexual differentiation, on the other. This all-too-brief reminder serves only to emphasize the apparent lessening of the importance of anatomy in the teachings of Lacan, approaching sex as he does from the point of view of *jouissance* and language and no longer in terms of development.

Lacan radicalized the tension between the supposedly natural difference between the sexes and its consequences for the subject. In the 1970s he began to speak of the subject's "sexuation" and sometimes of his or her "sexuated identification options." [3] The latter term points to a choice on the part of the subject, while "identification" indicates the intervention of the signifier. Sexuation is governed by a logic which has three temporal registers: first, that of the natural difference between the sexes; second, that of sexual discourse; and third, the register of the subject choosing a sex, that is, sexuation proper.

Two Reals

But before we approach this construction, we must point out the opposition of two reals, that of biology and that of psychoanalytical discourse.

In biology there are two sexes, recognizable by their anatomical attributes on the one hand and by their sex cells or gametes on the other. The nebulous area between sexes, which cannot be fully discounted, is continually being reduced by the spectacular progress now being made in the realm of chromosomal differentiation. These two biological sexes permit us to speak of sexual relations between gametes, leading to the goal of reproduction. This natural sex, even though rendered sophisticated by science and the instruments used to define it, nevertheless corresponds more or less to the Greek concept of *phusis*. Here, man is an animal among animals.

In psychoanalytic discourse, another real is in play, one that must take biology into account but that only encounters it in a way which is twisted by language. The psychoanalytic real of sex consists of the impasses created by the fact that here sex can only be approached through language. And language imposes one single signified on *jouissance,* namely the phallus. By speaking, the human being is transformed into the speaking being [*parlêtre*] and is no longer an animal like others. Sex ceases to be nature, *phusis,* and becomes *sexus,* which comes from the

Latin *secare,* meaning "to cut," the fact of the signifier. The psychoanalytic real of sex is summed up by the phrase "there is no relation between the sexes,"[4] which is equivalent to the phrase "there is a phallic function," a function in which each person can inscribe his or her *jouissance* or not and accept the consequences.

The Three Temporal Registers of Sexuation

The first register is that of natural, anatomical difference. In the old days, this used to be marked at birth, but the genotype is now mostly predicted using ultrasound, while waiting for the real choice of sex that will be made later. But this first register is a mythical real, inasmuch as it acquires its value only from the second phase.

The second register is that of sexual discourse. In effect, "nature" is only of value when interpreted, and no difference is imaginable without the signifier; perception itself is structured by it. Thus, "one" distinguishes "it" as being a boy or a girl. "One" here means the family, the doctor, and so on; in other words, the discourse of the Other. It is the source of an error Lacan calls the "common error," common because it is everybody's and because it creates a community, just as discourse creates a social link on the basis of the phallic universal.[5] Nature suggests a difference, but as soon as one says "it's a boy" or "it's a girl," one does so based on phallic criteria without even knowing it. "Boy" no longer means simply that it has a penis, but that it is capable of virility, of being a man, as one says. "Girl" loses its anatomical meaning to become simultaneously a synonym of privation and defect and also of femininity, beauty, perpetual mystery, and so on. Nature becomes a semblance. It succumbs under the weight of a single signifier which categorizes natural difference in terms of phallus and castration.

The natural organ has become an *organon,* a signifying instrument. What does the error of sexual discourse consist of? It changes the status of the phallus. The phallus is the signified of *jouissance,* J/ϕ, but sexual discourse makes it a signifier. These two things do not have the same value. Saying that the phallus is the signified of *jouissance* means that in *jouissance* we capture only the phallic signification. This does not stop other *jouissances* from existing or from being experienced by the subject, but they are silent, outside signification, and thus difficult to point

out and to differentiate. Some of these other *jouissances* include surplus enjoyment and the *jouissance* of the Other. A subject may be submerged in the phallic signified, which can be evoked by the vital flux,
the living being, the erect form, standing upright, the jubilation of the
mirror phase, and so forth, without being inscribed under the signifying
phallus—or, in other words, without accepting castration. One could
say of a psychotic like Schreber that he is submerged in a certain phallic
signified up until the death of the subject, while the phallus as a signifier
is foreclosed to him, and he does not inscribe his *jouissance* in the phallic
function. In this manner, the subject can accept or refuse the common
error of sexual discourse. If he (or she) refuses it, the result is psychosis,
or outside-discourse, and he will have to invent an untried sexuation.
We know that the push-toward-femininity [*pousse-à-la-femme*] occupies
an important place here. If he accepts it, he will reenter phallic human
society and inscribe his *jouissance* in the phallic function, which is the
only one that can signify sexual difference. This Lacanian solution, different from Freud's, nevertheless suggests an aporia: how do we write
two sexes with only one signifier? How do we further specify what now
is written Φ/boy, Φ/girl, and Φ/difference between the sexes?

A concrete example of this aporia is the screen memory of a young
homosexual male, who remembers that on the shelf of his childhood
bathroom there were two razors: his father's (for his beard), and his
mother's (for her legs). "And the two razors were the same!" he exclaims, perplexed. It is hard to find a clearer allusion to the phallic
mother or a more beautiful example of metonymy.

The third register is sexuation. There may be only one *jouissance* function for both sexes in language, but there are two ways to inscribe oneself in it, corresponding to two different modes of phallic *jouissance*. In
this way, Lacan resolves the aporia of one function to write both sexes.
The logical tool of quantification allows him to transcribe this second
degree of the mode of *jouissance* with respect to the phallic function. In
order to sexuate, a subject does not inscribe him- or herself in the function by declaring "I am phallic" or "I am not phallic," which would be
the same for both sexes and would therefore not be discriminating. The
subject inscribes him- or herself as a mode of *jouissance* of the phallus:
"In my relation to the other sex, I am completely caught in the phallic
function; therefore I am a man," or else, "In my relation to the other sex,

I am not-all inscribed in the phallic function; therefore I am a woman." Of course, these formulas are approximate, but they give an idea of the two modes of *jouissance* as regards this function. Freud, as we know, re-solved the aporia by a temporal inversion during the development of the Oedipus and castration complexes. Why does Lacan resort to logic? He does so because his definition of the real of sex is the impossibility of writing the relation between the sexes. He supposes then that existing logic attests to a formalization of the impossible, something that will be useful in writing sexual nonrelation.[6] This explains why he writes both sexes as formulas using symbols from modern logic, and why we must nevertheless in reading them return to the inventor of logic, Aristotle. Freud together with Aristotle, rewritten through modern logic: this is Lacan's attempt to define the sexes as two distinct modes of using the phallus in establishing a relation with the other sex, a relation that fails in different ways to make contact.

Aristotle with Freud

Lacan brings together Aristotle and Freud[7] in two ways. He juxtaposes, on the one hand, what both managed to express in their writings: in Freud, the Oedipus complex as a necessary link to the father, and in Aristotle, the logic of the universal, of "the all," based on the principle of contradiction. This is how Lacan writes the male side of the formu-las of sexuation: formal contradiction between the necessary existence of an exception to the phallic function (the father) and the rule of the phallic universal that creates man. The mode of *jouissance* of all-phallic man is the following: his phallic *jouissance* is the obstacle that keeps him from drawing pleasure [*jouir*] from the woman's body.[8] His phal-lic *jouissance* objects to a relationship with the other sex. This is a very clinical observation. Consider the "mistress" who simultaneously holds together and perturbs the married couple; this is the double composition of love described by Freud. But there are other possible forms of this obstacle: a subject who suffers from premature ejaculation must also in-voke the mental image of a phallus in order to have an erection when he is with his wife; this image immediately brings on ejaculation. He calls this homosexuality, but it is only a mode of expression of the phallic obstacle.[9]

On the other hand, Lacan also compares that which Aristotle and Freud both named but did not sufficiently explain. This is the enigma of femininity in Freud and the brief mention in Aristotle of the concept of the "not-all," an apparent dead end in his formal logic which he dropped during his development of syllogism for a theory of the universal and the particular. Of course, to rename an enigma with an unelaborated concept does not constitute a solution, and to affirm that the essence of femininity is not-all, without any explanation, may seem of little use to the practicing psychoanalyst. But this gives him an indication of a logic of discordance linked to enunciation, a logic of negation which does not result, however, in the construction of an existence: a logic of indeterminacy, of indecidability, of the contingency of the phallus, and so on.

Let us try now to use the three phases of sexuation to shed some light on the clinical analysis of transsexuality, of neurosis, and of female homosexuality, following some indications made by Lacan in the introductory lecture of his 1971–72 seminar, "Ou pire."

Transsexuality

Here we must refer ourselves to the second phase of sexuation, namely sexual discourse and the common error. The transsexual would like to change his anatomical sex and denounces the error of nature that has given him a woman's soul in the body of a man (or vice versa). Sometimes the analyst takes him at his word and endorses the operation. Sometimes, even if he is hesitant about operating, as in the case of Stoller, he accepts the transsexual's words at face value and develops a concept of gender, the "true" sex, that is opposed to the anatomical sex.[10] What determines the truth is the subject's intimate convictions about his sex, despite the fact that we know this is a sign of the absence of neurosis. The cause of gender in this case would be the mother's desire for a child-phallus, a desire not limited by paternal Law.[11] This often leads us to consider a diagnosis of psychosis in these cases.[12] The originality of these cases is that the patients are not delirious, except on this precise topic of "the error of nature," in which their madness is located. If we place ourselves in the second phase of sexuation, we can see that these subjects refuse the sexual discourse—in other words, the phallic categorization of the anatomical organ. "If my penis makes you think that I am male, even though I feel myself to be a woman, then put me under the knife," they say in effect. Therefore we are not dealing with an error of nature here but rather with a refusal on the order of foreclosure, of sexual discourse, and of common error which it implies: turning the phallus into the signifier of sex.

Neurosis: Identification and Sexuation

We have arrived at the third register of sexuation. The subject has agreed to enter into the community of sexual discourse where the phallus is the Master Signifier of sex. "One," that is, the sexual discourse, has categorized the subject as a boy or a girl. He or she can consent to or resist this distinction depending on whether his or her mode of *jouissance* leads him or her to stand on the side of the all-phallic or of the everywhere-phallic. This is why there is a choice, an option for the subject at this moment of sexuation, which can be contrary to anatomy and civil status. "The sexuated being only draws authority from him or herself," [13] says Lacan, which implicates some other people as well; the second register where one comes into play is crucial here. This choice, which affects the mode of *jouissance* in the phallic function (all or not-all), has a real value and is certainly not easy to modify, even if it is perhaps possible to do so. The sexuated identification option is, therefore, not one simple, signifying identification. But the neurotic is the one who mixes things up and may want to know nothing about his original choice, to reject it, in the sense of repression, or to cover it up with other identifications. Analysis, by disentangling these identifications, brings him back to this original choice, revealed for what it is. Hysteria is a clear example of masking the sexuated choice by a question which challenges it and by identifications with the opposite sex.

Feminine Homosexuality

Feminine homosexuality deploys another strategy in the face of sexual discourse. It holds tightly to its sex, and so, according to Lacan, "sustains sexual discourse with all sincerity." [14] Even so, it can only, in his words, "mumble" psychoanalytical discourse because of the specific nature of its relation to the phallus. Like the Précieuses in the seventeenth century, it wishes to "shatter the signifier in its letter" in order to reach the limit. The Précieuses formed a group in order to talk about love and also to eliminate from language all words that evoked sex. An enterprise as long as analysis! In order to underscore the refusal operating here, Lacan refers to *The Mammaries of Tiresias,* a surrealist play by Apollinaire. The heroine, Thérèse, no longer wants to be a married woman, but rather a man. She becomes Tiresias. So her husband produces babies on his own like a "daughter-father,"[15] and she herself becomes homosexual, a "man-madame"[16] [*homme-madame*], a ladies' man [*homme à dames*]. By the end, however, she comes back to him, once again becomes Thérèse, and he takes her back.

The two scenes that interest us are the ones in which there is a sex change. In the first, Thérèse refuses her husband's authority: "No Monsieur husband / You won't make me do what you want."[17] She makes a list of all of the things that she would like to be: soldier, minister, president, medical or psychological doctor (psychoanalyst?), and so on. Meanwhile, her husband says to her: "Give me bacon fat I tell you." And she answers, "Listen to him, all he thinks about is sex." Then she grows a beard and her breasts become detached. On stage this is represented by balloons (her "mammaries") flying away, and she says: "Fly away birds of my frailty. . . . After all vice is a dangerous thing / That's why it's better to sacrifice beauty / Which can give rise to sin / Let's get rid of my mammaries."[18]

The balloon-mammaries are detachable objects, feminine lures for the husband (he asks for bacon, but she knows what he really wants is sex). They are the invitation to sin, to sex. They represent both the *objet a* which Therese is to her husband and that which occupies the place of her own castration. They are the objects of her weakness, in that for him, she is precisely and only *objet a,* not-all. After rejecting her position as *objet a* and not-all, she becomes Tiresias, who is more virile than her husband and who vindicates the All: "And now the universe will be mine," she says.[19]

The second scene that interests us is the last one of the play. Tiresias comes back as a fortune-teller and undresses before the husband. "Don't you recognize me, husband dear?" she says, to which he replies, "Thérèse or should I say Tiresias?"[20] After recognizing her, he notes with regret the absence of her breasts: "You are as flat-chested as a bedbug."

She responds, "We need to love or else succumb," but he retorts, "Dear Thérèse, you can't remain / Flat-chested like a bedbug." He offers her some balloons, but she still does not want them: "You and I managed OK without them / Let's just carry on." And she lets them go once again, saying, "Fly away, birds of my weakness."

She comes back for an ideal love but still does not consent to being the *objet a* that renders her desirable to her husband, producing this comedy where each is deaf to what the other is saying.

From *objet a* to Not-All and the Other's *Jouissance*

One of the references in the play is to Ovid's *Metamorphoses,* which also relates the story of Tiresias changing sex twice.[21] He first goes from man to woman by striking two entwined snakes, and then reconverts by performing the same act again. His destiny is to know female *jouissance,* which surpasses man's, and to be blinded by Juno for revealing this *jouissance* to Zeus. He is blinded, therefore, because he is not blind to woman's *jouissance.*

Lacan's theory is that it is not by "letting go of the balloons"—in other words, what constitutes her as *objet a,* desirable to a man and also not-all—that a woman attains feminine *jouissance* beyond the phallus and so becomes absent. Rather, it is by "recuperating her balloons," which are her weakness, her castration lent to the other. Which means that the female homosexual wants to reach a more radical feminine *jouissance,* to reach her passion, by "letting go of her balloons"—in other words, by refusing the phallus, breaking it as it presents itself in its letter as the single, isolated signifier. This would prevent her from going very far into the analytical discourse, which assumes that the phallus in its letter will be encountered at every step, caught as it is in the net of metaphors and metonymies to which sexuality is reduced in the formulations of the unconscious. Analytical discourse implies confronting or even submitting to the law of castration. Analysis places the female homosexual in a constant struggle to break the phallus—remember the challenge posed by Freud's young homosexual woman—and makes her blind to the nature of feminine *jouissance,* whose secret she seeks with passion. Unlike Tiresias, she is blind to feminine *jouissance,* blinded by her own rejection of the phallus.

This rejection is of a singular nature: it is neither the foreclosure of transsexuals nor a repression to be deciphered through the symptom, such as, for example, the hysterical aversion to the male sex organ. But where the phallus is refused in its literal sense, it returns even more forcefully to inhabit and haunt *jouissance* as a real presence from which the subject cannot detach herself. The *Fi donc* [For shame] of the Précieuses, about which Lacan made a joke, illustrates this passage from challenge to one immutable conclusion: there you have it [*donc*]! The clinical studies of female homosexuality, such as the work done by Ernest Jones, reveal this obsessive, inescapable return of the phallus, driven out or defied, like the presence of a man as the invisible witness of amorous entanglements between women.[22]

In a case studied in analysis, the young woman's symptom was at first a compulsion to fight with men toward whom she was defiant. She professed a pure homosexuality, disconnected from all men, and found in it the apparent reason for her brutal and dangerous behavior, which had led her to seek treatment. Analysis revealed through a series of dreams and fantasies, which gradually became conscious, that orgasm for her was triggered by the idea of her companion being taken by a man who interrupts the women's love session. The displeasure of the symptom was the opposite of her phantasmatic surplus-enjoyment. The symptomatically struck phallus had taken on a determining role in sexual *jouissance*.

Female homosexuality fails the not-all through its attempt to eliminate the phallic signifier. All she is left with is either (1) love without desire, as in the case of Apollinaire's Thérèse, (2) a *jouissance* completely centered around the phallus of which she will always seek to rid herself, or (3), if she is theoretically minded like the Précieuses, the discourse of love itself. But she will not have access to feminine *jouissance* unless she accepts the "weakness" of being not-all for a man, who can only desire a woman as a partial being, or *objet a*.

Lacan's thesis here is to make the Other's *jouissance* (which is qualitatively linked to the absence of the phallus) paradoxically dependent on the presence of the phallus. This condition places woman as not-all under the aleatory control of the encounter with male desire.

Translated by Sina Najafi and Marina Harss

Notes

1   Sigmund Freud, "Some Psychical Consequences of the Anatomical Distinction be-
    tween the Sexes," in *The Standard Edition,* ed. James Strachey, vol. 19 (London:
    Hogarth Press, 1961), 243–58. Further references will be made to *SE.*

2   Sigmund Freud, *Three Essays on the Theory of Sexuality, SE,* vol. 7 (London: Hogarth
    Press, 1953), 220.

3   Jacques Lacan, "Les non-dupes errent" (unpublished seminar 21, 1973–74), lecture
    of 14 May 1974. The French terms are *sexuation* and *options d'identification sexuée.*

4   Lacan's statement "Il n'y a pas de rapport sexuel" is usually translated as "There is no
    sexual relation." This is sometimes misunderstood to mean that the sexual act itself
    is somehow impossible. Whenever "sexual relation" or "sexual nonrelation" appears
    later in the text, the phrase should be read in the context of a relationship between
    the sexes, and not as a statement about the sexual act itself [Translators].

5   Lacan, "Ou pire" (unpublished seminar 19, 1971–72), lecture of 8 Dec. 1971.

6   Lacan, "D'un discours qui ne serait pas du semblant" (unpublished seminar 28,
    1970–71), lecture of 18 May 1971.

7   Lacan, *The Seminar of Jacques Lacan,* book 20: *Encore,* ed. Jacques-Alain Miller,
    trans. Bruce Fink (New York: W. W. Norton, 1998), 62.

8   Ibid., 7.

9   Geneviève Morel, "L'obstacle du phallus," *Feuillets du Courtil* 11 (Oct. 1995): 25.

10 Robert Stoller, *Sex and Gender* (New York: Science House, 1968).

11 Ibid., chap. 9.

12 Morel, "Un cas de transvestisme féminin," *La cause freudienne* 30 (May 1995): 20.

13 Lacan, "Les non-dupes errent," lecture of 9 Apr. 1974.

14 Lacan, "Ou pire," lecture of 8 Dec. 1971.

15 Guillaume Apollinaire, *The Mammaries of Tiresias,* in *Three Pre-Surrealist Plays,*
    trans. and ed. Maya Slater (Oxford: Oxford University Press, 1997), act 2, scene 2,
    191.

16 Ibid., act 1, scene 7, 182.

17 Ibid., act 1, scene 1, 169.

18 Ibid., act 1, scene 1, 171.

19 Ibid., act 1, scene 4, 177.

20 Ibid., act 2, scene 7, 205.

21 Ovid, *Metamorphoses,* trans. Frank Justus Miller, Loeb Classical Library (Cambridge,
    Mass.: Harvard University Press, 1916), book 3, ll. 316–38, pp. 147–49.

22 Ernest Jones, "The Early Development of Female Sexuality," *International Journal of
    Psycho-analysis* 8 (Oct. 1927): 459–72.

3

Colette Soler | **The Curse on Sex**

Freud had no hesitation in repeating Napoleon's phrase "anatomy is destiny." Lacan, on the contrary, disagreed and proposed a thesis that seems to mark the end of any norms based on nature. If we take him at his word, subjects are free to choose whether they are men or women.

The Aporias of Sex

It would be easy enough to exploit the discrepancy between these two positions to point out the inconsistency of psychoanalytical doctrine. Instead, we would do better to read the discrepancy as evidence of the aporias of sex itself, with which psychoanalysis has continually been confronted. Notwithstanding, these aporias can be observed on the surface. Subjects identify with their anatomy to such a small degree that they are in fact inclined to be anxious about their sexual being. The extreme cases of transsexual delirium or transvestite illusions share much here with very common cases, where the male subject questions whether he is *truly* a man [*vraiment un homme*], to the point of sometimes feeling the need to prove himself. The female subject, meanwhile, is preoccupied with the question whether she is *a true* woman [*une vraie femme*] — a nuance of language we should pay attention to — and finds no other way to prove it but through "masquerade."

Psychoanalytical theory itself has for a century now faced the problem of defining what it is that determines sexual belonging, because it has had to accept that even if anatomy determines civil status, it holds no sway over desire or drive, as the existence of perversions has indicated for a long time. The initial presence or absence of a penis which defines anatomy will result in the naming of a subject as a boy or a girl and the subsequent routines of indoctrination, but evidence suggests that something else is also required to make someone into a man or a woman. Even Freud's formulation, contrary to appearances, does not come from any naturalism on his part. It refers more to "denaturalization" by language, to the fact that the natural difference between the sexes has subjective consequences only by being signified and only has repercussions at the level of the speaking being [*parlêtre*] by passing through the twists and turns of discourse.

Identification or Sexuation

The divergence between Freud and Lacan's responses to the question of sexual belonging can be expressed in shorthand by the opposition of two terms: identification and sexuation. This conceptual condensation obviously sacrifices the nuances and stages of their respective elaborations, but in my opinion, it delineates the major axis of difference.

After discovering the polymorphous perversity of children, Freud came up with his oedipal myth in order to explain how the perverse little child becomes unimorphously male or female. The oedipal phase is therefore, according to Freud, what "corrects" the polymorphous dispersion of drives by introducing unifying identifications, at the price, however, of certain sacrifices and failures—which is another way of saying that identification is the name he gives to the process by which the symbolic ensures its hold on the real.

With the Oedipus complex and the different identifications which it generates, Freud gave consistency to an Other of discourse. This Other connects its norms, models, obligations, and prohibitions with the original anatomical identity. It imposes a standard solution to the castration complex, a heterosexual solution, and rejects all other solutions as atypical or pathological. According to Lacan, an Other, by providing semblances capable of ordering the relation between the sexes, tells us what we should do as men or a women.

In order to be fair to him, one would have to describe all of Freud's nuances and details at length—first, because it is hardly true that he operates solely with the notion of identification, and he actually refers in each case to a trio consisting of drive, identification, and object choice; and second, because he himself became aware of the failure and limits of his solution when dealing with the resistance of repressed drives which incessantly return both in symptoms and in the inertia of what he called the death drive. Nevertheless, one can say in condensed form that for the Freud who came up with the myth of Oedipus, becoming a man or woman, with all the different modalities of desire and *jouissance* that implies, is a question of oedipal identification.

Moreover, regardless of the theoretical entropy that separates Stoller and Freud, the notion of gender so dear to Anglo-Saxons is, in this sense, oriented in the same direction. This is precisely the direction from which Lacan diverged when he went beyond the Oedipus complex, having spent years reformulating and rationalizing Freud's oedipal problematic in terms of language.

The term "sexuation," which Lacan proposed and whose formulas he provided in his article "L'étourdit," identifies man and woman on the basis of their respective modes of *jouissance*. These formulas of sexuation attest to and make sense of what we experience every day, namely that the authority of the Other's norms ends at the foot of the bed; as soon as we speak of sexual bodies, the order imposed by discourse proves incapable of correcting the "denaturing" of the speaking being and has nothing more to offer but the phallic semblance. The formulas show the distribution of subjects between two modes of inscription within the phallic function, which is nothing other than the function of *jouissance* insofar as the fact of language makes it fall prey to castration.

Man is the subject entirely submitted to the phallic function, from which it follows that castration is his lot, and also to phallic *jouissance*, to which he gains access through the mediation of fantasy. Woman is the opposite, the Other who has not fully [*pas tout*] submitted to the reign of phallic *jouissance* and to whom another *jouissance*, a supplementary *jouissance* without the support of any object or semblance, is available.

This distribution, as we see, is binary, like the sex ratio, which for some unknown reason distributes the species more or less equally between males and females. But the binary nature of sexuation is, according to Lacan, not simply the effect of biological distribution, but depends rather on a completely different logical necessity connected to the limits of signification. Curiously, these limits reduce the facticity of sex to a simple choice between the phallic all and not-all.

This thesis creates a strange homology between two heterogeneous alternatives—male-female and man-woman—both of which, however, are real: the first, that of the sexed organism, because it depends on nature and its established regularities; and the second, that of the speaking being, because it falls within the logical limits of language, which, by ceaselessly inscribing themselves, pass for the real in the symbolic order.

The Curse

"They have a choice" does not therefore imply any free will, but rather means, first of all, that the two alternatives are not isomorphous, and second, that the discord between one's official sex and one's erogenous sex emerges, as psychoanalytical practice has shown, in the discrepancy that divides the two alternatives. We can see then that anatomy does not determine the destiny of eros, even though for every speaking being it is an *a priori* handicap: in other words, there are males and females according to civil status who are not men or women as sexuated beings, hence the choice.

The word "choice" seems paradoxical, however, given that common experience attests more to a strong sense of constraint, either because the subject recognizes itself in its sexual aspirations to such a degree that it supposes them to come from nature, or, on the contrary, because they feel so constrained that the subject lives through them only as painful symptoms. In both cases, if there is a choice, it is a forced one, between the phallic all and not-all, in which the subject is less an autonomous agent than a pawn.

In his seminar "Les non-dupes errent," Lacan points out that subjects are forced to authorize themselves as sexual beings according to the directives of an unconscious that speaks. What a curse! This causes unhappiness, because the unconscious speaks sex badly, thus not always allowing us to recognize the phallic One, with its narcissistic attributes, and *never* allowing us to recognize what falls outside it, namely the Other itself, which for this reason ex-ists even more.[1] From this one can deduce that the unconscious is homosexual;[2] this is the curse that leaves the Other of sex foreclosed. The "lack of sexual relations," through which Lacan formulates what Freud says implicitly, means that in sexual relations, despite the presence of any love and desire, *jouissance,* insofar as it is phallic, does not permit any access to the *jouissance* of the Other.

Generalized Perversion or . . . the Other

From this point on we perceive a disjunction between the choice of *jouissance* and that of the object. Two figures from literature who illustrate this are Gide and Montherlant, who, without approaching women, did not cease to be men, glued as they were to the *jouissance* of the organ. More generally, one should not fail to recognize that, having crossed the limits of their respectives masquerades, not all gays are queens [*folles*] any more than all lesbians are dykes. We are here far from the oedipal standard of heterosexuality, which claims that, except in cases of deviation, men and women were made for each other, simply because their two signifiers, man and woman, copulate in the place of the Other, like the king and queen in "The Purloined Letter" by Edgar Allan Poe.

If, for the man, the lack of sexual relations means that access to the partner occurs only through a single fantasy, we can say that he is married to the object of his fantasy, with whom he cheats on his partner, be it male or female. So for each person, the real "lies" to the partner, as Lacan states in *Television.* The hidden object, the secret cause of *jouissance,* takes the place of the beloved. We can see that the major consequence of this generalized perversion is the relativization of the partner. Certainly the unconscious imposes the male or phallic norm; Freud realized this, but this norm does not impose any norms for the partner, except the surplus-enjoyment particular to each individual—the real partner of repetition, as it were. This partner can just as easily be found in a woman (heterosexuality) as in a man (homosexuality), or even, for some mystics, in God. This is the case, for example, in Angelus Silesius, who, if we are to believe Lacan's account, develops the aforementioned perversion as soon as he interposes the gaze between himself and God. As for the woman, insofar as she is not completely dedicated to phallic *jouissance* or completely caused by the fantasized object, she achieves *jouissance* through diverse partners; beyond man in sexual relations, through another woman, and in God himself if she is a mystic.

In this manner, there is no contradiction if we place men (heterosexual as well as homosexual), mystics, and even hysterical women preoccupied with the object of the male Other under the heading of "man" within the phallic all. Similarly, heterosexual and homosexual women, mystics like Saint Theresa, Hadewijch of Antwerp, or Saint John of the Cross, as well as psychotics of either sex, fall into the category of "woman." Partners can vary here without affecting the sexual belonging of the subject, which means that in each case, the true asexual partner of *jouissance* is veiled, as if waiting for interpretation.

This discrepancy, which separates the sex drive from love and their respective objects from each other, was recognized by Freud to be the source of all the disappointments of love life; he formulated it at first in terms of development, as the passage from autoerotic *jouissance* of one's own body to libidinally investing another object. It causes grave problems in relation to sex, but beyond that, it puts into question the social link in itself and, more specifically, love, because the problem is knowing how the drive, which never lets up, can be articulated in a stable and controlled relationship to one's fellows.

The seminar *Encore* addresses this very disjunction when it suggests, at the end of the first argument of the first chapter, that " 'the *jouissance* of the Other,' of the Other with a capital O, 'of the body of the Other who symbolizes the Other, is not the sign of love.' " [3] The idea "I love him or her, therefore I come" is not operative here. From that two further questions are opened by Lacan's statement: what is the source of the thing that responds in the form of *jouissance* in the sexual relations, and what is the true nature of love?

Hommosexual [*hommosexuel*] Love [4]

Lacan treats the question of love at the end as well as at the beginning of the seminar *Encore,* first to say that he is principally addressing the specular image long familiar to us, and also to add that this image comes from the unconscious and finds its jurisdiction in the perceived enigma of the subject, who, because it speaks, becomes the subject of the unconscious.

In a difficult passage in "L'étourdit," [5] Lacan had already asserted that where one finds the two of sex, or the inaccessible second lack, one also finds one's fellow man, the image of the mirror stage, who at once shows himself [*s'emble*] [6] and sows himself [*s'emblave*], tricking the libido and sowing his seed. This is the meaning of the verbs *s'embler* and *s'emblaver*. Thus fertilized, the image serves as a substitute, an imaginary replacement for the inaccessible Other, which should be written i(a)/$\cancel{A}$. In the same group of ambiguities, I will take the liberty of invoking here the notion of the sown field [*emblavure*], if this expression, an intentional neologism, makes us see in the theft or flight [*vol*] of the libido by the generic image of the species a structural blunder [*bavure*], which makes love "hommosexual" [*hommosexuel*], with two m's as Lacan writes it— without forgetting that Freud already understood this. By loving too much the covering that is the image, love remains "beyondsex" [*horssexe*].[7]

This is no less the case when love allows, in the absence of sexual relations and as the contingencies of the encounter dictate, a relation between subject and subject, which is the new definition of love offered at the end of *Encore*. If one needed proof that this exists, one would have only to watch a television show presented on Valentine's Day on the Arté channel about the phenomenon of "love at first sight" and to listen to the testimonials, running the gamut from male-female couples whose relationship is based only on love at first sight, to a recently married couple consisting of two obese African American lesbians, to the extreme case of a lifetime love that blossomed, as it were, on the verge of death, on the threshold of a Nazi concentration camp. The story is always the same: beyond all circumstances, the instantaneous certitude of having recognized one another.

Lacan associates this recognition with the vague understanding each person has of the manner in which he or she is affected by his or her destiny to be alone. Here, too, love goes from the same to the same, and not from one to the Other. It is no longer the sameness of the image which is at stake here, nor even the sameness of the usual destiny which the speaking unconscious reserves for each person, but another, more obscure sameness pertaining to how each person *qua* speaking being responds to his or her destiny and bears it. It consists in making a choice which we can only describe as ethical, singular, and original, and which psychoanalytic discourse subjects to its command to say well: to say well that which, drawn from the fantasy or the symptom, compensates for the foreclosure of sex.

One may ask how these conclusions fit in with our times. Through

the order it imposes between the sexes, through the "stability" of prejudices it fuels, through the offers of enjoyment [*offres à jouir*] it extends
to its subjects, discourse itself in effect attempts to tame the sexual impasse and the lack in the Other which does not exist, as Jacques-Alain
Miller reminded us in his lecture series this year. Discourse no doubt
stops at the foot of the bed, as I said earlier, at precisely the point where
Encore begins its exploration, but not without laying siege to the periph-
ery of this hole, where we can find its semblances, norms, and rules.
Each subject encounters them as a kind of foretaste of the deficiency
of civilization vis-à-vis sexuality, because the unconscious is not completely individual but is filled with the discourse that governs the community. Ours has promised, along with human rights, sexual equality,
which coincides (is this by chance?) with increasingly unisex lifestyles
determined by the market for new objects of pleasure available to everyone. One cannot fail to recognize that love relations today have been
profoundly transformed.

New Mores

The past few decades have revealed an unpredecented change in values,
pushed forward by legislation gradually legalizing sexual practices that
would have seemed insupportable only fifty years ago. It would not have
been possible for Claudel today to come up with his bon mot about tolerance that "there are houses for that sort of thing." I will leave aside
the question of what in our society conditions this liberalism. It is of
course not absolute, since it also elicits the opposite reaction, but it is
nevertheless a fact, and one that I think is irreversible. This liberalism is
not limited to finally accepting homosexuality, though the brief century
that separates the imprisonment of Oscar Wilde from our homosexual
marriages does give an idea of the speed of these changes. It no longer
prejudges any sexual practice, as long as it is one's fantasy and a partner
can be found.

The different sexual scenarios which Freud painstakingly discovered
at the heart of the unconscious are today exhibited for all to see—children and adults alike. His *Three Essays on Sexuality,* which in 1905 were
considered scandalous, are now widely seen as banal, while the supposedly perverse theories about children inventing their own response to
the sexual union of their parents appear daily on television. The whole

panoply of fantasies is now displayed there for our pleasure. Everything is as if the century had learned its lesson about the generalized masculine perversion which I described earlier. We now know, and psychoanalysis almost certainly has had a part in this, that everyone takes enjoyment from [*jouit de*] his or her unconscious and fantasies. Furthermore, one would like to be able to account for one's fantasies in words and actions (consider sexology and all of the efforts to talk about these things and have others do so as well), because now, sexual *jouissance* is held up as a right. This new cynicism is augmented by the fact that the paradigms of love that were elaborated in the past are no longer valid. Neither the Greek *philia,* nor the courtly model, nor divine mystical love, nor classical passion can captivate our present-day modes of *jouissance,* and we are left with love without any model, constructed as a symptom and attended only by the unpredictable conjunction of the contingencies of encounters and the automatons of the unconscious.

The Bachelor Ethic

There is only one question: Are all of these different symptomatic solutions by which subjects resolve the absence of sexual relations of equal value? Of course, this is a delicate question, but an inevitable one, since every form seen in the practice of psychoanalysis, whether it comes from neurosis, psychosis, perversion, or, more generally, from love, presupposes the ethical choice of the subject. The term "defense," which is present in the Freudian notion of the psychoneurosis of defense, implies the notion of "no treatment without an ethics." [8] Generalized perversion cannot escape this, because it too allows diverse ethical choices which analytical discourse must reveal.

I believe that we are witnessing today the rise of what Lacan felicitously named "the bachelor ethic." Greek friendship, the classical *philia,* illustrated this in the past; closer to our times, Henry de Montherlant embodied it; and Immanuel Kant made a system out of it in his "practical reason." By claiming to determine a will by excluding all motivations and so-called pathological objects of the senses, what the categorical imperative of moral law and its extremism ends up proscribing is evidently woman. This ethics is also "beyond sex" [*hors sexe*]; it short-circuits the Other in favor of the self.

In this option, one can see that the subject "removes itself from or fortifies itself against" [*se retranche*][9] Alterity in order to hole itself up in the refuge of the phallic One. It is a strategy for the eradication of the Other, an eradication in action which doubles its structural foreclosure but which is not necessarily incompatible with fascination with the supplementary *jouissance* of woman.

Subscribers to the Homosexual Unconscious

Let us not only assign homosexuals à la Montherlant (there are other types) to this bachelor ethic, but also all those who by other means avoid the approach of the Other, all those people we could call the teetotalers or strikers of the Other, a group that includes diehard masturbators, the sexless types that I have mentioned elsewhere,[10] and paradoxically perhaps even certain hysterical women. I call all of them "subscribers" [*abonnés*] to the homosexual unconscious in order to echo Lacan's description of Joyce as an "unsubscriber" of the unconscious [*desabonné de l'inconscient*], and to underscore that the homosexual unconscious does not force the subject into active homosexuality, though it forces it to justify heterosexuality itself.

In this regard, we see that feminine homosexuality is a completely different option: its ethic leaves a place for the Other of sex, without eliminating a secret link to man. This is why Lacan could say in 1958, *pace* Freud, that the eros of this kind of homosexuality, as illustrated by the Précieuses, works against social entropy through the information it conveys. And later, in 1973, he added that anyone who loves women is heterosexual regardless of gender, because even if there is no relation between the sexes, there is nevertheless sexual love, which is completely possible.

I call this ethics, which is one means of installing the Other of sex in the place of the symptom, hetero-ethical (but not heterosexual). This ethics is of course not to be confused with a valorization of conjugal values, because the latter has nothing to do with ethics. Rather, it constitutes another response to the impossibility of relations, a response that maintains an interest in the Other. Furthermore, by virtue of eros, this ethics grants the Other an existence, even though this does not help the relation between the sexes given that the unsuccessful encounter remains irreducible. All of a sudden, the "macho" seducer, the bête noire of all egalitarian ideologies, now takes on some positive characteristics, because despite his conquering arrogance, the feminine object, which he pretends to crush with his disdain, can only rise in his esteem.

One cannot help asking oneself what kind of pressures contemporary discourse exerts in this regard. It seems to me, at the end of the century, that as far as the regulation between the sexes is concerened, the overriding sense of our discourse seems to be complicit with the bachelor ethic. I would like to indicate the ways in which this happens; there are many, but one of them is related to the rights of man.

No Sexual Contract

I have spoken of the liberalism of values, and this in turn leads to the question of limits. We have no other limit to place against the possible excesses of the drive but that of human rights and its requirement of equality and respect. On the subject of sexuality, one could formulate its anti-Sadean dictum as follows: no one has the right to act upon the body of another without mutual consent. But the paradox is that no matter what kind of love pact exists, there is no possibility of a contractual relation with the sexual Other. There were once cultures in which kidnapping was elevated to the level of ritual, and where the real mutual agreements which had determined the marriage (and which affected a much larger group of people than just the bride and groom) were masked by the ritualized violence of a sham kidnapping of the bride, as if to symbolize the noncontractual portion of the sexual relations between the man and the woman. In our society, we go to court to denounce any sexual initiative that occurs without explicit mutual consent. Thus we have the unending trials for sexual harassment, and better yet, for date rape. So today, the respect due every subject reaches the most intimate space, and human rights tries hard to make generalized perversion submit to an ideology of contracts, which is itself no less generalized and universal today. And this is surely a good thing, because it would be outrageous to incriminate the ever-so-fragile barrier of human rights.

It is nevertheless clear in the light of analytical experience that this commendable desire for justice forgets a little too quickly that consents or refusals given by the ego often contradict those of the unconscious, and that this chasm is visible most clearly in the space of our relation to sex. How can we ignore the fact that our choices in love and the responses of *jouissance* are often a surprise to the aspirations of the ego, and that for this very reason, we might fear that laws claiming to constrain the partner within the norms of the ego simply give an exaggerated power to the faithlessness of hysterical intrigue? The rights of man are finally expanding to include the rights of women; this is laudable in itself, but they will never include the rights of the absolute Other. A woman, even if she is a subject, subjected as such to agreements of coexistence like any other subject, is incapable of negotiating with the Other that she is even to herself.

Foreclosure Redoubled

One question arises: what happens to the Other in the age of the contract? Is it not given over to the gag rule, since the Other is, by definition, antithetical to all legalization?

The Other to which I am referring here is of course not the Other of language, which does not exist, but a living Other, who, on the contrary, ex-ists [*ex-iste*] in and out of language. The two go together, since the first, the one with which one would want to strangle reality in order to bring order to the coexistence of different experiences of *jouissance*, renders everything which escapes it Other. This is how Lacan uses the term when he speaks of woman as an absolute Other, or, one could say, a real Other in that she is excluded from discourse. More generally, this Other takes on an existence each time configurations of *jouissance* appear that exceed the limits of the phallus and the norms and regulations of discourse—in other words, each time that drive goes beyond the limits imposed by the pleasure principle. In this sense, sex is not the only Other; we could even say that everyone is Other to the degree that he or she experiences *jouissance* foreclosed from phallic *jouissance*—"Other like everyone," as Lacan said in 1980.

Epiphanies of the Other are also varied: they appear between cultures (e.g., racism) and even within a single culture as symptoms of the failure of discourse to unify different *jouissances*, because it is to the extent to which there are failures in the One that parts of the Other are ejected as waste.

Today, it seems to me that the values of equality, along with the growing homogenization of the lifestyles of men and women, are reducing the di-mention [*dit-mention*] of heterogeneity as much as they misunderstand it. Women themselves participate in this process, now that they are fervent supporters of contractual and egalitarian ideology rather than mystics. Not content to rival men on the level of phallic achievements, a domain in which we now see women are not handicapped (since anatomy is not destiny), they have introduced the ideology of the contract into sexuality itself, as shown by the trials I spoke of before, which sometimes reach levels of absurdity. From there it is only a short step to thinking that by overly stressing this ideology, one in fact causes the unwelcome surprises that heterosexuals can hold in reserve.

In this context, what is the option represented by analytic discourse? After positing the unconscious as knowledge, Lacan cannot ignore that the unconscious knows nothing of the Other, and that it knows only the One—the ones who repeat themselves, or the One-saying [*l'Un-dire*] [11] of enunciation—to the point where we can say that the subject of the unconscious is in essence a bachelor. But psychoanalysis is not the unconscious, and its process, insofar as it tries to explore the Other of language in its inconsistency,[12] also pushes toward the Other [*pousse à l'Autre*] in the second sense (I am using this expression here by analogy to the push toward femininity [*pousse-à-la-femme*]). The psychoanalyst himself is in fact related to the logic of not-all,[13] whose structure is not that of a collection but of a series; it is a phallic series in which the Other only appears along the borders, or the margins, unless it is covered by the object *qua* semblance. Psychoanalysis must therefore know something about the Other; it is a way of naming the real, a real which it must deal with, which belongs to it, which is "extimate" [*extime*] and impossible to write—a real which is, however, embodied and therefore animated by the palpitation of *jouissance*.

The Ethics of Difference

The conclusion I can draw is that psychoanalysis, contrary to the dominant discourse, shuns all complicity with the rising bachelor ethic in its different forms. If Lacan could designate the desire of the psychoanalyst as "a desire of absolute difference," [14] it is because analysis makes the patient articulate in speech the singularity of the mode of *jouissance*, which for every subject compensates for its sexual gaping hole, in other words, the difference of the subject's symptom, taking this term in its largest sense. The unconscious conditions all symptoms, from the most autistic to the most externally oriented, whether they regulate solitary voluptuousness or that of the couple, whether they are related to psychosis or to generalized perversion. But an ethics of difference can only be opposed to the ethics of the same that governs the segregationist symptoms of the Other.

Lacan perceived the rejection of the Other as being at the very heart of psychoanalysis itself and stigmatized it as the "scandal of analytical discourse," [15] as I have pointed out elsewhere. [16] Even Freud could be accused of it, in that he used the same gauge for men and women. We can recognize this elision as something like an affirmation against the real and a desire to know nothing about it, which of course cannot be without effect, and which allows us to anticipate the risk of a return of the real as a result of the foreclusionary mechanism. Perhaps Montherland's suicide itself makes sense in this context.

It is impossible, however, simply to subscribe oneself to the Other; there is no directory assistance in the phone book of the unconscious. The question is what heteroethics can make of this Other with which it has no rapport and perhaps not even a relation. It can do no more than knot the Other into the unconscious, which means into the phallic order. This knot is one of the names of love, which means that, for a man, a woman is a symptom. This completes the model of per-version [père-version], written like this as two words (as Lacan does) to evoke the example of the function of the symptom which is the father. Perhaps there is no better use for this Other than to allow it to exist while tying it to the One.

Must we then predict that the less a civilization is able to maintain the knot of the One and the real Other, the more it will have to withstand the proliferation of other instances of the real, of a real untied from the phallic order, and the more it will have to come to the conclusion that as Others go, woman is definitely not as bad as it gets?

Translated by Sina Najafi and Marina Harss

Notes

A shorter version of this text was presented under the title "Otherness Today" at the European School of Psychoanalysis colloquium "The Clinical Limits of Gender" on 22 Mar. 1997 in London.

1   Jacques Lacan, "L'étourdit," *Scilicet* 4 (1973): 24.

2   The expression is from Jacques-Alain Miller, who made it the title of one of his annual evening lecture series at the Clinical division.

3   Lacan, *The Seminar of Jacques Lacan*, book 20: *Encore*, ed. Jacques-Alain Miller, trans. Bruce Fink (New York: W. W. Norton, 1998), 4.

4   *Hommosexuel* combines the French word *homme* (man) with the prefix *homo-* (the same) [Translators].

5   Lacan, "L'étourdit," 24.

6   This seems to be an invented word combining *sembler*, "to seem," and *d'emblée*, "at once" [Translators].

7   Lacan, *Encore*, 85.

8   I owe this expression to Jacques-Alain Miller.

9   Cf. Lacan, "L'étourdit," 24.

10   Colette Soler, *Lettre Mensuelle* 156 (Feb. 1997).

11   Lacan, "Ou pire," *Scilicet* 5 (1975): 9.

12   Lacan, "Compte rendu du Séminaire sur l'Acte psychanalytique," *Ornicar?* 29 (1964): 20.

13   This has been effectively proven by Jacques-Alain Miller.

14   Lacan, *The Four Fundamental Concepts of Psychoanalysis*, trans. Alan Sheridan (New York: Penguin, 1979), 276.

15   Lacan, "L'Étourdit," 19.

16   Colette Soler, "Le pastoute," *Revue de l'ECF* 21 (May 1992): 119.

PART II | **paternal**
prohibition

4

Freud's *Moses*

and the Ethics of

Eric L. Santner   **Nomotropic Desire**

It is perhaps ironic that at this historical moment when, at least in the United States, the cultural capital of psychoanalysis is at an all-time low, the work of Freud's that is enjoying the most widespread scholarly interest is the one that has been, up to now, nearly universally judged to be his most wildly, even embarrassingly, speculative. I am thinking, of course, of Freud's last completed book, *Der Mann Moses und die monotheistische Religion (Moses and Monotheism)*.[1] Why has a work whose basic premises, presuppositions, and arguments have nearly all been rejected or radically modified even within the psychoanalytic community claimed our attention now? To name the most important of these premises and theses: the idea that one can psychoanalyze a people as if it were an individual with a linear developmental history as well as conscious and unconscious memories; adherence to a Lamarckian hypothesis regarding the inheritance of acquired characteristics; the claim of totemic origins of religion and civilization, including the thesis of the primal patricide first presented in *Totem and Taboo*; the association of patriarchy with progress in intellectual and spiritual development; and finally, the speculative reconstruction of the Moses story itself. In Freud's view, Moses was an Egyptian priest of the short-lived monotheistic cult of the pharaoh Akhenaten in Egypt in the fourteenth century B.C., the so-called Amarna period; upon the demise of the cult in Egypt, Moses imposed it on the Hebrews, who, unable to bear the stringent burdens of the new religion, murdered Moses, only to internalize his stern command-

ments after many centuries of unconscious remorse. Among these difficult commandments were the worship of a single invisible deity inimical
to plastic representation, prohibition of sorcery and magic, elimination
of a death-denying cultivation of the afterlife, and the practice of circumcision. According to Freud, the rebellion against and murder of
Moses in response to these burdens repeats the plot of the primal patricide with which, in his view, civilization began.[2] These claims provide
the elements of what Freud took to be an awareness of an unnamed
trauma haunting the biblical narratives, a secret *Mit-Wissenschaft,* to use
Schelling's phrase, of what he refers to as the "historical truth," in contrast to the real or material truth, of the origins of Jewish monotheism.[3]

Because of the speculative nature of the Moses book, there has been
a tendency among scholars not to read it as a significant contribution to
any historiography other than that of the cultural pressures that might
have made Freud produce such a text, which, as is well known, he originally considered to be a kind of historical novel. In a word, scholars
have tried to historicize the book as a document of the tense, conflictual
nature of the German-Jewish formation on the eve of its destruction.
This argument is, of course, central to Yosef Yerushalmi's deservedly famous study of Freud's book.[4] Indeed, part of Yerushalmi's project has
been to undo Freud's lifelong "official" denials, made under the pressures of rising anti-Semitic sentiment in Europe; of a deep engagement
with Jewish sources and knowledge of Hebrew and Yiddish; and, above
all, of an abiding belief that psychoanalysis itself was a sort of godless
Judaism. That is, if the Moses book failed to be an enduring contribution to the "Wissenschaft des Judentums," it continues to be valuable
as a document manifesting, even secretly admitting, the Jewishness of
the strange science that continues to bear Freud's name. In defense of
this thesis, whose paradoxical nature has been discussed at length by
Derrida, Yerushalmi submits that one will understand it only by passing beyond the "false and insidious dichotomy between the 'parochial'
and the 'universal,' that canard of the Enlightenment which became and
remains a major neurosis of modern Jewish intellectuals."[5]

More recently, Daniel Boyarin has persuasively argued that Freud's
Moses ought to be read as an extended and—in a Freudian sense—displaced effort at assimilation, even at a sort of conversion on Freud's
part.[6] Because of the proliferation of anti-Semitic discourses circulat-

ing in popular culture as well as in so-called scientific communities—
discourses in which Jewish men, in particular, were figured as being
in some sense feminized, as being, in terms of their gender and sexuality, out of joint—Freud was under enormous pressure to construct an
image of Judaism that could pass muster as a cultural formation compatible with contemporary norms of masculinity and heterosexuality.
We might think of this as the way that "canard of the Enlightenment"
alluded to by Yerushalmi makes itself felt at the level of gender identity, the "parochial" being, of course, figured as feminine. As has been
well documented, these pressures rose enormously with the influx of
Eastern European Jews after World War I, for the *Ostjude,* this quasi-
"Asiatic" foreigner, was seen by many Germans—Jewish and Gentile
alike—as embodying the extremes of Jewish degeneration. (There was,
of course, a countermovement to this trend, one which instead idealized *Ostjudentum* as the last locus of Jewish authenticity and vitality;
one thinks above all of the work of Martin Buber.[7]) As Boyarin puts
it, "Freud's *Moses and Monotheism* is best read as part of a massive
sociocultural attempt by German-speaking Jews [beginning] in the nineteenth century to rewrite themselves, and particularly their masculine
selves, as Aryans, especially as Teutons." And further: "An entire Jewish collective—including its Orthodox members—engaged in a project
of the assimilation of Jewish culture to *Kultur,* and this included an assimilation of Judaism itself to Protestantism, the sublime faith. Rather
than the conversion of the Jews, the total conversion of Judaism was
the solution."[8] What Boyarin has in mind here are those passages in
Freud's *Moses* which characterize the essence of Judaism along the lines
of Hermann Cohen's Neo-Kantian conception of a religion of reason,
a religion that reaches, unlike its more "primitive" polytheistic precursor in Egypt, the "heights of sublime abstraction," as Freud puts it.[9]
Indeed, the image of Judaism one gets from Freud's book is of a religion that not only condemns the production of graven images and the
practice of magic and sorcery, but beyond that is essentially averse to
all forms of ritual, to all "carnal" practices aside from the elaboration and refinement of the original ethical commandments. In light of
Boyarin's reading, Freud's Judaism comes to resemble a sort of Haber-
masian *Verfassungspatriotismus* in which the Mosaic ordinances regulating ethical behaviors stand as the national constitution. According

to Boyarin, then, behind Freud's own conception of the "normative in-version"[10] of Egyptian cultural and religious practices instituted by the Mosaic laws and ordinances, an inversion that ultimately leads to a (compulsive) valuation of intellectual and spiritual virtues—of *Geistig-keit*—stands Freud's anxious efforts at passing as a good, virile German. This meant, as can be seen in Otto Weininger's notorious and highly in-fluential treatise, *Geschlecht und Charakter,* being a man of "Kantian" moral and intellectual self-mastery and sobriety. To quote Boyarin once more, "Jewish carnality, adherence to a law characterized by its passion-ate attachment to blood and flesh and thus described by antisemites . . . as feminine, is transvalued by Freud precisely into a . . . masculinist *Geistigkeit* or denial of the body itself."[11] We might call it, to use Max Nordau's famous phrase, *Muskeljudentum,* conceived as a moral and spiritual habitus, a resolute self-governance grounded in the multiple renunciations demanded by the Kantian conception of theoretical and practical reason.

Ilse Grubrich-Simitis has offered a less radical reading of the bio-graphical dimension of the book, but one which nonetheless salvages from it its value as a piece of Freudian self-analysis and fantasy pro-duction at a moment of extreme personal and political crisis.[12] Accord-ing to Grubrich-Simitis, the book documents the centrality of Moses in Freud's ego ideal, sustaining him in his lifelong struggle with anxieties pertaining to dependency and passivity, themselves residues of preoedi-pal traumas that never ceased to threaten Freud's psychic equilibrium. But against this background, Freud does something quite remarkable. At a point when his ego is most in danger, most in need of support, he subjects himself as well as his coreligionists to a sort of narcissistic in-jury: he claims that the original Jewish cultural hero was, as it were, not an original but rather an Egyptian priest or bureaucrat who, for purely contingent historical reasons, imposed his cult on the Hebrews. Let us briefly recall the opening lines of Freud's book, where he acknowledges the gravity of the narcisstic injury his thesis entails: "To deprive a people of the man whom they take pride in as the greatest of their sons is not a thing to be gladly or carelessly undertaken, least of all by someone who is himself one of them. But we cannot allow any such reflection to induce us to put the truth aside in favour of what are supposed to be national interests; and, moreover, the clarification of a set of facts may be expected to bring us a gain in knowledge" (Freud, *SE* 23:7).

We have here an indication of what might be seen as the categorical imperative proper to the Freudian response to historical crisis: at a moment of danger, counteract the natural tendency to protect the ego by means of imaginary self-aggrandizement. In a sense, Freud models a response to crisis that was diametrically opposed to what he was seeing all around him in Germany and Austria: while his Christian compatriots were busy fashioning themselves as original and pure Aryans by means of a narcissistic identification with Hitler and the grandiose fantasy of a millenial Reich, Freud introduced "impurity" and secondariness into the heart of Jewish cultural identity by suggesting that Jewish ethnogenesis begins with the contingent act of a willful Egyptian priest. In Freud's view, Jewish ego formation is ultimately grounded in a citation of occulted Egyptian authorities; where one would expect to find an essential core of indigenous drive—the id—Freud appears to install a (repressed) citational practice; call it the ibid. We might, then, say that Freud's strategy here elaborates, with cultural-historical materials, an alternative structural model of the (Jewish) psyche, one we might characterize as the ego and the ibid.[13] This "positive" reading of Freud's counternarcissistic gesture is, however, complicated by two considerations. In the last part of his book, Freud will argue that Jewish "narcissism" is recuperated on a level of symbolic, as opposed to imaginary, identification. That is, the result of mastering a profound narcissistic injury is often a "higher," symbolic form of narcissism or sense of spiritual superiority. And, as Boyarin suggests, this spiritual form of superiority was coded in terms that would have allowed Freud to "pass" as an Aryan man.

For Grubrich-Simitis, the most important aspect of Freud's claim that Moses was an Egyptian was ultimately a utopian one. By making Moses an Egyptian, she surmises, Freud hoped to deconstruct the boundary between Jew and Gentile, a boundary that had, in the Germany of the 1930s, assumed the rigidity of a paranoid construction. "Perhaps," she writes, "Freud had, in his secularized messianism, even imagined, in the register of a daydream, that his own theory of culture might help to facilitate this collective process of self-healing."[14]

Of all recent efforts at historicizing Freud's *Moses*, the one that opens itself up most to the radicality of Freud's theories concerning the "historical truth" of Jewish enthnogenesis is a work by the German Egyptologist Jan Assmann bearing the provocative title *Moses the Egyptian*. Assmann argues that only by taking Freud's arguments concerning the Egyptian origins of monotheism seriously can one hope to achieve the "messianic" dream alluded to by Grubrich-Simitis. "In this dream," as Assmann puts it, "the counter-religious institution of Moses' monotheistic revelation is revoked. It is a dream of reconciliation." [15]

Assmann's own commitment to this ostensibly Freudian dream is based on an understanding of monotheism as one of the primary impediments to cross-cultural translation in the modern world and thus as a major source of intolerance toward the beliefs, practices, and lives of others. According to Assmann, it is only with monotheism that we encounter the phenomenon of a counterreligion, that is, a religious formation that posits a distinction between *true* and *false* religion. Prior to that, the boundaries between polytheistic—or as Assmann prefers, cosmotheistic—cults were in principle open, the names of gods translatable from cult to cult because of a shared evidentiary base in nature, that is, in cosmic phenomena. Translatability is, in such a universe, grounded in and guaranteed by ultimate reference to nature. By contrast, monotheism, because it is grounded in (revealed) scripture, tends to erect a rigid boundary between true religion and everything else, now rejected as "paganism": "Whereas polytheism, or rather 'cosmotheism,' rendered different cultures mutually transparent and compatible, the new counter-religion blocked intercultural translatability. False gods cannot be translated" (Assmann, 3). According to Assmann, this rupture in patterns and possibilities of cultural translation, a rupture that has been codified in the West as the Mosaic distinction between Israel in truth and Egypt in error, must be understood as a profound historical trauma, and indeed as one that continues to haunt the West in the guise of violence against racial and cultural "others."

Once he has established this general principle concerning the role of monotheism in the ancient world, Assmann argues that Akhenaten's religious revolution in Egypt in the fourteenth century B.C. represents the advent of this disturbance—of counterreligious traumatism—in human history. This revolution was "not only the first but also the most radical and violent eruption of a counter-religion in the history of humankind. The temples were closed, the images of the gods were destroyed, their names were erased, and their cults were discontinued. . . .

The nonobservance of ritual interrupts the maintenance of cosmic and social order. The consciousness of a catastrophe and irreparable crime must have been quite widespread" (Assmann, 25). Because, by chance, the introduction of Akhenaten's cult, a cult in which the singular god was identified with the sun, coincided with the outbreak of a terrible epidemic throughout the entire Near East, Assmann concludes that "it is more than probable that this experience, together with that of the religious revolution, formed the trauma that gave rise to the phantasm of the religious enemy" (Assmann, 25). Assmann's core thesis is that the particular features of anti-Semitism in the West, above all the long association of Jews with disease and contamination, have been in large measure determined by this originally Egyptian trauma: "The Egyptian phantasm of the religious enemy first became associated with the Asiatics in general and then with Jews in particular. It anticipates many traits of Western anti-Semitism that can now be traced back to an original impulse. This impulse had nothing to do with the Jews but very much to do with the experience of a counter-religion and of a plague" (Assmann, 30). The "historical truth" of anti-Semitism, to use Freud's phrase, is thus to be located "not in idiosyncratic aversions of Jews and Egyptians but in the Mosaic distinction as such, *which was originally Akhenaten's distinction*" (Assmann, 5; my emphasis).[16]

To summarize this remarkable reconstruction, which is every bit as audacious as Freud's in *Moses and Monotheism,* Assmann argues that the traumatic disruption of the polytheistic cultural order by the violent imposition of monotheism in Egypt in the fourteenth century B.C.—a trauma almost immediately repressed in cultural memory after the collapse of Akhenaten's reign—formed a pathogenic core that would prove to be fateful in the later Egyptian encounter with the Jews. That encounter was, in a word, prefigured in the earlier, traumatic experience of a counterreligion which—and here lies the difficult heart of the matter—shared a number of structural similarities with the Mosaic formation.[17] In Assmann's view, the Egyptian encounter with the Jews in Hellenistic and Roman times must have been experienced as a return of the repressed trauma of Akhenaten's counterreligious revolution. In effect, Assmann appropriates the plot of Freud's *Moses* and posits it as an originally Egyptian story. Whereas for Freud, the rise and violent demise of Moses repeated, in certain structural features, the violent events of the primal horde experience, for Assmann, the Egyptian encounter with the Mosaic religion recalled an earlier (repressed) experience of what for Assmann is a *cultural violence internal to monotheism*. Affects (and their phantasmatic elaborations) left over from the Amarna experience, affects "unbound" or uncoupled from any object because of cultural repression,[18] were attached to the religion of Moses, who thereby became not so much Egyptian as *uncannily* Egyptian: both foreign and utterly familiar, an autochthonic alien. It is against the backdrop of this theory of counterreligious traumatism, repression, and return of the repressed that Assmann reads the various revisionist accounts of the Exodus story from Manetho to Tacitus. These are accounts in which the Exodus is figured not as a liberation of an oppressed people but as an expulsion of leprous aliens; these are generally understood to have laid the foundation of anti-Semitism in the West, to have provided the Western imagination with its core imagery of the diseased and degenerate Jew.

One of the paradoxes—really a sort of temporal loop—at work in this thesis is the claim that the phantasm of the religious enemy was formed in response to the introduction of the concept of the religious enemy by monotheism. According to Assmann, prior to monotheism there was no place for such a concept in the logical space of the ancient world. There were, of course, enemies, but not, Assmann suggests, of the type associated with counterreligious abomination. In Assmann's view, monotheism cleaves this space in such a way that the religious enemy—the essentially diseased other—becomes a possible object of experience. The paradox, then, is this: the real religious enemy is not so much the one seen as the bearer of the (newly conceived) "false" religion, but rather is the one seen as responsible for opening up this possibility of thought and affect in the first place. Anti-Semitism is, in this reading, directed at Jews not so much as the bearers of religious truth or error but rather as the bearers of the cultural formation that—and this is the real trauma— cleaved the universe into fundamentally incompatible domains of true and false religion. We might put it this way: if we call the distinction between true and false religion an *ontic* distinction, the difference between a world without such a distinction and one marked by it must be considered to be *ontological*. The Jews are the "carriers" of the event of this ontological distinction. The real trauma, according to Assmann, is not an ontic but rather what we might call an "ontological crime."[19]

But what is crucial for Assmann is that it was Akhenaten who, as it were, performed the original counterreligious cut in the ancient world. The persistence in the West of a discourse that presumes the Egyptian identity of Moses is understood by Assmann to be a kind of secret and displaced archive of this knowledge. By analyzing this archive, that is, the history of "Moses the Egyptian" as a figure of memory—Assmann characterizes this work as *mnemohistory*—one can, Assmann suggests, amplify Freud's views concerning the sources of anti-Semitism in the West:

> Not the Jew but monotheism had attracted this undying hatred. By making Moses an Egyptian, he deemed himself able to shift the sources of negativity and intolerance out of Judaism and back to Egypt, and show that the defining fundamentals of Jewish monotheism and mentality came from outside it. . . . Freud concentrates all the counter-religious force of Biblical monotheism in Akhenaten's revolution from above. This was the origin of it all. Freud stresses (quite correctly) the fact that he is dealing with the absolutely first monotheistic, counter-religious, and exclusivistically intolerant movement of this sort in human history. . . . *It is this hatred brought about by Akhenaten's revolution that informs the Judeophobic texts of antiquity.* (Assmann, 167; my emphasis) [20]

In the course of his mnemohistorical research on the figure of "Moses the Egyptian," research focused above all on works by late-Renaissance scholars and eighteenth-century Freemasons—he begins with John Spencer and ends with Gotthold Ephraim Lessing—Assmann discerns a common thread. The essential thrust of this textual tradition was to argue that despite "its obvious polytheistic and idolatrous appearance," Egyptian religion could be seen to contain "an esoteric and original monotheism or pantheism" (Assmann, 20). Moses was able to bring monotheism to the Hebrews because he had already been initiated into a monotheistic mystery cult—a kind of Spinozism—of the Egyptians. The discourses on "Moses the Egyptian"—and Assmann places Freud firmly within this tradition, indeed sees him as its culmination—are thus understood to be essentially efforts at dismantling the boundaries between revealed religion and cosmotheism. The "hidden agenda" of these discourses was, Assmann writes, "to deconstruct 'counter-religion' and its implications of intolerance by blurring the basic distinctions as they were symbolized by the antagonistic constellation of Israel and Egypt. 'Revelation' had to be (re)turned into 'translation'" (Assmann, 147; my emphasis). The opposition of Israel in truth and Egypt in error, of revealed, scripture-based monotheism and nonrevealed, nature-based polytheism, is superseded here by a conception of a *nonrevealed, nature-based monotheism*. And on the basis of his own analysis of Amarna theology, Assmann suggests that these discourses come very close to capturing the cosmotheistic kernel of Akhenaten's revolution:

> If the space of religious truth is constructed by the distinction between "Israel in truth" and "Egypt in error," any discoveries of Egyptian truths will necessarily invalidate the Mosaic distinction and deconstruct the space separated by this distinction. This method or strategy of historical deconstruction became especially important in the context of the Enlightenment, when all distinctions were viewed as opposed to Nature, and Nature came to be elevated to the rank of highest ideal. Spinoza's (in)famous formula *deus sive natura* amounted to an abolition not only of the Mosaic distinction but of the most fundamental of all distinctions, the distinction between God and the world. This deconstruction was as revolutionary as Moses' construction. It immediately led to a new appraisal of Egypt. The Egyptians were Spinozists and "cosmotheists." Ancient cosmotheism as a basis for intercultural translation was rediscovered. In the discourse of the Enlightenment, it was reconstructed as an international and intercultural mystery religion in the fashion of Freemasonry. (Assmann, 8)[21]

In the spirit of these efforts, and for the sake of its "potential consequences for the development of thought, society, and moral institutions," Assmann concludes his study by embracing the "return of Egypt and its cosmotheism *as the suppressed counter-religion of Biblical monotheism*" (Assmann, 218; my emphasis). By cultivating the cosmotheistic *content* of Akhenaten's revolution—the original counterreligion—one might, in other words, overcome the toxicity of its *form*, that is, the traumatogenic tendency of counterreligious formations to produce impassable barriers to cultural translation.

Whatever one might think of such a project, Assmann's view that it is one in which Freud participated represents a deep and in its own way important misunderstanding of Freud's project in *Moses and Monotheism* (by that I mean a misunderstanding that opens up a fruitful meditation on fundamental concepts).[22] There are two aspects to Assmann's mnemohistorical critique of monotheistic intolerance, only one of which, I think, is genuinely compatible with what Freud is up to in his *Moses*. The Freudian dimension of Assmann's project pertains to the recollection and working through of trauma, a labor he sees as crucial to the overcoming of anti-Semitism in the West and of religious abomination more generally. We might say that both Freud and Assmann see the cultural space carved out by the Judeo-Christian tradition as curved, in the manner of a traumatropism (according to the OED, "a peculiar growth or curvature of an organism . . . resulting from a wound"). The trauma is "present," exercises its influence, precisely *as* the curvature of this space. By "curvature" I mean the way an individual or a collective organizes its life as if in response to a spectral presence, to the trace of an event that has never achieved the full ontological weight of a historical reality, and so remains, effectively, "preontological" or "protocosmic." According to Assmann, the imposition of Akhenaten's cult in Egypt in the fourteenth century B.C. continues to "insist" (as a spectral presence) because, in a certain sense, it has not yet really taken place. Anti-Semitism is, Assmann suggests, one of the registers in which, beginning in the ancient world, this original trauma continued not to take place, a failure that has not ceased to produce catastrophic effects. Assmann's project is dedicated to giving the trauma a cultural space in which it might finally take place and thereby lose its demonic force. But there is another side to this project which strikes me as rather un-Freudian. It pertains to Assmann's assumption that a capacity for tolerance and empathy is compatible only with a sense of universality itself grounded in a worldview of the cosmotheistic type (this is the meaning of the (re)turning of revelation to a cosmotheistic basis of cultural translatability referred to above).

If I understand him correctly, Assmann's claim is that once we appreciate that "behind" biblical monotheism stands Akhenaten's revolution, we will be in a position to pass beyond the trauma of its originally violent imposition—a trauma that continues to haunt the West in the form of phobic fixations on religious enemies—and to appropriate the essentially cosmotheistic content of that revolution. It is that content alone which holds the promise of an opening to a future of genuine cosmopolitanism and religious tolerance. We might say that the dream of reconciliation alluded to by Assmann—a dream he ascribes to Freud—is cosmotheistic in its latent content. Assmann's crucial model for this dream of reconciliation is the effort made by various thinkers of the Enlightenment to discern within the biblical narratives traces of a cosmotheistic mystery religion.

But it is precisely here, where Assmann tries, as it were, to fill in the traumatic beginnings of monotheism with a secret, cosmotheistic doctrine in the spirit of eighteenth-century Freemasonry and Spinozism, that the distance between his project of reconciliation, of the restoration of a cosmotheistic basis of cross-cultural translation, and Freud's project of psychocultural genealogy becomes most evident (even though this is exactly the place where Assmann thinks himself to be most in sync with the spirit of Freud's work). We might characterize this distance (which may just be another version of the "Mosaic distinction" at the level of the theory of distinction) as that between two modalities of what I referred to as traumatropism. Recalling that Akhenaten's cult was essentially a form of sun worship, we might think of the difference between cosmotheistic monotheism and Jewish monotheism as that between a heliotropic and a nomotropic modality of that cultural "pathology."[23] By *nomotropism,* I mean the obsessive-compulsive preoccupation with *nomos,* with matters of law, justice, and ethics, which for Freud also comprised the compulsive dimension of the search for scientific truth, the *Zwang* internal to *Wissenschaft.* In the one case—cosmotheism—we find direct enjoyment of cosmic eros, of *deum sive naturam,* while in nomotropism "enjoyment" is conceived as an ambiguous libidinal tension strictly correlative to the ethicospiritual turn to the Law. In part, the question behind this disagreement is whether a nomotropic habitus can foster a genuine cosmopolitanism, which implies a fundamental openness *to* world and other, or whether it rather promotes a turning *from* world and other (and if so, for the sake of what?).

Freud wrote *Moses and Monotheism* in part to explain the seeming paradox he had noted in the preface to the Hebrew edition of *Totem and Taboo,* a paradox quite common among Freud's German-Jewish compatriots. There Freud wrote that although he is "completely estranged from the religion of his fathers . . . and . . . cannot take a share in nationalist ideals," he nevertheless feels that "he is in his essential nature a Jew." He added that "he could not now express that essence in words; but some day, no doubt, it will become accessible to the scientific mind."[24] *Moses and Monotheism* was in part Freud's effort to make this, his own "essential nature" as a Jew, an essence that somehow persisted despite his alienation from the liturgical and ritual practices of Judaism, accessible to the "science" of psychoanalysis. In the course of his investigation, Freud is led, however, not to the trauma of gods deposed and cults disbanded in the name of an encounter with the One *qua* Nature, but rather to a traumatic encounter with the grammar of injunction, of imperative speech acts charging the subject with ethical mandates.[25] The name Freud gives to this imperative dimension is, of course, *superego;* it figures as the psychic representative of an ultimately enigmatic and, as Freud would have it, paternal will.

In *Moses and Monotheism,* Freud develops the notion of the superego in conjunction with reflections alluded to earlier regarding the way in which a certain Jewish *Geistigkeit* appears to recuperate, on a symbolic level, a narcissism abandoned at the level of imaginary identification. Freud admits his perplexity at this peculiar conversion. "It is not obvious and not immediately understandable," he writes, "why an advance in intellectuality [*Geistigkeit*], a set-back to sensuality, should raise the self-regard both of an individual and of a people. It seems to presuppose the existence of a definite standard of value and so some other person or agency which maintains it" (Freud, *SE* 23:116). One cannot, he continues, "point to the authority which lays down the standard which is to be regarded as higher. . . . Thus we are faced by the phenomenon that in the course of the development of humanity [a development which, Freud assumes, took a quantum leap with the advent of monotheism] sensuality is gradually overpowered by intellectuality and that men feel proud and exalted by every such advance. But we are unable to say why this should be so" (Freud, *SE* 23:118).

This problem was, we should recall, a core issue of both Marx's and Nietzsche's philosophy: the problem of value, the value-form, and, above all, the problem of the value of values. The missing link in the genesis of value—the absence of a final value or justification grounding values and value exchange, the fact that value as such can never be finally substantiated (otherwise we would be faced with things and not values)—is filled, for Freud, by the "historical truth" of a paternal performative: "Going back to ethics, we may say . . . that a part of its precepts are justified rationally. . . . But what seems to us so grandiose about ethics, so mysterious and, in a mystical fashion, so self-evident, owes these characteristics to its connection with religion, its origin from the will of the father" (Freud, *SE* 23:122).[26] The superego thus marks the site of a paradoxical transmutation that in Freud's view figures in all religious thought and feeling. Indeed, we might call it the primordial figure. The missing reason—an answer to a final why-question— that would, according to the logic of theodicy, justify and so ground value, whether in the economic or ethical sphere, becomes a hypervalued, hypercathected placeholder of a lack of reasons: the father's willful word whose enunciation needs no rationale and is registered as an autopoetic "cause" that opens a field of values. The sovereignty of the paternal performative—the father's uncanny voice—is here linked to a breach in the logic of theodicy, a breach somehow constitutive of the possibility of life with values.

Earlier, Freud had linked this superego dimension of ethical feeling to a peculiar form of pleasure: "But whereas instinctual renunciation, when it is for external reasons, is *only* unpleasurable, when it is for internal reasons, in obedience to the super-ego, it has a different economic effect. In addition to the inevitable unpleasurable consequences it also brings the ego a yield of pleasure—a substitutive satisfaction, as it were" (Freud, *SE* 23:116–17). But it is in the final pages of the book that Freud really lays his cards on the table and suggests that the ethical genius of the Jews derives from a kind of perverse capacity for this sublime pleasure-in-pain, this *jouissance*: "In a fresh rapture of moral asceticism [*In einem neuen Rausch moralischer Askese*] they imposed more and more instinctual renunciations on themselves and in that way reached— in doctrine and precept, at least—ethical heights which had remained inaccessible to the other peoples of antiquity" (Freud, *SE* 23:134). The word Freud uses here, "rapture" or *Rausch*, bears distinctly Dionysian connotations of sensual excess and intoxication. The path of Jewish spiritual development traced by Freud turns out to have been shaped like a Möbius strip: in their attempt to structure a relationship to the mystically self-evident, nonsymbolizable dimension of their ethical commandments, the Jews rediscover, on a different level of experience and imagination, the "pagan" excesses which Judaism had ostensibly evacuated from the religious experience. The "secret treasure" of the Jews, as Freud refers to their "higher," ethicospiritual form of narcissism (Freud, *SE* 23:115), turns out to be dependent on an uncanny secretion of *jouissance* within the precincts of the moral law.[27] It is this "pagan" intoxication, this "carnal" enjoyment at the very core of what Freud characterizes as Jewish *Geistigkeit*—the spiritual and intellectual genius built around loss, instinctual renunciation, and deterritorialization—that represents, I think, the possibility of a rapprochement with Assmann's efforts to recuperate cosmotheism as a resource for reconciliation and the dismantling of phobic antagonisms, that is, antagonisms of the religious type.[28]

The crucial point, however, is that for Assmann, cosmotheistic "revelation" is that of a *shared substantial order* serving as the basis of intercultural translation; Freud, by contrast, focuses on a nontranslatable residue of *the process of ordering* itself, a residue that manifests itself as a certain drivenness, a certain compulsive energy endowing the symbolic order with uncanny animation. Freud thought that this uncanny vitality he discerned at the core of the Jewish tradition, and which he traces to a traumatic history, had been the secret of the survival of the Jews as a people. But it was also, he thought, the real object of hatred, revulsion, and envy in all anti-Semitism. What distinguished modern anti-Semitism from earlier varieties was largely the effort to isolate this surplus vitality as a genetic endowment, to biologize what was, in fact, a "life substance" that inhered not in the blood but, as it were, in the symbolic system itself, its specific way of binding—and so opening—the subject to its claims of normativity.

This notion of a kind of "Jewish uncanny" has immediate consequences for our understanding of universality. One of the central issues in any cultural crisis, at least since the Enlightenment—and Freud's *Moses* is, as Yerushalmi has rightly noted, an intervention in a crisis of post-Enlightenment civilization—is that of the definition of the community, the delimitation of the boundaries of the universals by which membership in the community of citizens is decided (one thinks here, for example, about the ongoing debates concerning membership in the various organizations of properly "Western" nations, nations whose political and economic structures are deemed compatible with Western notions of universality). Universalization, the expansion of the field of freedom, of human dignity, toward ever greater inclusiveness—to adapt the Freudian locution, geopolitical *Fortschritt in der Geistigkeit*—is, in the Mosaic paradigm, dependent not on reference to a primordially shared nature independent of any "positive" formulation of the universal, but rather on the surplus vitality immanent in the universal, in its contingent formulation. Every effort to reformulate the universal, to remap its boundaries, borrows, at some level, from the drive energies secreted within the universal, its secret "knowledge" or *Mitwissenschaft* of its own grounding in—and thus its debt to—a contingent, "parochial" locus of enunciation. It is this knowledge—really a sort of hauntedness by this debt—that is, Freud suggests, dispersed and elaborated in the biblical narratives, a knowledge comprising what we might call the "mythic" dimension of the biblical passage beyond myth, the "Egyptian" aspect of the exit from Egypt. The energies that attract and contract the subject to the rule of law are the same ones that perturb its functioning and push toward ever more expansive reformulations, new "Exoduses" from conditions stained by relations of domination. Freud clearly thought that it had, for utterly contingent reasons, become the historical task of the Jews to hold the place of—or, more accurately, to embody—this paradoxical vitality animating the struggle over ethico-political universals (by "embody" I mean that for Freud the Jews live this "task" as a kind of symptom, as a traumatropic passage through history). Which, of course, goes a long way in explaining why communities in crisis so often seem to discover that they are plagued by the so-called "Jewish question." Indeed, we might say that the real measure of the political maturity of a community lies in its capacity to claim this question as its own.

Perhaps another way of approaching this "disagreement" between Assmann and Freud is to recall Grubrich-Simitis's remark concerning Freud's "dream": "Perhaps," she writes, "Freud had, in his secularized messianism, even imagined, in the register of a daydream, that his own theory of culture might help to facilitate this collective process of self-healing."[29] Assmann, of course, characterized this dream as one of rec-

onciliation, in which the "counter-religious institution of Moses' monotheistic revelation is revoked." [30] The fundamental problem with these
views is that they attribute to Freud a messianism that is, at bottom,
singularly un-Freudian. If anything, Freud's understanding of culture in
general and of the Jewish cultural formation in particular suggests that
the best one can and ought to hope for is a working through of messianism, that is, of the fantasies contained in any vision of "last days." Indeed, Freud's *Moses* provides nothing less than the traumatic genealogy
of this "ought."

We might better appreciate the problem with converting Freud to
messianism, secular or religious, by recalling Michael Walzer's perspi-
cacious analysis of the difference between what he calls "Exodus thinking" and messianism proper. In his study of the Exodus narratives and
their legacy in Western political culture, Walzer has emphasized both
the radicality and the realism of these stories as presented in the Bible
and elaborated in rabbinic interpretation. [31] What is radical about the
Exodus narratives is that they open a field of temporal, emphatically historical experience beyond the closure of mythic time, thereby giving the
notion of "revolution" its modern sense of emancipatory movement into
a radically new future. The future opened by the biblical narratives no
longer cleaves to the rhythms of natural life and its cyclical patterns:
the lives and deeds of men and women no longer unfold according to a
system of correspondences extending "upwards, hierarchically, into the
mythic realm of nature and of nature's gods." Rather, Walzer argues,
"Biblical narrative generally, Exodus more particularly, breaks in the
most decisive way with this kind of cosmological storytelling" (Walzer,
13). The claim here is not that the relation to time elaborated in normative Judaism is devoid of a dimension of circularity and cycle. Rather,
the experience of cyclical time and natural repetition is transformed, by
the biblical narratives and their liturgical elaboration within the Jewish calendar, precisely into reminders of the break Walzer has noted,
that is, of the intervention of another temporality into human experience. The cycles of Jewish prayer, celebration, and remembrance are,
one might say, a mode of attunement to a noncyclical, postmythic temporality opened by the events—or, better, the event-structure—of deliverance and covenant. To use the terms introduced earlier, the Exodus
narratives uncouple temporality from its link to a cosmotheistic nor-

mativity, where the measure of human purposiveness is given and constrained by cosmic phenomena—by the rule of the sun—and bind it to
a nomotropic one in which human purposiveness is informed by a new
moral and political trajectory. This trajectory is, of course, the linear
procession out of slavery toward a promised land of freedom, a land
where the capacity to enjoy the milk and honey of one's labor is not—
ought not to be—impinged upon or corrupted by relations of lordship
and bondage.[32] To reiterate the Lacanian distinction, we might say that
in the promised land—or, better, in the orientation toward it—enjoyment is uncoupled from cosmic substance and is instead linked to, and
in a sense displaced by, covenantal enjoinment. After Sinai, what is enjoyed *in* milk and honey, what is, as a kind of permanent metaphorical
surplus, taken in or incorporated with these substances, is inseparable
from this enjoinment.

What is crucial, in the present context, is the distinction Walzer draws
between the nomotropic trajectory generated by the Exodus narratives
and more radical messianic strivings. The latter emerge from the patterns of thought and feeling established by the Exodus narratives but
also break with them in important and indeed fateful ways. Again, we
might think of the different conceptions of human purposiveness established by these "shapes of consciousness." Within the Exodus narratives,
human—or rather, Israelite—purposiveness is directed toward worldly
goals and tasks, that is, the emergence from bondage and the cultivation of covenantal responsibilities; messianic purposiveness, which has
its origins in the disappointments of the first and the vision of a second,
even greater Exodus, is directed toward the end of all worldly tasks and
goals: toward a beyond of purposiveness as such. It involves thinking
of the field of purposiveness as a delimited domain the boundaries of
which can be crossed. That is, while the Exodus narrative tells a story
of a historical procession from Egypt to Canaan, a procession structured according to a logic of promise and obligation, thereby including
the ever-present (logical) possibility of failure, messianic narrative tells
a story of a movement from history to a new Eden beyond the ethico-
temporal logic of promise and obligation. This is a movement not only
out of Egypt but out of Canaan and Sinai, too:

> Eden is a mythical garden while the promised land has latitude
> and longitude; Eden stands at the beginning and then, in messianic

thought, at the very end of human history, while the promised land is firmly located within history; and Eden represents the perfection of nature and human nature, while the promised land is simply a better place than Egypt was. . . . Freed from the specific opposition to Egypt, the picture of "the new heaven and the new earth" is worked out, instead, in opposition to this world, this life. It is not hard bondage but daily trouble, not the "evil diseases" of Egypt but disease itself, that will vanish when the messiah comes. (Walzer, 120)

It is in its difference from and resistance to the very messianic thinking that emerges from it that characterizes, for Walzer, the realism of Exodus thinking: "There is no ultimate struggle, but a long series of decisions, backslidings, and reforms. The apocalyptic war between 'the Lord's people' and 'their enemies' can't readily be located within the Exodus" (Walzer, 147). According to Walzer, then, the Exodus narratives provide the resources of a revolutionary politics that avoids the messianic temptation, that allows one to imagine and work toward "local deliverance" (Walzer, 146), toward "a great day that wasn't the Last Day" (Walzer, 130).

There are a number of problems with this otherwise rather appealing social-democratic reading of the biblical narratives. The obvious Freudian criticism would be that Walzer's conception of moral agency, as he sees it elaborated in the Exodus story, appears to have no place for unconscious mental activity and motivation. Indeed, there is a tendency in Walzer's reading to portray Exodus thinking as ego-thinking *tout court,* that is, as self-conscious, rational hopefulness evacuated of fantasy, while messianism is presented as fantasy triumphant over reasonable hope. One might even understand Walzer's reading as a kind of moral plea: where messianism was, there Exodus thinking shall (once more) be. What is clearly missing from this picture is that "shadow" (of) moral agency that was so crucial to Freud: the superego. And yet, by attending, as Freud does, to the superego dimension of Exodus thinking and the forms of consciousness and conscientiousness—of *Mitwissenschaft*—cultivated in normative Judaism more generally, we can, I think, deepen our understanding of the difference between the two senses of futurity opened by the biblical tradition.

Walzer comes closest to an awareness of this dimension in his dis-

cussion of the notion of consent he sees embedded in the canonical accounts of the covenant. As the commentaries on the covenant cited by
Walzer indicate, the covenantal agreement has the structure of a forced
choice: the Israelites are free to choose, provided they make the right
choice.[33] This sense is already clear in the Deuteronomic passage referred to by Walzer: "I call heaven and earth to witness against you this
day, that I have set before you life and death, blessing and curse; therefore choose life, that you and your descendants may live" (Deut. 30:19).
As Walzer himself asks, "how can anyone *not* fear an omnipotent God?"
(Walzer, 162). But the problem of consent assumes its real urgency not
in the imagined "primal scene" of covenantal agreement, but rather in
the organization of its transmission and transference across generations.
As Walzer notes, the problem of consent is a problem of succession, of
following, in both a temporal and normative sense: "Moses' success lies
in the fact that he finds successors not among the few but among the
many. The same competence that makes it possible for individuals to
join in the covenant in the first place also makes it possible for them to
introduce their children to the covenant. What they do is to 'remember'
the Exodus story [here follows a citation of Deut. 6:20–21]" (Walzer,
85). That is, covenantal enjoinment is at its origin an enjoinment to repetition. This "repetition compulsion," established in and, in a sense, *as*
the primordial revelation—what is revealed is, among other things, a
series of mnemotechnical procedures—can be understood as a displacement or deferral internal to the temporality of consent elaborated in the
Bible.[34] The compulsion to repeat the covenant and to enjoin each new
generation to repeat it co-constitutes the bindingness of the "original"
pact. Of that pact we can only say that it *will have been* binding in light of
future repetitions; what one does now and in the future directly affects
the truth of "what really happened" then.

The most famous statement or performance of this concept of consent
as repetition, as compulsive mnemotechnical procedure, is the *shema*,
the prayer taken from the sixth chapter of Deuteronomy that is repeated
every day by observant Jews.[35] The prayer begins with what is no doubt
the most famous—and most oft repeated—instance of interpellation in
Western history: "Hear, O Israel." Beyond the prayer's injunction to
Israel to love its singular God with all its heart, the prayer commands
Israel to repeat and to transmit the words of instruction issued by God
on "this day." These words of instruction include not only the Ten Com-

mandments but the rest of the Torah as well, which contains, of course, the very words of the prayer enjoining repetition. In this way, the injunction achieves a level of nearly pure self-referentiality that extends into practices of material (self-) replication, that is, the placing of the prayer in scrolls affixed to the exterior of the doorposts of Jewish homes and in the phylacteries worn by Jewish men during prayer: "And these words which I command you this day shall be upon your heart; and you shall teach them diligently to your children, and shall talk of them when you sit in your house, and when you walk by the way, and when you lie down, and when you rise. And you shall bind them as a sign upon your head, and they shall be as frontlets between your eyes. And you shall write them on the doorposts of your house and on your gates" (Deut. 6:4–9).[36] Walzer finally concludes that "we should perhaps say simply that the covenant is carried forward on a *flood of talk:* argument and analysis, folkloric expansion, interpretation and reinterpretation" (88; my emphasis). My claim here is that the superego dimension of the moral agency posited in the biblical narratives and conceived by Walzer according to a theory of consent and radical voluntarism is present precisely in and as the very excess—the flood—of talk he notes, an excess we might understand as a torrent of displacements forming the discursive register of nomotropic being.

This flood of talk that co-constitutes the covenantal agreement—that, we might say, co-constitutes it *at its origin*—recalls the alternative model of the psychic apparatus I have called "the ego and the ibid." With "ibid" I am trying to capture precisely this compulsive, iterative aspect of superegoic enjoinment. I am furthermore suggesting that the unconscious is best understood to be structured not so much like a language as like a citational system or "machine" in which the original signifier— the revealed word—to which the authority of all the others is referred is already a citation, already marked by ibidity.[37] Desire, in turn, might also be seen to be no longer simply libidinal, but also and from the start ibidinal: a projective opening to a future correlative to a persistent struggle to ground one's being in an original, authoritative word, a word that would be referred to no other and would thus provide an absolute beginning. Ibidinal desire is, we might say, the form in which one assumes responsibility for this missing word while coming to be haunted by its absence.[38]

Thus, we might understand the difference between Exodus thinking and messianism as one between two attitudes or postures toward the superegoic enjoinment inscribed within the original covenant. That enjoinment is, as we have seen, marked by repetition compulsion, by ibidity. Freud's basic claim in *Moses and Monotheism* would seem to be that the Jewish genius was to structure a way of life around this very ibidity, to discover in it a resource for the elaboration of an understanding of Being—of the *Seynsfuge* or "jointure" of Being, to use Heidegger's locution—grounded in commandment, the enjoinment to law and justice.[39] As is well known, this way of life came to include, as one of its most central features, the study and interpretation of commandment in all its facets: midrashic elaboration of an ibidity already present in the foundational, biblical archive. For Freud, messianism clearly signified a final sealing or closure of the "joints," a supersession or spiritualization of the superegoic enjoinment forming the kernel of Jewish "carnality," a carnality, in part, of (a "flood" of) gesture and speech. That is, the progress in *Geistigkeit*, in spirituality, represented by Christianity meant, for Freud, a spiriting away of spirits and specters, those phantasmatic remainders of the paternal will or voice which endow conscience with a quasi-material density and weight. To put it simply, the messianic "second Exodus" is motivated by a desire to be free of the superego pressures generated by the first one.[40] The resurrection associated with the last days signifies, then, not so much a reanimation of the dead as *a deanimation of the undead*, a putting to rest of their voices. And indeed, Freud understood the Jewish resistance to this absolution—the refusal of Christ as Messiah—as a kind of failure (with respect both to spiritual progress and to progress in spirituality) to which he was nonetheless deeply (need we say libidinally?) attached.

As we also know, Freud characterized this resistance in terms of the now familiar phylogenetic narrative: the Jewish attachment to superegoic enjoinment represents, for Freud, an inability to confess to the murderous deed, the killing of the primal father which the Israelites (must have) repeated on the person of the great man Moses.[41] The reproach of Christianity to the Jews, according to Freud, was thus: " 'They will not accept it as true that they murdered God, whereas we admit it and have been cleansed of the guilt.' " Freud goes on to say that it "is easy . . . to see how much truth lies in this reproach. A special enquiry would be called for to discover why it has been impossible for the Jews to join in this forward step which was implied, in spite of all its distortions, by the admission of having murdered God. In a certain sense they have in that way taken a tragic load of guilt on themselves; they have been made to pay a heavy penance for it" (*SE* 23:136). But even if we accept Freud's view that an account of moral agency—the agency we have to a large extent inherited from the biblical narratives— must include a recognition of the work of the superego, how might we finally evaluate Freud's commitment—we might say his "undying" commitment—to the phylogenetic genealogy of that spectral agency? Must there have been a murder for there to be ghosts in the symbolic machine, or does the symbolic system, the cultural archive, produce specters as a by-product of its own normal functioning, by-products on which "normality" in some sense depends?

We began our discussion of the difference between Exodus thinking and messianism with an eye to deepening our understanding of the gap we had noted between Freud's project in *Moses and Monotheism* and Assmann's mnemohistorical efforts at a revocation of the "Mosaic distinction." As we have seen, such a re-vocation aims at the "vocal object," attempts to exnucleate the traumatic kernel of nomotropic discourse, thereby opening a new libidinal economy—and possibilities of cultural translation—no longer bound to superegoic enjoinment. The suspicion motivating this project would seem to be that all "hearing of voices" culminates in psychotic delusion, that is, in paranoid constructions of the religious enemy.[42] But the disagreement is itself haunted by an ambiguity that has plagued and continues to plague all thinking about trauma, including Freud's. If I might borrow some terms suggested by Derrida, we might think about this ambiguity in light of the distinction between an archaeological and an archival gaze.[43]

One of the crucial questions regarding trauma is whether it is ultimately a historical event available to an archaeological gaze, that is, a "special enquiry" aimed at locating the singular and, as it were, datable imprint of an event or series of events on an individual or cultural formation, or a structural impasse, antagonism, or bind internal to the mental life of an individual or the cultural archive of a collectivity. With regard to the latter possibility, the question then becomes: in what sense does a structural impasse or antagonism "take place"? Does such an impasse have an event-structure? Where and when "is" it? In the context of Freud's *Moses,* this is, once again, the question of the status of what Freud refers to as "historical truth": to which sort of gaze is historical truth available? In Assmann's study, this ambiguity makes itself felt as an uncertainty or undecidability as to the locus of the traumatic impact of monotheism. Was it primarily the violence with which Akhenaten imposed his cult that was traumatic, or is the trauma rather to be located in a violence inherent in monotheism as such, in its way of making distinctions? Does the trauma which Assmann wants to make responsible for the emergence of the phantasm of the religious enemy pertain to the events of the Amarna period or to structural antagonisms inherent in counterreligious distinctions as such? Is the traumatic aspect of monotheism, crucial to both Freud's and Assmann's conception of this religious formation, part of a contingent developmental story—the way it was introduced along with whatever reactions or "actings out" that followed—or does it rather pertain to a logical or structural feature of monotheism as a symbolic system? Do the "acts" of the symbolic archive secrete their own forms of acting out, of traumatropic activity? In a word, is monotheism essentially or only contingently haunted? As I have been suggesting, Freud's own position on these questions in *Moses and Monotheism* remains fundamentally ambiguous. We might even say that this ambiguity is programmatic, that is, that the point of introducing a new conception of truth was to place this ambiguity into the foreground of our thinking, an ambiguity that blurs the boundaries between what is essential and what is contingent. Indeed, psychoanalytic thinking as such would seem to stand or fall with our capacity to acknowledge this ambiguity as a feature of human existence. At the very least we can say this: for Freud, historical truth is the truth of a trauma the event-structure of which does not correspond to normal historical time.

In the Moses book, Freud introduces what he characterizes as the unavoidable audacity of the hypothesis of phylogenetic inheritance in the context of a discussion of trauma. He notes there that "when we study the reactions to early traumas, we are quite often surprised to find that they are not strictly limited to what the subject himself has really experienced but diverge from it in a way which fits in much better with the model of a phylogenetic event and, in general, can only be explained by such an influence." He then specifies that the "behaviour of neurotic children towards their parents in the Oedipus and castration complex abounds in such reactions, which seem unjustified in the individual case and only become intelligible phylogenetically—by their connection with the experience of earlier generations" (*SE* 23:99). The phylogenetic events Freud has in mind here and really everywhere he invokes the term are events pertaining to the primal horde: domination by the primal father; his murder by the band of brothers; institution of the incest taboo and exogamy in the wake of the deed; and feelings of remorse over it. The phylogenetic events pertain, in a word, to the tumultuous passage beyond the primal horde pattern of succession—the cyclical and violent struggle to assume the father's singular place—to a first social pact establishing a basis of reciprocity among equals. In his cultural writings, from *Totem and Taboo,* where he first presented the hypothesis of the primal father and murder, up to *Moses and Monotheism,* Freud, however, remained uncertain about the final status of the phylogenetic events. And again, it was this uncertainty that called for a new category of truth.

In a recent monograph on Freud's essay, the anthropologist and psychoanalyst Robert Paul has made a crucial contribution toward clarifying the status of this uncertainty.[44] In essence, Paul's reading takes seriously Freud's hypothesis of the primal horde and murder but approaches it not as an event the traces of which would, in principle, be discoverable by an archaeological gaze, but rather as an event of fantasy, or, perhaps better, as an eventful fantasy embedded in the larger narrative structure of the Bible. By "eventful" I mean to say that it is not one fantasy among others but rather a fundamental one, one that sustains the distinctive range of human capacities that we call a "form of life." In the case of the Jews, the fantasy sustains possibilities of life organized around a divinely enjoined conscience and conscientiousness, possibilities which Freud understood as belonging within the range of the obsessive-compulsive personality.

Paul's reading depends on a distinction that he never explicitly draws but that is implied in his discussion, namely a distinction between foundational myth and fundamental fantasy, or between what Slavoj Žižek refers to as "symbolic *fiction* and phantasmatic *specter.*"[45] In the present context, the former constitutes the narratives and commandments making up the Torah—above all the Exodus, culminating in the covenant at Sinai—whereas the latter forms a sort of second-order myth secreted or encrypted by the first. That is, the status of the primal murder (and its repetition in Jewish ethnogenesis) in Freud and in Paul's post-Freudian reconstruction of the biblical narrative is spectral rather than symbolic. Its role, which must be reconstructed through structural analysis of the biblical narrative (along with its later mutations—for example, in the Catholic mass), is to contract a ground of passionate attachment where grounds, in the sense of reasons, give out. The work of fantasy forms the core of the (l)ibidinal economy on the basis of which "the Israelites [could say] *yes, yes.*" [46] This ground is for Freud the historical truth of a fantastic crime, a kind of structural *state of emergency* figured as a violent *act of emergence*. My basic claim here is that we are "in" a form of life, that is, truly animated by its spirit, not so much when we agree with its basic rules, values, and codes of conduct—its conception of the "good"—but rather when we are, as it were, haunted by its spirits. "For Freud," Paul writes,

> the memory of the hypothesized killing of the primal father, and the anxieties and defenses associated with it, are instilled anew in each generation of individuals by means of religious myths, rituals, and practices. The customs, ceremonies, and dogmas that are a distorted representation of the original memory or fantasy, defensively transformed and translated into primary-process symbolic imagery, can be unconsciously deciphered by new generations of participants in their parents' practices and thus acquired by them as well without the intervention of any conscious critical judgment. . . . What this theory tells us is that the supposed "memory" can be thought of as being actually *produced in individuals* by participation in the ceremonies and customs that express the dogmas of the mythic system. (Paul, 174)

By extension, this can be construed to mean that when one converts to Judaism, one acquires, in essence, a new set of unconscious, traumatic "memories" formally encrypted in its canonical texts. [47]

Paul's argument depends, however, on a fundamental adjustment to the story Freud tells in *Moses*. For Paul, "it is Moses himself who is the perpetrator of the primal deed. That deed is the rebellion against the pharaoh of Egypt and the liberation of the Israelites from Egyptian bondage." The further adjustments to the story follow from this initial reversal of Moses *qua* victim to Moses *qua* perpetrator. The primal horde corresponds to the life of slavery in Egypt, while the revelation at Sinai in the aftermath of the rebellion serves to establish a world structured around reciprocity and object relations. Freud's story of the primal crime and its consequences gives, in condensed form, the schema of the anarchic beginnings pulsating within the narratives forming the central archive of the Judeo-Christian tradition.

To summarize, the foundational myth of the Exodus narrative—a story of deliverance and covenant—is, at the level of fantasy, a sustained performance of the primal crime, a sustained state of emergency and emergence. The customs, laws, and ordinances the enunciation of which fills out so much of the text of the Torah are not simply religious and social practices commanded in a manner external to the details of the Exodus narrative, as if these same commandments could have been issued after a differently structured "plot," as if the commandments were already prepared and the Jews simply had to find a way to get to Sinai to receive them. Rather, the commandments are issued in relation to the acts performed in the Exodus narrative, acts, of course, commanded by God. The sense of the Sinaitic laws cannot be uncoupled from the violent commencement of the Israelite "separation-individuation" from Egypt. This beginning forms a kind of protocosmic background to the cosmos, articulated in and through the covenantal laws and ordinances.

It is important to keep in mind that in this fantasy, insofar as it pertains to the story of Moses, the emphasis is not so much on the primal horde and the incestuous *jouissance* ostensibly proper to it as on the cultural achievement of its supersession by way of an act of violent rebellion. The story of Moses is thus above all the story of the passage beyond the bad infinity of homogeneous "history," that is, of never-ending cycles of struggle over reproductive privilege, over succession to the status of senior male (or, in Freud's formulation, the primal father). Egyptian kingship was, as Paul notes, imagined against the backdrop of the mythic triad Isis-Osiris-Horus in which Horus, the model for the living pharaoh, accedes to the place of Osiris, the mythic prototype of the deceased precursor. As "an elementary transformation of the horde pattern," this model of succession "can be interpreted to mean that the pharaoh is depicted as an oedipal victor: that is, as a son who has succeeded his father and become senior male. By virtue of having accomplished this momentous feat, the son is seen as fit to rule over his fellows" (Paul, 31). The shift to the Mosaic paradigm thus marks, in a sense, the advent of the failed or hindered Oedipus, the figure whose oedipal strivings are, paradoxically, anti-oedipal: "The pharaonic model can thus be seen as what happens when the junior male emerges victorious from a struggle for succession, as opposed to what happens when a junior male *rebels to end the system of succession itself,* as Moses does" (Paul, 31–32; my emphasis).[48] The fundamental impasse, the traumatic kernel, as it were, of the Exodus story is, ultimately, the fact that this rebellious and violent overcoming of the system of succession leaves a haunting stain of transgression on the civilization thereby established. In this view, to be Jewish means, at some level, to be haunted by this transgression. To hear the repetitive call of the *shema,* the "Hear, O Israel," to be drawn into the covenantal enjoinment, is also to hear another voice, a phantasmatic call to act out, or rather, to have already acted out a transgression. Whereas the voice at Sinai enjoins, this other voice seems to command a primal horde–like *jouissance.* Paul's Freudian point is that these two commands are two sides or aspects of a single one, aspects which, in the course of the biblical narratives, undergo various kinds of decomposition. The effectiveness of the covenantal interpellation, its success as a performative speech act in-forming the Israelites as a people, is sustained, in other words, by its spectral supplement, an imperative that would seem to say, "Enjoy!" Once they have given their consent to be enjoined by God, they have also assumed responsibility for this other enjoyment, which now acquires the status of "pagan." That is, it is only with the Sinaitic covenant that the Israelites become susceptible to the guilt of failing to overcome paganism.[49] But because the covenantal bond is sustained by a "remainder" of pagan *jouissance*—that is, because this remainder is in some sense irreducible—a certain failure is inscribed in the Sinaitic pact from the start (for Walzer, this logic of failure accounts for the realism of Exodus thinking as distinct from messianism; the latter emerges out of the desire to be done, once and for all, with this remainder).

Paul understands this dilemma in terms suggested by Freud's own analysis, that is, as a dilemma pertaining to the law of the talion or (equitable) retributive justice, which is the negative face of the principle of reciprocity enacted, above all, in the exchange of gifts.[50] According to Freud, the principle of reciprocity emerges only with the band of brothers who commit the primal murder and renounce the ambition to assume his place and absolute reproductive privilege, that is, his unlimited access to sexual *jouissance* (the primal father does not engage in any form of exchange and so cannot be said to inhabit a world of object relations, which is, in essence, what we mean by "world"; the primal father is thus an emphatically protocosmic being). But the advent of the principle of reciprocity also introduces a new affect into the world, namely guilt: "Before the rebellion, there was no such thing as guilt. The brothers acted unanimously, each motivated by the single purpose of getting what he desired for himself and, with the help of his fellows, eliminating the obstacle to it. After the rebellion the brothers felt guilty, because they then became a society ruled by reciprocity. Killing, no matter of whom, became a crime that merited an equal, retributive punishment" (Paul, 75). But this means, in effect, that "the founding deed itself demands just retribution by virtue of the law it brings into effect. The cosmogonic deed of the culture hero, insofar as it is a disruption of the previous order, not only brings the law into existence but also thereby condemns itself with the same law" (Paul, 75). It was no doubt in response to this structural necessity that Freud posited the murder of Moses as the traumatic secret at the heart of Jewish monotheism. Indeed, something about Moses had to be made to disappear, to vanish, to be finished off.

I would like to call this dilemma "last-cannibal syndrome" after a witticism: "There are no more cannibals; I ate the last one." Moses is such a "last cannibal" in that the deeds he performs in God's name leading to the revelation at Sinai are transgressions in the context of that same revelation. Paul summarizes the narrative and psychological structure of Moses's last-cannibal syndrome:

[the] destruction of Egypt is . . . a crime on Moses's hands. . . . Moses's rebellion is at once a patricide, since Pharaoh is Moses's father; a deicide, since Pharaoh is a living god; a regicide, since Pharaoh is the ruler of the Egyptian empire; and a revolt of the servant against the master, since Moses leads the enslaved Israelites against their overlord and taskmaster. . . . Because of the guilt engendered by this deed the covenant on Mount Sinai is instituted,

and from that guilt the Law gains its compulsory force. According to the Mosaic Law—which is, however, a statement of the more general human social principle of reciprocity—justice demands like for like: punishment, in talionic fashion, must match the crime. . . . Because this debt remains uncollected, the Israelites are violators of the Law by virtue of the very events that led to its promulgation. The Law itself, no matter how restrictive it may seem, protectively wards off the as-yet unexecuted and dreaded talionic punishment for the original crime. (Paul, 210)

Not only the laws and ordinances pertaining to social relations (which, of course, demand the self-mastery and sacrifice associated with the passage beyond the primal horde and toward a society of reciprocity), but more openly and obviously the animal sacrifices instituted by Moses can be seen as attempts to structure a livable relation to this inaugural guilt. By combining a yearly festival meal with the ritualized transmission of the Exodus story, the Passover sacrifice serves as a poignant induction into the (l)ibidinal economy of superegoic enjoinment. "It . . . perpetuates and brings to life the overt commemoration of joyous liberation, together with the more covert acknowledgment of the guilt entailed thereby and the obligation to make sacrifices for it" (Paul, 211). By receiving the cultural transmission (of the Exodus story) one is simultaneously inducted into a transference pertaining to "events" the material truth of which is not essential.

And again, the fundamental argument of messianism is that none of this will suffice—not the Law, not substitutive sacrifice, not the nomotropic habitus of Jews. Messianism, whether Jewish or Christian, offers itself as a source of relief from the pressure of Jewish nomotropism. Christianity, in particular, "holds out the promise . . . that a time will come in which the crime that underwrites the social contract, making the contract necessary and inescapable, will be adequately atoned for" (Paul, 213). It was in this regard that Freud was able to see in Christianity a progress in *Geistigkeit* with respect to Judaism. That is, Christianity spirits away not so much an ostensible Judaic legalism as the specters that shadow it. To bring it to a point, we might say that if Moses is the last cannibal, Jesus offers himself as the last meal that could finally resolve the last-cannibal syndrome driving and sustaining Jewish nomotropism.

Last-cannibal syndrome ultimately derives, of course, from a self-splitting or inconsistency in the behavior of God, who both dispatches Moses to initiate the violent break with Egypt and, as the one who prohibits the sort of patricidal violence committed in his name, ultimately prevents Moses from reaching his destination, the promised land of milk and honey (I am assuming in all of this that as the leader of the rebellion, Moses bears the brunt of the responsibility for the violence, even though it is God who, as it were, pushes the button). This is a split between a God who prohibits ("pagan") enjoyment, the acting out of affects proper to the primal horde, and a God who demands of his people, through his prophet, that they perform deeds which are, from the point of view of the Law, transgressions.[51] For Judaism, this apparent inconsistency is no doubt at least in part what accounts for the vitality, the *Lebendigkeit*, of its God, and thus what keeps the divinity from becoming a mere cosmic principle and Judaism from becoming cosmotheism.

There are resonances in all of this with recent debates concerning trauma, posttraumatic stress, and associated phenomena of childhood sexual abuse, recovered memory, and multiple personality disorder. In a sense, Freud's reading of the history of the Jews in *Moses and Monotheism* might be characterized as kind of recovered-memory syndrome. In the process of trying to understand the enigma of his own "essential nature" as a Jew—and for Freud, this nature included, of course, a compulsive hermeneutic drive and an "oedipal" obsession with the clarification of enigmas and the decoding of cryptophoric signifiers in the name of the search for truth—he "recovers" the traces of trauma: the imposition of the Mosaic law and the fateful, homicidal response. I have indicated the extent to which Freud himself announces uncertainty, even a kind of structural undecidability, apropos of these traumatic "scenes," which leads him to posit the historical, as opposed to real or material, truth of the traumas he claims to have inherited with and, indeed, as the very core of his Judaism (or, rather, his "Jewishness"). I have characterized this process of transmission not as one of acquired characteristics or experiences, as Freud was often tempted to do, but rather as a kind of transference or *Übertragung* of "spirits." And no doubt the prospect of engaging in a kind of spiritism was in part what pushed Freud to his Lamarckian hypothesis: better controversial science than occultism.

But there can be little doubt that Freud's understanding of the workings of the human mind and culture cannot dispense with the dynamics of haunting. Put somewhat differently, Freud's project in *Moses and Monotheism* is not to discover "what really happened," to reconstruct the material truth of how the Jews got monotheism (i.e., by way of an Egyptian priest), but rather to show how the biblical story of how the Jews got monotheism secretes another kind of truth—historical truth—which can in turn be narrated in the way Freud does. But historical truth pertains to "events" that do not properly take place; they are what I have been calling protocosmic, comparable to quantum events that can only be constructed mathematically and on the basis of the behavior of matter in the world. We might say that *Moses and Monotheism* presents a kind of quantum historiography of the Jews; their behavior in the world and the canonical texts providing the normative framework of that behavior are shown to be haunted by residues of protocosmic events.

In his work on recent debates about trauma, recovered memory, and multiple personality, Ian Hacking has touched on the matter of historical truth without naming it as such.[52] One of the strengths of Hacking's presentation is his emphasis on the background of normativity that is required if we are to be able to register an event as having taken place at all. In a sense, the field of normativity (rather than a spatiotemporal point or grid) is the true site of an event's "taking place." We have to be able to be right or wrong about certain questions if we are to be able to speak of an event at all: What happened? How did it happen? Why did it happen? Hacking suggests that recent debates about sexual abuse and multiple personality disorder are troubled by a failure to understand the ontology of events, which ultimately means the logical relation between temporality and normativity. In Hacking's terms, we can only speak of there *being* an event in relation to a descriptive vocabulary allowing for normative commitments (we can be right or wrong, there is a fact to the matter of our claims). In all of this, Hacking is interested in the historical emergence of the diagnostic nexus of terms linking trauma, childhood sexual abuse, and so-called multiple personality disorder.

If all actions (and Hacking is, as we have been here, interested in events linked to human actions) are actions "under a description," then the introduction of new kinds of descriptive vocabularies, new concepts for thinking actions, opens the space for new event-entities: "When new descriptions become available, when they come into circulation, or even when they become the sorts of things that it is all right to say, to think, then there are new things to choose to do. When new intentions become open to me, because new descriptions, new concepts, become available to me, I live in a new world of opportunities" (Hacking, 236). With such innovation, the space of normativity is altered: "Inventing or molding a new kind, a new classification, of people or of behavior may create new ways to be a person, new choices to make, for good or evil. There are new descriptions, and hence new actions under a description. It is not that people change, substantively, but that as a point of logic new opportunities for action are open to them" (Hacking, 239). A corollary of this view is that prior to the introduction of such opportunities, one cannot feel constrained or limited by their lack: "It is a trivial, logical fact that I cannot form those intentions. This fact cannot make me feel confined, or make me regret my lack of power. I cannot feel limited by lacking a description, for if I did, in a self-aware way, feel limited, then I would have at least a glimmering of the descriptions of the action and so could think of choosing it" (Hacking, 236). According to Hacking, then, the past itself is indeterminate to the extent that new kinds of descriptions may retroactively "produce" events that were *not there* to be experienced at the time of their occurrence:

> It is almost as if retroactive redescription changes the past. That is too paradoxical a turn of phrase, for sure. But if we describe past actions in ways in which they could not have been described at the time, we derive a curious result. For all intentional actions are actions under a description. If a description did not exist, or was not available, at an earlier time, then at that time one could not act intentionally under that description. Only later did it become true that, at that time, one performed an action under that description. At the very least, we rewrite the past, not because we find out more about it, but because we present actions under new descriptions. (Hacking, 243)

The view I have been proposing here is a modification of Hacking's approach, where, after all, one descriptive vocabulary merely follows upon another, ad infinitum. I would argue instead that the discourse of trauma is not simply one descriptive vocabulary among others for determining the past (though it may emerge into our vocabularies at a certain historical moment); rather, I am suggesting that a trauma is fundamentally linked to the emergence of new descriptive vocabularies, to what remains unaccountable in such emergence. A trauma is an event that continues not to take place precisely insofar as it radically shifts the ground of historical experience, changes the field of possible events (not all such shifts need be traumatic, though all traumas do, I think, involve such shifts). Even the determination of the past as traumatic—bringing it under that description—does not fully eliminate the undecidability of its event-structure. It persists as an event which is, as I have been suggesting, protocosmic, that is, constitutive of world yet not fully *of* the world (understood as a normative field of object relations). Traumas are the event-equivalents of anamorphotic distortions in paintings that only assume a shape when looked at from the side. In a sense, *Moses and Monotheism* attempts to look at the Bible from the side.

The ongoing debate, for example, about the possibility of representing or imagining the Holocaust (historiographically or aesthetically) might be understood as an indication that the events subsumed by that name did not merely occur in history but rather changed our very conception of history, of what is possible in history. The uncanny sense that the Holocaust is not yet past, that it persists as a haunting proximity, means that it has, in a certain sense, not yet taken place: we are still trying to respond not so much to a historical event as to a shift in the ground of the normative space in which historical events can be located.[53] No matter how much we attempt to circumscribe the Holocaust with historiographical information, there persists an anxious awareness that we have missed the essential thing, that what transpired there has not yet found a conceptual or linguistic representation. This is what is meant, I think, by the claim for the metahistorical significance of the Holocaust: that it was an event that affected our capacity to orient ourselves in our existing structures of thinking. (The insistence that we can and do continue to orient ourselves in these structures would in this view have to be understood as a mode of defense.) This claim has absolutely nothing to do with Holocaust denial; we know perfectly well what happened in terms of the real or material truth of the events, as Freud would say. The point is that this truth can never fully account for what transpired. In response to each account our feeling is, this is not *it*.

To put it another way, though every past is contingently indeterminate—its determination depends on the availability of descriptive vocabularies—the traumatic past is logically indeterminate or undecidable, and its persistence is a function of this undecidability. To return to *Moses and Monotheism,* Freud's view apropos of the historical truth of Jewish ethnogenesis would be, then, that the exit from Egypt in some sense continues not to take place, continues to haunt the Jews, and the West more generally, not because of the presence or lack of a descriptive vocabulary adequate to the events of the Exodus, but rather because the space opened by this exit is structurally perturbed by its traumatic beginnings. More precisely, a structural perturbation internal to Jewish monotheism splits its tradition into a dominant narrative organized around, on one hand the Exodus and its social, political, and moral consequences, and on the other, a spectral fantasy of traumatic and transgressive beginnings—a split that endows the tradition with an uncanny vitality. Freud's guiding intuition in *Moses and Monotheism* was that Jewish survival could only be explained by reference to such an uncanny vitality; the normal vitality of a national, ethnic, or religious tradition would not have sufficed. This split is mirrored in Freud's distinction between material truth and historical truth, between what is registered and not registered—or registered virtually, spectrally—in the Jewish archive.[54] What I have been trying to capture by the term "ibidity" might, then, finally be understood as the subject's inscription in such virtual archives; our reasons for doing what we do are ultimately substantiated—given substance and density—by reference to, by citation of, what is registered there.

For Freud, the exit from Egypt was, in essence, a passage out of cryptophoric symbolism and the form of life associated with it. Freud's crucial discovery, however, was that the compulsive dimension of this passage—and its interminability—were to be understood as a perpetuation of cryptophoric symbolism on another level, that is, as *symptom,* a modality of what we earlier referred to as the mythic dimension of the passage beyond myth. The story of the primal murder and its repetition with Moses are Freud's efforts at unpacking the content of this mythic residue, of uncovering the historical truth from which nomotropic desire turns as it turns toward the law. Our reading of *Moses and Monotheism* has helped us to appreciate the temporal paradox of this tropism: the turn toward the law secretes a remainder of that from which the tropism turns, which is not so much paganism as such—Egypt—as the pagan dimension of the turning. In a sense, then, Freud's method in *Moses and Monotheism* transcends the opposition that has guided us thus far, the opposition, that is, between an archaeological and an archival perspective. Freud's study seems rather to be guided by the paradoxical gaze of a spectral or virtual archaeology, a search for singular and eventful impressions left by the structural binds of a certain life with normativity, the ethically inflected monotheism of the Judaic tradition. The cosmos of monotheism, as elaborated in its dominant symbol and liturgical practices, carries with it, secretes within itself its own protocosmic beginnings, which it can thus never fully metabolize nor forgive itself for. For Freud, this is the ultimate source of what he clearly considered to be the neurotic majesty of Judaism. Historical truth thus pertains to the mnemonic traces of the spectral eventfulness of structural binds.[55] These "spectral memories" are the stuff of what Freud felt compelled to posit as phylogenetic inheritance.

Another way to approach this inheritance is to return to what constitutes the real breakthrough in Freudian thought, the notion of the dream-work. Crucial to Freud's conception of the dream is the distinction between what he called the latent dream-thoughts and the dream-work proper, which was for Freud the true locus of the unconscious wish generating the dream. Freud famously castigates his fellow analysts for forgetting this distinction in a footnote added to the 1925 edition of *The Interpretation of Dreams*:

> But now that analysts at least have become reconciled to replacing the manifest dream by the meaning revealed by its interpretation, many of them have become guilty of falling into another confusion which they cling to with an equal obstinacy. They seek to find the essence of dreams in their latent content and in so doing they overlook the distinction between the latent dream-thoughts and the dream-work. . . . At bottom, dreams are nothing other than a particular form of thinking, made possible by the conditions of the state of sleep. It is the dream-work which creates that form, and it alone is the essence of dreaming.[56]

The key, then, to a properly psychoanalytic understanding of the dream is the focus not on the "secret *behind* the form but *the secret of this form itself* . . . the process by means of which the hidden meaning disguised itself in such a form." This secret, as Žižek further notes, is "not 'more concealed, deeper' in relation to the latent thought, it is decidedly more 'on the surface', consisting entirely of the signifier's mechanisms, of the treatment to which the latent thought is submitted." [57]

Another way of putting this is to say that the dreaming subject is *doing* something by dreaming, by cutting up and reassembling words, images, and scenes according to relations of similarity and contiguity. This emphatically creative and performative dimension of the dream-work was underlined by Lyotard in an important essay on Freud's theory of the dream. As he puts it, "The dream is not the language of desire, but its work. . . . Desire does not speak; it does violence to the order of utterance. This violence is primordial: the imaginary fulfilment of desire consists in this transgression, which repeats, in the dream workshop, what occurred and continues to occur in the manufacture of the so-called primal phantasm." The true locus of desire, of the wish and its fulfillment, is not, ultimately, some scene of satisfaction produced by the dream, but rather "the imaginary activity itself. It is not the dream-content that fulfils desire, but the act of dreaming, of fantasizing, because the Phantasy is a transgression." [58] Here, as the title of his essay indicates, Lyotard undertakes a slight modification of Freud's claim that the dream-work is a form of thinking. What is misleading about Freud's claim is that it can lead to a view of the dreaming subject as a sort of rational agent, a mind within the mind, engaged in Sartrian bad faith, that is, a picture of the mind in which desire attempts to disguise itself *by means* of the dream-work. Against such a view, Lyotard maintains that "desire is a scrambled text from the outset. The disguise does not result from the alleged deceiving intent of desire; the work itself *is* disguise because it is violence perpetrated on linguistic space. There is no need to imagine that the id has an idea at the back of its head. . . . The mobility of the primal process is deceptive in itself; it *is* what deceives, what sends the 'faculties' using articulated language into a spin: the figural versus the mind." [59] This passage captures the meaning of my claim that in the turn toward the law constitutive of nomotropism, the pagan element that really haunts Israel is, in the end, not some substantial realm of affects, beliefs, and practices from which Israel turned—that is, a self-contained pagan cosmos called Egypt—but rather an aspect of this turning or tropism itself. This is the ultimate reason why the danger of pagan backsliding never ceases to haunt Israel.

To return to the discourse of archivization, we might say that the dream-work is the attempt to draw the events, thoughts, and feelings of daily life—material registered in the ego archive, material in principle available to consciousness—into the orbit of the virtual or spectral archive in which the quantum events of protocosmic being are registered. The dream-work attempts to make the latent dream-thoughts, thoughts which are fully *of* the world we inhabit consciously, bear the burden of what is registered in the virtual archive. But again, the virtual archive exists only in the form of the distortions generated on the latent dream-thoughts, on the documents or acts of the ego archive. Freud's fundamental point would seem to be that when we try to unpack, by means of narration, the kernel of historical truth manifest in these distortions, we are ultimately led to oedipal impulses and crimes, to eros and destruction. It comes as no surprise, then, that in the course of his presentation of the dream-work as the tropological activity par excellence, Lyotard cites the passage in *Moses and Monotheism* where Freud compares the compositional procedures that produced the Bible to a kind of violence, indeed to murder. The passage is well known: "In its implications the distortion [*Entstellung*] of a text resembles a murder: the difficulty is not in perpetuating the deed, but in getting rid of its traces."[60]

In this passage, Freud is attempting to link the documentary hypothesis of biblical authorship to his own theory of doublets, his claim, that is, that the Jewish people were formed from two groups, only one of which had experienced the Exodus under the leadership of Moses as well as that leader's violent demise. In the context of these reflections, Freud somewhat off-handedly suggests that "the Israelites of that earliest period—that is to say, the scribes of Moses—may have had some share in the invention of the first alphabet." To this suspicion he adds the footnote, "If they were subject to the prohibition against pictures they would even have had a motive for abandoning the hieroglyphic picture-writing while adapting its written characters to expressing a new language" (Freud, *SE* 23:43). The conclusion to which we are led by this strange grouping of topics is a simple and startling one: for Freud, what the dreaming subject is ultimately doing by engaging in this "literalist" symbolic mode, this "hieroglyphic" thinking that plays with the surface features of the letter (and thereby undoes the achievement of the Mosaic scribes), is comparable to the scriptural distortions which Freud explicitly compares to a murder and its occultation. That is, the undoing of the alphabetic script(ure), its submission to hieroglyphic manhandling, whether by the dreaming subject or the biblical redactors, is, at the level of formal procedures, a displaced performance of patricide and incest, the oedipal crimes. With regard to the dream, this means that the dreamer does not have to dream of patricide and incest; the activity of dreaming, the mental activity Freud called the dream-work, *is* already patricidal and incestuous. No matter what we dream about, that is, no matter what the representational content of the latent dream-thoughts, we are dreaming the oedipal crimes insofar as that representational content is submitted to the primary processes of the dream-work. In other words, the phylogenetic inheritance persists not as this or that set of propositional attitudes or thoughts stored in deep memory, but rather as the content of the *form* of the dream.

Robert Paul's speculations apropos of the so-called waters of Meribah episode in the Bible (Numbers 20) may be of some help here. During their wanderings in the desert, the Israelites quarrel (yet again) with Moses and Aaron, this time because of thirst. Moses produces water for the rebellious Israelites but in a way that violates God's instructions. Rather than raising Jethro's rod and ordering the rock to yield water, Moses strikes the rock directly. On the basis of this violation, Moses is prohibited from entering the promised land with his people. Paul's reading of the apparent disproportion between the crime and its punishment brings together the various strands of our argument and allows us to appreciate what we might call the *eventfulness of a symbolic mode.* By invoking, as it were, his phallic power directly—by striking the rock—Moses claims a kind of oedipal victory vis-à-vis God (as Paul suggests, we can understand the rock as the withholding breast compelled to yield its goodness): "When Moses strikes the rock with his rod, he is giving expression to erotic, sadistic, and destructive impulses, of a combined oral and phallic nature, that he ought to have controlled." But the crucial point here is that Moses violates God's command in a very particular way, that is, by refusing the dimension of speech: "At the waters of

Meribah, Moses disobeys the paternal injunction to speak, to use language, and reverts to a preoedipal demand for the breast and its withheld bounty. It is thus for a symbolic incestuous infraction of the oedipal law of the father that Moses is punished."[61] The shift in symbolic modes, from the miracle of authorized speech to direct magical intervention into nature, is already transgressive in the post-Sinaitic world, a "violence perpetrated on linguistic space," a violence now coded as "pagan." For that transgression, which is emblematic of his status as the last cannibal, Moses is prohibited from entering the promised land. But the transgression at Meribah is directed not only *against* the nomotropic curve of desire instituted by God's commandments; it is a transgression *internal to it*. In a certain sense, then, each time we awake from a night spent in dream-work, this daily, eventful shift of symbolic modes, we share in Moses's fate. Not only does the dreaming subject labor, as it were, in the protocosmic depths from which we turn with each awakening; insofar as wakefulness is nomotropic, that is, informed by repetitive, compulsive turning, the dreaming subject—the subject of the unconscious—persists in it.

Yerushalmi's study of *Moses and Monotheism,* to which we referred at the beginning of this chapter, concludes with a "Monologue with Freud," a sort of conjuration of Freud's spirit in the service of clarifying unresolved issues of interpretation.[62] By means of this monologue, as Derrida has noted, Yerushalmi "repeats in an exemplary fashion the logic of the event whose specter was described and whose structure was 'performed' by the historical novel [i.e., Freud's *Moses*]."[63] I would put it this way: just as Freud's study of the Jewish tradition suggests that one is truly in a form of life not so much when one agrees with its public values, beliefs, and dogmas as when one comes to be haunted by its ghosts, so one only truly enters into Freud's own text when one finds oneself unsettled, compelled, by its deep and animating enigmas. Only then does one become responsive to them and thus, in a sense, responsible for them; only then has one registered the historical truth of the project, assumed the phylogenetic inheritance it transmits. It has been the fundamental wager of this essay that to be thus unsettled may also mean to have entered more deeply into the debts and depths of the Jewish inheritance.

Notes

This essay first appeared in *October*, no. 88 (1999).

1 I will be quoting from *The Standard Edition*, ed. James Strachey, vol. 23 (London: Hogarth Press, 1964). Further references will be made to *SE*, followed by volume and page number.

2 For those unfamiliar with the details of Freud's argument, I cite here the text of his letter of 6 Jan. 1935 to Lou Andreas-Salomé in which he offers a concise summary of the book: "What you have heard about my last piece of work I can now explain in greater detail. It started out from the question as to what has really created the particular character of the Jew, and came to the conclusion that the Jew is the creation of the man Moses. Who was this Moses and what did he bring about? The answer to this question was given in a kind of historical novel. Moses was not a Jew but a well-born Egyptian, a high official, a priest, perhaps a prince of the royal dynasty, and a zealous supporter of the monotheistic faith, which the Pharaoh Amenhotep IV had made the dominant religion round about 1350 B.C. With the collapse of the new religion and the extinction of the 18th dynasty after the Pharaoh's death this ambitious and aspiring man had lost all his hopes and had decided to leave his fatherland and create a new nation which he proposed to bring up in the imposing religion of his master. He resorted to the Semitic tribe which had been dwelling in the land since the Hyksos period, placed himself at their head, led them out of bondage into freedom, gave them the spiritualized religion of Aten and as an expression of consecration as well as a means of setting them apart introduced circumcision, which was a native custom among the Egyptians and only among them. What the Jews later boasted of their god Jahve, that he had made them his Chosen People and delivered them from Egypt, was literally true—of Moses. By this act of choice and the gift of the new religion he created the Jew. . . . These Jews were as little able to tolerate the exacting faith of the religion of Aten as the Egyptians before them. A non-Jewish scholar, Sellin, has shown that Moses was probably killed a few decades later in a popular uprising and his teachings abandoned. It seems certain that the tribe which returned from Egypt later united with other kindred tribes which dwelt in the land of Midian (between Palestine and the west coast of Arabia) and which had adopted the worship of a volcano god living on Mount Sinai. This primitive god Jahve became the national god of the Jewish people. But the religion of Moses had not been extinguished. A dim memory of it and its founder had remained. Tradition fused the god of Moses with Jahve, ascribed to him the deliverance from Egypt and identified Moses with priests of Jahve from Midian, who had introduced the worship of this latter god to Israel. . . . In reality Moses had never heard the name of Jahve, and the Jews had never passed through the Red Sea, nor had they been at Sinai. Jahve had to pay dearly for having thus usurped the god of Moses. The older god was always at his back, and in the course of six to eight centuries Jahve had been changed into the likeness of the god of Moses. As a half-extinguished tradition the religion of Moses had finally triumphed. This process is typical of the way a religion is created and was only the repetition of an earlier process. Religions owe their compulsive power to

the *return of the repressed;* they are reawakened memories of very ancient, forgotten, highly emotional episodes of human history. I have already said this in *Totem and Taboo;* I express it now in the formula: the strength of religion lies not in its *material* [*reale*] but in its *historical* truth" (*Sigmund Freud and Lou Andreas-Salomé Letters,* ed. Ernst Pfeiffer, trans. William and Elaine Robson-Scott [New York: Harcourt Brace Jovanovich, 1972], 204–5).

3   See the new translation by Judith Norman of the second draft of F. W. J. Schelling's "Ages of the World," in Slavoj Žižek, *The Abyss of Freedom: Ages of the World* (Ann Arbor: University of Michigan Press, 1997). Norman translates *Mitwissenschaft* as "co-science/consciousness" (114). For Freud, this peculiar knowledge is registered in and as *conscience.*

4   Yosef Hayim Yerushalmi, *Freud's Moses: Judaism Terminable and Interminable* (New Haven: Yale University Press, 1991).

5   Yerushalmi, *Freud's Moses,* 98. See Jacques Derrida, *Archive Fever: A Freudian Impression,* trans. Eric Prenowitz (Chicago: University of Chicago Press, 1996).

6   See, for example, Daniel Boyarin, *Unheroic Conduct: The Rise of Heterosexuality and the Invention of the Jewish Man* (Berkeley: University of California Press, 1997). Boyarin's project is, of course, indebted to Sander Gilman's work on the various modalities of Jewish self-hatred.

7   See Paul Mendes-Flohr, "Fin de Siècle Orientalism, The *Ostjuden,* and the Aesthetics of Jewish Self-Affirmation," in Mendes-Flohr, *Divided Passions: Jewish Intellectuals and the Experience of Modernity* (Detroit: Wayne State University Press, 1991), 77–132.

8   Boyarin, *Unheroic,* 246–48.

9   Freud, *SE* 23:19.

10 Jan Assmann describes normative inversion as the practice of "inverting the abominations of the other culture into obligations and vice versa." Jan Assmann, *Moses the Egyptian: The Memory of Egypt in Western Monotheism* (Cambridge: Harvard University Press, 1997), 31. I discuss Assmann's work below.

11 Boyarin, *Unheroic,* 260.

12 Ilse Grubrich-Simitis, *Freuds Moses-Studie als Tagtraum: Ein biographischer Essay* (Frankfurt a.M.: Fischer, 1994).

13 Here I am borrowing the title of G. W. Bowersock's review of Anthony Grafton's *The Footnote: A Curious History* (Cambridge: Harvard University Press, 1998), published in the *New Republic,* 19 Jan. 1998. I have written extensively on Freud's use of footnotes as a locus for the acting-out of influence anxiety in *My Own Private Germany: Daniel Paul Schreber's Secret History of Modernity* (Princeton: Princeton University Press, 1996).

14 Grubrich-Simitis, 58–59 (my translation).

15 Assmann, 166. Further references will be made in the body of the text.

16 We might say that Assmann argues that the answer to the question as to what anti-Semites really hate about the Jews ought to be *ibid,* in the sense of "see Akhenaten."

17 Assmann makes no clear arguments as to the causes of such similarities. Indeed, the

absence of any clear statement or manifest commitment on the question of influence or debt is one of the odd features of the book.

18 It was only on the basis of archaeological discoveries in the nineteenth century that these events and the nature of Akhenaten's cult could be reconstructed.

19 In his recent study of Nazi Germany, Saul Friedländer introduced the notion of "redemptive anti-Semitism" in an effort to capture the specificity of that hatred in the Third Reich (*Nazi Germany and the Jews,* vol. 1, *The Years of Persecution* [HarperCollins: New York, 1997]). Assmann's claim might ultimately be understood to mean that redemptive anti-Semitism is the hatred for those who introduced into the world the notion of redemption in the first place, i.e., the idea that the world is in need of redemption. Redemptive anti-Semitism thereby signifies the paradox of a longing for redemption from the very notion of redemption.

20 Assmann adds that "this time the source of intolerance is enlightenment itself. Akhenaten is shown to be a figure both of enlightenment and of intolerant despotism, forcing his universalist monotheism onto his people with violence and persecution" (Assmann, 167).

21 What Assmann never considers is that it may have been precisely this "revolutionary" character of the "deconstruction" and abolition pursued in this new phase of the Moses-Egypt discourse which inaugurated what Paul Rose has called "revolutionary anti-Semitism." See Paul L. Rose, *Revolutionary Antisemitism in Germany from Kant to Wagner* (Princeton: Princeton University Press, 1990).

22 Assmann writes that "while it is true that many arguments of the 'idolators' lived on in the discourse of anti-Semitism, and that the fight against the Mosaic distinction seemed to have anti-Semitic implications, it is also true that many of those who, in the eighteenth century, attacked Moses' distinction, such as John Toland or Gotthold Ephraim Lessing, fought for tolerance and committed themselves to the equality of the Jews. The struggle against the Mosaic distinction could also assume the character of a fight against anti-Semitism. The most outspoken destroyer of the Mosaic distinction was a Jew: Sigmund Freud" (Assmann, 5).

23 In his analysis of Amarna theology on the basis of the hymns discovered in the nineteenth century, Assmann writes, for example: "It was the discovery that not only light, but also time is to be explained as manifestations of solar energy. With this discovery, *everything* could be explained as workings, 'emanations,' or 'becomings' of the sun. In this system, the concept of 'One' has not a theological but a physical meaning: the One is the source of cosmic existence. . . . What Akhenaten actually discovered, what he was probably the first to discover, and what he certainly experienced himself as a revelation, was a concept of *nature.* With regard to the Divine, his message is essentially negative: God is *nothing else than* the sun, and he is also nature" (Assmann, 188–89).

24 Freud, *SE* 13:xv.

25 Slavoj Žižek has formulated this distinction in terms immediately relevant to the present discussion, namely as the difference between a Spinozistic and Kantian: "In Lacanian terms, Spinoza accomplishes a kind of leveling of the signifying chain, he

gets rid of the gap that separates S_2, the chain of knowledge, from S_1, the signifier of injunction, of prohibition, of NO!: the Spinozist substance designates universal Knowledge as having no need for support in a Master-Signifier, i.e., as being the met-onymical universe of 'pure positivity' prior to the intervention of the negativizing cut of the paternal metaphor. The attitude of the Spinozist 'wisdom' [the 'wisdom' of Assmann's cosmotheism—E.L.S.] is therefore defined by the reduction of deontology to ontology, of injunction to rational knowledge, and, in terms of speech-acts-theory, of performative to constative. . . . Kant, on the contrary, affirms the primacy of prac-tical over theoretical reason, which means that *the fact of injunction is irreducible*: we, as finite subjects, cannot ever assume the contemplative position which would en-able us to reduce imperative to constative" (*Tarrying with the Negative: Kant, Hegel, and the Critique of Ideology* [Durham: Duke University Press, 1993], 217). In his most recent work, Žižek has put the matter precisely in the terms of Freud's narrative of Jewish ethnogenesis. The whole point of Freud's myth of the murder of Moses, Žižek suggests, is that cosmotheism—the Freemasonic religion of "Moses the Egyptian" in Assmann's account—still needs to be *subjectivized*: "The old Egyptian Moses be-trayed and killed by his people was the all-inclusive One of *logos*, the rational sub-stantial structure of the universe, the 'writing' accessible to those who know how to read the 'Great Book of Nature,' not yet the all-exclusive One of subjectivity who imposes His unconditional Will on His creation" (*The Ticklish Subject: The Absent Center of Political Ontology* [London: Verso, 1999], 319; I am grateful to the author for making the uncorrected proofs of this new volume available to me).

26   Freud is concerned here, in other words, not with justice per se but rather with the source of what Levinas has called "the unlimited responsibility which justifies . . . concern for justice" (Emmanuel Levinas, *Nine Talmudic Readings*, trans. Annette Aronowicz [Bloomington: Indiana University Press, 1994], 50). In the context of Marx's genesis of the money form of value, we might say that his concern is not with gold but rather with what makes gold gold, i.e., with what endows it with the "stuff" of value.

27   Jean-Joseph Goux, in his analysis of Freud's first text on Moses, the short essay on the Moses of Michelangelo, writes that the "ambiguity of the *Moses*, simultaneously in motion and immobile, furious and calm, is revealed in what connects the impera-tive of the superego to the *jouissance* of the sublime. The superego's eternal decree is the self-denying *jouissance* of the sublime: superior *jouissance*" (*Symbolic Economies: After Marx and Freud*, trans. Jennifer Curtiss Gage [Ithaca: Cornell University Press, 1990], 144).

28   I say deterritorialization because Freud understood diaspora to be structurally com-patible with Judaism, indeed even demanded by it, as a link in a chain of separations, departures, cuts informing this cultural formation: of the deity from plastic repre-sentation; of spirituality from magic, animism, and sexual ecstasy; of thinking from the fantasy of the omnipotence of thoughts; of the passions from their violent enact-ments. The condition of diaspora was for Freud simply the next link in this chain: the separation of a people from a territory conceived as proper to them.

29 Grubrich-Simitis, *Freuds Moses-Studie,* 58–59.

30 Assmann, *Moses the Egyptian,* 166.

31 Michael Walzer, *Exodus and Revolution* (New York: Basic Books, 1985). References will be made in the body of the text.

32 In a critique of Yerushalmi's insistence on Israel's unique privilege or election as bearer of this postmythic temporal consciousness, as the singular locus of the religious and cultural imperative to remember the promise of future emancipation, Derrida has offered his own promising revision: "Unless, in the logic of this election, one were to call by the *unique* name of Israel all the places and all the peoples who would be ready to recognize themselves in this anticipation and in this injunction. . . . Like the question of the proper name, the question of exemplarity . . . here situates the place of all violences. Because if it is just to remember the future and the injunction to remember . . . it is no less just to remember the others, the other others and the others in oneself, and that the other peoples could say the same thing—in another way" (Derrida, *Archive Fever,* 77). To put it in its simplest terms, we might say that only in Judaism does the nomos of nomotropism signify Torah.

33 Walzer cites the *Book of Doctrines and Beliefs* of the medieval Jewish philosopher Saadya Gaon: "God . . . gave man the ability to obey Him, placing it as it were in his hands, endowed him with power and free will, and commanded him to choose that which is good" (81). A more explicit characterization of the forced choice is found in the following midrashic tale cited by Walzer: "It was not quite of their own free will that Israel declared themselves ready to accept the Torah, for when the whole nation . . . approached Sinai, God lifted up the mountain and held it over the heads of the people . . . saying to them: 'If you accept the Torah, it is well; otherwise you will find your grave under this mountain'" (161). It is as if God were saying to the Hebrews, "Your paganism or your life!" The option that is thereby excluded is, of course, a pagan life.

34 Walzer characterizes this displacement as the "philosophical difficulty" contained in the shift of pronouns in Deut. 6:20–21: "The son asks about the laws that God 'hath commanded *you,*' excluding himself from the obligation to obey. The father replies, '*We* were Pharaoh's bondsmen, . . .' including his son in the covenantal history" (Walzer, 85). Interestingly, while reflecting on the mimetic relation of later political covenants to the Sinaitic model, Walzer ventriloquizes a repetition into the original: "All these are genuine covenants, depending for their force on the consent of a free (newly free!) people, and all of them look back, more or less distantly, to that moment at Sinai when the Israelites said *yes, yes*" (Walzer, 89; my emphasis).

35 See Jan Assmann's brilliant discussion of Deuteronomy as a paradigm of cultural mnemotechnics in his *Das kulturelle Gedächtnis: Schrift, Erinnerung, und politische Identität in frühen Hochkulturen* (Munich: C. H. Beck, 1997). There Assmann argues that is precisely the mnemotechnical procedures elaborated in Deuteronomy, procedures that make superfluous the "natural" frameworks and supports of collective and cultural memory—territory, temple, monarchy—that allowed for the survival of the Jews in the diaspora. In effect, these procedures constitute the Jews as a people whose

foundational *lieux de mémoire* are uncoupled from territory, architecture, and political institutions. Such a deterritorialization of cultural memory is, of course, part of what Freud had in mind when he spoke of a Jewish "progress in spirituality" (Freud, of course, believed that such progress could be sustained and even amplified without the mnemotechnical procedures elaborated in Deuteronomy).

36 In a brilliant reading of Freud's *Moses,* Robert Paul (*Moses and Civilization: The Meaning behind Freud's Myth* [New Haven: Yale University Press, 1996]) borrows Richard Dawkins's notion of "memes," the equivalent, in a symbolic system, of genetic codes in cellular life, to capture the recursive dimension of biblical commandment. Noting that both memes and genes belong to a wider class of "replicators," meaning "anything in the universe of which copies are made," Paul suggests that "a 'memic' or cultural replicator accomplishes its work by channeling the motivation and capacities of human actors into activities that result in the reproduction of copies of the meme. . . . People who have been significantly informed by the same memic instructions can be said to be like each other and, indeed, to be related in a way directly analagous to the way people are genetically related: that is, by being realizations of, and providers of future copies of, the same instructions" (186). Paul notes that the Torah as a whole is well suited to function as "an uncaused cause of replication at the memic level. . . . It is a symbol whose meaning, and ability to instruct authoritatively, comes from its own status as a self-created, self-referential symbol, or meme, and thus as a fixed point in relation to which all other symbols derive meaning, that derives its own meaning from nothing except itself" (187). Finally, apropos of the *shema,* Paul is led to compare its recursive power to that of a computer virus which "intimates to the practitioner an infinity of reproduction and thus of a vast fecundity suitable to produce a sense of the infinity of the Deity himself: a Deity who introduces himself to Moses with that most self-referential and recursive of statements: 'I am that I am'" (188). We will return to Paul's reading later in the discussion.

37 Such a citational system was imagined, on the basis of an endopsychic perception that earned envious admiration on the part of Freud, by the psychotic judge Daniel Paul Schreber. His term for this textual machinery was *Aufschreibesystem* or "writing-down-system" (see my reading of Schreber's memoirs—and Freud's relation to "ibidity" in *My Own Private Germany*). Friedrich Kittler has argued that such endopsychic perceptions only became possible through the advent of new technologies of writing and models of the mind that developed in synch with them. See his remarkable study, *Aufschreibesysteme: 1800-1900* (Munich: Wilhelm Fink Verlag, 1987). We might perhaps understand Derrida's notion of *différance* as the submission of signification, of all discursive operations, to the effects of ibidity. The fundamental wager of psychoanalysis would seem to be that the human subject is introduced into these effects through the castration complex; the primordial encounter with ibidity is, in this view, the revelation of the phallus as the primary citation of sexual value.

38 This is, I think, what Heidegger means when he speaks of Dasein's primordial guilt, of its being the null ground of a nullity. See *Sein und Zeit* (Tübingen: Max Niemeyer, 1993), 285.

39 In the spirit of Heidegger's orthographic idiosyncracies, we might write: *enjoynment.*

40 Citing Freud's early distinction between primary and secondary defenses, Robert
Paul suggests that Christianity as a whole "corresponds to a system of secondary defenses, in the sense that the first self-reproaches—the Mosaic Laws—now themselves
seem to be the primary danger, since they accompany the impulses that led to the
original deed with a need for inexorable and dreadful punishment. The ceremonials
and penances to which Christianity is driven may be understood as defenses against
Judaism, its prophet, and his Law. These, in turn represent a level of primary defense
against the patricide" (Paul, *Moses and Civilization*, 218).

41 Freud's claim about the history of the Jews is a genuine "turn of the screw": the claim
that the murder of Moses recalled the primal crime, that it signified a "revival of an
experience in the primaeval ages of the human family which had long vanished from
men's conscious memory" (*SE* 23:129), means, in effect, that Judaism represents a
return of the revenant, a reanimation of the undead (primal) father, in a word, an
uncanny renewal of a primordial uncanniness.

42 Such an "ex-nucleation" would seem to be the attempt to reverse the process that
Assmann has referred to as the "ex-carnation" effectuated within the Jewish tradition. According to Assmann, Judaism displaced the performative force of the king's
Machtwort, the kingly utterance that establishes law in an emphatic sense, into the
Torah. In this way the Book of Law effectively replaces the king and assumes—in-
corporates—the charisma of his carnal being. In Assmann's view this process of ex-
carnation/incorporation entered a new stage after the Babylonian Captivity, when
the cultural continuity of Judaism came to depend more and more on the hightened
normativity of texts requiring the mnemotechnical procedures—the "memic replica-
tions"—elaborated in Deuteronomy. As Assmann puts it, "the 'wise and understanding people' (Deut. 4:6) learned the written Torah, and indeed learned it by heart."
In a word, Assmann here traces the passage of the king's charismatic body into the
ibidity of superegoic enjoinment, really a kind of "hearing of voices." See Jan Assmann, "Wenn die Kette des Nachmachens zerreisst: Fünf Stufen zur Überlieferung:
Tradition und Schriftkultur im alten Israel und frühen Judentum," *Berliner Zeitung*,
3 Dec. 1997 (my translation).

43 See, once more, Derrida, *Archive Fever*.

44 References to Paul's *Moses and Civilization* will be made in the text.

45 Slavoj Žižek, "'I Hear You with My Eyes'; or, The Invisible Master," in *Gaze and
Voice as Love Objects*, ed. Renata Salecl and Slavoj Žižek (Durham: Duke University
Press, 1996), 111.

46 Walzer, *Exodus*, 89.

47 Paul adds the stronger psychoanalytic claim that "the 'memory' produced by partici-
pating in the appropriate religious practices must seem convincing by virtue of its
correspondence to fantasies, as well as to conflicts, impulses, anxieties, and defenses
generated by the interaction of an infant human with its nurturing environment. . . .
The myth gives shape to the individual fantasy, while the psychological energy of
individuals is transformed through ritual symbolism into the fuel that animates the
cultural symbol system" (Paul, 174).

48 Jean-Joseph Goux has put forth an elegant and persuasive argument that Oedipus

himself is already the first anti-Oedipus, the first mythic figure in Greece whose assumption of kingship breaks with the normal mythic pattern of royal investiture and succession elaborated in other myths of the Indo-European cultural space. See Goux, *Oedipus, Philosopher,* trans. Catherine Porter (Stanford: Stanford University Press, 1993).

49   Slavoj Žižek has noted a similar paradox apropos of the dialectic of Enlightenment. Žižek notes that enlightenment modernity can be conceived according to two mutually exclusive narratives: according to the first, only with the advent of modernity does the conception and requirement of the neutral symbolic Law emerge, the Law no longer permeated by a specific form or life; according to the second, Foucauldian counter-narrative, modernity marks the birth of disciplinary power, which, as obscene superego supplement, supplants the traditional judicial Law with the compulsive regulation of bodies and populations. Žižek proposes that one "conceive of these two narratives as the two complementary ideological gestures of resolving/obfuscating the underlying deadlock which resides in the fact that the Law was smeared, stigmatized, by enjoyment *at the very moment of its emergence as the neutral-universal formal Law.* The very emergence of a pure neutral Law, free of its concrete 'organic' life-world support, gives birth to the obscene superego underside, since this very life-world support, once opposed to the pure Law, is all of a sudden perceived as obscene" (*The Plague of Fantasies* [London: Verso, 1997], 11–12).

50   Freud appeals to the law of the talion in his interpretation of the death of Jesus. See *SE* 23:86.

51   It is this self-splitting of the deity that Freud registers as the various doublings in the Jewish tradition (some of which, of course, are Freud's invention): "Jewish history is familiar to us for its dualities: *two* groups of people who came together to form the nation, *two* kingdoms into which this nation fell apart, *two* gods' names in the documentary sources of the Bible. To this we add two fresh ones: the foundation of *two* religions—the first repressed by the second but nevertheless later emerging victoriously behind it, and *two* religious founders, who are both called by the same name of Moses and whose personalities we have to distinguish from each other. All of these dualities are the necessary consequences of the first one: the fact that one portion of the people had an experience which must be regarded as traumatic and which the other portion escaped" (Freud, *SE* 23:52). For a good summary of the theory of doublets and its implications for an understanding of biblical authorship, see Richard Elliott Friedman, *Who Wrote the Bible?* (New York: HarperCollins, 1997). In a suggestive discussion of Theodor Reik's thoughts on the Jewish practice of blowing the shofar in conjunction with the Yom Kippur ritual, Slavoj Žižek has appealed to this notion of a split god, a god who both prohibits and commands enjoyment. By evoking the sound of the dying primal father—we might say the primal father *qua* undead father—the shofar condenses the " 'pagan' superego dimension of God" and his function as guarantor of the symbolic pact and Law. What is crucial is that within Judaism this split is sustained, even cultivated, rather than dialectically superseded: "This voice *qua* reminder/remainder of the dying father, of course, is not something that can be erased once the reign of the Law is established: it is constantly needed as the

ineradicable support of the Law. For that reason its reverberation was heard when Moses was receiving the Commandments from God—that is to say, at the very moment when the reign of (symbolic) Law was being instituted (in what Moses was able to discern as the articulated Commandments, the crowd waiting below Mount Sinai apprehended only the continuous, non-articulated sound of the shofar): the voice of the shofar is an irreducible *supplement* of the (written) Law. It is only the *voice* that confers on the Law its performative dimension, that is, makes it operative: without this support in the senseless voice (voice *qua* object), Law would be a piece of powerless writing obliging no one. By means of the shofar *qua* voice, the Law acquires its *enunciator,* 'subjectivizes' itself, thereby becoming an effective agency which *obliges.* In other words, it is the intervention of a voice which transmutes the signifying chain into an act of creation" (*The Indivisible Remainder: An Essay on Schelling and Related Matters* [London: Verso, 1996], 153–54).

52   *Rewriting the Soul: Multiple Personality and the Sciences of Memory* (Princeton: Princeton University Press, 1995); references will be made to it in the body of the text.

53   One of the most interesting efforts to approach this dimension of the Holocaust is Dan Diner's essay "Historical Understanding and Counterrationality: The *Judenrat* as Epistemological Vantage," in *Probing the Limits of Representation: Nazism and the "Final Solution,"* ed. Saul Friedländer (Cambridge: Harvard University Press, 1992), 128–42. Diner argues that it was the Jewish councils in the ghettos, the bodies charged with negotiating with the Nazis, that were most directly exposed to the mutation of the space of reason which the "final solution" represented.

54   Once again, Derrida's *Archive Fever* is largely a meditation on the status of such virtual or spectral archivization. The "texts" of what is thus archived are "not readable according to the paths of 'ordinary history' and this is the very relevance of psychoanalysis, if it has one" (65).

55   In an essay on *Moses and Monotheism,* Marianne Schuller speaks of "die unheimliche Ereignishaftigkeit eines unsichtbaren, un(be)greifbaren Einschnitts" ("the uncanny eventfulness of an invisible, ungraspable cut"; see "Gesetzes-Text: Zu Freud," in Schuller, *Moderne: Verluste* [Frankfurt a.M.: Stroemfeld/Nexus, 1997], 107).

56   Freud, *The Interpretation of Dreams,* cited in Žižek, *The Sublime Object of Ideology* (London: Verso, 1989), 14.

57   Žižek, *Sublime Object,* 15, 13.

58   Jean-François Lyotard, "The Dream-Work Does Not Think," trans. Mary Lydon, in *The Lyotard Reader,* ed. Andrew Benjamin (Oxford: Basil Blackwell, 1991), 19, 26.

59   Lyotard, "Dream-Work," 25. See also Jonathan Lear's lucid rejection of this picture of the dreaming subject as a kind of rational agent that is simply in conflict with the ego in "Restlessness, Irrationality, and the Concept of Mind," in *Open Minded: Working Out the Logic of the Soul* (Cambridge: Harvard University Press, 1998).

60   Freud, *SE* 23:43.

61   Paul, *Moses and Civilization,* 106.

62   See once more Yerushalmi, *Freud's Moses.*

63   Derrida, *Archive Fever,* 67.

5

Darian Leader

Beating Fantasies and Sexuality

Psychoanalysis shows us the singular nature of each subject's fantasy, different in the modes of its use and the pathways of its construction despite what may appear to be a "common" imaginary content. Freud was particularly sensitive to the problems of generalizing about fantasy content, and yet he saw the ubiquity of certain fantasy sequences as a research problem. He devoted much attention to the vicissitudes of the rescue fantasy and the beating fantasy, and I have commented elsewhere on how Freud's study of the rescue motif may illuminate questions of male and female sexuality.[1] The beating fantasy has been much discussed in the analytic literature, yet more so in relation to perversions than to sexuation as such. Although it would be unwise to assume that the establishment of sexed positions in childhood can be studied *without* reference to perversion, as Lacan demonstrated in his seminar on object relations,[2] Freud's discussion of the beating fantasy can shed light on other aspects of sexuality that have perhaps received less attention within this context. In particular, if sexuality and language are as closely bound up as Lacan argues, it can help to clarify the nature of some of the relations between the libido and the signifying mechanisms introduced by symbolic functioning.

The Context

Why did Freud write "A Child Is Being Beaten" in 1919? There are three immediate answers to this question. First, there is the proximity of his publication of the analysis of the Wolf Man, in which the beating fantasy plays a crucial role in the reconstruction of the patient's infantile neurosis.[3] Second, there is the clinical proximity of the analysis of Freud's daughter Anna, the first phase of which ran from October 1918 to the spring of 1922. She would in fact publish an account of beating fantasies in a young girl almost three years after her father's paper, although we now know that when she presented this case to the Vienna Psychoanalytic Society there would be another six months before she was to see her first analytic patient.[4] The case, in fact, was her own, and given that her analysis with Freud was taking place in 1919, it is clear that the material Freud dealt with in his study of the beating fantasy was rather close to home.[5] Third, there is the more general question of the theory of perversion. As the notion of a developmental ladder became more frequently appealed to in analytic theory, perverse fixation was sometimes explained in terms of a stagnation of the developmental sequence: the pervert was just someone who got stuck before the Oedipus complex had really got going. Freud's examination of the beating fantasy aimed at impeaching this view, showing how the perverse residue manifest in the beating fantasy is in fact an end-product [*Endausgang*], in the same way that a ray of white light is a composite product rather than an original and elementary "raw material." Pursuing this analogy, Freud would evoke the image of the lens as comparable to that of the Oedipus complex itself. In an argument which would later be refined by Hans Sachs, Freud is showing how such fantasies are in fact the end-product of a complicated development that cannot be separated from the Oedipus complex.[6]

The Sequence

Freud's first point in the 1919 paper is the ubiquity of the beating fantasy: distributed through different clinical structures, it emerges with surprising frequency, despite the reticence of his patients to "confess" to its presence. Six cases are evoked, four female and two male, and although Freud discusses the diagnostic possibilities of five of these, the sixth, curiously, remains unmentioned. We also know that all of the female cases discussed were virgins, as Freud informed Marie Bonaparte in an unpublished letter.[7] Although the fantasy seems to be set in the verbal form "A child is being beaten," Freud shows how it in fact supposes a complex sequence of phases. The fantasy his patients describe is the most elaborated form of this sequence and will be elaborated in different ways for the boy and the girl.

In the first phase of the female version of the beating fantasy, a child who is not the subject is being beaten by the father. Freud gives this phase the wording, "My father is beating the child" (hereafter 1). Since this child tends to be a sibling, he adds to the initial formulation "whom I hate," with the suggestion that hence the father "loves only me." He is unwilling, however, to claim that phase 1 has the dignity of a fantasy as such: rather, it may simply consist of recollections or desires from early childhood. The second phase, in contrast, is identified unambiguously with a fantasy. The apparent sadism of phase 1 seems converted into a masochism, where it is now the subject who is being beaten, to give the formulation "I am being beaten by my father" (hereafter 2). This fantasy is accompanied by a high yield of pleasure, yet Freud stresses that it is never remembered as such, but must be reconstructed [*rekonstruiert*]: "This second phase," he writes, "is the most important and the most momentous of all. But we can say of it in a certain sense that it has never had a real existence. It is never remembered, it has never been brought to consciousness." [8]

The third phase complicates the initial sequence by pluralizing the subject, changing its sex, and introducing the motif of the "representative" (or "delegate"): "child (many children) is being beaten by a representative of the father [*Vatervertreter*]" (hereafter 3). The children tend to be boys, and Freud notes how in this phase, "The situation of being beaten, which was originally simple and monotonous, may undergo the most complicated alterations and embellishments." [9] The boys involved are simply substitutes [*Ersetzungen*] for the child herself. Freud's emphasis here is on the *jouissance* involved in the scenario: great masturbatory pleasure is linked to this third phase, and the subject fails to recognize herself in the scene—she seems to have no place except as an onlooker: "I am probably looking on."

Freud devotes less attention to the male versions of the beating fantasy. The sequence here seems to begin with the same formulation as phase 2 for the girl, "I am being beaten by my father," although he modifies this to posit a first phase in order to generate symmetry with the female version: "I am loved by my father." This will become transformed into a second phase, "I am being beaten by my mother," which then translates into "I am being beaten by a mother substitute" (the term for substitute is *Ersatz*). The activity of this reformulation is described by Freud as a "remodeling" [*Umarbeitung*].

Phase 1 of the female sequence would appear to articulate a demand for exclusive love from the father: he does not love the other child, only the subject herself. This incestuous bond is not yet linked to the genitals, although, Freud argues, the genital organization has been reached. The sex itself is mysterious, even if the child realizes that it is somehow connected to the parental relation. The work of repression and the presence of guilt introduced by the incestuous tendency generate the second phase, in which the overall attitude seems to be masochistic: the subject is herself being punished. But this punishment is also the vehicle of a regressive satisfaction, as the force of repression generates a debasement of the genital organization: sexual love and guilt converge. The sexual love is shifted to another register, producing a regressive substitute in anal-sadistic terms for genital tendencies. The third phase remains masochistic to the extent that the other children are substitutes for the child herself, as she turns away from the incestuous link with the father to become a boy. The "feminine role" is abandoned, and she gives up her sex in distancing herself from her incest.

As for the boy, the first unconscious phase articulates the thought "I am loved by my father," a feminine attitude which succumbs to repression.[10] To avoid his homosexuality, the agent of the beating becomes the mother, allowing the boy to retain a feminine position while keeping the homosexual currents at a distance. Despite the difficulties in generating any clear symmetries between the fantasy sequence for the boy and that for the girl, Freud argues that the key to both is the incestuous link to the father. Despite his later revisions to the theory of the Oedipus complex, he leaves this fundamental point unmodified.

However, before we examine the logic of these sequences, it is worthwhile to pose a number of questions. First of all, if the girl relates to a paternal representative and the boy to a mother substitute, is there a difference in status between a representative and a substitute? And if so, what can this tell us about sexuation for the boy and the girl? Secondly, if the key motif seems to concern being loved, why do we not find a more explicit love scenario, and, taking into account Freud's later formulations of the original link to the mother, why do we not find a note to this effect or some development on this theme? Why should this archaic fantasy always seem to revolve around the father? And to what extent does the activity of logical transformation involved in the fantasy sequence *depend* on the presence of the paternal agency?

Lacan's Perspectives

Lacan comments on Freud's article several times, and we can try to sketch the changes in perspective from the 1950s to the 1967 seminar on the logic of fantasy. The first detailed commentary appears in the context of a discussion of perversion in the seminar on object relations.[11] Lacan is interested in the perverse valorization of a single image, an isolation of a particular imaginary element which is separated from the dialectical considerations introduced by symbolic functioning. With Freud and Sachs, he is arguing against the conception of perverse formations as being some sort of raw leftover and showing how they result from the passage through the oedipal network. The frozen image here is linked in particular to phase 1 of the female fantasy: "My father beats the child" is situated on the imaginary axis aa' of schema L, whereas the latent symbolic message "he loves only me" finds its place on the axis AS. The interpretation of the fantasy at this point in Lacan's seminar thus uses the disparity of imaginary and symbolic registers to situate the clinical material, with the accent being on the message articulated beyond the apparently frozen and isolated nature of the image of beating.

Just one year later, in 1958, Lacan's focus has changed considerably. The emphasis now is on the action of the symbolic in the fantasy sequence to abolish the subject. In the first phase, the subject is erased at the symbolic level, with beating taking on the dignity of a "symbolic act" par excellence.[12] As Freud had pointed out, witnessing a real scene involving the beating of another child fails to automatically generate any pleasure, indicating the erotization of the symbolic accent itself. But how exactly is this presence of the symbolic indexed? Here Lacan adds a detail which is not to be found in Freud's discussion, the presence of the instrument of beating—the whip, the rod, or the staff used by the father—a detail which we find in other clinical reports of the fantasy. In the same way that Lacan had shown in his commentary on Hans how an imaginary element could be elevated to symbolic functioning, he sees the rod as indexing the symbolic itself, a mythic, symbolically rich element which is added to the fantasy scenario. Melitta Schmideberg had in fact emphasized the way in which the instrument of beating is often highly elaborated: the cane or staff may be contained in an expensive traveling case, with gold or ivory handles.[13] It is thus *separated* from the other imaginary elements in the beating scenario and given a special value, a symbolic density which is indexed by the elaborate and rare nature of its form.

This evocation of the symbolic becomes even more convincing if we remember the close link between expressions of beating and expressions that designate the effects of language on the organism. As R. B. Onians showed in his classic book *The Origins of European Thought,* the action of words is formulated quite literally as a beating: the blows of fate, the chains or bonds of destiny, and so on.[14] Where human life is seen as ordered by a larger design, this design is conceived as a form of speech (for example, as a prophecy or a sentence) which is imposed with violence on the subject. Thus, the action of the symbolic is materialized in these images as an action on the body. These ideas were implicit in William Niederland's apparently startling conclusion to a clinical study dealing with the beating fantasy that the blows gave form to acoustic force, to the voice, an auditory presence linked to the father: what strikes the child may well be an empirical object like a whip, but this object is serving to embody the symbolic dimension of language.[15] As he points out, there is a "close relation and possible interchangeability of sound and beating,"[16] suggested linguistically by such terms as *beat, strike, blow, bang,* and *hit.* Niederland, like Onians, evokes the *Iliad* to support his observation of a convergence of terms designating the effects of beating and acoustic presence.

This perspective helps to clarify the logic of the sequence of fantasies. The imaginary world of rivalries represented in the first phase of the fantasy, in which the sibling is being beaten, becomes valorized into the symbolic world, the universe of the law, with its consequent embodiment in the figure of the father.[17] The imaginary register is what allows the shift of the child from the first phase to the second, from the sibling to the subject, but in the precise sense of a move in the direction of the symbolic. The rival of phase 1 may be hated, but the subject will slide into his or her place, the place of a subject as abolished, as not recognized by the symbolic except as barred.

Such uses of the imaginary are a major concern in Lacan's work in the 1950s, perhaps the two most striking examples being the way in which the image of the mirror phase becomes reformulated in terms of symbolic shifts and the way in which Hamlet, in Lacan's reading, is able to momentarily assume his desire through his capture in the image of the mourning Laertes.[18] This passage from imaginary to symbolic may also be seen in the phenomena of what linguists call "overextending." At the single-word stage, children will often use the same word for several different objects or events in their environment, a practice which seems based first of all on perceptual similarities: "moon," for example, may be used for the crescent-shaped object in the night sky, then for a grapefruit segment, and then for a portion of a circle. In this first overextension, the shifts are based on similarity at the level of the image (the crescent shape), but soon this will pass to the level of proper symbolic functioning when properties of objects and links with other words start to function in a more autonomous way.[19] The move into the symbolic world, with its necessary distance from the image and any features of perceptual identity, is supported precisely through the use of this initial identity to engage with verbal chains. However, what Lacan's observations make clear is the lack of any real continuity between these domains: rather, there is a violence in the disruption and modification of the imaginary by the symbolic register, a violence which we see quite clearly in the beating scenarios.

The sequence of beating fantasies thus becomes the narrative of the passage of the imaginary into the symbolic, the story of the effects of language on the subject. Although this may appear to be a structural abstraction, distanced from the field of subjectivity, Freud's discussion shows that affects and emotions are entirely caught up in such a process. The subject may be beaten in the second phase but is loved to the extent of being recognized. This rereading also responds to the question we posed earlier about the place of the mother, who is missing from the female sequence. Post-Freudian commentators have often stressed the preoedipal roots of the beating fantasy sequence, and Lacan is far from ignoring the mother's structural role.[20] He argues that the first phase only makes sense if we suppose the presence of the mother and her desire and the child's notion of the phallic object. The principle of substitution relies on the registration that the mother is lacking something, which may take on the form of the image of the sibling. This convergence of phallus and child would allow us to make sense of the addition Freud made to the beating fantasy theory in 1925, when he claims that since the problematic of penis-having predates sibling rivalry, the formula of the fantasy ought to be adjusted to "A clitoris is being beaten."[21]

This surprising reformulation is in fact also a consequence of the Freudian series child-penis, and we could ask why it did not feature in the 1919 text, particularly given the clinical material from the analysis of the Wolf Man that produced exactly these results. The Wolf Man's masochistic fantasies, Freud claims, followed the formula "A penis is being beaten." After his sister's seduction attempt, he is captured in the relation "to have the penis touched," which reverts to its anal-sadistic form after the castration threat from Nanya. He tries at first to realize the touching relation with her, but her refusal and articulation of the threat send him back to the beating fantasy. The father now becomes its object, with the reversal from the sadistic direction to the masochistic, generating the new relation "to be beaten on the penis." The tension here with the 1919 article is in the identity of the agent: in the Wolf Man sequence as reconstructed by Freud, the initial image concerns a woman, whereas in the discussion of the male beating fantasy it is the father. Although this may appear to be a contradiction, the resemblance disappears when we introduce the Lacanian distinctions of imaginary and symbolic. The father is present here not as an empirically based figure in the fantasy, but rather as the index of the imposition of the symbolic order, something which will always be distanced from the world of images through which it operates.

With this new emphasis on the symbolic, Lacan can link the beating fantasy sequence to the oedipal passage itself. As the phallic image linked to the mother becomes barred, the only way it can pass into the symbolic is precisely as abolished, as beaten. The beaten child thus becomes an embodiment of the barred child-phallus, with the rod indexing the action of the symbolic in the act of abolition. We see here how Lacan's notion of the phallus is primarily the marker of a loss, something that Freud's students grasped in their own particular way. The recent literature on the 1920s debates on the function of the phallus tends to miss what was probably the key question. Jones, Horney, Klein, and Deutsch did not agree with all of Freud's formulations of sexual development, but what they did not dispute was the existence of an early phase of *Penisneid*. Neither did they dispute the existence of a castration complex in women. The problem was not to determine whether either of these was really operative, but rather to understand the nature of the relation between them. The debates of the 1920s and 1930s share this one underlying question: *is there or is there not a causal connection between penis envy and the castration complex?* Women might have a concern with loss of love and with ideas of adding and subtracting something from the body, and girls might spend some time comparing their own genitals with those of the boy, but what was the relation between these two sets of interests? What Jones, Horney, Klein, and Deutsch could not accept was that the one was the cause of the other. Something, they thought, had to happen in between, and they formulated this something in their own, individual ways. If the castration complex in women was sometimes identified with the term *Penisneid,* what this meant was that there was more than one castration complex.

The first, apparently anatomically based comparison of genitals might generate a little envy, but something had to happen to this envy to give it the powerful form of the castration complex as such. Karen Horney had the idea that after the initial penis envy, the girl had to deal with the tragedy of her failed, disappointed romance with the father. This frustration would search for a symbol, and so the first penis envy would become recathected and function now as the representative of the loss of love.[22] Jones agreed more or less with this formulation, except that he followed Klein in making the tragedy not the failed romance with the father but the impossibility of sharing the father's penis with the mother in coitus. "The disappointment at never being allowed to share the penis in coitus with the father, or to thereby obtain a baby, reactivates the girl's early wish to possess a penis of her own."[23] For both Horney and Jones, the anatomical penis of the initial penis envy would become reanimated as the symbol of another and quite distinct loss. An organ would thus pass to the level of a symbol:

$$\text{Organ} \rightarrow \frac{\text{Symbol}}{\text{frustration/impossibility}}$$

This would seem to explain, they thought, how the transitory and apparently contingent episodes of anatomical comparison could generate the more global and structural complex of castration. The phallus replaces the penis not as an anatomical attribute but as a symbol of what the child has to give up. In Lacan's terms in 1958, it marks the effects of the symbolic, the loss introduced by the network of language and the law: as he says, it becomes the symbol of the effects of language on the subject. And hence the interest of linking the phallic motif with linguistic considerations of signifier and signified.

The Name-of-the-Father

The link to the father here is clear given Lacan's framework in 1958: his function is to intervene to pass the imaginary object of the mother's desire to the level of the symbolic, abolishing and forbidding it simultaneously for both mother and child. Thus, where one finds the abolition of the imaginary phallus, one will find the index of the symbolic network, the father, accounting for the ubiquity of the paternal presence in the fantasy sequence. In one sense, this is a consequence of interpreting the beating sequence as a representation of the effects of the symbolic on the imaginary. Despite the introduction of these new considerations, which were absent from Freud's discussion, Lacan's results here are entirely Freudian in the sense that they link the beating fantasy sequence not with some preoedipal developmental stagnation but rather with the actual passage through the Oedipus complex itself.

If we formulate the beating fantasy as a dramatization of the effects of the symbolic on the imaginary, we have a clue as to the presence of the motif of substitution. We noted earlier how the third stage of the fantasy for the girl involves the passage from the father to a representative of the father: she is no longer being beaten by her father, but other children, who are her "substitutes," are being beaten by a paternal representative. Now, if one of the principles of the symbolic world is precisely that of substitution, as the imaginary is collapsed by the symbolic, the substitution of one term for another would be introduced. More exactly, what the fantasy sequence shows is how the presence of the symbolic function of paternity, the Name-of-the-Father, is what allows the *possibility* of substitution. In 1958, Lacan still holds the view that this operator is what authorizes the signifying system, what gives it its law. Hence it is perhaps not surprising to find Freud introducing his notions of the normative nature of the Oedipus complex at the point in his discussion where he turns to the function of the father.[24] To find a clinical illustration of these apparently abstract ideas, we can turn to the paper Anna Freud read to gain admission to the Vienna Psychoanalytic Society in 1922, a case history which, as we noted earlier, is her own. It is also with little doubt one of the six cases which Freud evokes in the 1919 paper.

"Beating Fantasies and the Daydream" deals with a case that generated an "artistic superstructure," a set of stories which gradually became distanced from beating fantasies and their masturbatory accompaniment. If it began with a beating fantasy that did involve masturbation, it is thus a question of tracing the signifying transformation from one story to another and the loss of enjoyment which ensued. Given the nature of Anna Freud's later work, it is perhaps surprising to see her concern in this early paper with questions of logic: the *derivation* of the daydream from the fantasy, its *dependence* on the beating fantasy, and its *proof* during analytic treatment[25] — in other words, how a fantasy linked with masturbation is transformed into a daydream without masturbation.[26] It is thus a narrative of the relations between libido and signifying mechanisms.

The first phases of transformation concern the passage from "A boy is being beaten by a grown-up person" to "Many boys are being beaten by many grown-up persons." In each instance, both the boys and the grown-ups are indeterminate, and the scenarios are accompanied at their close by masturbation. The daydreamer had tried for years to separate the fantasy from its masturbatory accompaniment, but with little success, indicating one of the key implicit problems of the article: the dependence and independence of libido from a signifying scenario, or how the libidinal charge of a fantasy framework can be drained or not drained. Anna Freud had tried to defer the tabooed climax indefinitely, adding description after description to the scenario, a tactic that neatly shows one of the functions of human desire. Perpetuating the fantasy framework with these additions, the *jouissance* of the masturbatory act is deferred, making desire equivalent to a limit or defense against *jouissance*.

It is curious to note how the details added to the initial framework concerned institutions, schools, and reformatories in which the scenes of beating were imagined to take place. Anna Freud was later to found the Hampstead Clinic for psychoanalytic work with children, an initiative which seems in no way at odds with the basic structure of her fantasy. Her systematic attempts to separate the fantasy from its masturbatory climax led her to try suppressing the scenario itself, and it was between her eighth and tenth year that an important nuance introduced itself into these efforts. The beating fantasy metamorphosed into what she calls "nice stories," in which the indeterminate names and faces of the earlier fantasy were filled in. Masturbation ceased, and she thus indulged "without guilt" in this new form of daydreaming, the "artistic superstructure" which she set out to analyze in its derivation from the initial sequence.[27] This link was entirely the result of analytic treatment, as she had established no link whatsoever between the two series at the time: "The two were kept apart very carefully—even in regard to time: for every reactivation of the fantasies of beating had to be followed by a temporary renunciation of the 'nice stories.'" Again, this introduces considerations of logic, perhaps best modeled in topological terms, as what is in question is the separation of sets of signifying elements. If a topology is an order imposed on signifying elements (the various sequences of the nice stories and the initial fantasy), for them to be kept apart and then, in the course of analysis, linked implies a change of topology, a modification of the barriers which separate certain elements from others.

Anna's nice stories were continued in a long and complex series, yet she singles out one of them as "the cardinal and most important." It persisted for a number of years and underwent various transformations; other stories would branch off from it "just as in legends or mythology." In an image that evokes the Brontë sisters' construction of the imaginary kingdoms of Angria and Gondal from their chance encounter with a boy's set of toy soldiers, she describes the inspiration for the new stories on finding a boy's story book. Appropriating various details from its narrative, she constructs the following skeleton plot: "A medieval knight has for years been at feud with a number of nobles who have leagued together against him. In the course of a battle, a noble youth of fifteen (the age of the daydreamer) is captured by the knight's henchmen. He is taken to the knight's castle and there kept prisoner for some time,

until at last he gains his freedom again."[28] This story constituted the
"outer frame" [*ausseren Rahmen*] for her daydreams: "Into this frame
she inserted a wealth of scenes, every one of which was organised like
an independent story, containing an introduction, development of the
plot and climax . . . She was free at any moment to choose between the
different parts of the tale according to her mood: and she could always
interpose a new situation between two others which had been finished
and previously joined up with each other."

Anna is describing here what may be called a *grammar* of the fantasy.
Just as many commentators have remarked on the grammar of the transformations of Freud's fantasy sequence, we find here a set of transforma-
tional principles which rely on addition, substitution, and combination
but all within the same basic framework. Freud had noted the change of
author, object, and signification in the fantasy sequence, even suggesting to some commentators that a Chomskyan tree diagram should be
introduced; this stress on grammar may be found implicitly in the early
paper by Schmideberg where she refers to the "assortments" of the fantasy scenario, in which terms could be shifted around and displaced. If
such linguistic operations are serving to organize libido and keep desire
going in the various scenarios, it shows how a fantasy may be construed
as a signifying organization of libido, a way of treating *jouissance* with
a particular signifying chain with its own rules. This would constitute a
sort of minimal grammar. We will turn later on to the question of why
Lacan would refer to what he called a "logic" of fantasy as distinct from
a simple grammar. In other words, why is the grammatical reference not
enough to account for the function of fantasy?

One of the central motifs of Anna Freud's framework involves the relationship between the knight and the youth. The knight is harsh and
brutal, the youth noble and pleasing, and there is antagonism and hostility between them. Anna gives a special importance to the "fear" and
"helplessness" of the youth when confronted with the knight, and we
can note that in their first encounter the youth is threatened with the rack
in order to force him to confess his secrets. This interesting detail evokes
the dimension of secrecy that Freud had stressed in his discussions of
female sexuality and also reminds us of Jones's observation about the
place of confession, of saying, in the sexual life of the female.[29] Despite
wishing to harm the youth, the knight still grants him one favor after

another, and as this occurs, the daydreamer shares the youth's "feelings of fear and fortitude in a state of great excitement." As Anna puts it: "In every instance the structure . . . was as follows: antagonism between a strong and a weak person; a misdeed—mostly unintentional—on the part of the weak one which puts him at the other's mercy; the latter's menacing attitude giving rise to the gravest apprehensions; a slow and sometimes very elaborate intensification almost to the limit of endurance of the dread and anxiety; and finally, as a pleasurable climax, the solution of the conflict, i.e. a pardon for the sinner, reconciliation, and, for a moment, complete harmony between the former antagonists." [30] It seems that an erotic charge is linked to this motif of the menace of punishment, even if the threatened punishment in fact fails to take place. This excitement will turn into pleasure at the moment that the anger and rage of the torturer become kindness and pity. As these periods of excitement fade to the memory of their transformation into kindness in other stories, she has to invent new variations of the scenario, new configurations allowing her to maintain desire.

How does this structural framework derive from the earlier beating fantasy? They seem to differ in that the first fantasy scenario ends in beating, whereas the second ends in reconciliation, although in both, as Anna Freud points out, there are both a strong and a weak figure, an indeterminate misdeed, and a period of dread and anxiety. The menace of punishment echoes, she thinks, the earlier scenes of beating, although they now exist in the form of an unrealized possibility. The "essential difference," however, lies in the fact that "in the nice stories affectionate treatment takes the place of the chastisement contained in the fantasies of beating." The passage from the one to the other is favored, she thinks, by the fact that in the beating scenario the girl was invariably represented by a boy, and the latter scenarios bring out the latent motif of a bond of love, the same bond that Freud had privileged in his own discussion of the beating sequence.[31] If the beating fantasies represented a return of the repressed incestuous wish, the nice stories form their sublimation, the tender emotional tie which is the result of an effective repression.

But what happened to the daydreams to make them eventually fade away? The response to this question can give us a clue not only to the supposed sublimation at play but also to the function of the paternal operator in the fantasy. Some years after the first emergence of the nice stories, Anna wrote down one version, a narrative which took the form of a short story. "It began with a description of the torture (the youth) underwent and ended with the prisoner's refusal to try to escape from the castle. His readiness to remain in the knight's power suggested the beginning of their friendship. In contrast to the daydream all the events were laid in the past and appeared in the form of a conversation between the prisoner's father and the knight." [32] This last detail is crucial. The story has become the *story of a story*, a sort of second-order version of the initial fantasy scenario, and what allows one story to become the object of another story is the presence of the youth's father. We can also note that the term used for the castle which imprisoned the youth is *Burg*, perhaps evocative of the *Berggasse* address which has become almost synonymous with her father. In the new version of the story, this signifier *Burg* is now linked in a chain to the term *Vater*. As this chain is constructed, the youth becomes an object of exchange in the conversation between the father and the knight. With this written version, the whole daydream fades away, and there is a real loss of enjoyment. Reading the story now has no more effect on her than as if it had been "produced by a stranger." Anna Freud explains this strange vicissitude in terms of the desire to communicate: her previous "private pleasure" has now been given up in exchange for her pleasure in "the impression she could create on others." Although it would be unjustified to assume that the fantasy frame vanished as such, its form in terms of the nice stories proves no longer valid, as if she has gone outside the frame of the initial sequence, an exit that is reflected in her reference to the story's production by a "stranger." There is thus a link between the presence of the father as speaking, as indexing the symbolic, and the motifs of the exchange of one form of enjoyment for another and the fading of the story's intensity.

Anna Freud, however, was to return to her analysis with her father some two years later for reasons which were probably linked to the non-exhaustion of the beating fantasy. The nice stories would continue to plague her, invoked apparently as a compensation for the distress involved in attending Schilder's ward rounds in Wagner-Jauregg's University of Vienna Psychiatric Clinic. As she wrote to Lou Andreas-Salomé, "The reason for continuing was the not entirely orderly behaviour of my honourable inner life: occasional unseemly intrusions of the daydreams combined with an increasing intolerance—sometimes physical as well as mental—of the beating fantasies and of their consequences which I could not do without."[33] Although the final version of the nice story we have discussed indicates a structural change of perspective, this later revival poses all the questions of reanimation, regression, and repression that would preoccupy Freud in the later years of the 1920s.

Grammar of Fantasy or Logic?

The story of youth and knight functions as a language for the day-dreamer. The elements can be rearranged, combined, and transformed in a certain number of ways while preserving overall rules which govern the fantasy framework. Presumably, it will be through pinpointing and defining these rules that one would be able to construct the grammar of the fantasy. When Lacan turns to renew his study of fantasy in 1967, he argues that fantasy is a phrase—in the sense of "A child is being beaten"—yet one which "only has grammatical sense."[34] The immediate difficulty here would seem to be the word "only": surely fantasies mean something beyond the rules of their grammar? Yet Lacan is careful to emphasize their function as being beyond or separate from meaning as such. A fantasy is a grammatical structure in which the index of subjective attribution, the "I" which would confer meaning, is absent. And yet, surely one would expect a fantasy to be a deeply personal wish, one in which we would find the true place for the "I"?

This assumption becomes less evident when we realize that the Freudian paradigm of "A child is being beaten" involves a sequence, one in which the second and unconscious phase is never remembered by the subject. As Freud writes, "This second phase is the most important and the most momentous of all. But we may say of it in a certain sense that it has never had a real existence. It is never remembered, it has never been brought to consciousness. It is a construction of analysis, but it is no less a necessity on that account."[35] The fantasy exists only in the terms of a construction: in other words, the fantasy excludes the "I," the subjective index which would assume the thought in question. With phase 2 ("I am being beaten by my father"), the "I" is never actually there to articulate it.

If we take this nonassumption of phase 2 of the beating fantasy seriously, it becomes possible to clarify the nature and function of desire. Phase 2 is constructed in between two other terms in a series. This aspect of the beating fantasy has gone unnoticed, the fact that it is not simply a question of a latent fantasy behind some more or less conscious one, but rather is situated *in between* two of them. Assuming that this is not an accident, we are led back to the idea of fantasy as excluding the "I." When something cannot be thought, when an "I" cannot be attributed to whatever is too unbearable to think, instead of forming some kind of prepositional and subjectively attributed phrase—for example, "I want to"—it will take on the form of a relation between two other terms. As the structuralists once pointed out, when it is not possible to formulate something as a meaningful statement, it will take on the form of a relation between other elements. In the famous Lévi-Straussian example, the inability to make sense of the contradiction between the fact that man is born of woman and born from the earth will generate the ciphering of this impossibility in terms of the further contradiction between overevaluation and underevaluation of a kinship tie. Each set of terms is self-contradictory in the same way. A literary example can make this clearer.

The "play within a play" in *Hamlet* has always constituted something of a puzzle. The main plot concerns a son commanded to avenge his murdered father. In the midst of his indecision and hesitancy, he hits on the idea of staging a play before his guilty uncle Claudius in which the murder scene is played out. The miniplay, however, makes the nephew the king's murderer, not the brother, as in the main narrative. Countless interpretations of this episode have been put forward in the literature on *Hamlet*, but the first question that we can ask is, why it was necessary to add the extra play at all? What, structurally, is its function? To be suitably dogmatic, suppose for a moment the presence of some oedipal material, the kind of thing that the best and the worst psychoanalytic commentators on the play have always emphasized. Little boys want to murder their daddies, so when someone else actually does, all the unconscious currents become especially reanimated: the uncle, in this sense, is in the place of the unconscious desire of Hamlet himself. We do not find this oedipal desire expressed as such in the play. What we have instead are two contradictory plots, and this very contradiction can suggest that when an unconscious wish is impossible to assume, it will take the form of pieces of material that cannot be fully superimposed, the one on the other. There is a margin between them, and the failure to map the one onto the other can suggest a definition of desire as being exactly this failure. Two stories thus cipher an initial point of impossibility, something that cannot be thought because it is so unbearable: that the son is himself in the place of the father's murderer. In other words, what the play-within-a-play shows us is that when a wish cannot be expressed as a proposition ("I want to kill Daddy"), it will take the form of a *relation*, a relation in which the "I" is missing.

If we take such an argument seriously, we can then try to apply it to clinical material, to interpret it in a Hamletian way. A young woman has two dreams on the same night. In the first, there is a violent struggle with a man. In the second, her father turns to her and says, "What you did was round," or, as it is specified, "You killed him in a shape that's round." Now, just as we asked why there are two plots and not just one in the literary reference, we can ask the same question of the dream material: why is there not just one dream? Since there are two, we might conjecture that a *relation* is at stake, that something that cannot be said is taking the form of a contradiction. This something is being articulated not as a proposition, but as a relation, something that emerges not in one or the other dream, but in the space between them. Now, we can dogmatically conjecture a murderous struggle with the father, as other associative material at the time suggested. This does not emerge as such in the dreams, but in the tension between the first dream and the second dream. In the second dream in particular, we have less a clear statement than an absurdity, a logical mistake: how can one kill someone in a shape that is round? Now, clearly, the word "round" resonates with the word "wrong," but taken at the letter it is still absurd. If we examine the dreams from the perspective of the mutual impossibilities we have been discussing, it is the impossibility evoked by the first fragment—the underevaluation of a kinship tie, the murder of Daddy—that translates into the logical impossibility of the second, the absurdity of the "round." A piece of nonsense thus responds to a point of prohibition, like the double plot motif in *Hamlet*. And surely it is not by chance that in the chapter Freud devoted to absurd dreams in his *Interpretation of Dreams*, nearly all of the examples he gives concern the dead father. Where something cannot be explicitly formulated in words, it will take the form of an absurdity, a point of nonsense in language, not a direct expression but a relation.

This introduces a new perspective on the beating fantasy series discussed by Freud. Phase 2 is never assumed by the subject, and we may question, with Freud, its "real existence" in terms of a proposition. Rather, it exists as the construction, the inferred term in between phase 1 and phase 3. Whereas one might have chosen to read the sequence 1–2–3 as chronological, with each phase following the next in time, this perspective would suggest that phase 1 and 3 are in fact only generated by the impossibility of formulating phase 2. Because the thought cannot be assumed subjectively, it takes on the form of the *relation* between 1 and 3. Hence Lacan's designation of phase 2 as "a time of angst" and his insistence that there is a "radical inadequation of thought to sexual reality."[36] This indicates one way of understanding Lacan's suggestion to study the logic, as opposed to simply the grammar, of fantasy: where meaning stops, where the subject fails to generate a signification, logic steps in with its relational structures. Given the fact that sexuality for a human being is something which seems to exclude meaning, which cannot be given any ready answer beyond the phallic signification, this would suggest that human beings treat sexuality with logic, and hence, that in order to study sexualities, logical considerations will have a special place, exactly as Lacan would argue in his seminar *Encore*.[37]

The Logic of Sexuation

Let us review the discussion so far before turning to the question of sexuation. We have seen how the beating fantasy sequence may be understood as the imaginarization of the imposition of the symbolic, with its special emphasis on the signifier of the phallus and the name of the father. Now, what are the consequences here as to the choice of *jouissance?* And what can we deduce from Freud's introduction of the terms "representative" and "substitute" in the third phase of the fantasy? Why is the paternal figure a representative or delegate rather than a substitute? Anna Freud had interpreted the substitution of the youth for the daydreamer as a simple oedipal defense: the sexual love scenes of the beating scenario could become the nice stories on condition that sexual difference was abandoned. As girl became boy, the menace of the incestuous wish was weakened.

This sort of argument, put forward by Freud himself in the 1919 paper, was indeed quite frequent in the 1920s and early 1930s. Karen Horney, for example, theorized the girl's "flight from womanhood" in terms of a comparable defense: accepting her own sex would intensify the terrible oedipal desires and guilt, but if the girl changed into a boy she could distance herself from them.[38] The change of sex in phase 3 of the fantasy sequence would thus be understood as a way out of the conflict generated by the Oedipus complex, an explanation that would make sense of Freud's comment to Marie Bonaparte about the women in question being virgins. As virgins, they may not have made the choice to assume their sex as women. Even if one accepts this kind of argument, there is still the question of why the boys are a plural here and why the father is replaced by "a representative taken from the class of fathers."[39]

When Princess Bonaparte asked the first of these questions, she would see the presence of the boys as less the expression of a "masculinity complex" than an elaboration of the series *feces-money-child-penis* that Freud had commented on, so that the child and the penis are in a relation of symbolic equation in the fantasy.[40] This is particularly interesting since it shifts the focus from the register of substitution to that of displacement, from the idea of "boy" replacing "girl" to that of a series of terms that are metonymically linked. As Bonaparte points out, the girl may substitute the boy for herself because of the wish to be a boy, but also, and above all, "because she wishes her father to beat what is equivalent to the child in her unconscious, namely her small male phallus, the clitoris multiplied as a royal (!) plural in the final beating fantasy."[41] She argues that rather than seeing the fantasy scenario as a block to femininity, it in fact opens up the possibility of "full vaginality," since the clitoris is now a passive organ. "The clitoris will thus finally surrender to [the penis] and the blows of the father's rod . . . will be kept for the vagina." The beating fantasy is thus the path to vaginal sensitivity rather than the contrary. What is beaten in the scenario, as she says, is the phallus, be it penis or clitoris.[42]

Other commentators have tackled this problem by claiming that the children of phase 3 simply represent the parents, as opposed to the subject herself. Although there may be some clinical evidence for this in certain cases, there are good reasons to think that one of the key principles of the fantasy chain is the multiple position of the subject, who may be in the place of the beater or the beaten or both.[43] It is perhaps no accident that soon after her paper on the beating fantasy, Anna Freud would elaborate her well-known theory of "identification with the aggressor," thus formalizing exactly the principle of multiple place. Indeed, in a hysteria, it is usually evident that the subject is in both of these positions simultaneously, without forgetting the third place implied by Freud when he tells us that the girl is in the position of the spectator of the whole event. Part of the analytic process involves allowing the subject to register such identifications and to confront the consequences of being in more than one place at the same time.

But how should we make sense of the reference to a representative taken from the class of fathers? It would seem as if a substitute—the boy(s)—relates to a representative, and the juxtaposition of these terms, which index symbolic functioning, seems particularly significant. In Freud's account of chronological development, the libidinal link with the father is treated by this procedure: the class of fathers takes the place of the father, and the girl can then situate herself in relation to it. The problem, of course, is that phase 3 of the sequence suggests that she is in fact situating herself as a boy, or indeed, as several boys. One immediate explanation may be offered here in terms of the distribution of *jouissance* if we include the figure of the spectator: where the plural boys incarnate the side of phallic *jouissance*, the isolated spectator incarnates the place of the exception, another form of *jouissance* which is separate from the boy's. Similarly, one may evoke the triangulation often discussed by Lacan where the girl, to elaborate the question of the enigma of her sex, takes the place of the man and relates to the woman from his place.[44] Whatever interpretation we choose here, it seems that the girl does not relate to her object "as herself," precisely because she is in the place of a substitute. In the male scenario, the boy relates to his object as a boy, although the object is a substitute, but the girl relates to her object as someone else. Her own place may be localized to the look of the spectator, absent in one sense from the sexual scene and generating a division, the effects of which may be seen in the notorious problems of pinning down a woman's subjective place in relation to the currents of sexual life.

However, as Bernard Burgoyne has shown, the initial argument which supposes the reference to the "class of fathers" must be put in question, since what Freud writes in the German text is *Vaterreihe*, the *series* rather than the *class* of fathers.[45] This detail is crucial: where the boy changes the sex of his object from the father to the mother in the fantasy sequence, the sex remains unchanged for the girl, yet the father is now linked to a series. If there is a class of mother substitutes, the father representatives are linked less to a class than to a series, an idea which might explain the male valorization of traits (a woman is attractive if she has blonde hair, green eyes, etc.) in contrast to the often apparently disparate series of partners a woman has. This would suggest that the way in which transferences function in female sexual life may not be identical to the way in which they function for a man, or, more precisely, that class functioning may not be the whole story when it comes to object choice.

This formulation generates a peculiar tension with the standard accounts of the Freudian Oedipus, in which it is the girl who has to change not only her object but its sex (mother to father, and then father to man), while the boy only has to change object (mother to woman). Thus, as Burgoyne points out, where the boy opts, in a sense, for the easy solution, choosing the mother and thereby avoiding the conflictual situation of being in the position of an object for the father, the girl remains in a conflictual relation with the series of fathers. One implication of this argument is that it would be erroneous to reduce the dynamics of female sexuality to the motif of substitution, however appropriate this term may be to describe the path of the boy. Hence Freud's implicit separation of "substitute" and "representative" in the 1919 paper. The difference between these terms indicates a difference at the level of repression, where substitution supposes that a repression has operated and representation or delegation that it is partial. If that is the case, the importance of barriers and the accentuation of the sense of guilt in female sexuality becomes clearer: left with the relation to the series of delegates of the father, a woman's oedipal conflicts may remain very close to the surface. And just as there are problems when a diplomat starts to behave like a substitute for his or her government rather than as a delegate, when a woman's partner starts to behave like a substitute, there is a recipe for trouble!

The common assumption that the key concept of female sexuality is substitution is exactly that: a recipe for trouble. To argue that a man is substituted for the father or that the father is substituted for the mother fails to do justice to the phenomenon. If we opt instead for the notion of a series, many of the transfers involved in unconscious sexual life start to make more sense, and we have a clue as to why Lacan used the term "transference" to describe the girl's shift from mother to father.[46] Thus, the third phase of the fantasy does not mean that the girl has abandoned her oedipal love for the father, as Freud at one point seems to suggest, to enter the masculinity complex as a boy, but rather that there is an engagement with the series of representatives which will remain conflictual and which will invite its own series of solutions, solutions that will not be elaborated in the register of substitution. The link of masturbatory *jouissance* to this third phase implies, in addition, that there is a special bond between enjoyment and the idea of delegation, whereas for the boy the masturbatory *jouissance* is rendered possible precisely by the fact of a substitution. Which suggests that it is women and not men who understand the meaning of the word *serious*.

Notes

The idea for this paper was suggested to me by reading Bernard Burgoyne's unpublished paper "The Class of Fathers," and I have tried here to develop some of the themes of his fascinating study.

1   See Darian Leader, *Promises Lovers Make When It Gets Late* (London: Faber and Faber, 1997), 83–92, 101–4.

2   See Jacques Lacan, *La relation d'objet* (Paris: Seuil, 1994).

3   Sigmund Freud, *From the History of an Infantile Neurosis*, in *The Standard Edition*, ed. James Strachey, vol. 17 (London: Hogarth Press, 1955), 46–47. Further references will be made to *SE*, followed by volume and page number.

4   Elizabeth Young-Bruehl, *Anna Freud: A Biography* (New York: Summit, 1988).

5   See the discussion in Rachel Blass, "Insights into the Struggle of Creativity: A Rereading of Anna Freud's 'Beating Fantasies and Daydreams,'" *Psychoanalytic Study of the Child* 48 (1993): 67–97.

6   Sigmund Freud, "A Child Is Being Beaten," *SE* 17:79–204 (*Gesammelte Wer* [hereafter *GW*], 12:197–226); Hans Sachs, "On the Genesis of Sexual Perversions" (1923), in *Homosexuality*, ed. Charles W. Socarides (New York: Aronson, 1978), 531–46.

7   Marie Bonaparte, *Female Sexuality* (New York: International Universities Press, 1953), 87.

8   Freud, "A Child Is Being Beaten," *SE* 17:185 (*GW* 12:204). I sometimes alter Strachey's translation.

9   Freud, "A Child Is Being Beaten," *SE* 17:186 (*GW* 12:205).

10   The relation here of repression to regression is arguably the key concern of Freud's

subsequent work in the 1920s. See Darian Leader, *Freud's Footnotes* (London: Faber and Faber, forthcoming).

11 Lacan, *La relation d'objet*, 111–29.

12 Cf. Jacques Lacan, "Les formations de l'inconscient" (unpublished seminar), 23 Apr. 1958.

13 Ibid., 303.

14 Cf. R. B. Onians, *The Origins of European Thought* (Cambridge: Cambridge University Press, 1988), 321–33, 378–82, 386–87.

15 Cf. William Niederland, "Early Auditory Experiences, Beating Fantasies, and Primal Scene," *Psychoanalytic Study of the Child* 13 (1958): 471–504.

16 Ibid., 480.

17 For the opposite opinion, cf. Ethel Spector Person, ed., *On Freud's "A Child Is Being Beaten"* (New Haven: Yale University Press, 1997), 105.

18 Cf. Jacques Lacan, "Désir et son interpretation" (unpublished seminar), 1958–59.

19 Cf. M. Bowerman, "The Acquisition of Word Meaning: An Investigation into Some Current Conflicts," in *The Development of Communication*, ed. N. Waterson and C. Snow (New York: Wiley, 1978), 263–87.

20 E.g., Edmund Bergler, "Preliminary Phases of the Masculine Beating Fantasy," *Psychoanalytic Quarterly* 22 (1938): 514–36; and W. A. Myers, "The Psychodynamics of a Beating Fantasy," *International Journal of Psychoanalytic Psychotherapy* 8 (1981): 623–47.

21 Freud, "Some Psychical Consequences of the Anatomical Distinction between the Sexes," *SE* 19:254.

22 Karen Horney, "The Genesis of the Castration Complex," in *Feminine Psychology*, ed. H. Kelman (New York: W. W. Norton, 1967), 37–53.

23 Ernest Jones, "The Early Development of Female Sexuality," in *Papers on Psychoanalysis* (London: Balliere Tindall, 1948), 438–51.

24 Freud, "A Child Is Being Beaten," *SE* 17:188.

25 Cf. Anna Freud, "The Relation of Beating Phantasies to a Daydream," *International Journal of Psychoanalysis* 4 (1923): 89–102; "Schlagephantasie und Tagtraum," *Imago* 8 (1922): 317–32.

26 Anna Freud, "Schlagephantasie und Tagtraum," 318.

27 In her careful study, Rachel Blass ("Insights"), shows how there are certain contradictions in the material concerning the link from masturbation to the beating fantasy and the nice stories. At some moments the masturbation is linked to the former, at others to the latter. Similarly, whereas Freud stressed that guilt was linked not to masturbation but to the accompanying fantasy, Anna Freud seems to come to exactly the opposite conclusion.

28 Again, Blass points out contradictions here in Anna Freud's text, given a kind of symptomatic representation in the running head to the English translation of the article: "Beating-Phantasies in a Daydream." The "in" is precisely what Anna Freud seeks to be denying with her separation of the two sets of sequences.

29 Jones, "Female Sexuality," 441.

30 Anna Freud, "The Relation of Beating Phantasies to a Daydream," 94; "Schlagephantasie und Tagtraum," 321.

31 Anna Freud and Freud do not share the same opinions about the place of sexual as opposed to affectionate currents in the beating sequence. See Blass for discussion.

32 Anna Freud, "The Relation of Beating Phantasies to a Daydream," 100; "Schlagephantasie und Tagtraum," 330.

33 Young-Bruehl, *Anna Freud*, 122.

34 Jacques Lacan, "La logic du fantasme" (unpublished seminar), 1966–67.

35 Freud, "A Child Is Being Beaten," *SE* 17:185.

36 Lacan, "La logique du fantasme." Cf. the summary in *Ornicar?* 29 (1984): 13–18. The research of Novick and Novick using the Hampstead Clinic Index arguably supports this interpretation; cf. Jack Novick and Kerry Kelly Novick, "Beating Fantasies in Children," *International Journal of Psychoanalysis* 53 (1972): 237–42.

37 Cf. *The Seminar of Jacques Lacan,* book 20: *Encore,* ed. Jacques-Alain Miller, trans. Bruce Fink (New York: Norton, 1998).

38 Cf. Karen Horney, "The Flight from Womanhood" (1926), in Kelman, *Feminine Psychology,* 54–70.

39 Freud, "A Child Is Being Beaten," *SE* 17:196 (*GW* 216). Strachey translates "representative/delegate" as "substitute." The German is *Stellvertreter.*

40 Bonaparte, *Female Sexuality*, 83.

41 Ibid., 84.

42 Ibid., 90.

43 Freud's multiple place model can be found in his "Hysterical Phantasies and Their Relations to Bisexuality," *SE* 9:159–66.

44 As can be seen, for example, in Daniel B. Schuster, "Notes on 'A Child Is Being Beaten,'" *Psychoanalytic Quarterly* 34 (1966): 357–67.

45 Cf. Bernard Burgoyne, "The Class of Fathers," unpublished paper.

46 Jacques Lacan, *Écrits* (Paris: Éditions de Seuil, 1966), 686.

6

The Collapse of the Function of the Father and Its Effect on Gender Roles

Paul Verhaeghe

The year 1970 saw the publication of Germaine Greer's famous book *The Female Eunuch*. It was without doubt an intellectual landmark within what is called the second feminist wave.[1] In scope, both the book and the wave surpass feminist territory alone and aim at liberation as such, since they are directed against authoritarian political structures, the nuclear family, and power in general. Greer expresses this quite clearly in the last paragraph of her first chapter: "The anti-feminists have complained that the emancipation of women will imply the end of marriage, the end of morality, and the end of the state. . . . When we reap the harvest which the unwitting suffragettes sowed, we shall see that the anti-feminists were after all right."

Meanwhile, a quarter of a century has elapsed, we are ready to reap this harvest, and indeed Greer's prophetic words have turned out to be true. However, there is one snag: she herself does not seem to be very happy with the result. Quite the contrary. In an interview with the *Sunday Times Magazine*,[2] she tells us that if women were in charge, the United Kingdom would return to the status of a kind of Third World country. The rest of the interview follows the same lines.

Since this reversal is rather a surprise, one is tempted to look for reassuring *ad hominem* explanations: she is probably frustrated, it has something to do with her age, and so on. Strange as it may seem, we find an analogous although more subtle reversal in the work of another prominent figure of that movement, namely Doris Lessing. Anybody who has read her *Martha Quest* tetralogy cannot doubt her literary talent or her left-wing feminist commitment. Nevertheless, in her recent autobiography and the ensuing interviews, she distances herself from the movement and even goes so far as to say that she deplores its impact on her personal life.[3]

The crowning touch came in 1990, when Camille Paglia stormed onto the scene with her *Sexual Personae*, which immediately turned her into a cult figure. Indeed, her message was loud and clear: being a woman and a confirmed lesbian, she wrote a polemic plea in favor of the male cause and described femininity in a way no man had dared to do since Otto Weininger's *Geschlecht und Charakter*.[4]

I mention these three women in my introduction because they express quite clearly the contemporary malaise concerning such issues as gender, patriarchy, and feminism. In this respect, our century has seen a striking reversal. During the first fifty years, a popular interpretation of Freud turned the authoritarian father into the source of all evil, both at an individual and at a sociological level. Authority had to be banned; freedom was the word. The obvious success of this movement from the 1960s on gave rise to its exact opposite: nowadays, popular opinion is asking, sometimes even begging, for a return of law and order, that is, a return to the authoritarian father, again both at the individual and at the sociological level. No wonder Colette Soler defines our century as the one in which we wanted to educate fathers into their role.[5] Of course, this proposition affects the way in which gender roles are viewed, or, more precisely, the difficulties with or even the decline of those roles. The two main characters in question are the father and femininity. The purpose of this essay is to show that Freud and Lacan present us with different answers.

Freud and the Primal Father

The father of psychoanalysis is without doubt the man who elevated the importance of fatherhood to a hitherto undreamt-of level. This was not new in itself; it had been done before, albeit within a religious context. What was new was the fact that a liberal, nonreligious Jew endorsed this traditional religious view from a scientific standpoint. The analogy with religion goes even further: followers who tried to privilege the position of the mother were to be banned from the orthodox analytical church. There was no room for mothers and women.

Both in his case studies and in his theoretical work in general, Freud places the accent entirely on the real father. Nevertheless, there is a striking difference between real fathers in his clinical practice and the way in which he depicts the father role in his oedipal theory. In his classic case studies, we meet a father who is living on his wife's fortune, a second who travels in a state of total depression from one mental institution to another, a third who is utterly dominated by his wife, and a fourth who is ill but nevertheless is capable of offering his daughter in exchange for his mistress to the latter's husband.[6] The fact that in his clinical studies these real fathers turn out time and again to be total failures does not prevent Freud from cultivating the idea of the oedipal father as a feared, menacing character whose threat of castration has to be taken seriously. In order to close the gap between clinical reality and his theory, Freud invented the myth of the primal father. The myth runs as follows: once upon a time, there must have been a real such father, an *Urvater*, and the phylogenetic memory of this father is stronger than any weak incarnation of it. Further, every real father, strong or weak, occupies this terrifying oedipal position owing to this collectively inherited myth.[7] The result is the omnipresent Oedipus complex, which divides humans by gender into two binary categories: one that has the penis and is always in danger of losing it, and one that does not and develops envy of it. Again, we have to stress the fact that for Freud, both the father and the penis are taken as real, which means that Freudian gender differentiation belongs to what is usually referred to as "essentialism." It is the same essentialism that returns in Freud's perception of the failure of the analytic process, that is, the "biological bedrock" he is talking about in his *Analysis Terminable and Interminable*.[8]

For Freud, this biological and consequently real bedrock is backed up by his myth of the primal horde and its leader. Moreover, for him, this myth was not so much a myth as a historical reality. He developed two versions of the story, and a comparison between them is fascinating. In the version in *Totem and Taboo*, we have the primal father in total possession of all females; a conspiracy of sons kills him in order to make the women sexually available. The net result of the murder is rather surprising: they discover themselves to be brothers with a common sense of guilt and install the incest prohibition, which then becomes the corner-stone of human society. From this point onward, the father figure fills the picture; he is the one that has to be obeyed, revered, and so on.[9]

This first version is not very convincing, even for a hard-core Freud-ian: there is no mention of castration, the mother figure is not mentioned at all, and the acute sense of guilt is surprisingly unaccounted for. The second version of the story, which is found in *Moses and Monotheism*, is much more elaborate. This time, Freud describes a number of stages. The first contains only the primal father and his women; there are no mothers, and language is absent. In the second stage, the primal father is murdered, which unexpectedly results in the establishment of matri-archy. The third one gave Freud a lot of trouble. As a transitional phase it contains a strange mixture of matriarchy, mother-goddesses, clans of brothers, and an emerging totemism. The fourth and last stage reintro-duces the primal father-patriarch thanks to an intermediate figure: the son. In one way or another, the son installs the cult of the father, and thus patriarchal power.[10]

This is the process which Freud recognizes at the heart of every mono-theistic religion, that is, in Judaism, Christianity, and Islam. Each of them has its own son, Moses, Jesus, or Muhammad, and all three of them reinstall the father figure. Moses installed the one and only father against pagan polytheism, Jesus endorsed the father figure as indepen-dent from any motherly involvement, and Muhammad finished the job with Allah. Now, there is something strange about these stories; instead of the murder of a primal father, more often than not we find a son who has to sacrifice himself in order to (re)install this father figure. Indeed, if we take a closer look at Freud's second version, it becomes obvious that the son needs the father in order to defend himself against the threat and power that he fears from femininity. The primal oedipal anxiety is not directed toward the father; on the contrary, the father is needed as a defense against the mother.

From a Lacanian point of view, the second myth is read as the in-stallation of the symbolic function, through which the subject will be protected from the *jouissance* of the first Other and directed toward the ever-shifting dialectics of desire. This is all the more obvious if one pays attention to Freud's casual remarks about language acquisition and its relationship to the inheritance of the sense of guilt. These remarks are to be found in the very same essay wherein he develops his second version.[11]

In the second version, it becomes clear that the son is in need of the symbolic function of the father. Hence, the observation that all sons try to saddle their fathers with precisely this symbolic function becomes comprehensible. In this respect, Freud's myth is very reassuring for every neurotic: once upon a time, there was a real father who, and so on. This is the message he conveys to Hans, the little boy in one of his case studies.[12] Lacan stresses this need and renames it: the father is a symptom of the son.

The effects of what I would term the patriarchal-monotheistic complex come down to a binary installation of the gender roles. On the one hand, sons and potential fathers; on the other, daughters and potential mothers. In such a system, gender characteristics must be described in terms of opposites, strong-weak, clever-stupid, brave-cowardly, and so forth. At the same time, such a system tends to create a situation that produces these characteristics, so the whole thing becomes a self-fulfilling prophecy. No wonder the daily prayer of the traditional Jewish man contains the following exclamation: "Blessed art Thou, O Lord our God, King of the Universe, that Thou hast not made me a woman."

Today, in spite of Freud's allegedly real myth, we are witnessing a very strange phenomenon: the massive collapse of the father figure. Historically, the function itself used to remain intact; only the embodiment changed ("The king is dead, long live the king"). Thus the belief in the unique system as such was kept intact, and the replacement of one figure by another did not affect the system or the gender roles. Nowadays, we are living in a period when the symbolic father as such is murdered, together with the belief in him. It is no coincidence that the prevailing attitude today is so-called postmodern cynicism, which epitomizes above all widespread distrust and lack of belief in any symbolic function whatever. From a Freudian point of view, this confronts us with the reversal of the primal myth, and thus with the loss of protection against *jouissance* and consequently a return to original chaos. The original myth installed binary gender differentiation; therefore, its reversal must have serious effects on this differentiation.

In order to understand these effects, first of all we have to understand the problems for which the father function used to be the solution. Following Freud, we know that the central problem for every hysterical subject is the *Spaltung,* that is, the fact that he or she is divided between a conscious and an unconscious, an ego and an id, a true and a false self. This division emerges over and over again at exactly the same moment: whenever the subject is required to identify a solution to his or her own existence. These moments were discovered by Freud in their developmental stage, in other words, when children were confronted with them. They are threefold: first, sexual differences, especially female sexual identity; second, the role of the father, especially concerning the origin of the subject; and third, the sexual rapport between parents. This Freudian description was redefined in a structural way by Lacan: thus, the subject is always a divided subject $, owing to a structural lack in the symbolic order. This division emerges at the same characteristic points: feminine identity, authority, and sexual rapport. This was summarized by Lacan in his formula S(A) and evoked in his three provocative statements: the Woman does not exist, the Other of the Other does not exist, the sexual rapport does not exist. This is a structural problem: while the three of them *do* exist in the Real, they do not find an appropriate answer in the Symbolic. As a result, the subject has to fall back on solutions in the Imaginary.[13]

The classical solution for the hysterical subject had already been discovered by Freud, although we need Lacan's reinterpretation. This is of course the Oedipus complex. From a Lacanian point of view, the oedipal solution consists in setting up an Other, who guarantees a certain feminine identity and thus allows the possibility of a sexual rapport. The recurrent problem for the hysterical subject is that this Other who guarantees can never do so enough: the series starts with the father, but it does not take long for the subject to realize that every father fails; at that point, the endless chain of big Others is started. Usually, the oedipal series is carried over into religion or ideology, where the hysterical subject continues to look for an undivided big Other who will function as a guarantee. Hence, from a structural point of view, the hysterical subject is essentially a *believer*. He or she needs an Other to believe in, in order to put an end to doubting. Paradoxically, this belief is concealed behind a more eye-catching characteristic, namely the hysterical subject's aptitude for questioning and undermining authority, that is, someone else's authority. Being the quintessential zealot, the hysterical subject will always fight another religion or ideology in the name of his or her own "true faith." This fight will be all the more violent if it takes place between similar and thus competing beliefs. Just think of the scene in *Monty Python's Life of Brian* (Terry Jones, 1979), in which a member of the Jewish Freedom Fighters cries out "The enemy!," whereupon his companion asks "The Romans?," to which the indignant response is, "No, the Jewish Liberation Front." In this sense, the hysteric is not so much a revolutionary as the essential supporter of authority, albeit from time to time a so-called alternative authority. This relationship can be understood in a structural sense using Lacan's discourse theory, in which the discourse of the Master and the discourse of the hysteric are in perfect balance. From a clinical point of view, the main problem for the hysteric is that those who incarnate authority are never fully up to the mark, hence the typical dissatisfaction of the hysteric and his or her ever-shifting desire.

Thus, the hysterical divided subject is looking for an ironclad guarantee from the Other without a lack, who knows for certain. This is the basis of normal group formation, as described by Freud in his *Group Psychology and Analysis of the Ego*. The leader takes the place of the external object, with whom the members of the group-to-be identify; more precisely, the identification focuses on the ego ideal, which blots out the individual egos.[14] This is why subjects who were originally very different start resembling each other. This often finds expression in similar clothing and in the development of a common jargon. They have become what Lacan describes with a pun as *des égos/égaux,* that is, a group of identical followers. Normally—that is, according to the norm, and thus oedipally—this position of the leader is the original oedipal paternal position and embodies a very necessary function. To put it succinctly: it gives the subject the opportunity to come to terms with his or her own desire and *jouissance,* usually by elaborating and eventually throwing away the terms of the father and choosing his or her own. This used to be the normal evolution of what I would like to call developmental hysteria, starting with the belief in the almighty father in childhood, provoking and destroying him during puberty and adolescence, and coming to terms with him in adulthood. Thus, the differentiation made by Lacan between the real father, the imaginary father figure, and the symbolic function of the father is a very useful one.

However, this normal evolution is no longer the case. This brings us to what is probably the biggest problem today, and not only for the hysterical subject: namely the fact that the symbolic father function itself has become questionable. Its guaranteeing and answer-providing function is not very convincing any more, to say the least. As a result, the number of hysterical subjects who are on the run, looking for a new master, is on the increase. Moreover, since it is the function itself which is affected, the possibility of coming to terms with it is seriously hampered, because one is forced to stick with the real father and is without the symbolic father function. This situation is very aptly described by Slavoj Žižek in terms of a reversal of the original Freudian primal myth.[15]

Normally, it should be the real primal father who is done away with, with the result that the symbolic paternal function can be established; the sons can then identify with the latter in order to take up their position as men. In the reversed version, instead of the real primal father, it is the symbolic function which is destroyed, thereby setting loose what Žižek calls the primal anal father, a figure who is only on the lookout for his own *jouissance*. Owing to the collapse of the symbolic paternal function, it is this primal anal father that the hysteric will meet during his or her search, especially in his paranoid version (besides the perverse one). There are abundant contemporary examples, from the return of fundamentalism on a mass scale to the success of smaller sects. The two share a number of typical characteristics, among them the installation of an absolute big Other with an irrevocable authority. This big Other is the incarnation of an absolute, albeit obscure, truth, which always concerns ethics, that is, desire and *jouissance,* and enforces a sexual rapport, in which women are assigned a submissive position.

From a structural point of view, this reversal of the primal myth explains several typical contemporary phenomena on the gender level. Contemporary sons have great difficulties in regarding their fathers as representatives of ancient patriarchal authority. As a consequence, the security and protection associated with that authority has disappeared, resulting in ever-increasing levels of anxiety and thus aggression in the sons. The absence of the possibility of identifying with the symbolic function itself condemns the contemporary male to staying at the level of the immature boy and son, afraid of the threatening female figure, which once more assumes its atavistic characteristics. These sons are just wandering around, staying forever in the same position, owing to the lack of an identificatory figure; thirty-year-old kids and adolescents of forty are no longer the exception. On the psychopathological level, we are confronted with a new category: the so-called borderline state. From our point of view, this is the hysterical subject stuck at the preoedipal, anxiety-loaded level. For lack of a masculine identificatory figure, a number of men proceed in the opposite direction and become perfect . . . mothers. Recent developments in this respect can literally be seen on the screen. In *Kramer vs. Kramer* (Rober Benton, 1979), it sufficed for the hero to take the motherly role, but later, *Mrs. Doubtfire* (Chris Columbus, 1994) required a complete metamorphosis of a man into a woman.

On the feminine side, we also find a drastic change. The disappearance of the old-style masculine superiority implies at the same time a disappearance of feminine inferiority. This is demonstrated by university enrollment lists and soft-porn movies: in both, women take the upper position. The absence of the security-enhancing symbolic law regulating desire and enjoyment invests woman with all the ancient masculine fears, which results in a turnaround: today, we have woman-the-hunter and man-the-hunted. Thus, the daughters are turned into hunter-gatherers for whom every male is free game, and indeed, the men are fleeing.

At the root of the myth, we meet the real *Urvater*. The loss of classical patriarchal authority forces the sons to look for alternatives. Hence, primal fathers are popping up everywhere, on the lookout for their own *jouissance* and attracting anxious sons who are hoping for protection. Moreover, the collapse of the symbolic father function is not without an effect on the symbolic order as such: ever-increasing analphabetism is mirrored by the introduction of pictograms on a worldwide scale.

What of the mothers? As a category, they are more and more marginalized, condemned to stay behind with the children, among whom, more often than not, they count their partner of the moment. While their sons trouble them the most, there is a new coalition in the making with their daughters.

Thus, these shifts in gender roles form part of a wider confusion, in which anxiety is predominant. The predictable Freudian remedy is perfectly illustrated by Freud's interventions in his case study on Little Hans: Freud will try to reinstall the real father. From a historical point of view, this is very ironic, because this solution inevitably leads to phallocratic fascism. It reminds one of the famous scene in *Cabaret* (Bob Fosse, 1972) in which the depiction of decadence is exemplified by the moment when a pure boy in SS uniform stands up in the audience and starts to sing, announcing the new order. The imaginary fathers of fascism are nothing but attempts to bridle femininity and *jouissance*. It is no coincidence that the great masters of totalitarian regimes could only tolerate child-women as partners. The biographies of Hitler and Mao are quite clear on this point, and they find a contemporary reflection in ever-increasing pedophilia. This is a clear indication of the anxiety of men when they are confronted with women as sexually active, desiring, and enjoying subjects.

The effect of this classical solution is a neat distribution of gender roles: the male warrior and son, the pure maiden, the childbearing mother, and the omnipresent primal father. This was studied and described in detail by Klaus Theweleit in his classic, *Male Fantasies*.[16] This book charts the rise of fascism by concentrating on "trivial" material: publicity, posters, literary productions, pamphlets, and so forth. In this material, the distribution of gender roles is very clear. Men are represented as the defenders of law and order, fighting for their country; women are incarnated pureness, fair virgins, passively waiting for their one and only task: the production of new sons. Nevertheless, woman's dangerous alter ego appears in the background: the devouring vamp, origin of a dangerous enjoyment in which every man risks annihilation and against which he has to defend himself by establishing an ever more intimate brotherhood. The very fact that Theweleit undertook this study in order to come to terms with a fascist father turns the book into a psychoanalytic cure, which goes further than Freud himself. As we already have shown, Freud stuck to the father, and thus to the classical solution.

The Freudian solution is exemplified by the relationship between Sigmund Freud as the hysterical subject and Wilhelm Fliess as the paranoid master.[17] From a structural point of view, the relationship between the hysterical and the paranoid subject is a perfect match: the divided hysteric is looking for a guaranteeing big Other without a lack, who knows for certain; the paranoid subject is looking for followers and believers. Indeed, the paranoid subject is not divided at all and shows no lack whatever: he knows. Owing to his psychotic structure, he has never accepted the oedipal answers. This is why Freud described the paranoid as the quintessential unbeliever. His refusal of the oedipal structure, which Lacan terms the foreclosure of the Name-of-the-Father, forces him at a given stage of psychotic development to produce answers of his own. These answers concern the same questions as the hysteric's—feminine sexual identity, the guaranteeing role of the father, and sexual rapport—but they will be treated in a totally different way. Whereas the hysterical subject is always in doubt, never sure about the choices he or she has made, by contrast, the paranoid subject knows for certain and transforms this knowledge into a system. From a psychiatric point of view, this typically gives rise to delusion, megalomania, lack of doubt, lack of self-reflection, and complete certainty. The message is clear: he is a master without any lack whatever. The basic fault or lack will always and irrevocably be ascribed to the other, while the paranoiac is incarnated innocence. He is not only innocent, he is convinced of the malevolence of the other who accuses him and persecutes him. Colette Soler has termed this the typical *innocence paranoïaque*.[18]

Thus, the problem of the all-knowing paranoid master is completely different from the one faced by the forever doubting hysterical subject. So long as he is the *only one* who knows, his status as all-knowing is rather precarious. Freud saw this clearly in his study on Schreber, when he asked himself what the difference was between him and Schreber. This question was especially pertinent in view of the fact that some of his contemporaries were accusing Freud of producing delusional theories. Freud's answer to this question runs as follows: Schreber's theory is only believed in by one person (i.e., Schreber), while mine is at least believed in by a group of people who are ready to try it out in practice. Hence the typical problem of the paranoid subject: as long as he is the only one who is convinced of his knowledge, his status as master is rather precarious, and he is in dire need of convincing others. A historical example is again provided by Schreber; he wrote his memoirs in order to convince the world of the correctness of his *Weltanschauung*.[19] This explains why a considerable number of paranoid subjects start writing or lecturing. It is the psychotic's attempt at installing a social bond, exactly the thing that he lacks. It is lacking because every social bond is heir to the oedipal structure, and this has been rejected by the paranoiac. As a result, the psychotic stands outside normal social relationships. In psychiatric terms, the psychotic is the quintessentially different other, even the uncanny other. For Lacan, the psychotic stands outside the four discourses and therefore outside the social relationships; and for Freud, psychosis is a narcissistic neurosis, that is, a neurosis without the normal object relations. The paradoxical result of this situation is that it is the paranoiac who is most in need of an audience such as a group, in order to "keep his sanity," that is, to avoid a psychotic breakdown. The group functions as a "suppletion," the typically psychotic complement to this lack.

Lacan and "The Other of the Other Does Not Exist"

The Freudian solution is a very conservative one, because it tries to reinstate the father figure with the resultant classical gender roles. This reinstatement is particularly important for the hysterical subject in general and for men in particular, since it provides them with security. Nevertheless, such a reinstatement is virtually impossible nowadays, because its very basis, the symbolic father function, has been destroyed. Hence, Freud's solution can create only primal fathers with a primal horde of their own. Apart from this ever-failing solution, there should be other possibilities. What has Lacan to say in these matters?

If one studies Lacan in this respect, it becomes clear that his last theory differs radically from his first conceptualizations. Specifically in matters of oedipal theory, his famous "return to Freud" turns into a new theory. Indeed, Lacan's subsequent elaborations of the Freudian oedipal complex characterize his entire development.

Initially, he follows Freud, albeit with a Hegelian *Aufhebung* (sublation), when he interprets the Freudian oedipal complex as the paternal metaphor. Indeed, with this very idea of metaphor, he distances himself from the idea of the real father and stresses the *function* beyond the actual father figure; the metaphor installs an organizational principle through which the transition from duality to triangularity is inaugurated, that is, the desire of the mother is answered by the Name-of-the-Father. The main goal is the separation of the child from the mother.[20] It is important to note that in this early Lacanian theory, the emphasis is placed on the level of desire, which corresponds to a singular lack. The distance from Freud's real father becomes even clearer in Lacan's seminar "The Ethics of Psychoanalysis," where the Name-of-the-Father is explicitly described as a sublimation ("To introduce as primordial the function of the father is a sublimation"), together with a question that had already been asked by Freud: what is the basis of patriarchal authority?[21]

The turning point comes in 1963, with the seminar "Les noms du père," a seminar that with the exception of its first lesson was never given, as a result of Lacan's expulsion from the International Psychoanalytic Association.[22] This historical context, combined with the fact that for years after Lacan keeps alluding to this phantom seminar without actually delivering it, presents us with a magnificent illustration of its subject: the not-existing seminar functions as a structuring lack. The very fact that Lacan has made the transition from the singular to the plural (from "le Nom-du-Père" to "les noms du père") accentuates the lack and breaks through the at-least-one [au moins un] aspect of the Name-of-the-Father. In this respect, the new formula is very significant: "the Other of the Other does not exist."

In 1969, with the seminar "L'Envers de la psychanalyse," Lacan breaks radically with Freudian oedipal theory. The second part of it is titled "Beyond the Oedipus Complex."[23] Freudian oedipal theory is described as Freud's dream, his answer to the desire of the hysteric: the installation of an idealized father figure, who produces knowledge on the level of truth in matters of desire, jouissance, and gender. It is the same character that makes its appearance in the hysterical transference neurosis: the subject supposed to know. Coming to terms with this subject implies coming to terms with (the Name-of-)the father and is an essential goal of Lacanian analysis. For Freud, its installation was something like the end in itself, albeit a never-ending one.

It is this end which was to preoccupy Lacan for the rest of his career. In the seminar "R.S.I.," he considers the number of names of the father to be "indefinite," and he stresses their function, that is, to keep the real, the symbolic, and the imaginary distinct from each other. The operative principle in this function is the act of naming.[24] A Name-of-the-Father functions as the fourth knot which binds the real, the symbolic, and the imaginary in such a way that they remain distinct. Hence, we reencounter the function of separation. It is this function which is focused upon in Lacan's theory on the end of an analysis.

To summarize, we can say that the Lacanian subject is constituted in an ever-alienating relationship with a first Other, from which it is separated by the intervention of a second Other. The advantage of our formulation is that it is neither developmental nor gender related. The idea of separation is central and takes place through name giving; the real father is superfluous in this function.

This idea is endorsed in historical anthropology, where one finds separation and separation rules long before the concept of fatherhood arises. Within the maternal clan structure, separation was originally based on food taboos; sexual taboos are much more recent. Based upon these rules and the accompanying name giving, separate clan groups were established among which exchange was possible. The initially maternal clan gave way to the matrilineal family, which in turn changed into patriarchy. The further development is such that the separation function coincides with the function of the father and is directed against the union between mother and child, especially against the union between mother and son. Each individual father is invested with both the function and the accompanying authority within the larger framework of patriarchy and monotheism whose representative he has become. Compared with the clan structure, the kinship system formally remains the same: at a given age, a child is segregated from one group and introduced into another, an event which is endorsed by name giving. Contemporaneously with the evolution from clan structure to patriarchy, there is another shift in accent, that is, from food to sex.[25]

During the ensuing evolution, kinship groups tend to become smaller and smaller, diminishing from the enlarged patriarchal family to the nuclear family of our century. In turn, the individual as such comes to the fore. Today the function of separation has reached its zenith with omnipresent egocratia: the subject is separated from one Other, but the step toward a second Other is not very convincing.

In the light of this historical evolution, and combined with a clinical point of view, the Freudian oedipal father and even the Lacanian Name-of-the-Father come down to a hypothesis which is especially apparent in the symptoms of the neurotic. The father as a symptom on the level of the individual is mirrored by a collective symptom on the level of society—that is, the individual belief in the father is based on a collective belief. This hypothesis of the neurotic is based on the idea of an exception, a founding figure, the *x non phi de x*, the *au moins un*, which is the Lacanian counterpart of Freud's primal father. Even Freud was aware of the fallacy in his reasoning. Indeed, when he tried to explain monotheism and the Oedipus complex through the function of the father, he had to ask himself what the basis was of this base. In order to find an answer, he had to fall back on an expression used by a church father: *Credo quia absurdum* (Tertullian).[26] But Lacan goes much further than this when he states that "the Other of the Other does not exist." There is no guarantee-providing exception; the father and the Oedipus complex come down to creationalist sublimation, which enables the subject to come to terms with the other lacking signifiers, that is, femininity and *jouissance*.[27]

This Lacanian reinterpretation of the Oedipus complex—where the sexual identity is decided—leaves Freudian essentialism behind and opens new perspectives in matters of gender identity. Since the subject is always characterized by a structural lack of being [*manque-à-être*], it has to find its identity in the Other. This brings us to the very opposite of essentialism and creates the impression that Lacan belongs to constructivism, where gender identity is a mere effect of the joint venture between the Symbolic and the Imaginary, that is, the Other.

This Other is the contemporaneous union of signifiers which predominates within a certain grouping and functions as a guarantee because the individual members of that grouping believe in this Other. In this respect, gender identity is an arbitrary convention, and there is the possibility of choice for every subject; however, the choice has already been made for him or her by the group, the community to which he or she belongs, resulting in a series of conventions; each subject has to acquire in his or her own way the conventions of the group; changes are possible, but they take place within a temporal evolution.[28]

If we compare Freud's mythical construction of a primal father to Lacan's structural theory, it is quite clear that this shift from the real father to the function of naming frees us from the paranoid-fascist solution with its ever-present incarnation of the primal father. The constructivist part of Lacanian theory permits us to understand the difference between present gender identifications and those of the past. The collective convention based upon a common belief as a symptom used to be far greater in Freud's time. Nowadays, this collective experience is fragmented into much smaller "peer groups," each with a convention of its own. The difference between then and now can be understood perfectly in terms of the difference between monotheism and polytheism.

The belief in the one and almighty created a far larger community with a much stronger impact on its members, hence their idea of being essentially right. Polytheism, on the other hand, necessarily results in diversity, with an accompanying element of wider choice at the level of the individual. In this respect, the typical Freudian idea that monotheism is a further step in human evolution is rather doubtful. Karen Armstrong's study *A History of God* clearly demonstrates that monotheism inevitably leads to cruel holy wars in the name of the one and only truth, banning and killing all others—*Gott mit uns!*[29] Fundamentalism and fascism are therefore one and the same, and it is no coincidence that women are always regarded as inferior in these monotheistic groups. Polytheism, on the other hand, has to be tolerant, in line with its starting point, and, not surprisingly, this tolerance is not without an effect on the position of women.

As we have already said, this leaves us with the impression of Lacan as a constructivist, considering gender as a mere construct, to be changed virtually at will, although it takes some time. This was one of the major beliefs of the post–May 1968 generation, framed within the larger belief of the constructibility of man in general and the accompanying demand for equality. In the meantime, both have been proved wrong.

At this point, we have to commence another reading of Lacan: contemporary with the shift in the theory on the Name-of-the-Father/names of the father described above, Lacan turns his attention from desire to *jouissance* and from castration to the structurally determined loss of *objet a*, meaning that the category of the real comes to the fore. The effect is that Lacan moves beyond the original debate between constructivism and essentialism. Indeed, originally the real of the drive insists in a non-gender-specified way; the opposition does not reside in female versus male, but in the real versus the symbolico-imaginary; it is this ever-insisting gap, caused by a double lack, that will determine the constitution of the subject.

This new theory was elaborated in Seminar 11, where Lacan starts his discussion of the causation of the subject with something which is already familiar to his audience: the proposition that the drive revolves around a lack. However, at this point, he surprises his audience by stating that there is not one but two lacks. The first is the lack in the chain of signifiers. This is the typically hysterical and thus Freudian level, where desire can never be fully represented and expressed, let alone satisfied. In Lacanian terms, this means that the subject, confronted with the enigma of the desire of the Other, tries to verbalize this desire and thus constitutes itself by identifying with the signifiers in the field of the Other, without ever succeeding in filling the gap between subject and Other. This process of alienation results in the advent of the subject [*l'avènement du sujet*].[30]

However, this lack is only a retake of another lack, which Lacan terms anterior and real in comparison to the one described above. It has to be understood in the context of the advent of living being [*l'avènement du vivant*], that is, the emergence of sexual reproduction in phylogenesis, which is repeated with every ontogenesis. This anterior lack concerns the price life has to pay for the acquisition of sexual reproduction. From the moment an organism becomes capable of reproducing itself in a sexual way, it loses its individual immortality, and death becomes an unavoidable necessity. The individual loses something at birth that will be represented later on by all the other substitute objects. Lacan depicts this primary loss with his myth of the lamella, the object that flies away at birth, and suggests that this is nothing but pure life instinct, beyond gender as such.[31]

Lacan's new conceptualization can therefore be summarized as follows: the real of the drive is not a gender-specific insistence, and it cannot be constructed from a male-female opposition. Rather, it consists in an opposition between the real on the one hand and the combined symbolic and imaginary on the other, each one with a lack of their own. It is this double lack that determines the ever-insistent gap between the real and the symbolico-imaginary, and thus the constitution of the subject.

This theory confronts us this with a more essential "essentialism" than the Freudian. It sets a task for every culture, that of providing a more or less collective solution for this typically human condition. The attempts to answer this double lack give rise to the differentiation between two different positions of the subject and especially to the relationship between them. Normally—that is, according to the collectively endorsed norm—we expect a male and a female position; following Lacan, these are nothing more than attempts to symbolize the lost core of our being. Owing to the structural character of the primary lack, these solutions will never be satisfactory, nor will they ever be resolved. They belong to the category of *ce qui ne cesse pas de ne pas s'écrire* [what does not stop not being written].

One of the basic characteristics of the Freudian drives is their conservatism: they wish to return to a previous state, to repair the original loss. It is this theory that Lacan develops further with his theory of the double lack. The annihilation of the lack is operated through the installation of a certain relationship between subject and Other, in which one is used to fill the lack of the Other. If this process takes place in a nonmediated, dual way, the result is that the subject is totally usurped and reabsorbed, without any chance of escape. This is the level of *jouissance* that can be found in a particular relationship between mother and child, usually resulting in child psychosis. If this process takes place in a mediated, triangular way, then the subject will be used in a limited way, just as it uses the other subject. This is the level of desire and phallic *jouissance*.[32]

Hence, the relationship between two subjects, in which one functions as an object for the other, is not in the first place a relationship between two subjects with different genders; in the primal relationship, there is not even any gender differentiation involved as such. The basic relationship is one between *active and passive,* and the main question is: who takes whom as an object?

This brings us to a major Freudian theme—one that has been largely neglected.[33] Time and again, in his quest for the definition of gender identity, Freud arrives at the active-passive opposition, and time and again, he has to admit that the male-female differentiation cannot be reduced to this opposition. Nevertheless, from his patriarchal point of view, femininity comes down to passivity. His obstinacy in this respect becomes all the more apparent when he discusses the failure of (Freudian) analysis to go beyond a certain point. Indeed, in *Analysis Terminable and Interminable,* his essentialism brings him to the conclusion that no analysand can go beyond the biological rock of castration. He considers this a biological and thus a general principle, which can be understood in terms of "repudiation of femininity" and which applies to both sexes. Nevertheless, the elaboration in this very text makes it obvious that femininity is not to be equated with castration, but, again, stands for passivity.[34] The passive position is the most dreaded, for every subject, whichever its gender. Another thing made obvious by this text is

Freud's patriarchal stance and his ensuing adherence to the father position, although he is dimly aware that the very process of analysis opens up the possibility of something beyond this position. What he fails to see is that his patriarchal stance has two adverse consequences: his insistent failure in the analytic transference process and his simplistic reduction of femininity to passivity.

This brings us to our conclusion, where the present fin de siècle and the end of analysis can be compared in matters of gender and patriarchy.

Freudian analysis ends in a paradoxical way, since it tends to endorse patriarchy and the traditional gender roles. The individual symptoms must be replaced by the collective ones, thus replacing idiosyncratic "hysterical misery" by "common unhappiness."[35] For Lacan, analysis ends with a very particular identification of the subject with his or her symptom. This particularity resides in the fact that this identification is an identification not with (the desire of) the Other, but with an aspect of the real. Gender identity—that is, the way in which a subject comes to terms with the drive—contains two quite different parts: the real of the drive, and the part dependent upon the Other. Previously, the subject had identified with/alienated itself from the desire of the Other based on his or her belief in this Other, with a consequent typical gender position. The discovery made by the analysand during the analysis that this Other is just a symptom, a homemade construction that does not exist, discloses at the same time the symptomatic character of the subject itself and its entailing nonexistence. This paves the way to the real being of the subject, *son être du sujet*. From that point onward, the subject can no longer be considered a mere "answer to or from the Other" [*réponse de l'Autre*]; on the contrary, the subject is now an "answer to or from the real" [*réponse du réel*].[36]

Here we can invoke Lacan's reasoning on creation. Indeed, in my opinion, the "identification with the real of the symptom" has to be understood via the idea of creation. The essential argument can be recognized in Lacan's earlier ideas on sublimation and *creatio ex nihilo* in his seminar "The Ethics of Psychoanalysis." The subject can "choose" to elevate nothing to something and to enjoy this: "The object is elevated to the dignity of the Thing."[37] Applied to the end of analysis, this means that the subject has actively created his or her own symptom in the real and proceeds by identifying with it. In this way, the symptom takes the place of the ever-lacking object. Finally, it takes the place of the lacking sexual rapport and furnishes a self-made answer to it, instead of the previous Other-made ones. Lacan accentuates this shift by introducing a neologism. The subject has to become a *sinthome,* a combination of symptom [*symptôme*], holy man [*saint homme*], and Saint Thomas (the one who did not believe the Other and went for the Real Thing): "On the level of the *sinthome* . . . there is relationship. There is only relationship where there is *sinthome.*"[38]

Contemporary society has also discovered the nonexistence of the Other. There are inevitable consequences in matters of gender and law. In an earlier age, there were collectively accepted and endorsed rules within the patriarchal-monotheistic complex which governed the distribution of *jouissance* (food, sex) in a binary way (male-female). Today, these collective rules have lost their authority and are more and more open to question. Typical reactions are a generalized feeling of meaninglessness and depression (i.e., mourning for the death of the Other) or a postmodern cynical position (anything goes). More creatively, the former collective rules tend to be replaced by strictly individually determined arrangements—"rules" is a too strong word—between two particular individuals. This is of course the "mutual consent" or "informed consent" of our time, between partners who are supposed to be equals. A number of these relationships will reinstall the same alienating subject-Other relationship, albeit on a smaller scale; a smaller number will go beyond this repetition and join the Lacanian sinthome. Owing to the particularity of this sinthome, predictions and generalizations are impossible.

It is crucial to stress this symptomatic part: there is no solution as such, and we remain in the realm of what does not stop not being written. The major change in comparison with the patriarchal-monotheist complex is the change in the binary opposition. Instead of male versus female, the present terms are *active* versus *passive*—so much for equality! At the level of contemporary society, this is clearly demonstrated by the fact that the two major themes in clinical sexology are sexual abuse or trauma and pedophilia. These two themes, important as they may be, tend to divert our attention from the underlying structure, which is not interpersonal. The interpersonal realm is none other than the expression of the *internal* antinomy: each subject has either to cope *actively* with the real of his or her own drive or to undergo it in a *passive* way.

This seems to me the major theme of a new theory on gender.

Notes

1   Germaine Greer, *The Female Eunuch* (London, 1970).

2   *Sunday Times Magazine,* 3 Mar. 1996.

3   Doris Lessing, *Children of Violence,* book 1: *Martha Quest;* book 2: *A Proper Marriage;* book 3: *A Ripple from the Storm* (London: Panther Books, 1966); *Children of Violence,* book 4: *Landlocked* (London: Panther Books, 1967); *Under My Skin* (London: Harper and Collins, 1994).

4   Camille Paglia, *Sexual Personae: Art and Decadence from Nefertiti to Emily Dickinson* (New York: Vintage, 1990); Otto Weininger, *Geschlecht und Charakter: eine prinzipielle Untersuchung* (Wien: Braumüller, 1905). Weininger is described thus by Freud: "Weininger (the young philosopher who, highly gifted but sexually deranged, committed suicide after producing his remarkable book, *Geschlecht und Charakter* [1903]), in a chapter that attracted much attention, treated Jews and women with equal hostility and overwhelmed them with the same insults." Sigmund Freud, *Analysis of a Phobia in a Five-Year-Old Boy,* in *The Standard Edition,* ed. James Strachey, vol. 10 (London: Hogarth Press, 1955), 36 n.1. Further citations will be to *SE,* followed by volume and page number.

5   Colette Soler, "Abord du nom-du-père," *Quarto: Bulletin de l'École de la Cause Freudienne en Belgique* 8 (1982): 58.

6   Respectively, the fathers of the Rat Man, the Wolf Man, Little Hans, and Dora.

7   This is elaborated by Freud in his case study on the Wolf Man, where the gap between the real father and the dreamt-of oedipal father is very large indeed. This case study can be considered his last attempt to find a basis in the Real for neurotic symptoms. Twenty years after his search for real seductions, Freud was looking with the same tenacity for a primal scene which had really been observed, even if only with dogs. The most remarkable thing about this polemical search, directed against Jung, is that Freud, when he had the answer in hand and was ready to vouch for the authenticity of a scene which really happened, chose this very moment to bring us a new answer: the primary fantasy (Sigmund Freud, *From the History of an Infantile Neurosis, SE* 17:57–60). Primary fantasies are supposed to replace a missing reality: the child who has never seen a primal scene will imagine one. Therefore, these primal scenes appeal to a prehistoric, phylogenetic reality: seduction, primal scene, and castration were once, in the childhood period of humanity, a reality that was all too real. As such, they belong to the phylogenetic heritage of every human child (Sigmund Freud, *Introductory Lectures on Psycho-Analysis, SE* 15–16:371). In Freud's opinion, their importance is very great: in a number of cases, individual reality is changed under just the influence of this phylogenetic heritage. Thus, the Wolf Man saw his father as the castra-

tion authority, in accordance with the phylogenetic scheme and contrary to his own experience in which the threat of castration came exclusively from women (Freud, *From the History of an Infantile Neurosis, SE* 17:119). It is quite clear that, in doing this, Freud subordinated an individual reality to a relationship operating structurally between the real and the symbolic.

8 Freud complained that when one is trying to persuade a woman to abandon her wish for a penis on the grounds that it is unrealizable, or when one is seeking to convince a man that a passive attitude to men does not always signify castration, one gets the impression of hitting a biological bedrock. See Sigmund Freud, *Analysis Terminable and Interminable, SE* 23:250–52.

9 In 1908, Freud wrote an introduction to Otto Rank's *Der Mythus von der Geburt des Helden.* Written originally within this significant context, it was published separately as *Family Romances* (*SE* 9). In my opinion, this small paper was the precursor of as well as the transition to the theory that he elaborated in 1912 in *Totem and Taboo.* From a certain point of view, it provides us with the hidden meaning of his essay on the primal father. Sigmund Freud, *Totem and Taboo, SE* 13:140–43.

10 The central subject of the book on Moses is the rewriting of the myth of the primal father. Freud tries it twice, without ever reaching an end. See Sigmund Freud, *Moses and Monotheism, SE* 23:80–84, 130–32. There is another important difference from *Totem and Taboo.* When Freud had finished the third essay in 1912, he considered it the best he had ever written, and he always maintained this opinion. *Moses and Monotheism,* and especially the third essay, was depicted by him as the worst thing he had ever written. This is a strange reversal, which cannot be considered in isolation from its counterpart, all the more because it is a reworking of this counterpart.

11 Freud, *Moses and Monotheism, SE* 23:80, 82, 132.

12 The case study itself was conducted by the father of the little patient, and during the whole "treatment," Freud intervened only once in person: "Long before he (i.e. Hans) was in the world, I had known that a Little Hans would come who would be so fond of his mother that he would be bound to feel afraid of his father because of it; and I had told his father this." See Freud, *Analysis of a Phobia in a Five-Year-Old Boy, SE* 10:42. This intervention is not an interpretation, it is a suggestive construction of something missing. What Freud is introducing here is nothing but the missing part of the paternal metaphor. The beauty of the case is that he introduced it not only for the little boy, but also for his father: "and I had told his father this." Which, in view of the parental situation, was highly necessary.

13 The content of this paragraph is a main theme of a much larger study. See Paul Verhaeghe, *Does the Woman Exist? From Freud's Hysteric to Lacan's Feminine* (London: Rebus Press, 1997).

14 Sigmund Freud, *Group Psychology and the Analysis of the Ego, SE* 17:111–16.

15 Slavoj Žižek, *The Metastases of Enjoyment: Six Essays on Woman and Causality* (London: Verso, 1994), 205.

16 Klaus Theweleit, *Male Fantasies: Women, Floods, Bodies, History,* trans. Stephen Conway (Minneapolis: University of Minnesota Press, 1990); *Male Fantasies 2: Male*

Bodies: Psychoanalyzing the White Terror, trans. Chris Turner et al. (Cambridge: Polity Press, 1989).

17   Freud's poem in his letter to Fliess of 29 Dec. 1899 speaks for itself: "Hail, To the valiant son who at the behest of his father appeared at the right time, / To be his assistant and fellow worker in fathoming the divine order. / But hail to the father, too, who just prior to the event found in his calculations / The key to restraining the power of the female sex / And to shouldering his burden of lawful succession; / No longer relying on sensory appearances, as does the mother, / He calls upon the higher powers to claim his right, conclusion, belief and doubt; / Thus, at the beginning, there stands, hale and hearty, equal to the exigency of error, the father / In his infinitely mature development. / May the calculation be correct and, as the legacy of labor, be transferred from father to son and beyond the parting of the centuries / Unite in the mind what the vicissitudes of life tear apart."

18   Colette Soler, "Innocence paranoïaque et indignité mélancholique," in *Quarto: Bulletin de L'École de la Cause Freudienne en Belgique* 33-34 (1995): 23-24.

19   Daniel Paul Schreber, *Denkwürdigkeiten eines Nervenkranken* (Leipzig, 1903). Sigmund Freud, *Psychoanalytic Notes on an Autobiographical Account of a Case of Paranoia (Dementia Paranoides), SE* 12:9-84.

20   The main references for this period are Jacques Lacan, *The Seminar of Jacques Lacan,* book 3: *Psychoses (1955-56),* ed. Jacques-Alain Miller, trans. Russell Grigg (New York: W. W. Norton, 1993) and "On a Question Preliminary to Any Possible Treatment of Psychosis," in Jacques Lacan, *Écrits: A Selection,* trans. Alan Sheridan (New York: W. W. Norton, 1977), 179-225.

21   Jacques Lacan, *The Ethics of Psychoanalysis (1959-1960),* book 7, ed. Jacques-Alain Miller, trans. Denis Porter (New York: W. W. Norton, 1992), 143. Trans. modified.

22   Elisabeth Roudinesco, *Histoire de la psychanalyse en France,* vol. 2 (Paris: Seuil, 1986), 328-68.

23   Jacques Lacan, *Le Séminaire,* book 17: *L'envers de la psychanalyse (1969-70),* ed. Jacques-Alain Miller (Paris: Seuil, 1991), 99-166.

24   Jacques Lacan, "R.S.I." (unpublished seminar), 11 Mar. 1975 and 15 Apr. 1975.

25   For this historical evolution, see Evelyn Reed, *Woman's Evolution: From Matriarchal Clan to Patriarchal Family* (New York: Pathfinder, 1975), and Christopher Knight, *Blood Relations: Menstruation and the Origins of Culture* (New Haven: Yale University Press, 1991).

26   Freud, *SE* 23:118.

27   See Lacan, *The Ethics of Psychoanalysis,* book 7.

28   Ferdinand de Saussure, *Cours de linguistique générale (1906-1911)* (Paris: Payot, 1972), 104ff.

29   Karen Armstrong, *A History of God* (London: Mandarin, 1993), 51-94.

30   See Jacques Lacan, *The Four Fundamental Concepts of Psychoanalysis,* ed. Jacques-Alain Miller, trans. Alan Sheridan (London: Hogarth Press and Institute of Psychoanalysis, 1977), 197-205. I have elaborated this elsewhere; see Paul Verhaeghe, "Causation and Destitution of a Pre-Ontological Non-Entity: On the Lacanian Sub-

ject," in *Key Concepts of Lacanian Psychoanalysis,* ed. Dany Nobus (London: Rebus Press, 1998), 164–89.

31   Of course, this reopens the debate on the drive theory, especially on the opposition between death and live drives. I have elaborated this in the third essay of "Love in Times of Solitude," in *Love in a Time of Loneliness: Three Essays on Drive and Desire* (New York: Other Press, 1999).

32   Both levels are described by Lacan in his discourse theory, each with a typical disjunction: impossibility for the level of desire, impotence for the level of *jouissance.*

33   In Freud's earliest conceptualisations, active-passive stood for masculine-feminine, with "passivity" as the most difficult component. Indeed, Freud meant it to represent femininity on the psychological level, but in the final analysis, it only demonstrated the lack of a specific signifier for the woman (Sigmund Freud, "Extracts from the Fliess Papers, Draft K, *SE* 1:228; "Draft M," *SE* 1:251; and *Three Essays on the Theory of Sexuality, SE* 7:160, 219–20). In Freud's later work, there is an important shift: passivity also denotes a certain enjoyment in the mother and child relationship. The attempts of the child to make the transition to the pole of activity must be understood as a running away from the position of passive object of enjoyment to an active form of pleasure (Sigmund Freud, *Female Sexuality, SE* 21:235–36).

34   Sigmund Freud, *Analysis Terminable and Interminable, SE* 23:250–53.

35   This is what Freud tells us in the very last paragraph of his *Studies on Hysteria, SE* 2:305.

36   Jacques Lacan, "L'étourdit," *Scilicet* 4 (1973): 15.

37   Lacan, *The Ethics of Psychoanalysis,* book 7, 112.

38   Jacques Lacan, "Le Séminaire XXIII, Le sinthome (1975–76)," ed. Jacques-Alain Miller, in *Ornicar?* 8 (1976): 20 (my translation).

PART III | **feminine exception**

7

Geneviève Morel | **Feminine Jealousies**

If we believe what Freud says on the subject, women are much more jealous than men. This heightened jealousy in women is supposed to be the classic outcome of penis envy transformed into a permanent character trait, the definitive consequence of nostalgia for the lack of having.[1]

Strangely enough, the Freudian woman shares this trait with an eminent figure [*personnage*]: the mythical father of the primal horde.

The Jealous Father and the Envious Daughter

The Darwinian father, who possessed "all the women" before he was killed by his sons, jealously defended his property against all other men. In *Totem and Taboo,* Freud, along with Andrew Lang, calls him "the jealous Sire."[2] I am not bringing together these two extreme figures, however, just to cause a surprise: the ultimate possessor (the rich father) and the forever deprived (the poor daughter) are united by the concept of "having," in a positive sense for the first and a negative one for the second. Jealousy has something to do with "the proprietor mentality," as Paul Benichou called it.[3] One might also think of the definition given by Claude Lévi-Strauss in *The Jealous Potter:* "Jealousy can be defined either as a feeling emanating from the desire to hold on to something or someone that is being taken away from you or as the desire for something or someone you do not possess."[4] The more you have, the more afraid you are of losing everything; the less you have or have had, the more attached you are to your possessions, or the more you covet your neighbor's possessions. In this sense, jealousy and envy are very similar. In fact mythical thinking sometimes uses the two terms interchangeably, and the languages of so-called primitive peoples often use the same word to denote avarice, jealousy, and envy.[5] Furthermore, he who possesses is not immune to the lack of having, as demonstrated by the insatiability of the miser or the anguish of the jealous legitimate owner, who is never sure of possessing everything that he owns: "O curse of marriage!" cries Othello, "that we can call these delicate creatures ours / And not their appetites!"[6] In other words, to a man, to the "jealous Sire," the act of possessing a woman does not mean that he is the owner of her drives, her desires, or her feelings; she is never completely his. Just as in Achilles' race with the tortoise, something eludes him each time, ad infinitum. The woman as not-all reserves this infinity for the Other, and even God may come to fill the place of this *jouissance* concealed from the woman's partner. "In Venice they do let God see the pranks / They dare not show their husbands," says Iago to Othello in order to malign virtuous Desdemona.[7] But perhaps behind his deception there lies a truth: the eternally elsewhere, or Other, nature of woman is the source of jealousy in the man who loves her, and in the woman who loves her in the case of feminine homosexuality. This is certainly more convincing than the projection by which Freud tries to explain Othello's jealousy.[8] Lacan completes the notion of projection by associating it with an imaginary identification which is essential to *invidia*, which he also names *jalouissance*.[9]

Jalouissance

Jalouissance is the jealous hatred provoked by the confrontation of the subject with an ideal image that possesses the desired object which the subject lacks. The example used by Lacan is that of Saint Augustine, in his childhood, contemplating his foster brother at his mother's breast, which is the desired object, or *objet a*. In *jalouissance*, there is *jouissance* in the form of the torments of jealousy, the "fatal poison,"[10] the "monster / Begot upon itself, born on itself,"[11] a *jouissance* that is torturous pain and that maintains itself through contemplation and imaginary confrontation. One can denote the relations of some women to their penis-bearing partners as *invidia-jalouissance*. Here we are not talk-ing about sexual jealousy, but of a rivalry with the man, which implies a constant castration of the virile partner, a refusal of everything that comes from him, and which in many ways makes daily life even more difficult.

Since Lacan's example of *jalouissance* is sexually rather neutral, the matrix that characterizes it can be found in the jealousy of both sexes. For example,we find it in men who fall into the category defined by Freud as the "injured third party." [12] These are men who love women who belong to someone else. According to Freud, their passion culmi-nates in jealousy, which is a "need" for them. But this jealousy is not aimed at the legitimate possessor of the beloved, but at strangers who are in a similar position to that of the lover himself, thus completing the narcissistic, mirroring condition of the lover and the object of his jeal-ousy.

This narcissistic jealousy is very common in women. It is described well by Jane Austen, especially in *Mansfield Park*. The lovelorn hero-ine, who has been temporarily abandoned for another, spends her time watching her rival, searching out her faults and her dissimilarities from herself. She falls prey to an intense moral suffering, which she attempts to overcome by trying not to calculate or make comparisons, but she cannot help doing exactly that. In the end, she finds that the only thing they have in common is their love and "value for Edmund," who is pos-sessed by the other and not by her. [13]

One sometimes finds another kind of "mirror" situation between two women where one is jealous of the other. Here, the place of the envied *objet a* is occupied not by a man but by a love child. This is the situation in "Roman Fever," a story by Edith Wharton, and in *The Old Maid* by the same author. [14] In both cases, the woman who has everything that she could wish for, the one with the legitimate claim on the man that both she and the other woman love, envies the other, less fortunate woman. What she envies is a daughter who she discovers was conceived in a night of passion "stolen" from her. The legitimate lover, who thought that she had "everything," feels a violent jealousy toward her rival and her *agalma*, the prized object which is denied her.

But let us move past penis envy and the proprietary mentality so disparaged by the Précieuses of the seventeenth century, and also past *jalouissance,* even if it is almost always present in jealousy in the form of jealous hatred and a specular relationship with the rival.

Let us leave behind the concept of "having," which defines Freudian sexuality, and consider the new perspectives on feminine jealousy made possible by the diversity of Lacanian approaches to the relation between the sexes. Lacan offers an explicit thesis on the subject, but before we get to this, we will uncover other, more implicit theses from his teachings.

Indeed, in 1958, Lacan delineates the relationship between the sexes along the axes of "being" and "having," referring not to the penis but to the phallic signifier.[15] The problematic notion of a feminine essence is replaced by "being the phallus," which makes her predisposed to masquerade. In addition, the absence of an essence on which to base a well-defined femininity exposes woman (more than man) to identification, especially in the case of hysteria.

Masquerade and Identification

Masquerade, when linked to jealousy, often has a comic edge. This comic aspect is related to the phallus and its peekaboo games, which are a function of its nature as a signifier that appears and disappears, and also of the effects of substitution which result from this. This is very different from the sadness associated with *Penisneid.*

A story by Boccaccio from *The Decameron* describes to great comic effect how woman's jealousy makes her unfaithful.[16] In the story, the woman is actually jealous of herself. *La celosa de si misma* (The Woman Jealous of Herself) is also the title of a play by Tirso de Molina. A young man is in love with Catella, a married woman who loves her husband. Her only weakness is that she is very jealous of her beloved husband, and so the young lover develops a plan. He pretends to court another woman in order to gain Catella's confidence, and then one day tells her that his fiancée is being pursued by Catella's husband. Catella does not believe him but, like all people afflicted with jealousy, is willing to go along with a test. The young man invites her to come, veiled, to the baths, where her husband supposedly has a rendezvous with the other woman. Of course, our young lover is there, lurking in the darkness. Catella arrives and makes love to him, convinced that he is her husband who has mistaken her for the other woman. She finds him more amorous than ever before, and becomes enraged. The man then takes off his mask: he was not himself, she was not herself, but the wife who was jealous of herself discovers that she has been unfaithful and has liked it! Let us point out here that this theme of the woman jealous of herself, who discovers herself to be a "woman" through the eyes of a man, stages Lacan's 1958 thesis that "man here acts as the relay whereby the woman becomes this Other for herself as she is this Other for him."[17] Access to femininity as an absolute alterity requires mediation through a man. Hysteria would be not an access through *jouissance,* as is the case here (being the Other), but an epistemic access through knowledge (knowing oneself to be Other). Lacan makes this distinction in *Encore* in 1973.[18]

We can find a prototype of jealousy through hysterical identification in the dream of the beautiful butcher's wife, taken from Freud by Lacan and reinterpreted in "The Direction of the Treatment," also from 1958.[19] In this case, the woman identifies with the man in order to pose her question about the other woman. But this question takes the form of interrogating the man's desire for the other woman and is therefore a jealous interrogation. In *L'envers de la psychanalyse* (1970), Lacan shows that the motivating force behind the dream is a scandalous and unnoticed surplus-enjoyment of the subject: leaving the husband's penis to another woman by refusing herself "the bliss of the phallus [*le bonheur du phallus*]."[20]

A few years ago, I analyzed a young woman whose symptom consisted of a tormenting jealousy caused by a consuming passion for her exquisitely beautiful cousin. The woman had chosen as a partner a man who knew her cousin; she spent her time spying on him and watching him for signs that he actually preferred the other woman. This symptom dissipated after analysis permitted her to construct a fantasy about a young boy beaten to death in front of her. This was her version of "a child being beaten." Freud in fact links feminine jealousy to this fantasy, and it was clear in the case of this young woman, who had four younger brothers, that this was how she held back her claiming of the penis.[21] The surplus-enjoyment in this fantasy was her making a martyr of her lover, who was constantly put to the test, and to whom she had proposed that he sleep with her cousin.

The woman who is jealous of herself, like the jealous hysteric, aims at the woman through the man. This is also true in the case of masculine jealousy in its Othello version: everything is focused on the woman. These two types of jealousy (male and female) are therefore not symmetrical. But if masculine jealousy stems from the woman as not-all whom it is impossible to ever fully own, and if the woman jealous of herself sees herself as an inaccesible Other (therefore also as not-all), the jealous hysteric embodies rather a question about woman as *objet a* of man, about woman's status in male fantasy.

Up to here we have not encountered any thesis by Lacan which is specific to feminine jealousy, since *jalouissance* was not sexuated. There is one, however, that first appeared in 1958[22] and was then reformulated in 1972 in the context of sexuation and the concept of the woman as not-all.[23]

The Demand for Fidelity

Lacan does not speak of feminine jealousy, but of what logically precedes it: "the demand for . . . fidelity,"[24] or, later, "the demand for love," and the desire to be considered "the only one," "apart."[25] The emphasis is therefore not on the character flaw, "such baseness as jealous creatures are [made of],"[26] as Desdemona puts it, but rather on an ethical position which evokes the lady of courtly love and her faithful knight. Furthermore, in the two passages in question we find the expressions "servitude of the conjoined" and "serving" applied to men, which evokes the superego position taken by woman vis-à-vis man: woman as "superego *qua* better half" [*surmoitié*] of man.[27]

Another point of departure from Freud is that this demand for fidelity or unity is not based on a lack, on *Penisneid*, but rather on a positive, feminine *jouissance*. It is the specificity of feminine *jouissance* which, requiring fidelity, creates a basis for jealousy.

In 1958, Lacan's thesis was based on the "duplicity of the [feminine] subject,"[28] the duplicity of love and desire, which are focused on only one man, who is, however, not loved where he is desired and not desired where he is loved. She desires the fetishized penis of her partner, but loves in him the castrated Other, the "castrated lover," "the dead man," or "the victim of castration." Furthermore, feminine *jouissance* is conditioned by her adoration of this figure, behind which can be found the locus of paternal Law. This is "the true motive for the particular character of the demand for the fidelity of the Other on the part of the woman." It is the sole right not so much to the partner's penis which is demanded as to the castrated Other, who is loved by the woman and is the condition of her *jouissance*. Infidelity, which "constitutes the male function" and which leads him to desire a girl-phallus distinct from his love partner, is not, as one might have thought, the "real motive" behind feminine jealousy. Clinical cases demonstrate that betrayal in love is much more brutally felt than betrayal in desire, but that the subject usually does not know that this is because the love of the castrated partner is the basis of her *jouissance,* even in the sexual act.

In 1972, Lacan reformulated his thesis around the concept of the woman as not-all: "On the other hand, it is as the only one that she wants to be recognized: we know this too well." [29] In effect, men feel this requirement as a superego constraint. The point is not that she wants to be the only sexual partner. But, through sexual union, the loved man allows her to reach that Other *jouissance,* which outmeasures the phallic *jouissance* of coitus, and where in any case she is alone without her partner, not-all to him. It is feminine *jouissance,* therefore, now located by Lacan beyond the phallus, which forms the basis for the demand for fidelity.

Tragic Jealousy

Lacan's radical thesis, which bases the requirement of fidelity on woman's *jouissance* and not on her fear of castration (as Freud held), makes the failure to meet this requirement much more serious than any character flaw, even an invasive one.

In fact, woman's *jouissance* is outside the Law and is not in itself regulated by castration, as in the case of men.[30] Jane Austen perceptively notes of her protagonist: "he was not yet so much in love as to measure distance, or reckon time, with feminine lawlessness." [31]

But if feminine *jouissance* is obtained as a supplement to phallic *jouissance* through the man, the relation with him, framed by the fantasy and the phallic function, will contain and retain this Other *jouissance.* To obtain this, the female subject must agree to occupy the place of *objet a* in the man's fantasy and to give her castration up to him. She, of course, has her own fantasies, which have determined her choice of partner and which allow her to desire that particular man and to articulate desire and the law of castration. If this complex frame is brutally shattered by the man's betrayal of the demand for fidelity, woman's *jouissance* outside the Law, which has up to that point been contained by her love, will be revealed in all its excesses. These are the excesses about which tragic poets have sung and which clinical cases of impassioned states have described.[32] Jason himself remarks that eros is the only thing which dominated Medea before the tragedy.[33] This is why Lévi-Strauss can say that jealousy, seen here as a demand for fidelity, "tends to support or create a state of conjunction whenever there is a state or threat of disjunction."[34] The conjunction is maintained by fantasy, thanks to the contingency of love that establishes the phallic mediation. The disjunction in tragedy corresponds to the shattering of the frame of fantasy and of the Law and to the rise of an uncontrollable jealous passion, which is the worst torture, according to Racine's Phaedra, who is full of avenging wrath.[35] She is described as a feminine monstrosity, which is actually the sudden unchecked spreading of feminine *jouissance* through the world. "[R]id the world of one more monster now,"[36] cries Phaedra, adding, "He knows, I let him see, the full extent / Of my insane desires. The boundaries / Of modesty, austerity, are passed."[37]

The tragedy of Medea is without a doubt the most famous example of this phenomenon. Lacan refers to it when he speaks of the vengeance of Madeleine, Gide's wife, when he took another lover for the first time. Lacan describes "the gaping hole that the woman's act was meant to open up in her being" of burning one by one all the letters she had received from him.[38] These letters were not only her most precious possessions but also a "doubling of Gide himself," in other words his *objet a*.

Indeed, the feminine loss of control brought on by betrayal, which we encounter in tragedy (but also in life), has specific characteristics that are not found in masculine jealousy, which is based on the passion of the phallus, dressed up as manly honor and blinded by the imaginary alienation of *jalouissance*. We see this kind of jealousy in Othello when he is betrayed by Iago.

On the one hand, hatred arises on its own and is independent from its ambivalence toward love. Lacan describes ambivalence as the bastard concept of psychoanalysis.[39] This hatred goes beyond all love, including even a mother's love for her son, which Freud considered to be the only uncorrupted love.

On the other hand, hatred, which is undoubtedly a passion for ignorance of the self, nevertheless renders the person lucid vis-à-vis others.[40]
This lucidity allows the betrayed woman to aim at the very heart of the
other's being and desire and to shatter him in his most intimate recesses.
And the lawless nature of the *jouissance* which controls her makes the
impossible act possible, as when Medea kills not only her rival but also
her most prized possessions, her children with Jason, the carriers of the
blood of their father's race, who therefore embody *objet a* for him as
well. Medea acts voluntarily and not, as in the case of Othello, in a state
of mental aberration: "I tore your heart for you because you deserved
it."[41] And she says to her nursemaid, "It is the way I can most hurt my
husband."[42]

The tragedy of Medea was rewritten in various forms in the seventeenth century, but always as a moral denunciation of the alienating
characteristics of jealousy, the "double passion of love and anger,"[43]
"jealous fury," "double ardor" "which causes terrible convulsions of the
mind," even "an animal fury."[44]

Racine's heroines—Phaedra, Hermione, and Roxane—take revenge
out of a feeling of jealousy but are less radical than Medea. They kill the
object of their love instead of aiming at his heart by targeting his *objet a*.
They are divided and are sometimes deceived—like Roxane, who wants
to be loved by Bajazet. They remain partially attached to the Law and
hesitate. Sometimes they deny their act as soon as it is accomplished and
are inconsistent, as in the case of Hermione, when she chastises Orestes
for a crime which she has made him commit: "Why kill him? For what
crime / What had he done? What was he guilty of? / Who told you to?"[45]

The Myth of the Jealous Woman

Racine's heroines are more human, more modern, more divided, and
closer to us than Medea, who one could say is "all woman" and who
is also a sorceress, a descendant of the sun, and quasi-divine. Medea
is a myth which exemplifies in fictional form a structural trait, namely
Lacan's thesis that feminine jealousy is grounded in the loss of control
over the Other part of *jouissance*, something that leads inexorably to her
"demand for fidelity from the Other," the demand to be the only one.

Medea is a myth, elements of which can be found in American myths
collected by Lévi-Strauss in *The Jealous Potter*: Mother Earth is a super-

natural being descended from the Serpents, from whom she has acquired her wisdom. She is a jealous deity who only shares this wisdom with her potters in exchange for their chastity; sometimes she even takes their lives in order to keep them near her. In this manner, she shows a "lover's or an owner's jealousy" toward her protégés.[46] One can find other elements of the myth of the jealous woman in literature. In Goldoni's Le donne gelose (The Jealous Ladies), for example, there is a female character of whom it is said that "she wants all the men for herself," as if she were the mirror image of the Freudian father who possesses all the women in the horde.[47]

But myth is not the prototype of the jealous woman; there is no clinical archetype, but rather different feminine jealousies which can be studied in their diversity. A woman can even dream of the jealous woman who, like Medea, would go beyond her concepts of honor and moral law in order to avenge herself. This is the case in Rebecca West's novella, "There Is No Conversation." A woman, the ex-wife of a man described as a "desert," imagines that a rich American woman whom the man left after a brief affair has avenged herself by ruining him financially and by forcing him to sell his most precious art objects.[48] The American woman has supposedly extracted her revenge after overcoming her own capitalist principles. The narrator (the ex-wife) is later disappointed to discover that what actually happened was much more trivial, and that, in a hysterical reaction, she has imagined a monstrous, jealous woman, a sort of Medea, in order to elevate the man in her own eyes.

Is there perhaps even a feminine myth of jealous Woman, as Lacan says of Don Juan?[49] What does the contemporary practice of psychoanalysis reveal about this subject? If women are always preoccupied by love and by the quality of a man's love, it seems to me that jealousy occurs in the discourse of analysands too infrequently. They are more tormented by their envious rivalry with men, or by their hysterical denunciations of the castrated master or of the castrated father. There could be different explanations for this: either they reserve their jealousy for their partners, finding in this a fantasmatic predilection that they are not so easily predisposed to reveal in analysis, as it is a symptom which does not disturb them; or else feminine jealousy is less and less of an issue because of the evolution of customs and the changes in the relationship between the sexes, especially after Freud. This does not mean that we should forget its real place within the structure of the subject, or fail to see woman as not-all, if we have read Lacan correctly.

In a word, masculine jealousy is an expression of man's inability to *have* or possess woman as not-all. Feminine jealousy is the result of her *being* not-all in relation to her *jouissance*. *Jalouissance* or *invidia* super-imposes itself in the imagination.

Translated by Sina Najafi and Marina Harss

Notes

1   Sigmund Freud, *Some Psychical Consequences of the Anatomical Distinction Between the Sexes,* in *The Standard Edition,* ed. James Strachey, vol. 19 (London: Hogarth Press, 1961), 254. Further citations will be made to SE, followed by volume and page number. "Of course, jealousy is not limited to one sex and has a wider foundation than this, but I am of opinion that it plays a far larger part in the mental life of women than of men and that this is because it is enormously reinforced from the direction of displaced penis-envy."

2   Sigmund Freud, *Totem and Taboo, SE* 13:126.

3   Paul Benichou, *Morales du grand siècle* (Paris: Gallimard, 1948), 239. [Translated into English as *Man and Ethics: Studies in French Classicism,* trans. Elizabeth Hughes (Garden City, N.Y.: Anchor, 1971). The above translation is our own.—Translators]

4   Claude Lévi-Strauss, *The Jealous Potter,* trans. Bénédicte Chorier (Chicago: Chicago University Press, 1988), 173.

5   Ibid., 35.

6   William Shakespeare, *Othello* (Baltimore: Penguin, 1958), act 3, scene 3, p. 94.

7   Ibid., 111.

8   Sigmund Freud, *Some Neurotic Mechanisms in Jealousy, Paranoia, and Homosexuality, SE* 17:224.

9   Jacques Lacan, *Le Séminaire,* book 20: *Encore* (Paris: Éditions du Seuil, 1975), 91. [The French word *jalouissance* is a neologism that combines *jalousie* (jealousy) with *jouissance.*—Translators]

10   Jean Racine, *Phèdre,* trans. Margaret Rawlings (New York: Penguin, 1961), act 3, scene 6, p. 113.

11   Shakespeare, *Othello,* act 3, scene 4, p. 108.

12   Sigmund Freud, *A Special Type of Choice of Object Made by Men (Contributions to the Psychology of Love I), SE* 11:166.

13   Jane Austen, *Mansfield Park* (London: Oxford University Press, 1970), 73.

14   Edith Wharton, "Roman Fever," in *The Selected Short Stories of Edith Wharton* (New York: Charles Scribner's Sons, 1991), 342–52; *The Old Maid (The 'Fifties)* (New York: D. Appleton, 1924).

15   Lacan, "The Signification of the Phallus," in *Écrits: A Selection,* trans. Alan Sheridan (New York: W. W. Norton, 1977), 289.

16   Giovanni Boccaccio, *The Decameron*, trans. Guido Waldman (Oxford: Oxford University Press, 1993), Day Three, Story 6, pp. 200–207.

17   Lacan, "Guiding Remarks for a Congress on Feminine Sexuality," trans. Jacqueline Rose, in Jacques Lacan, *Feminine Sexuality*, ed. Juliet Mitchell and Jacqueline Rose (New York: W. W. Norton and Pantheon Books, 1985), 93.

18   Lacan, *Encore*, 79.

19   Lacan, "The Direction of the Treatment and the Principles of Its Power," in *Écrits: A Selection*, 261–62.

20   Lacan, *Le séminaire*, book 17: *L'envers de la psychanalyse* (Paris: Éditions du Seuil, 1991), 85.

21   Freud, *Some Psychical Consequences*, SE 19:254.

22   Lacan, "Guiding Remarks," 96.

23   Lacan, "L'étourdit," *Scilicet* 4 (1973): 23.

24   Lacan, "Guiding Remarks," 95.

25   Lacan, "L'étourdit," 23.

26   Shakespeare, *Othello*, act 3, scene 3, p. 103.

27   Lacan, "L'étourdit," 25.

28   All quotes in this paragraph are taken from "Guiding Remarks," 95, and from "The Signification of the Phallus."

29   Lacan, "L'étourdit," 25.

30   Lacan, "D'un discours qui ne serait pas du semblant" (unpublished seminar 18, 1970–1971), 18 May 1971.

31   Austen, *Mansfield Park,* 85.

32   Cf. Daniel Lagache, *La jalousie amoureuse* (Paris: PUF, 1947).

33   Euripides, *Medea*, in *Three Greek Plays for the Theatre*, ed. and trans. Peter Arnott (Bloomington: Indiana University Press, 1961), 43.

34   Lévi-Strauss, *The Jealous Potter*, 173.

35   Racine, *Phèdre*, act 4, scene 6, pp. 135–39.

36   Ibid., act 2, scene 5, p. 87.

37   Ibid., act 3, scene 1, p. 95.

38   Lacan, "Jeunesse de Gide ou la lettre et le désir," in *Écrits* (Paris: Éditions du Seuil, 1966), 761. See also Jacques-Alain Miller, "Sur le Gide de Lacan," *La cause freudienne* 25 (Sept. 1993): 7.

39   Lacan, *Encore*, 84.

40   Lacan, "Seminar on 'The Purloined Letter,'" trans. Jeffrey Mehlman, in *The Purloined Poe: Lacan, Derrida, and Psychoanalytic Readings*, ed. John Muller and William Richardson (Baltimore: Johns Hopkins University Press, 1988), 52.

41   Euripides, *Medea*, 71.

42   Ibid., 54.

43   Jean-Paul Camus, "La jalousie précipitée," in *Dom Carlos et autres nouvelles françaises du XVIIᵉ siècle*, ed. Roger Guichemerre (Paris: Gallimard, 1995), 92.

44   Jean-Paul Camus, "La mère Médée," in *Dom Carlos et autres nouvelles*, 89.

45   Jean Racine, *Andromache*, trans. Eric Korn (New York: Applause Theatre Book Publishers, 1988), act 5, scene 3, p. 85.

46 Lévi-Strauss, *The Jealous Potter*, 33.

47 Carlo Goldoni, *Le donne gelose,* in *Tutte le opere di Carlo Goldoni,* vol. 4 (Rome: Arnoldo Mondadori, 1940), act 2, scene 3, p. 386.

48 Rebecca West, "There Is No Conversation," in *The Harsh Voice: Four Short Novels* (London: Virago Press, 1982), 127.

49 Lacan, *Encore,* 15.

8

Elisabeth Bronfen | **Noir Wagner**

Nothing seems to fascinate us in quite the same way as does a narrative of fatal attraction, of *Liebestod,* with Richard Wagner's opera *Tristan und Isolde* undoubtedly the most resilient modern version of this tale of adulterous passion. In part, the seductive effect of this story of fated love resides in the fact that, as Walter Benjamin argues for all tales of death, owing to the flame of passion which consumes its protagonists, their destiny vicariously affords us a brilliance and heat that we can never experience in our drab everyday reality. We are attracted to such fatal tales in the hope that we might satiate our desire for transgressive enjoyment by feeding on the death we read about.[1] What this also implies, however, is that the seductive quality of the *Liebestod* narrative is contingent upon the reliability of its outcome. There can be no doubt in the mind of the reader that the hero and heroine are caught in a love relation that can only end in self-expenditure. The closed circuit of the performative structuring of the *Liebestod* scenario, owing to which the adulterous couple comes to exist as a product of the discursive formation which declares its demise from the very start, does not, however, merely play through our cultural convention of linking storytelling and death in such a way that a story is told either because its narrator is about to embark on a dangerous quest or because the demise of the protagonist requires a narrative explanation. Rather, what is at stake is the fact that the reader is set up from the start to expect fatality. In the same way that the hero and heroine of the *Liebestod* romance find themselves caught in a sequence of events which, from the very beginning, can only go one way, the reader is confronted with a narrative that declares its finality before it even begins. Even while the adulterous lovers are consumed by their forbidden passion, they are also framed by a predetermined narrative trajectory whose final stop is inevitably the cemetery.

Thus, while this narrative promise of reliability affords pleasure, it also opens up the question of duplicitous articulation. For the logical consequence of its promise also means that its tale of fated love is purely rhetorical. The heroic couple performs a transgressive passion that is nothing but a scene of repetition, with their bodies in a twofold sense simply functioning as the host for a pregiven script—they play through the tragic story fate has preordained for them, but they also play through a preexistent narrative of a love which is fatal not only because it must end in death, but also because it removes the lovers from the realm of symbolic law. At the same time, owing to such a rhetorical dominant in a narrative which, manifestly at least, presents itself as a tale about heated and brilliant passion, this fatal love scenario raises the question whether this fantasy of a law-endangering and self-destructive enjoyment does not actually serve as a protective fiction, shielding this passion from a traumatic knowledge whose scene is located elsewhere. Furthermore, given that the tale of *Liebestod* has proven to be one of the most resilient fantasies of our cultural image repertoire—whose aim is to help us organize our desire for transgressive enjoyment in relation to the law, but which does so in the form of a scenario in which radical enjoyment inevitably and necessarily leads to an existence beyond the law—what alternative subject positions within the symbolic does it foreclose?

In the midst of all its predetermined fatality, the *Liebestod* scenario is thus far more ambivalent than it appears to be. A powerful older man hires a younger and more attractive man of superior strength to find the woman he wishes to marry. This representative is to watch her, court her in his name, and bring her to him. And yet the hero's name in a sense already anticipates the fateful outcome of any quest he might undertake. For, as Denis de Rougement notes, the name Tristan solidifies into a signifier the fact that this powerful knight was born of sadness: his father died just before he was born, his mother did not survive his birth, and he was raised as an orphan by his uncle.[2] All his subsequent deeds of prowess are undertaken under the sign of this originary lack of a home and family; or, put another way, they are inscribed by an instability subtending his position within the symbolic community. In Wagner's libretto, this fact of prior scenes of traumatic wounding and loss subtending the *Liebestod* scenario is further enhanced by the fact that his narrative not only begins in medias res—Tristan is about to hand Isolde over to King Marke—but also offers as the setting for the scene of fatal attraction a site which has no fixed locality: a ship travel-ing from Ireland, the home of his prisoner, to Cornwall, the home of his employer. Insofar as this site is a kind of non-place, located between the bride's homeland and her designated place of exile, it functions along the lines of what Foucault has called a heterotopia. In distinction to utopias, which present society in a perfected form but are fundamentally un-real spaces, a heterotopia is a countersite, "a kind of effectively enacted utopia," a place outside all places, different from all the sites that it re-flects and speaks about, even though it nevertheless does exist in reality. And indeed, Foucault significantly calls the ship the heterotopia par ex-cellence, which as "a floating piece of space, a place without a place, that exists by itself, that is closed in on itself and at the same time is given over to the infinity of the sea" has been for our civilization not only "the great instrument of economic development" but perhaps more crucially "the greatest reserve of the imagination." [3]

And it is precisely because the ship is a place without a place that it can serve so perfectly as the scene for the enactment of both Tristan's and Isolde's fantasy of fatal romance. Because what we discover within the first act is that Tristan's mission of courting a beautiful woman for another man is nothing other than a repetition of a series of earlier scenes of wounding and healing, which Isolde in her angry confronta-tion with her captor calls forth out of the past. As she reminds Tristan, not only has he met her before, but this is also not the first time that he has betrayed her. Having killed Morold, the man she was to marry, Tris-tan had come to her under the guise of an assumed name, and, rather than killing him, she had administered the potion that had healed his seemingly incurable wound. For some reason unknown to her, she had felt for Tristan an attraction that was stronger than her desire for re-venge, only to find him betraying her forgiveness by capturing her for another man. Although throughout the voyage Tristan has avoided her presence, once she forces him to come to her, something unexpected and yet fatefully predetermined happens. It is as though both of them were bewitched, for their anger at and disdain for each other suddenly turn into an equally violent and insurmountable romantic attraction. They are as if transfixed in a realm beyond symbolic codes and find they can do nothing other than give in to their transgressive desire. They enter into the fantasy of *Liebestod,* in the attitude of one who says, "I know it's wrong, but I can't help it. I know you are bad for me but I don't care." In the case of Tristan, caught between his allegiance to the law of his master and his seemingly irresistible love for the forbidden woman, the object of his desire is nevertheless ambivalent. Does he desire the woman who has so fatally seduced him, or does he desire the transgression of the law which the adulterous betrayal of his master entails? Or are we to understand *Liebestod* as a desire not for the consummation of irresistible passion, but rather for self-expenditure, screened by the protective fiction of romantic love? Her initial desire for revenge at Tristan's betrayal not only invokes mad anguish. Rather, finding herself the prisoner of the man she once cured of his fatal wound allows her to indulge in a fantasy of destruction involving both herself and this intermediary.

The magic moment, when this enjoyment of revenge turns into the equally consuming fantasy of reconciliation, entails a transformation of her anger at his betrayal into a betrayal of their mutual master, the king, even as she now gives herself up completely to the very agent whom she had previously hated with such a passion for having twice betrayed her. Their nocturnal love leads them to imagine for themselves an existence beyond space and time, beyond the constraints of symbolic laws, conventions, and codes, and they conceive of this future as the fulfillment of their preordained destiny. What they tell themselves is that by transgressing the law, by crossing their master, they are simply following an old melody they heard prior to ever having met. However, the love they are able to proclaim to each other in this heterotopic site is sustained by a nostalgic note in another sense. For it knots together the recollection of past recovery from woundings with a fantasy of salvation from present wounds that is utopically projected into the future. And yet, once Brangäne has crossed her mistress's intentions by exchanging a death potion with a love potion and the two lovers no longer heed the law, a chain of betrayals and delusions, of willful ignorance and fatal delaying sets in, until the law finally catches up with them.

Thus, like Tristan, the fatal seductress Isolde also finds herself the host of an ambivalent desire. The seamless interchangeability of revenge and love not only engenders a fantasy where transgressive enjoyment is conceived as the longed-for curative release from the unbearable constraints of symbolic law. Rather, the fact that death is so explicitly inherent to this transgressive love raises the question whether the *Liebestod* fantasy does not use the narrative of romantic self-expenditure to screen out and yet obliquely articulate another desire, namely for a penetration by the paternal law itself. In the midst of all this crisscross of desire, only one thing is not equivocal. Once Tristan and Isolde have fallen into each other's arms, it is straight down the line for both of them.

Lit for Night

The wager the following essay explores is that if Wagner's libretto for *Tristan und Isolde* is perhaps the most provocative modern version of the *Liebestod*, its most compelling postmodern refiguration occurs in the realm of what has come to be known as film noir. As Paul Schrader suggests, while the label *film noir* does not refer to a genre, in the sense of referring to conventions of setting and conflict, but rather to "more subtle qualities of tone and mood," it also designates a specific, though unwieldy, period of film history. While it includes Hollywood films of the 1940s and early 1950s "which portrayed the world of dark, slick city streets, crime, and corruption" it also harks back to earlier periods, notably the 1930s gangster film, the French "poetic realism" of Carné and Duvivier, and German Expressionist crime films like Lang's *Mabuse*.[4] Seeking, nevertheless, to isolate the conditions in Hollywood in the 1940s which were most influential in bringing about film noir, Schrader names four: (1) the war and postwar disillusionment, as a response to the artificial optimism of war propaganda as well as the difficulties soldiers, small businessmen, and housewives/factory employees were faced with when called upon to return to a peacetime economy; (2) postwar realism, answering to a desire on the part of Hollywood audiences for a more honest and harsher view of American society once the patriotism called forth by the war was no longer required; (3) the hard-boiled tradition, which came to offer the perfect scripts for a cultural condition seeking to emphasize the tough moral understratum of

American culture; and finally (4) the German influence, fed by the influx of German expatriates to Hollywood in the previous decades, so that, as Schrader puts it, "when, in the late Forties, Hollywood decided to paint it black, there were no greater masters of chiaroscuro than the Germans."[5]

In this essay, however, I want to shift Schrader's argument slightly by suggesting a different German influence for film noir's negotiation of the transition between wartime and peace, namely the late-romantic pathos of Wagner's *Tristan und Isolde*. Like the libretto by Wagner— with its emphasis not only on a nocturnal setting but on a chiaroscuro tone enveloping the entire plot, which revolves around the adulterous love of his two *Nachtgeweihte*—the scripts of film noir play through a love of self-expenditure beyond the law, where the lovers acknowledge that their story has been predetermined by a fate they cannot escape. Indeed, as Walker notes, entering a noir world means stepping outside "the normal, 'safe' world," because the noir world is "associated with a dissolution of the self, with a surrender to dangerous and disturbing passions."[6] And yet, as the noir scripts present narratives about how the hero and his fatal seductress cede to this other law of destruction, they deconstruct the *Liebestod* even as they play with our fascination for a romantic world beyond safe normalcy. The noir inflection reintroduces two elements which, though inherent to Wagner's libretto about enraptured ecstasy, function like a concealed yet shared secret, screened out by the overwhelming power of a score whose aim is to call forth in the audience an experience of collective transfiguration in the face of a dual death. On the one hand, the noir scripts argue that any narrative about an escape from the harsh constraints of the law requires a figuration of evil; on the other hand, they also insist that any transgressive enjoyment can only be thought of as the obscene inversion of an inconsistent, fallible paternal law, rather than a radical severance from it. At the end of the line, what reemerges is precisely the impossibility of real transgression, for even though the *Liebestod* scenario sustains a fantasy of stepping outside the world of strife so as to shed all traumatic knowledge about one's past, traces of this past prove to be ineffaceable, indeed return to haunt the protagonists with a vengeance. Furthermore, in the noir world, ultimately it is not fate which catches up with the fatal night-devoted lovers at all, but rather the law in all its obscene fallibility.

One aspect of the speculative wager I am proposing is that, insofar as both Wagner's libretto and the scripts of film noir offer an aesthetic figuration of transgressive enjoyment, whose aim is to negotiate the relation between the harshness of symbolic law and the harshness of the death drive inherent to it, they both devise narratives in response to a double crisis subtending modern culture. First, by presenting a fallible father, who cannot speak for himself but must be represented by a son, they engage with a crisis in paternity. This paternal representative, furthermore, is himself fallible, given his readiness to cede to the fatal woman's seduction and her plan of crossing the very authority he allegedly represents. At the same time, however, these scripts also stage a crisis in feminine articulation within this paternalistic system of masculine bonds. As the fatal woman finds that she cannot assert herself, her passivity turns into a vengeance which is both self-destructive and destructive of the representatives of symbolic law. It is so as to negotiate this double crisis that our cultural image repertoire has come to circulate the narrative of *Liebestod*—of a feminine enjoyment beyond space and time, beyond the constraints of a fallible symbolic law, beyond the difference of the castrative third voice, troubling the fantasy of plenitude staged by the narcissistically informed romantic couple.

The second aspect of the speculation I am proposing is, however, that mapping the scripts of film noir onto the libretto of *Tristan und Isolde* allows one not only to trace the similarities between the Wagnerian and the noir couple as both find themselves caught between giving in to their transgressive *jouissance* and abiding by the fallible law of paternal authority. Rather, teasing out the implications of the transformation that takes place in the noir inflection of Wagnerian *Liebestod* also allows one to deconstruct the grand narrative of a curative atonement and salvation that Wagner's opera installs, by privileging dimensions of the libretto that tend to be overlooked in favor of the all-engulfing score.[7] For what the noir scripts also perform is a recognition that the grand promise at stake in Wagner's game of fated and fatal love, staged so as to organize our desire for redemption and transfigured rapture, does not come out as intended. Indeed, these scripts insist instead that the nostalgic scenario of fated and yet liberating love is not merely a protective fiction, but, because the traumatic knowledge it seeks to cover up can never fully be effaced, also an untenable fantasy. At the same time, reading Wagner's libretto against the noir script points to the impasse upon which this narrative of ecstatic salvation is based and allows one to locate a fissure in Wagner's own libretto, out of which an alternative to his totalizing narrative of healing and redemption emerges. In Wagner's libretto, Brangäne, who continually seeks to cross fate's master plan, gives voice to the question whether, as one finds oneself irrevocably and inevitably bumping into one's past, one might not have a choice between embracing transgressive enjoyment, ceding to the violence of the laws of fate, and negotiating the fatality of symbolic law.

Crisscross of Desire

As the figure who engenders the transformation of hatred into love, who beguiles the errant knight and induces him to follow her into a noir world where, at the end of their mutual adventure, they find themselves embracing both death and the law, Isolde, along with her noir sister, the femme fatale, can be read as one of the most prominent figurations our cultural image repertoire has to offer of what Lacan designates as feminine *jouissance*. Juliet Flower MacCannell notes that there is no adequate equivalent for the French term in English that would illustrate how radical enjoyment conjoins the "usufruct or surplus value of an object or property" with the "bliss of sexual orgasm" such that extreme pleasure emerges as being inseparable from enjoying the profits of something belonging to another.[8] For Lacan, *jouissance* is precisely what is excluded from the symbolic, what the subject must renounce as it acquires language and a position within the symbolic by accepting the castrative law of paternal authority and handing radical enjoyment over to this Other; "castration means that *jouissance* must be refused, so that it can be reached on the inverted ladder of the law of desire."[9] At the same time, Lacan uses the term to illustrate that while pleasure implies an acceptance of the limitation which cultural prohibitions impose on the realization of one's libidinal wants and desires, such curtailment calls forth a desire to transgress these laws, to enjoy what belongs to the agent of forbiddance, to the paternal figure of authority, so that *jouissance* can only be considered in relation to the very law it seeks to transgress. As Bruce Fink points out, "Desire is subservient to the law! What the law prohibits, desire seeks."[10] Furthermore, although the subject constantly seeks to transgress the prohibitions imposed on his enjoyment, this prohibition is, as Dylan Evans notes, "of something which is already impossible. Its function is therefore to sustain the neurotic illusion that enjoyment would be attainable if it were not forbidden." [11] Precisely because the prohibition constitutive of the subject's position within the symbolic also creates the desire to transgress it, *jouissance* represents that part of the libidinal economy of the subject aimed at transgressing the law, at moving beyond the pleasure principle toward an excess enjoyment, which is why Lacan ultimately designates *jouissance* as "the path toward death." [12]

Yet while Lacan aligns the masculine position with an acceptance of the loss of full enjoyment and an identification with the phallic signifier, the feminine position does not fully exist within the masculine realm of the symbolic register organized under the aegis of the phallus. Woman, he claims in his seminar on feminine sexuality, is not-all [*pas tout*], nonexistent [*la femme n'existe pas*], and more than her reference to the phallic signifier [*encore*] because, even while the idealized woman of courtly love inspires a fantasy about how plenitude can be gained through romance, a defamed woman like the femme fatale is also disturbing proof that the loss and renunciation constitutive of subjectivity are irrevocable and insurmountable. [13] In other words, the romantically desirable though also dangerous woman comes to represent both a protective fiction, meant to mitigate a knowledge of the fundamental loss and alienation upon which an existence within the symbolic realm is based, and a horrific message broadcasting the fallibility and inconsistency of this phallic law. Yet insofar as Lacan excludes the feminine position from the symbolic by claiming that woman is not-all, he indicates that woman has a desire that exceeds phallic economy. She not only seeks to enjoy what belongs to someone else, namely to the figure of paternal authority. Rather, her desire is also aimed at something more than this phallic signifier. To say she is not-one means that woman has a negative (because no fixed) place in the symbolic order, given that her function is to point out the implenitude at the heart of human existence, just as the "not-all" refers to the fact that any system of representation is never fully totalizing or all-inclusive because it harbors a recognition of its own limitation even while it seeks to cover up this traumatic knowledge. In other words, to argue that woman is not-all implies that the function ascribed to the feminine position is that of performing the conjunction between more than one psychic order, of articulating that which is in excess of any one order, because, as Lacan suggests, the feminine position insists from beyond and against any totalizing symbolic system: "On the one hand, woman becomes, or is produced, precisely as what man is not, that is sexual difference, and on the other, as what he has to renounce, that is, *jouissance*."[14] As Flower MacCannell comments, "the *jouissance* of woman is less what remains free of or goes beyond language and the law than what exceeds the phallic fantasy of totalization on the part of the male, of his version of 'the' woman."[15]

This other or feminine *jouissance,* articulating the fact that the phallic function has its limits (which is to say that the castrative signifier calling for renunciation of enjoyment is not everything there is to know about satisfaction), thus serves two purposes. On the one hand, as Bruce Fink argues, in that it seems to go "right off the map of representation, [its] status is akin to that of a logical exception, a case which throws into question the whole thing." On the other hand, feminine *jouissance* plays through the ambivalence so persistently attached to our cultural construction of femininity. Even as it is positioned against an acceptance of a limitation to enjoyment, it promises an impossible satisfaction of the enraptured ecstasy the transgression of phallic law seeks. This leads Fink to formulate the rhetorical impasse upon which Lacan's designation of feminine *jouissance* feeds. In contrast to phallic *jouissance,* other or feminine *jouissance* is asexual, designating above all a position beyond the castrative symbolic phallic law. As such, he notes, "We can discern a place for it within our symbolic order, and even name it, but it nevertheless remains ineffable, unspeakable." Feminine *jouissance* thus brings back into play the primal enjoyment of pleasure and pain, initially given body in the unmediated mother-child unity, even while it also signifies the traumatic overproximity of the real, against which the subject must defend itself. And yet, incommensurability is written into the promise feminine *jouissance* affords, for as Fink concludes, there is "no proportionate relationship between jouissance sacrificed and jouissance gained, no sense in which the Other jouissance makes up for or makes good the inadequacy or paucity of phallic jouissance."[16]

One could say that, translated into the language of Wagner's *Liebestod,* feminine *jouissance* gives voice to the promise that an originary wound, upon which all fantasy work as well as all symbolic obligations and debts build, can be healed, even while the mise-en-scène of desire it performs only serves to play through the impossibility of this promise. At the same time, the path toward death the fatal woman's *jouissance* traces, as it moves beyond phallic law, entails not only crossing over into another realm. Rather, the desire to cross the demand imposed on her by the paternal figure of authority engenders a series of double crossings, in the course of which all those involved find that they have been betrayed, that their desire has been crossed out and appropriated to satisfy a desire that is not their own. However, even though the libretto sustains this crisscross of desire by pitting homoerotic bonds against the fatal love of the transgressive heterosexual couple, the *jouissance* subtending its plot of fate is indeed an asexual one beyond phallic enjoyment, with love screening a traumatic drive toward an overproximity of death.

Indeed, Isolde's first monologue translates her desire to transgress the castrative law imposed on her by the representative of paternal authority into a revenge fantasy. She calls upon her noir magic power, the maternal gift she has inherited, to reawaken her "bold violence." She hopes to gain control over the waters and command them to demolish the ship because it constrains her freedom—"Air! Air! My heart is suffocating within me! Open! Open wide there!" she calls out (act 1, scene 1).[17] And significantly, the figure under whose auspices she gives voice to her desire for violence is precisely the mother over whose body the initial, originary experience of *jouissance* is figured, even as this revenge fantasy breaks out in the heterotopic site of the sailing ship, crossing from her maternal homeland into a paternal site of exile. Like the femme fatale, she is willing to kill all men who cross her; yet unlike her noir sisters, who go back to their husbands of their own accord, fully assured that the paternal representative will ultimately come round and help them fulfill their murderous plots, Isolde aims her transgressive *jouissance* at the representative who betrayed her on two scores. Having been destined for her, he was then lost to her not only when he left her, but also when he boasted to his uncle that he could fetch this bride for him and then returned to claim her for his master. In so doing, he has turned her into a gift, signifying both his prowess and the stability of the bond between the older king and the younger warrior, which is why she designates herself a "corpse-like bride" (act 1, scene 2). But, as she explains

to Brangäne, Tristan's head and his heart are "consecrated to death" because she will pay him back in the same coin. Like her noir sisters, she
recognizes that she is nothing other than the stake for which the men
play, the prize bestowed upon the winner—indeed, that she is forced to
repeat the lot of her betrothed, Morold, who, having gone to Cornwall
to claim the tribute due to Ireland, was not only slain by Tristan, as she
has figuratively been slain by his betrayal. His head was hung up in Ireland "as tribute paid by England," much as, in this crisscross game of
wounded and dead bodies, she will be symbolically hung up in England
as Marke's wife, signifying that Ireland has been forced to accept the
English king's mortifying false claim. Put another way, Isolde recognizes
that as long as she is in the phallic realm of paternal law she must accept
the castration which turns her into an object of desire for the Other. And
like the femme fatale, she recognizes that the only position open to her
in this fatal exchange is to produce a counterstake—the dual corpse of
herself and her captor—which serves to cross the authority of the paternal law by exceeding its demands, even while it radically performs the
obscenity subtending the phallic bond between uncle and nephew.

The transformation of Isolde's revenge fantasy into the *Liebestod* so
ecstatically played through in the second act, is, however, significantly
embedded within two homoerotic bonds: a feminine alliance in the first
and a masculine one in the third act. For, in contrast to her noir sisters,
who are all on their own when they first charm the errant knight and
then bring death to him once he has fallen into the love trap, Isolde does
not operate alone. Indeed, Brangäne has not only been sent to accompany her in her exile because she knows how to administer the magic
powers of healing woes and wounds ascribed to feminine knowledge.
"Know you not your mother's arts?" she asks. "Think you that she . . .
would have sent me with you to a strange land without her counsel?"
(act 1, scene 3). Rather, it is as though in the Wagnerian libretto the
femme fatale were divided into two figures. As Isolde calls for the maternal potion that will help her attain "vengeance for treachery," in the
form of the "draft of death," Brangäne counters by offering her the other
juice of feminine *jouissance,* the unrestrained power of seduction, which
is sure to bind the faithless lover by an all-encompassing and inescapable spell. What this split into two figures—where a drive toward death
is pitted against a drive toward fatal seduction—affords is an articula-

tion of the complexity of the crisscross of desire at stake in the *Liebestod* scenario. Brangäne's sleight of hand illustrates how the draft of death, posing as a drink of atonement, represents a double phony claim, because it screens out Isolde's equally strong romantic desire for Tristan. Her anger at his betrayal, after all, not only involves the offense involved in his willingness to sacrifice her to the desire of his uncle, but also addresses the fact that, in so doing, he refuses to requite her love. The interchangeability of revengeful betrayal, reconciliation, and the consummation of transgressive love, which Brangäne's replacement of one potion with the other performs, also suggests that perhaps Isolde's desire is aimed beyond both fantasy scenes—whether atonement of guilt or subsumation of revenge into love. Instead, what Brangäne seems to know, yet seeks to deflect, is a recognition that the *jouissance* gained in any one of the scenarios proposed by Isolde can never make up for what has been lost, even while it is this primal, asexual *jouissance,* located before and beyond all laws, which subtends the complex play of desire.

While Isolde seeks to cross the bond between Tristan and his uncle by imposing upon her fickle lover the role of groom, in a perversion of the marriage ritual whose alleged aim is not a sexual consummation of passion but rather a dual death, what Brangäne achieves is a deflection of her mistress's courtship of death. And yet, as Tristan accepts Isolde's draft of atonement—in the hope, as he exclaims, "that today will heal me completely . . . Sole balm for endless grief, oblivion's kindly draught, I drink thee without flinching!" (act 1, scene 5)—he leaves open whether he, too, seeks the death she wishes to give him in return for his betrayal or hopes that she has forgiven him and will with this potion release him from all guilt. Thus, the outcome of Brangäne's defection from her mistress's orders is that Tristan, far from being healed, is instead infected with the feminine *jouissance,* which, aimed beyond phallic law, will actually complete the path toward death initially undertaken in the name of paternal authority. Indeed, in a manner film noir will cinematically embellish, once Tristan, who has been avoiding the gaze of his prisoner, looks at Isolde, the enchantment begins to work. As they fall into a silent embrace, their ambivalent courtship of death and defiance of death—in the course of which the scarred warrior conveys a corpselike bride to his master—is covered over by a different articulation of death. They enter the noir world of an enraptured nocturnal love outside the parameters of paternal space-time, in which, knowing only each other, they have "escaped from the world" in "supreme joy of love."

This inversion of Isolde's revenge fantasy, so elaborately staged in the second act of Wagner's opera, seeks to name feminine *jouissance*, to discern a place for it within the symbolic realm. As Isolde, not heeding Brangäne's warning, extinguishes the light of the torch, she wishes to extinguish all boundaries between herself and her lover as well. The logic of this foreclosure of symbolic difference also works by pitting the phallic realm of day against what is conceived as a return to the realm of primal *jouissance*, the fusion of separate bodies into one undifferentiated whole, the relinquishing of all tension in favor of the inanimate state out of which we come and to which we return, such that the nocturnal garden functions as the heterotopic enactment of nostalgic utopia par excellence. Indeed, the desire to move beyond the law of symbolic difference goes hand in hand with the desire to foreclose all ambivalence of feeling on the part of the individual lovers. Thus all those aspects of Tristan that disturb Isolde's desire for total fusion with her lover are relegated to the phallic realm of day. "Was it not the day in him that lied when he went to Ireland to woo, to win me for Marke," she asks her lover, who is quick to assure her that it was "the envy that day awoke in me" that allowed him to betray his clandestine love for Isolde and the *jouissance* she represents, for which, to paraphrase Fink's definition, a place can be discerned within the symbolic realm while it nevertheless remains ineffable, unspeakable. Accordingly, the *jouissance* she infected him with as she cured his wound, which has been reactivated by the love potion, remains something that can only fully take shape in a site beyond the symbolic logic of distinctions and categories. It is a knowledge which he has preserved "darkly locked away in chaste night . . . unknown and unimagined," a vision he has "not dared to gaze on," and which turns into falsity once it is brought forth and exhibited by "the light of day" to foster symbolic interests such as ambition, jealousy, and honor (act 2, scene 2).

And yet the short circuit upon which Isolde's odd logic is based is that the night is not only the realm in which her unspeakable, ineffable love for Tristan can find its adequate articulation. It is also the realm into which she wanted to draw him so as to put an end to his deception, so as "to drink eternal love to you, you united to me I longed to dedicate to death." And much like the noir hero, whose desire for the femme fatale is inflamed not despite her murderous ambition but rather precisely because of it, Tristan confesses that what seduced him was the recognition that she desired to give him death: "then there gently spread within my breast the noble sway of night: for me day was at an end." In other words, for both of them transgressive *jouissance* implies a conflation of indulging in an enjoyment forbidden by the law and seeking to escape the law of life entirely, such that the love potion, the phony draft, has simply deferred this aim and given day back to those who sought "only death." If the night is designated as a "wondrous realm" which is able to repulse "day's deceiving light" such that Tristan's nocturnal [*nachtsichtig*] eye is finally able to truly perceive the *jouissance* Isolde has infected him with, this other noir vision not only renders visible the paucity of phallic law but also calls up a desire to return to what is conceived as primal *jouissance,* beyond the economy of the phallic signifier, in the sense that this primal union is also a final union, conjoining the originary with the eternal. As Tristan declares, having looked lovingly at death's night, "the lies of daylight honor and fame, power and profit, glittering so bright—are scattered like barren dust in the sun. Amid day's empty fancies one single longing remains, the longing for holy night." The odd logic of *Liebestod* is such, however, that even though it takes its impulse from a need to show that phallic law is not all there is to enjoyment, the scenario it enacts has recourse to just that totalizing rhetoric which it seeks to break open. As the two lovers sing their duet, celebrating the fantasy of engulfment in an abundant proximity of the other, where, "never more to awaken," they enjoy a "delusion-free, sweetly known desire," the move beyond the phallic law of day they herald spells out a psychotic fantasy foreclosing all identity designations based on symbolic castration. At the acme of their enraptured duet they cancel out each other's symbolic designation. "You Tristan, I Isolde, no more Tristan," he explains, and she responds, "You Isolde, I Tristan, no more Isolde," until both declare "No names, no parting . . . ever, unendingly, one consciousness; supreme joy of love."

But paradoxically, this fantasy of total self-expenditure in the beloved, where death can be experienced in the midst of life, namely as an unending mutual sleep of all-engulfing love from which they need not awake, is also conceived as the effective enactment of a pregiven narrative titled

"The eternal love of Tristan and Isolde." The logic of this other *jouissance,* in the course of which the lovers move beyond symbolic existence and live exclusively in a deathlike state of total love, proves to be based on tautology. The proof that *Liebestod* allows one to experience the impossible—living death by enjoying the other forever, beyond all symbolic constraints, differences, and distinctions—relies on a conundrum. Tristan insists that, even though he seeks to die, "how could love die with me," given that theirs has been designated by fate as an "ever-living love," so that he can conclude, "So, if his love could never die, how could Tristan die in his love?" And yet, as Slavoj Žižek astutely notes, "fantasy is the primordial form of *narrative,* which serves to occult some original deadlocks," so that "the answer to the question 'Why do we tell stories?' is that *narrative as such* emerges in order to resolve some fundamental antagonism by rearranging its terms into a temporal succession. It is thus the very form of narrative which bears witness to some repressed antagonism."[18] The rhetorical circularity subtending Wagner's *Liebestod* indeed renders just such a fundamental antagonism visible. Not only does the fantasy of enacting what one must renounce in the form of an enraptured ecstasy prove to be in itself a totalizing narrative; the only realization of this fantasy means quite concretely going right off the map of symbolic, which is to say mortal, existence. The *Liebestod* fantasy thus finds itself unable to avoid the suicide it seems to deflect and defer. Rather, it keeps revolving around this fundamental antagonism by refiguring a scene of conquest into one of revenge and then one of all-engulfing love.

Perhaps more significant, however, is another incommensuration, which emerges as a result of the narrative impasse the *Liebestod* scenario enacts. In Wagner's libretto, feminine *jouissance,* conceived as designating the voice that speaks from beyond and against totalizing systems, must be sought elsewhere. For in its aim at pointing to the limitations and paucity of the phallic law, Wagner's *Liebestod* simply exchanges the exclusiveness of death's law for the symbolic law the lovers transgress. But in so doing, this fantasy merely proves the impossibility of an effectively enacted transgression. Simulating an unmitigated bond between two beings, which is to say, existing in the real before and beyond symbolic distinctions, proves to be nothing other than a scenario which can only be thought from within the symbolic, as a belated fantasy of primal *jouissance,* indeed an inherited narrative, conceived so as to resolve the fundamental incommensurability between *jouissance* lost and *jouissance* gained. As though to highlight the impossibility of sustaining this fantasy, Marke suddenly appears, and though the confrontation between him and the two adulterous lovers only confirms the fallibility of his law, it also serves to bring them back into his symbolic realm and at the same time into the cycle of real death. Performing the acme of crisscrossed desire, Melot double-crosses Tristan, allegedly to punish him for his betrayal of the king. And yet Tristan, for whom suicidal desire, desire for symbolic honor, and desire to be caught by the phallic law he both represents and transgresses are never clearly severed, actually walks into the outstretched sword of his opponent unarmed, taking upon himself yet another wound, only to sink into the arms not of Isolde but rather of his friend Kurwenal, who carries him to his home in Kareol.

This homoerotic bond, which, in the final act, predominates over the fated fusion of the two transgressive lovers, could in fact be seen as a mirror inversion of the allegiance between Isolde and Brangäne. In the first act Kurwenal warns Tristan to beware of Isolde's dangerous powers; indeed, he responds to Brangäne's request that the warrior go to speak to her mistress by answering in his name: "Say this to the lady Isolde: He who bestows Cornwall's crown and England's realm to Ireland's maid cannot be at the beck and call of her whom he himself brings his uncle as gift" (act 1, scene 2). He then taunts the power of the two women by singing a song about Morold's death and decapitation, a misogyny which film noir scripts will embellish as they pit the male bond against the solitary will of the femme fatale. But if Brangäne is the one to convert a death potion into a love potion, only to repeatedly warn Isolde that the bliss of *Liebestod* cannot last, Kurwenal is the one to sustain the fantasy of the transgressive love he initially warned against. His function is to forewarn Tristan of Isolde's arrival. Nevertheless, the misogynist stance subtending this homoerotic bond is sustained, for what Kurwenal supports is Tristan's nostalgic desire for the return to a lost bliss. It is to him that the wounded lover addresses the fragmentary narrative about his noir enjoyment of the "fearful bliss of death," all the while emphasizing its ineffability, as it is he who sustains Tristan's desire for Isolde as the agent who will liberate him from the pain of having reawakened into the "falsely bright and golden" light of day (act 3, scene 1). And yet,

desire, as Fink notes, is precisely what comes into being "in place of satisfaction, as a defense against jouissance."[19] The inverted relationship of
Brangäne and Kurwenal to the *jouissance* played through in the *Liebestod*
scenario is such that, while the former transforms Isolde's drive toward
an unmitigated enjoyment of destruction into a fantasy about the experience of radical enjoyment as death in life, the latter seeks to sustain Tristan's life by promoting a fantasy that once the woman for whom he has
sent to heal Tristan's fatal wound arrives, the nostalgically longed-for
fusion with his beloved can be recuperated. But what Kurwenal seeks is
to win Tristan back into the symbolic realm, and by defending him to the
end against death, he is also seeking to shield him from the dangerous
realm of femininity, the source for the entire fatal game with *jouissance*.
As he watches over the wounded lover, he curses the power of Brangäne and thereby also implicitly privileges the filial love between him
and Tristan over the adulterous *Liebestod*: "O love's deceit! O power of
love! The world's sweetest illusion, what have you wrought? Here he lies
now, the blissful man" (act 3, scene 1).

It is precisely by filtering the scene of final transfiguration through the
delusional vision of the two protagonists that Wagner's libretto allows
for an ironic distanciation in relation to the double corpse with which
his noir romance ends. For insofar as the final act presents an effective
enactment of the transgressive *jouissance* the two lovers have so vocally
been celebrating, it does so in the guise of hallucination. Isolde's ship
lands only after Tristan has described at length his vision of her arrival, explicitly positioned against Kurwenal's day-infected blindness:
"Do you not see it yet?" (act 3, scene 1). In other words, Isolde's actual
presence is crossed out by his fantasied vision of her, even while Tristan, one last time, crosses both Kurwenal and Brangäne's plea for survival under the aegis of symbolic constraint by tearing the bandage from
his wound, allowing his blood to "flow joyfully." Similarly, Isolde's narrative about her transfixed rapture at Tristan's resurrection is not only
clearly marked as a delusion. It also invokes the very words Tristan had
used to pit his hallucination against symbolic reality: "How gently and
quietly he smiles, how fondly he opens his eyes! Do you see, friends?
Do you not see?" (act 3, scene 2). The irony of the final act, of course,
resides in the fact that no one need have died. And yet, infected by a
narrative about fated love, willing to privilege a hallucinatory fantasy of

Liebestod that promises to solve the incommensurability between the enjoyment lost upon entering into the symbolic and the enjoyment gained by transgressing its law, no one is willing to listen to the representative of paternal authority. Kurwenal kills Melot and is fatally wounded himself because he will not heed Brangäne's reason, preferring instead to follow Tristan in his death. Isolde can no longer hear Marke's declaration that he not only has forgiven her but is willing to wed her to the man she loves. Instead, "taking in nothing around her," fixing "her eyes on Tristan's body with growing ecstasy," she is finally consumed by her own hallucinatory narrative. Read against the scripts of film noir, in which the death of the fatal seductress is the one variable which is never put into question, Isolde's simulated death offers an example of pure hysteria, perfect down the line. With no real organic lesion or injury to be found on her, she dies by enjoying not Tristan's body but rather her hallucination of his resurrection. She enjoys a penetration not by his erected member but rather by a melody only she can hear, which "sounding from him, pierces me through," and finally allows her "to sink unconscious—supreme bliss!"[20] Radically undercutting the narrative promise upon which his libretto feeds, Wagner leaves the actual death of his femme fatale open, directing her merely to sink, "as if transfigured, onto Tristan's body."

In this section I have sought to trace what sustains the *Liebestod* scenario. I will use the last section to explore the fissures over and against which Wagner is able to sustain his narrative of fated love. Before doing so, however, I will turn to the noir inflection of *Liebestod*. The crucial paradox subtending my proposed cross-mapping consists in the fact that since the noir script designates the femme fatale's insistence on her other *jouissance* as the source and agent of all evil, while the Wagnerian libretto relies on the innocence of the adulterous couple and is, indeed, bereft of all notions of evil, the inevitability of destruction in each takes on a very different tone. While in Wagner's libretto giving in to fate means abdicating all responsibility for one's actions, the noir scripts play through fantasy scenarios in which renouncing choice—believing in fate rather than contingency—actually designs moments of subjective agency such that the narratives they propose resolve by acknowledging the antagonism between desire and the law.

Accidentally on Purpose

The noir script usually begins in the second act, after Isolde has married Marke.[21] In Jacques Tourneur's *Out of the Past* (1947), the hero, Jeff
Bailey, is hired by the gambler Whit Sterling to find and bring back the
woman who ran off with $40,000 after having shot him four times with
his own gun. He explains to the younger man, "When you see her, you'll
understand." Indeed, the moment Jeff spots her coming out of the sun
into the dark interior of the shabby café La Mar Azur in Acapulco, the
fatal enchantment sets in, and though Kathie Moffett crosses him by returning to Whit even as Jeff tries to begin a new life in the small town
of Bridgeport, 350 miles outside Los Angeles, their past romance inevitably catches up with both of them. In Robert Siodmak's *Criss Cross*
(1949), the hero, Steve Thompson, returns to his hometown, thinking he
has finally gotten his divorced wife, Anna, out of his system, but when
he sees her dancing to the sensual waves of Latin American music, the
old magic takes over again. She, too, crosses him, by marrying the gangster Slim Dundee, and yet the fatal attraction between them is so strong
that Steve crosses both masters, the company he works for and Dundee,
with whom he has planned a robbery, in order to be reunited with her.
In Billy Wilder's *Double Indemnity* (1944), the hero, Walter Neff, finds
that he suddenly cannot stop thinking about the way an ankle bracelet
cuts into the leg of the beautiful wife of one of his clients. What begins with an apparently innocent pass made at Phyllis Dietrichson while
trying to sell her car insurance turns into a fatal scam, in the course of
which he kills the husband whose fatal accident he has also helped her
insure.[22]

All three of the noir scripts I have chosen as transformations of Wagnerian *Liebestod* use the voice-over of the hero, who, in an effort to explain a scene of violence revolving around theft and murder, conceives
of a narrative to resolve the fundamental antagonism at the heart of
his desire to transgress the very law he also seeks to sustain. And even
though the individual figurations of the *Liebestod* theme differ in significant ways, four elements structure all of these noir narratives:

1. Things that seem to happen accidentally prove to have taken place
on purpose, although the one orchestrating the events is sometimes the
adulterous couple, sometimes the crossed husband, while sometimes the
fatal events are the result of pure contingency.

2. In contrast to the Wagnerian libretto, the femme fatale has no position outside the narrative her lover offers of these fateful events. And yet the noir script stages the way in which she infects the hero with her transgressive *jouissance* in a manner that undercuts the masculinist prejudice it apparently installs even as it dismantles the romantic delusion upon which the hero's tale of fated love is based.

3. As in the Wagnerian libretto, the fantasy of perfect love conceived by the noir couple seeks to foreclose symbolic law, and not only by stealing from the figure of paternal authority. Equally important, this *jouissance* can only be sustained in a heterotopic realm outside symbolic reality, be this Mexico in *Out of the Past*, a place the lovers once inhabited and wish to return to; an undesignated place the lovers believe they might escape to in *Criss Cross;* or the psychic journey Phyllis insists Walter share with her in *Double Indemnity,* when she explains, "Nobody is pulling out. We went into this together and we're coming out of it together. It's straight down the line for both of us."

4. While in Wagner's libretto transgressive *jouissance* is restricted to a betrayal of honor and a suicidal desire on the part of the adulterous lovers that ends in self-destruction, noir scripts redirect this destructive energy. Their plots hinge on the projected murder of the father as a strategy of survival on the part of the femme fatale.

In *Out of the Past,* Jeff Bailey, tired of running and wishing to clean up the obligations that tie him to his past employer, Whit, responds to his call to visit him at his home, only to find that the woman Jeff once stole from him is "back in the fold now." When Kathie tries to seduce him once more, explaining, "I couldn't help it, Jeff," he points out to her that she has always presented herself as one who is powerless before the law of fate. "You can never help anything, can you? You're like a leaf that the wind blows from one gutter to another. . . . You can't help anything you do; even murder." Yet in the narrative he offers to the woman he loves, Ann, for whom he imagines he might build a home that would be beyond all things that happened in the past, he emphasizes his own tendency to relinquish responsibility and give in to fate, knowing full well that this is a narrative he constructs to cover up the ambivalence of his own feelings toward the phallic law he is meant to represent. For example, when he finds that the post office is closed, so that he is not able to send a telegram to Whit to inform him that he has found his wife, he presents this as an accident that he is nevertheless glad about because it allows him to turn an issue of choice into a question of preordained destiny. Similarly, like Tristan, Jeff knows that the woman who has enchanted him with her beauty will not hesitate to betray and destroy those who cross her, and yet, when Kathie asks him whether he believes that although she hates her husband she has not stolen from him, he laconically retorts, "Baby, I don't care."

Indeed, as in Wagner's libretto, Kathie and Jeff's fantasy of transgressive love is both engendered and sustained by the heterotopia which Mexico, with its dark cafés, gambling halls, and beaches, represents to the two North Americans. In this place of interim exile, they can indulge in the fantasy that symbolic law can be transformed into the law of fate, even while they know that everything they do happens accidentally on purpose. Jeff is willfully blind to the fact that Kathie's seduction is a ploy to release him from his obligation to take her back to her husband, constructing their meetings as though they were contingent even though he knows precisely when and where "she would show." And although, in contrast to Isolde, Kathie willfully uses her seductive powers as the love potion she administers to her adversary so as to cover over her destructive *jouissance*, the noir world that opens up is only a nocturnal world; as Jeff notes, "I never saw her in the daytime. She seemed to live at night." These nightly meetings on the beach also take place in a site where time seems to be suspended, with the two lovers hovering between past obligations and future projects. "What were we waiting for?" Jeff wonders in retrospect. "Maybe we thought the world would end." They could escape, and yet their transgressive enjoyment seems to feed off the threat of the very law they seek to move beyond, as though they were hunting for what also haunts them. The logic of fate which Jeff employs as he rearranges the contingent events of the past into a narrative for Ann serves to weld any effort at escape to the payment of past debts. During this confession also, these lovers find themselves in a heterotopic site—a car, driving at night toward the figures who have come out of the past to claim Jeff, reduplicating in the frame the story he is narrating as a flashback. For the day that Kathie and Jeff are about to embark on a ship to take them to San Francisco, Whit arrives, and although Jeff is able to stall his adversary and bar him from seeing Kathie, Whit's sudden appearance signifies that the law of symbolic obligations, which the two fated lovers sought to evade, will always catch up with them. Whit's response to Jeff's wish to terminate their bond is as ambivalently fatalistic as the latter's declaration of love to Kathie had been: "You started this and you'll end it."

Jeff closes his confession to Ann by describing the scene in which Kathie actually realizes the destructive *jouissance* Isolde converts into a fantasy of fated love. She shoots his old partner Fisher, who has found out their hiding place and has come to blackmail them. The scene is crucial, however, not because it casts Kathie in the role of the ruthless woman who will destroy whoever threatens the success of her transgressive romance. Her explanation, "he would have been against us," foreshadows the multiple betrayals and deaths with which the film closes. Nor is the scene seminal in revealing how Kathie's other *jouissance* speaks from beyond phallic law in the sense that in the end she looks out only for herself, leaving Jeff to deal with his ex-partner's corpse. Rather, at stake is the fact that by insisting that she had to kill Fisher, that she had to act according to her transgressive desire, she pits her ruthless drive for survival at all costs against his romantic delusion that their noir romance could be sustained against all odds. In other words, her decision to act allows us to recognize obliquely that she is not only more than what the narrator knows or is willing to tell us about her. She also has a knowledge which exceeds the narrator's in the sense that she acknowledges that they can never be free of the past. In so doing, however, she points out to him that her position exceeds both the scenario of fated love she has infected him with and the scenario of revenge that ties her to the husband she has betrayed, and thus dismantles the very fantasy she has been sustaining on two scores. The manner in which Jeff narrates the story to Ann suggests that he is seeking to cover over not only the narcissistically wounding message the femme fatale has broadcast to him, but also the fundamental antagonism inherent to his fatal romance: he assures Ann, who trusts him unconditionally and thus gives stability to his floating existence, that he no longer feels any passion for Kathie.

And yet, drawn back into her seductive presence, Jeff once more succumbs to the fantasy of *Liebestod* the other woman plays to him. When they find themselves caught in a complex plot of double crosses, the contradictions the noir hero has sought to repress are brought to the fore. Against the pressing recognition that they can escape neither Whit's plan to turn Jeff into the fall guy, so as to cover up his own crimes, nor the police, who are searching for Fisher's murderer, they once more evoke the heterotopic scenario of a love beyond symbolic reality. "I've never stopped loving you," Kathie proclaims. "We can be together again, the way we were. We can go back to Acapulco, start all over, as though nothing had happened." And even while, or perhaps precisely because each lover knows that he or she will ruthlessly sacrifice the other, so as to look out for his or her own interests—in Jeff's case the wish to get clear of the past and unite with Ann, in Kathie's case the wish to get clear of a husband who pushes her around—they passionately embrace. Infected by the woman's transgressive *jouissance,* Jeff finds his own desire exceeding any one totalizing romance narrative. He desires both a life under the sign of phallic law (the house he plans to build for Ann in Bridgeport) and a transgression of the law (an undetermined existence with Kathie). He wants to get clear of the past and he wants the past to consume him. Put into more radical terms, the noir inflection of the *Liebestod* is such that, far from being innocent, all the figures involved—the betrayed husband, his duplicitous representative, and the femme fatale—not only double-cross each other, but constantly renegotiate whom to sacrifice to the law. At the same time, the two adulterous lovers are also irrevocably tied to each other, precisely because they know that consuming an enjoyment beyond the law and betraying each other to the law may end up converging.

If we, then, compare the relation of characters presented in this noir script with the Wagnerian libretto, several significant transformations emerge.[23] The representative of paternal authority has been split up into two figures.[24] Tourneur presents to us a fallible representative of the law, the sheriff, Jim, who has had to accept that Ann prefers Jeff to him, even while he cannot bring himself to arrest the man his high school sweetheart loves. His counterpart, Whit Sterling, in turn represents the obscene underbelly of phallic law, for though he gambles and withholds funds from the Department of Internal Revenue, he is the paternal figure of authority from whom Kathie steals and whom she betrays. As they support their adulterous love by theft and murder, Kathie and Jeff cross both the legitimized and the perverted agents of symbolic law; but while Kathie, in contrast to Isolde, not only operates alone but also undergoes different alliances, which she adroitly shifts according to her needs, Jeff, like Tristan, is supported by a helper, the deaf and dumb Kid, who, like Kurwenal, repeatedly warns him against danger. Indeed, as in Wagner's libretto, the Kid brings about the accidental death of Whit's helper Jo, who, much like Melot, has gone after Jeff to kill him—though, in contrast to the Wagnerian plot, Jeff's partner does not follow him in his death. Instead, the Kid proves his love for his boss by refusing to resolve into a sentimental story the antagonism of desire for which his master ultimately paid with his life. To Ann's question of whether Jeff was going away with Kathie when the police caught up with them, he nods in affirmation, forcing her to recognize that she was not all there was to her lover's desire. As he watches her getting into the sheriff's car, the Kid salutes the sign above the gas station carrying Jeff's name, as though to signal that their oblique homoerotic bond has won in the end against both the reality of Jeff's fatal embrace with Kathie and the protective fiction of Ann's romantic trust. The disillusioned bride, in turn, takes on Brangäne's position, for throughout the noir script she is the one who pleads for a peaceful solution. She defends Jeff against Jim, and she repeatedly assures Jeff that she trusts in his love. At the same time, she argues against the narrative of fated love by insisting that they can realize his fantasy of a home cleansed of all traces of the past even while she refuses to accept Jeff's version of Kathie as an embodiment of evil. And like Brangäne, she is also the one who colludes with the constraints of the law, telling the sheriff about her love for Jeff, yet ultimately ceding to his authority once the Kid has shattered her belief in Jeff's fidelity.

Most striking, however, is the fact that the noir script endows its femme fatale with one significant attribute which Wagner had reserved for her helper. For Kathie not only voices her desire from a position beyond the phallic system—be this the fallible law of the police who finally shoot her after she has shot at them, Whit's obscene plan to hand her over to the law to protect Jeff (which she crosses by killing him instead), or Jeff's logic of fated love, according to which he will go with her but only after he has notified the police about their escape. Rather, her *jouissance* undercuts any totalizing system by giving voice to what is in excess of each of the narratives told by the different figures of paternal authority, in part when she plays one man off the other, but most significantly in the final confrontation with Jeff. For as she insists, "I never told you I was anything other than I am. You just wanted to imagine I was. That's why I left you," she radically troubles the premises of his narrative of fated love by showing that, in contrast to his willingness to abdicate choice and give himself up to accident, she actually could "help it" all along. It is at precisely this point that the noir script dismantles the misogynist encoding which its narrator installs, by making it horrifically clear that what renders the woman's *jouissance* evil in the noir world is her insistence on agency. Kathie forces Jeff to realize that the stain of the past will always haunt him because it is the very motor of his desire. And even if he ends up crossing her urge for survival, he does so only after acknowledging the nonviability of the totalizing fantasy of perfect love he sought to enact with Ann. Describing to him her plan that he should go away with her, as she had done once before in Mexico, Kathie explains, "You're no good for anyone but me. You're no good and nor am I. We've been wrong a lot, and unlucky a long time. I think we deserve a break." With his response, "We deserve each other," the noir script indicates that if his entrance into the noir world began when her beauty infected him with a fantasy of fated love as a move beyond the obligations and constraints of everyday reality, his exit from this world occurs precisely when he acknowledges his own agency, in an act in which accepting the constraints of symbolic law and ceding to a *jouissance* whose path leads to death proves to be the same thing.

In *Criss Cross*, the narrative of *Liebestod* which the hero tells himself as he drives an armored truck carrying $100,000 cash to the site he has designated for the holdup also emphasizes his helplessness before the logic of purposeful accident. Against his conscious wish to forget the woman with whom he had a troubled marriage, against his mother's prohibition and his best friend's warnings, Steve claims, "It was in the cards, or fate or whatever you want to call it. But right from the start it all went one way." And as in Wagner's libretto, this fantasy is sustained by the seductive voice of the forbidden woman promising him a nostalgically tinged utopic state of happiness, in which all stains from the past and all conflicts from the present will have been eradicated. For the entire flashback sets in with what is also the very first scene of the film—Anna's urgent voice, insisting, "All those things that happened before, we'll forget it. You'll see, I'll make you forget it. After it's all over and we're safe. It'll just be you and me. The way it should have been from the start." And yet the Tristan whom Siodmak's film refigures is not at all the valiant man Tourneur depicts, resolute in his search for Kathie Moffit, fully aware of the danger she represents, not caring, because it is this destruction he also seeks. Rather, his is the wounded Tristan, who floats aimlessly along the shore of Ireland, only to find himself unwittingly in the presence of the woman he has himself injured by killing her bridegroom. Throughout the script, Steve repeatedly finds himself in situations where, although this was never intended, he accidentally meets the very woman he tells himself he is not looking for—first in the bar they used to frequent, which he seems to float into almost unconsciously, then again at the train station, after she has broken her obligation to him by marrying the crook Slim Dundee. In a similar manner, the plan to rob the armored car, with him as the inside man, is something he comes up with suddenly, once he finds his opponent sitting in his parents' living room, challenging the adulterous lovers, saying, "Hello, baby—you know, it don't look right." Indeed, without any premeditation, Steve simply ties together the odd remark he heard in the locker room about how it is impossible to steal from an armored car with Anna's insistence that they need money to escape from Slim's jealous rage.

By highlighting this lack of clear purpose, however, Siodmak brings to the fore that aspect of Wagner's *Liebestod* scenario which allows one to conceive of Tristan as an ultimately disempowered pawn in the game played between the two captured women, willlessly ceding to whichever script infects him, Isolde's revenge fantasy or Brangäne's love fantasy. Even though Steve is utterly uncritical in his love for Anna and still holds on to the illusion, even when everything is lost, that all he wanted was an untroubled union with her—"I never wanted the money. I just wanted you. I just wanted to hold you in my arms"—he is also easily swayed in believing the bad things others say of her. At the beginning of the story, when she is still trying to convince him that they should get together again, he hesitates, worrying about the fights they used to have in the past because he cannot foreclose his mother's warning, "You had trouble with her once." And to the end, the crisscross of his own desire is such that, even as he holds on to his blind love for her, he also confronts her with the suspicion his friend Pete has infected him with, namely that, rather than supporting him in his plan to betray Slim Dundee, she has been in on her husband's plan to double-cross him all along. The most significant refiguration of the Wagnerian libretto which *Criss Cross* plays through, however, involves the position of Marke. As in other noir scripts, the figure of paternal authority is split between an obscene representative of the law, the gangster Slim Dundee, and a legitimate representative of symbolic law, Steve's high school friend, the detective Pete Ramirez. However, Pete is, like Kurwenal, also Steve's best friend, warning the errant knight against the danger that the femme fatale embodies. As in Wagner's libretto, he is willing to use verbal violence to separate his friend from the woman he believes can only spell trouble. "I know it when I see a bad one," he explains. "Leave that girl alone." His version of taunting the seductive woman is not, however, to remind her of past shame, but rather to threaten to frame her for a crime so as to get her locked away in prison. At the same time, after the robbery has failed, he will ruthlessly leave the wounded Steve unguarded in a hospital room so as to use him as bait to catch Slim Dundee. One could say that what Siodmak embellishes in his noir refiguration of the crisscrossed desire played out in Wagner's libretto is the way phallic law, even when it is legitimate, is obscene in its castration of woman's subjectivity. For it relentlessly reduces her to a stake in a game of masculine bonds of honor, rivalry, jealousy, and camaraderie that utterly crosses out any agency of her own. In one of the subtly poignant moments Siodmak uses to introduce the femme fatale's position outside the masculinist narrative, he shows Anna lying on a couch, asleep, while the men plan the holdup. She, who is barred from taking part in the robbery, is also not allowed to leave the room.

The most compelling twist Siodmak introduces, however, as he supports the cultural climate of his time in its wish to paint the system of symbolic codes as black as possible, is that the phallic law which the femme fatale resists finds as its staunchest and most adamant representative the figure of the mother. She not only repeatedly warns Steve against Anna's fatal charms, but she is behind Pete Ramirez's threats to find illegal means for arresting the daughter-in-law she does not want. The fated lovers thus find themselves caught between two aspects of the law which uncannily coincide in their desire: a mother seeking to ensure her notion of propriety against all odds, and a cuckolded husband seeking to indulge in his jealous rage at all costs. It is to cross them both that

Steve ultimately cedes unconditionally to the feminine *jouissance* Anna represents, explaining to Pete, "I'm going to do anything I please. And you and Dundee and nobody else is going to tell me what to do." Given the claustrophobic bleakness with which Siodmak presents all figures of symbolic authority, it is not surprising that *Criss Cross* offers one of very few noir scripts in which the betrayed older man does not get killed but actually does the killing. During the holdup, one of the burglars kills Steve's partner, against his explicit orders, and, suspecting that Slim wanted all along to double-cross him, Steve shoots him in the leg but is himself then shot in the arm. Because he is able to return half of the money to the armored car and protect it from the robbers until the police come, he becomes a local hero. But Slim sends Nelson, his Melot, to the hospital to kidnap the wounded man and use him as bait to find Anna, who had been designated to handle the stolen money.

Like her noir sisters, she, too, is in excess of any one order. She is asked merely to watch the men as they design their crisscrossed schemes —Steve suggesting a robbery to maintain his romantic illusions, Slim going along with his plan so as to destroy his opponent. Yet for one brief moment, after she has stolen away to the kitchen with Steve to finalize their own getaway, the camera shows her standing alone, looking out at nobody. We are meant to recognize that she is enjoying a scheme of her own, but we are also forced to realize that she will not be reduced to the either-or scenario which Pete Ramirez will present to the wounded hero during his visit to the hospital; "If she double-crossed you, you're all right. If she double-crossed Slim, he'll get you." Instead, by introducing a third alternative, that of double-crossing both but waiting to see how things turn out "accidentally on purpose" (which is to say, being fully prepared to act upon contingency), what she illustrates is that her *jouissance* exceeds any one totalizing scenario, be it Slim's narrative of jealous love or Steve's narrative of naive love. Above all, however, her jouissance also exceeds the logic of fated love. For even though in contrast to other femmes fatales she is not evil—she is right to want to run away from a husband who beats her, as she is right to flout the narrow-minded sense of propriety espoused by Steve and his family—she is a ruthless realist, looking out for herself by playing through the extreme consequences of the very law of capitalist values she has transgressed.

As in *Out of the Past*, what turns the seductive woman fatal is her insistence on agency. In the final scene, recognizing immediately that Nelson, who has brought Steve to her, will turn around and betray them either to Slim or to the police—in other words, finding herself caught between two sides of the law—Anna also confronts the hero with the naïveté and nonviability of his romantic illusions. She not only points out to him the foolishness in his having come to her, but also explains that, under the new circumstances, she must get away immediately with the money, leaving him behind because in his wounded state he would not last a day without medical help. The music sets in to signal that Steve, like Tristan, has now fully entered into the hallucinatory fantasy of a love which could have worked out but did not because it was in the cards, explaining more to himself than her, "All those things you said to me, you weren't lying. You meant it. I know you meant it. You love me." Against this delusion she violently pits her realist rendition of the antagonism at the heart of symbolic existence: "Love, love, You have to watch out for yourself. That's the way it is. I'm sorry. What do you want me to do? Throw away all this money?" But as his transfixed gaze watches her finish packing and moving to the door, he no longer heeds her narrative about practical survival; "I'm sorry. I can't help it if people don't know how to take care of themselves." And yet, perhaps the most disturbing aspect of the logic of feminine *jouissance* to which the femme fatale gives voice is that it performs the contradiction of betraying and loving at the same time. What Anna's final gesture illustrates is that just because she believes in the narrative that "you have to watch out for yourself," that does not mean she has relinquished the fantasy that escape from the constraints of phallic law are possible, that "after it is all over and we're safe, it'll just be you and me. The way it should have been from the start." As she sees Slim limping up to the cabin, she returns to Steve and falls into his embrace. The double corpse which the camera frames into a picture of perfect union between the two fated lovers before it draws back to show us Slim's face as he hears the approaching police sirens signifies not only that fully ceding to the other *jouissance* beyond phallic law ultimately means entering upon a path to death. It signifies an ethical act, which, as Žižek explicates, involves traversing a point of absolute freedom, when "what a moment ago appeared as the whirlpool of rage sweeping away all determinate existence changes miraculously into supreme bliss—as soon as we renounce all symbolic ties." By turning to Steve, fully aware that his notion of love is a delusion that can be sustained only by screening out all contradictions and antagonism, in other words, moving beyond desire, and in so doing turning away from any further negotiation with the law—be this Slim's gun or that of the police—Anna renounces renunciation itself. As Žižek notes, however, this also means "becoming aware of the fact that we have nothing to lose in a loss."[25] Even though this renunciation sustains the *Liebestod* in which Steve so fervently and so fatefully believes, the *jouissance* it displays persists in its radicality because it also crosses the totalizing gesture of this masculinist narrative.

Billy Wilder's *Double Indemnity* is framed by the wounded Walter Neff, who, having found refuge in his office, narrates his version of past events into a dictating machine before trying to get across the border to Mexico. The memorandum he addresses to his partner Barton Keyes, whom he describes as "wolf on a phony claim," begins with the confession of murder: "I killed Dietrichson. I killed him for money and for a woman. I didn't get the money and I didn't get the woman. Pity, isn't it?" And yet the irony around which Wilder's film so brilliantly revolves is that the hero's narrative itself is a phony claim. For, as the story unfolds, we are obliquely shown that his fatal enjoyment lay neither in enjoying the forbidden woman nor in enjoying the money, but rather in cheating the law and getting caught by the very man he sought to trick. The poignancy of Wilder's refiguration of Wagner's *Liebestod* scenario thus consists first and foremost in the way he recasts his fated hero, who is neither Tourneur's Jeff, giving in to what is bad but not caring, nor Siodmak's Steve, naively drifting into a fatal seduction. Rather, Walter Neff's fetishistic sexual fantasies, spurred on by the ankle bracelet Phyllis Dietrichson wears on her left leg, is simply a protective fiction, screening his wish to share in Phyllis's enjoyment of transgression. Even as he feigns indignation at her proposal that he sell her accident insurance for her husband without the latter knowing it and walks out on her that afternoon, the fact that she has infected him with the plot of a "morgue job" also clearly excites him. As he confesses, "I was all twisted inside and . . . then it came over me that I hadn't walked out on anything at all. That the hook was too strong, that this wasn't the end between her and me. It was just the beginning."

Like a phantasmatic fulfillment of precisely this transgressive desire,

Phyllis visits Walter that very night in his apartment, using her seductive powers to win him over. Yet the manner in which Wilder stages their embrace, corresponding to the moment when Tristan and Isolde enter into the noir world of *Liebestod,* brilliantly emphasizes the asexual nature of their *jouissance.* After the initial kiss, Walter quite deliberately disentangles himself from Phyllis's arms, and instead, we are shown how both get off on their respective narratives. Inspired by Walter's story about the woman who tried to kill her husband in the bathtub and ended up in prison, Phyllis not only offers him a glimpse at her own domestic malaise—she quietly responds, "Perhaps it was worth it to her"—but also indulges in her fantasy of a fatal accident happening to the husband, who has mistreated her and written her out of his will. Walter, in turn, counters with a double fantasy, for he not only assures her that Keyes knows all the tricks, thus signifying that it is the enjoyment of beating the company that he is after. He also admonishes her "if there is a death mixed up in it you haven't got a prayer. They'll hang you as ten dimes will buy a dollar." Only after having added, "And I don't want you to hang baby. Stop thinking about it," does he take her in his arms. The smile that suddenly lights up his face as he presses her face to his right shoulder and looks out over her head, once more avoiding her kiss, thus signifies his pleasure at the thought that he can come up with the one trick his partner does not know, even as, by virtue of his explicit denial, it implicitly also refers to his pleasure at the thought of seeing her hang. Walter Neff is, indeed, the Tristan of the first act, the one who desires Isolde for her vengeful, murderous desire, for the death she wishes to give him, and the Tristan who bonds with his friend Kurwenal to shame, taunt, and at least symbolically destroy the power of his female adversary.

Two things are particularly striking about the way Wilder films the deflection of a sexual consummation of passion on the part of his fated lovers. At this point the camera draws back from their embrace and cuts to Neff, speaking into his dictating machine in a room lit for night. It pans up to his face, which glows with some inner fire, as he explains the details of his fantasy of transgressive enjoyment: "it was all tied up with something I'd been thinking about for years, since long before I ran into Phyllis Dietrichson. Because, you know how it is, Keyes, in this business you can't sleep for trying to figure out all the tricks they could pull on you. You're like the guy behind the roulette wheel watching the customers to make sure they don't crook the house. And then, one night, you get to thinking how you could crook the house yourself, and do it smart because you've got the wheel right under your hand . . . and suddenly the doorbell rings, and the setup is right there in the room with you."[26] What is so significant about this mise-en-scène is the fact that, while on the one hand it occludes and postpones the second part of Neff's fantasy (his desire to enjoy Phyllis's corpse), by embellishing only the first part, on the other hand it screens out a visual rendition of their lovemaking, replacing it instead with the image of a different bond, namely the one between him and Keyes. This too is a form of the other's *jouissance* because it is spoken as an apostrophe, even while the bond it confirms is based on his getting off on the thought of crossing this forbidden lover as well. Given that the camera does not cut back to the fated lovers until their phallic enjoyment has taken place—Walter is leaning back on one arm of his couch, smoking, watching Phyllis putting on her lipstick—we recognize that the fantasy subtending his adultery with Phyllis in fact revolves around a different transgressive enjoyment, the enjoyment of the male body.[27] Wilder's particular noir inflection of the Wagnerian *Liebestod* thus consists in pointing to the way the masculinist narrative is sustained by first appropriating feminine *jouissance* as a way to enjoy one's forbidden destructive drives, only to end up by seeking to cross out the feminine position entirely. Phyllis's corpse can be seen as embodying the fact that the sadism played through was always one of misdirection. For as the murderous scheme unfolds, what becomes clear is that Walter merely uses Phyllis's plot against her husband to enjoy a different scene of wounding, in which the part she is allocated is that of being the stake toward which the men direct their sadism, even though the wound that counts—which, in accordance with Wagner's libretto, is the one the lover both inflicts and heals—refers to a different scene, one that occurred long before Walter met Phyllis Dietrichson. As the object of desire, which Walter erects so as to protect himself from this other *jouissance*, Phyllis is also the figure that must be sacrificed before the two men can finally unite in their forbidden embrace.

Although both Walter and Phyllis pretend to each other that they have conceived of the scheme to kill Dietrichson and collect the double indemnity so as to assure an unconstrained consummation of their passion for each other, going through with their plan actually keeps them apart.

Indeed, they now meet only "accidentally," in a designated supermarket. Phyllis reiterates her love for Walter only in conjunction either with expressing her excitement at the fact that they are about to go through with the murder, or once the deed has been successfully completed. Wilder stages this misdirection of crisscrossed desire perhaps most poignantly, however, in the scene where Keyes visits Walter unexpectedly one night to inform him that he is convinced "something has been worked on us in the Dietrichson case." Phyllis, who overhears their conversation as she approaches Walter's apartment, hides behind the door opening out into the corridor as Keyes leaves. For several moments Walter remains suspended between his two forbidden lovers, the woman with whom he has broken the law at his back, the man he has betrayed in front of him, waiting for him to light his cigar. Several moments later, after Keyes has left, Phyllis will once again stand behind Walter, place her arms around him, and force him into an embrace, but only after he, standing in front of her without turning around, has already admonished her that "Keyes can't prove anything. Not if we don't see each other."

When Walter finally allows himself to enjoy the second part of the fantasy he disclosed to Phyllis the first time they embraced on his couch, he does so explicitly in references to signifiers given him by Keyes. For this representative of symbolic authority had asserted the infallibility of his power to break phony claims by offering Walter a narrative about how transgressive *jouissance* inevitably traces a path to death. Speaking of the murderers, though as yet unaware that he is actually addressing one of them, he assures Walter, "They'll be digging their own graves . . . they are stuck with each other and they have to ride together all the way to the end of the line. It's a one-way trip and the final stop is the cemetery." Wilder offers us perhaps the most perfidious version of the *Liebestod* script, where inflicting and healing a wound so strangely correspond. For, supported by Keyes's story in fantasizing "how it would be if she were dead," the cure Walter comes up with is to turn the murderous desire with which the femme fatale infected him against her and thus purify himself of this stain. In their final nocturnal confrontation, both Walter and Phyllis renounce the protective fantasy of fated love they had proclaimed to each other on the night of their first embrace and admit that, instead of an eternal union with the other, each wishes to enjoy the death of the other. However, as in the other noir scripts I have discussed, the final articulation of feminine *jouissance* consists in speaking in excess of any one order. Walter merely seeks to exchange one protective fiction for another. To motivate his own killing, he offers Phyllis a narrative about how he has decided to believe that she and her daughter-in-law's fiancé, Nino Sacchetti, had planned the murder all along. Phyllis, however, exchanges her radical dismantling of the romantic fantasy with an ethical gesture which consists in declaring the paucity of phallic law, but also in the radical recognition that she has nothing to lose in a loss. After she has fired the first shot, she admits, "No, I never loved you nor anybody else. I'm rotten to the heart. I used you just as you said until a minute ago, when I couldn't fire that second shot. I never thought that could happen to me." [28] In this brief moment, the full radicality of a feminine *jouissance* speaking beyond and against any totalizing system can be heard. In imitation of Tristan's hallucinatory transfiguration—yet unlike Steve or Jeff, who both remain transfixed in their nostalgic fantasy of the perfect love that could have been, if fate had not worked against them—Walter is utterly caught up in a delusion one could call the sadistic reversal of *Liebestod*. "Sorry, I'm not buying," he explains, as his shots penetrate the woman who has begun to hold him close to her body, embracing him with both her arms. But then, he was not only using her as she was using him. His asexual *jouissance* was aimed at a different *Liebestod* scenario from the very beginning.

Thus the most compelling refiguration of the Wagnerian *Liebestod* offered by Billy Wilder involves the figure of paternal authority, who is once again split between the abusive, crude, and sexually indifferent husband, Dietrichson, on the one hand, and the infallible detector of phony claims, Barton Keyes, on the other. As in *Criss Cross*, the representative of the phallic order is also a recasting of Kurwenal, the man who warns the hero against the fatal seduction of the woman, who taunts her and is willing to risk everything to destroy her. However, as many critics have noted, the fact that Keyes, who will not carry his own matches because "they always explode in my pocket," repeatedly asks Walter Neff to light his cigar is perhaps the key trademark of a homoerotic bond. What is particularly relevant to the way this other, deflected homoerotic *jouissance* is played through in Wilder's noir refiguration of the *Liebestod* scenario is the fact that it, too, requires the presence of the very law it seeks to transgress. With the exception of the first and the last exchange of fire between the two men, each instance implies the presence of Phyllis—in Neff's office, when Phyllis is on the telephone, telling him of Dietrichson's accident; in front of Neff's door, when Phyllis is standing behind Neff, signaling her presence by pulling at the doorknob he is holding in his right hand; in Keyes's office, when the older man assures Walter that he will get Phyllis on her false claim. By implication, Phyllis—as an object of desire and as the catalyst for a plan to crook the company—is necessary as the demarcation line whose transgression allows Walter to enjoy his forbidden partner. In line with the perfect symmetry structuring *Double Indemnity,* the final exchange between the two men both echoes and completes the first conversation we hear between Neff and Keyes, in the course of which the former accuses the latter that he is "so darn conscientious, [he's] driving [himself] crazy" and continues to jest at his partner's scrupulous pedantry until Keyes replies, "Now that's enough of you, Walter. Get out of here before I throw my desk at you." Bemused, Walter watches while his friend touches first the pockets in his vest, then those in his trousers, looking in vain for a match, only to offer him fire from one of his own matches, adding, "I love you too." And if Neff's narrative begins with the phony claim that he wanted a forbidden woman and money that did not belong to him, it ends on a phony demand. Walter, who asks Keyes not to call an ambulance because he says he needs four hours to get to the border, collapses before he can even get to the elevator. Given the fact that roughly the same amount of time has passed between his arrival in the office and the arrival of Keyes, what is implied is that if he had relinquished his desire to make a confession to Keyes and instead gone across into Mexico, he would have survived. His desire, therefore, was never to escape, but rather to be caught in a libidinal impasse, where ceding oneself to symbolic law and ceding to transgressive enjoyment prove to be the same thing.

In this final scene, Keyes, representing both aspects of the law, does penetrate Walter by turning the gesture of giving fire back onto the wounded hero, even while he fully dismantles any romantic illusion that there can be an escape from either the police or death. Having called an ambulance, explaining, "Yeah, it's a police job," Keyes kneels beside his wounded friend, who says, "You know why you couldn't figure this one, Keyes—because the guy you were looking for was too close.

Right across the desk from you." Now Keyes directly expresses what his search for matches had obliquely signified in the first scene. "Closer than that," he confesses, to which Neff responds as before, "I love you too." Pushing a cigarette between his lips but finding that he no longer has the power to light his own match, Walter turns to Keyes, who takes the match, lights it with his thumb the way Walter used to, and lights the cigarette. The last image of the film resonates with the full ambivalence of this exchange, for as Walter looks beyond Keyes, it is as though he, too, had recognized that there is nothing to lose in a loss. In this sense the femme fatale has succeeded in infecting him with her radical *jouissance*. Receiving Keyes's punishment as an oblique confession of love, is, finally, the perfect plot, straight down the line. And this is, of course, also the position in which Wagner's hero ends—Isolde holding Tristan's corpse in her arms, through her hallucination reinvigorating his dead body. It was their fatal love all along.

Out of the Wound

"There was one chance in a million we'd bump into our past," Jeff explains to Ann in *Out of the Past*. Yet, what the noir scripts articulate so convincingly is that this enjoyment of pure contingency is the clandestine kernel of the *Liebestod* scenario, which emerges once the fated lovers have traversed the double fantasy of a perfect love beyond the constraints of symbolic reality and its inversion, the enjoyment of murderous desire. Similarly, both Isolde and Tristan obsessively reiterate a past scene of injury, where an inflicted wound never fully healed, designating this as the primal scene around which their *Liebestod* scenario revolves. Initially, in response to the song Kurwenal sings about the death of Morold to shame her, Isolde explains to Brangäne that her captor, Tristan, is the man who once came to her, "sick and stricken, near to death" under the assumed name Tantris. Once she discovers that in his sword there is a notch which fits exactly a splinter she had found in the head of Morold that had been sent back to her, she at first wishes to strike him dead with his own sword. But, "as he looked up . . . looked into my eyes, his anguish touched my heart." Instead of killing him, in order to heal the psychic wound his murder of Morold has inflicted upon her, she decides to heal the wound inflicted on Tristan by Morold, so as to recuperate from another wound Tristan has inflicted on her, namely having been pierced by his eyes: "so that in health he could travel homeward and trouble me no more with his gaze!" This chain of woundings and healings is then turned one twist further when Tristan returns, wooing her for "Cornwall's weary king," because Isolde is forced to recognize that she has engendered her own shame, "It was I who in secret brought this shame upon myself! Instead of wielding the avenging sword, I let it fall harmlessly!" (act 1, scene 3). And yet, when Isolde confronts Tristan with her narrative of the same scene (act 1, scene 5), she addresses the short circuit of this fated economy of wounding recuperations more directly. Explaining to him, "I tended the wounded man so that, restored to health, he should be struck down in vengeance by one who had won Isolde from him," she signals yet another turn of the screw. If she is the creator of her own shame, she wishes him to fulfill the death she has designed for him, hoping thus to heal her multiple wounds. Explaining to him, "You yourself may now utter your fate!" she offers him not his sword, but the drink of fatal atonement.

Their fantasy of a totally encompassing love which would allow them to enter into a state beyond all difference is thus conceived as a release from this economy of psychic woundings. Having twice refused to wound him mortally with his own sword, having failed to mortally wound them both with a drink of atonement, Isolde has instead engendered a psychic state owing to which both believe that, by expending themselves in the other, they can move beyond any situation of recuperation, though healing a past wound can never obliterate the scar of this cut. And yet—as the noir inflection of *Liebestod* so insistently plays through—any fantasy of escape must be thought as a protective fiction, as a phony claim to an originary state. For the economy of psychic recuperation is structured by the fatalistic law that any cure simply engenders more woundings, precisely because the entire exchange takes place on the level of after-pressures, without ever touching upon the actual originary wound. Put another way, any real primal scene or wounding lies beyond the realm of representation, even beyond a metaphoric rendition, such as the maternal-nocturnal womb as originary site of dwelling, which Tristan designates as "the dark land of night from which my mother sent me forth when he whom in death she conceived in death she let go into the light" (act 2, scene 3). The value of a primal scene of wounding is purely structural, for it functions as the kernel of traumatic knowledge from which all subsequent psychic representations feed without ever having full access to this scene of originary shock, and as such it exceeds all belated scenarios and figurations. In the libretto, this chain of recuperative woundings is played through in the second act not only in the sense that Melot repeats Morold's act, when he once more inflicts a mortal wound on Tristan's body. More crucially, Tristan and Isolde's delusion of escape has as its return the wounding of Marke. As he explains, confronting Tristan, "why, wretched man, have you now wounded me so sore . . . with never a hope that I could ever be healed" (act 2, scene 3). By referring to the betrayal of his trust, more than the actual adultery, Marke insists that the significant wounding occurs in relation to the infallibility of his symbolic authority, which is to say, in the introduction of deceit and suspicion on the symbolic level of exchange, not to any romantic desire for Isolde. In so doing, he in turn wounds the fated lovers' delusional trust in the exclusive significance of romantic bonds.

As Bruce Fink suggests, "We can imagine a kind of jouissance before the letter, before the institution of the symbolic order (J_1)—corresponding to an unmediated relation between mother and child, a real connection between them—which gives way before the signifier, being canceled out by the operation of the paternal function." Any narrative about an enchainment of wounding and healing comes to serve as a protective fiction which both shields the originary cut from the maternal body and yet, like the navel, marking the scar that remains after a cut, also harks back to this impossible knowledge. For, as Fink adds, "some modicum or portion of that real connection is refound in fantasy (a jouissance after the latter, J_2), in the subject's relation to the left over or byproduct of symbolization. This second-order jouissance takes the place of the former 'wholeness' or 'completeness,' and fantasy—which stages this second-order jouissance—takes the subject beyond his or her nothingness . . . and supplies a sense of being."[29] Indeed, when Tristan offers his narrative of this alleged primal scene of recuperative wounding to Kurwenal (act 3, scene 1), he explicitly refers it back to the fatal wound at the beginning of life. Fearing that Isolde will not arrive, he recalls that the old melody he now hears is the same one he heard as a newborn child, when it heralded the death of his parents. Recalling how Isolde healed and closed his wound only to tear it apart again with his sword before dropping this fatal instrument, and then again, how she gave him a poison draft to drink, which, intead of finally curing him of his fated yearning, came instead to cast "the direst spell . . . that I should never die but should be left in eternal torment," Tristan exposes how the kernel of the *Liebestod* scenario consists in a traumatic antagonism underwriting human existence. For even as the fantasy staging of a second-order *jouissance* seems to supply the fated lovers with a sense of being beyond the symbolic alienation *qua* castration, which is the trademark of all human existence, its content bespeaks the paucity and fallibility of this promise. One could say that the *Liebestod* scenario—which Tristan designates as "Dying, still to yearn, not of yearning to die. What never dies now calls, yearning, for the peace of death"—stages the psychic impasse Freud has theoretically formulated as strife between the pleasure and the death principle, where the former seeks to preserve a life-sustaining balance of tension, and with it an economy of deferred desire aimed at a release from this tension, while the later is aimed at a tensionless state of existence, which is, however, coterminous with deanimation.[30]

Discussing the way in which the Lacanian subject is decentered in relation to the death drive inherent to all its psychic processes, Žižek suggests that *jouissance*, functioning as an expression of the human drive to move beyond the balanced tension of the symbolic, "is thus the 'place' of the subject—one is tempted to say: his 'impossible' Being-there, *Da-Sein*." In that the most radical and elementary experience of decenterment occurs with regard "to the traumatic Thing-*jouissance* which the subject can never 'subjectivize,' assume, integrate," Žižek concludes, "*jouissance* is that notorious *heimliche* which is simultaneously the most *unheimliche*, always-already here and, precisely as such, always-already lost." Engendered in a heterotopic site between home and exile, conjuring up a psychic state where that which was fated to be always-already lost can be enjoyed as something always-already here, the fantasy of *Liebestod* transposes a traumatic knowledge about the inevitability of contingency into a narrative of fate, which allows its two fated to lovers to speak about the primordial loss subtending all efforts of recuperation, even while it functions as a protective fiction, allowing them to misrecognize, and thus continually transpose, the void.

And yet, addressing the traumatic kernel at the heart of human desire, *jouissance* can never be contained nor effaced, even as it also exceeds any one narrative of fate. As I have already suggested, Wagner's libretto splits the femme fatale into two figures—the vengeful Isolde, over whose body a protective fiction of enraptured ecstasy comes to be enacted, and Brangäne, who engenders this transformation of pure death drive into a second-order *jouissance*. It is precisely in the second figure, who warns against the all-encompassing and thus also all-exclusive drive of the *Liebestod,* that I want to locate the voice of feminine *jouissance* in Wagner's libretto. The radicality of this position consists in the fact that, although Brangäne speaks not beyond but from within the symbolic, it is precisely in the way she refuses the temptation of totalizing narratives that she articulates that which is in excess of any one order. In the first act she pits reason against Isolde's mad and vain frenzy, arguing first in favor of Marke's nobility and then, once she recognizes that Isolde's anger is in part fueled by Tristan's requital of her love, invoking the power of her love potion. Finally, after having voiced her horror at Isolde's wish to administer the draft of death, she is also the one who introduces their first duet of love by declaring that the narrative of enraptured passion they are about to proclaim to each other is nothing other than "foolish devotion's deceitful work," a lamentation of "eternal want and pain" (act 1, scene 5). In so doing, she offers us the possibility of ironic distanciation toward both Tristan's belief that his past rejection of Isolde was nothing other than the "deceitful spell of malicious cunning" and Isolde's assurance that her fear that her lover was lost to her was nothing other than "idle and foolish anger." From the start, Wagner's libretto uses Brangäne's repeated interventions to allow for a multiplicity of positions in relation to the *Liebestod* scenario, for she is also the one who explains to the two fated lovers that their sudden ecstasy is nothing other than the result of the draft of love. Although she intends this message to be understood as the reason why they should renounce their enjoyment, the two lovers choose to hear a different message: the permission to cede unconditionally to transgressive *jouissance.* While Isolde falls unconscious into his embrace, Tristan declares, "O rapture rich in deceit! O bliss consecrated to guile!"

In a similar manner, Brangäne warns Isolde in the second act that her drive toward unconditional enjoyment deludes her senses, allowing her to hear only what she wants to while she remains blind to those around her who are planning to betray their transgression to the king. In their debate over whether to extinguish the torch or not, she once more pits the voice of reason, pleading for a self-conscious enjoyment of transgression from within the symbolic, for a recognition that passion is a fiction, resulting from a deceptive draft ("O leave the warning flame, let it show you your danger"), and against Isolde's reckless foreclosure of symbolic law and renunciation of agency. Isolde's banishing of Brangäne's light is meant to signify her total subjugation to the goddess of love—"I have become her property, now let me show my obedience" (act 2, scene 1). Indeed, Brangäne's intervention, admonishing the fated lovers, with her solitary voice, to "Take care! Soon the night will pass" (act 2, scene 1), functions like the castrative law of paternal authority in its effort to break up their dyadic fusion. And yet her broadcast that the ecstasy they are experiencing is not only the fantasy of second-order *jouissance* but necessarily one contained within the symbolic, whose law will inevitably disrupt what cannot be infinitely maintained, only feeds their wish to transgress prohibitions by enjoying the fantasy of an eternal life in death. Put another way, her voice of warning is what guarantees their fantasy of being able to foreclose castration, to renounce renunciation within the realm of human *qua* symbolic existence. Finally, in the third act, her voice speaks out against the collective delusion that has taken hold of all those involved in the *Liebestod* scenario—warning Kurvenal that Marke and his court have come with peaceful intentions, explaining to Isolde that she has revealed the secret of the potion to the king. The ironic distanciation thus introduced by the libretto consists in the following: precisely because her voice not only offers an alternative to the tragic outcome, declaring that no one needs to die, but also represents the position no one heeds, it marks the voice of alterity, against which the delusion of fated love is erected. As such a mark of difference, however, it also gives voice to a contingency which undercuts the narrative of *Liebestod*. Things could have happened differently.

Her intervention is fruitless, of course, because the narrative promise sustaining any cultural representation of the "eternal love between Tristan and Isolde" works with the tacit understanding that the two lovers will abide by the script of fatality that has been preordained for them. And yet the inclusion of Brangäne's voice, engendering, supporting, guarding, but also warning against the totalizing fantasy of

Liebestod, whose fatal deception ultimately consists in the illusory be-lief that the incommensurability between second-order *jouissance* and an enjoyment of the traumatic Thing-*jouissance* can be resolved, calls forth an ineffaceable fissure in Wagner's celebration of recuperative healings. Although the score seeks to seduce us away from the position of reason she represents, Wagner's libretto offers us the choice of this other femi-nine position as both catalyst of fantasy and that to which fantasy must be deaf and dumb so as to play itself out straight down the line. Against the preordained script of fated love—the old melody Tristan hears at birth, signifying the fatedness of his lot, and then again as he lies dying; the melody Isolde in her hallucination hears resonating from Tristan's corpse—she gives voice to the law of pure contingency. Take care! Pre-cisely because night invariably gives way to day, everything could always still turn out differently. Her voice offers a different promise than the *Liebestod,* less enjoyable, perhaps, but also less circular—the promise of agency and intervention. She, too, knows there is nothing to lose in a loss, because the traumatic knowledge of our radical decenterment, which is to say the impossibility of any full mortal *Da-Sein,* is as ir-recuperable as it is ineffaceable. Yet renouncing a renunciation of this knowledge in her case means accepting the symbolic for what it is: the catalyst for viable narratives we construct so as to live, because without such a fallible protection against an unconditional and overabundant proximity of *jouissance* there would be no representation of any kind— no score, no script, no fantasy. In her voice, the gesture of accepting our fate of radical alienation within the symbolic and the gesture of living in ironic distanciation from any one law of fate, though crisscrossed, rest side by side.

Notes

1   Walter Benjamin, "Der Erzähler," In *Illuminationen: Ausgewählte Schriften* (Frankfurt a.M.: Suhrkamp Verlag, 1977), 402.

2   Denis de Rougemont, *L'amour et l'occident* (Paris: Plon, 1972), 27.

3   Michel Foucault, "Of Other Spaces," *Diacritics* 16, no. 1 (spring 1986): 24, 27.

4   Paul Schrader, "Notes on *Film Noir,*" in *Film Noir Reader,* ed. Alain Silver and James Ursini (New York: Limelight Editions, 1996), 53f.

5   Ibid., 54–56. For a discussion of the difficulties involved in defining film noir as a genre, see Michael Walker's excellent "Film Noir: Introduction," in *The Movie Book*

of Film Noir, ed. Ian Cameron (London: Studio Vista, 1992), 8–35. In the same collection of essays, see Richard Maltby, "The Politics of the Maladjusted Text," 39–48,
for a discussion of the postwar climate in Hollywood in the late 1940s, as well as
Deborah Thomas's "How Hollywood Deals with the Deviant Male," 59–70, for a
discussion of how film noir dramatizes points of crisis in the lives of its male protagonists, one of which is the transition between wartime and peace.

6   Walker, "Film Noir," 13.

7   In so doing I follow Cathérine Clément's attempt to explore the ideologically en-
coded family romances played through in nineteenth-century-opera libretti divorced
from the explicit intentions of the composer as well as the librettist in *L'opéra ou la
défaite des femmes* (Paris: Grasset, 1979) without necessarily agreeing with the readings she offers. See also David J. Levin's excellent collection of essays *Opera Through
Other Eyes* (Stanford: Stanford University Press, 1994), where a privileging of the
libretto in view of literary and cultural theory over the more canonical readings by
musicologists serves to uncover overlooked fissures and ambivalences in well-known
operatic texts.

8   Juliet Flower MacCannell, "Jouissance," in *Feminism and Psychoanalysis: A Critical
Dictionary,* ed. Elizabeth Wright (Oxford: Blackwell, 1992), 185–87.

9   Jacques Lacan, "The Subversion of the Subject and the Dialectic of Desire," in *Écrits:
A Selection,* trans. Alan Sheridan (New York: Norton, 1995), 324.

10 Bruce Fink, *A Clinical Introduction to Lacanian Psychoanalysis: Theory and Technique*
(Cambridge: Harvard University Press, 1997), 207. *Jouissance,* he argues, is to be
thought of as a pleasure "beyond the pleasure principle, for it already implies the
existence of other people, their demands, injunctions, desires and values—all of those
things that tie pleasure up in knots, inhibiting it and impeding it" (226). Insofar as
it can be conceived as the "living out of a fantasy regardless of its consequences for
others," the transgression that *jouissance* engenders implies a knowledge of these consequences.

11 Dylan Evans, "Jouissance," in *An Introductory Dictionary of Lacanian Psychoanalysis*
(London: Routledge, 1996), 92.

12 In his formulation, *Le séminaire,* book 17: *L'envers de la psychoanalyse* (Paris: Éditions de Seuil, 1991), 17, Jacques Lacan reformulates Sigmund Freud's discussion of
the death drive as giving articulation to something in the psychic apparatus of the
subject which forces it to move beyond the pleasure principle toward the state of in-
animation and tensionlessness from which all existence emerges. For a discussion of
the gendering implicit in both Freud's concept of the death drive and Lacan's refiguration, see my *Over Her Dead Body: Death, Femininity, and the Aesthetic* (New York:
Routledge, 1992).

13 Jacques Lacan, *Le séminaire,* book 20: *Encore* (Paris: Éditions de Seuil, 1975).

14 Cited in Jacqueline Rose's very informative "Introduction II," in *Feminine Sexuality:
Jacques Lacan and the École freudienne,* ed. Juliet Mitchell and Jaqueline Rose (New
York: W. W. Norton, 1982), 49.

15 Flower MacCannell, "Jouissance," 187. For a discussion of feminine *jouissance,* see

also Danielle Bergeron, "The Letter Against the Phallus: Analysis of the Masculine Position in *Fatal Attraction*," *American Journal of Semiotics* 7, no. 3 (1990): 27–34.

16 Bruce Fink, *The Lacanian Subject: Between Language and Jouissance* (Princeton: Princeton University Press, 1995), 122.

17 In the following I have adapted Lionel Salter's excellent translation of Wagner's libretto, accompanying the recording of the production of *Tristan und Isolde* at the Berliner Staatsoper, under the direction of Daniel Barenboim (Teldec, 1994).

18 Slavoj Žižek, *The Plague of Fantasies* (London: Verso, 1997), 10.

19 Fink, *Clinical Introduction,* 241.

20 For a discussion of cultural configurations of this strangely elusive yet resilient performance of excessive psychic states, see Elisabeth Bronfen, *The Knotted Subject: Hysteria and Its Discontents* (Princeton: Princeton University Press, 1998).

21 For an excellent presentation of the plot summary and analysis of the films belonging to this genre, see Alain Silver and Elizabeth Ward, *Film Noir: An Encyclopedic Reference to the American Style* (Woodstock, Conn.: Overlook Press, 1992).

22 As Elisabeth Cowie, "*Film Noir* and Women," in *Shades of Noir,* ed. Joan Copjec (London: Verso, 1993), compellingly argues, " 'femme fatale' is simply a catch phrase for the danger of sexual difference and the demands and risks desire poses for the man. The male hero often knowingly submits himself to the 'spider-woman'—as Neff does in *Double Indemnity*—for it is precisely her dangerous sexuality that he desires, so that it is ultimately his own perverse desire that is his downfall" (125).

23 As Walker, "Film Noir," 23, notes, the typical noir script is based on a configuration of three interlocking sexual triangles. In the predominant one, the femme fatale is positioned between a husband/order male and the hero. In the second triangulation the hero is positioned betweeen the femme fatale and a domestic woman, and in the third the domestic woman is positioned between the hero and a respectable man. I have argued that, by contrast, Wagner's libretto places the fallible figure of paternal authority between the surrogate son and the reluctant wife, who both betray him, even while each is in turn bound to a same-sex friend, such that the adulterous triangle is structurally counterbalanced by a quartet of two homoerotic couples.

24 I take this point from Slavoj Žižek, who in *The Plague of Fantasies,* 11, argues that one of our most consistent cultural narratives is the one "according to which, with the advent of modernity, the law rooted in concrete traditional communities, and as such still permeated by *jouissance* of a specific 'way of life,' gets split into the neutral symbolic Law and its superego supplement of obscene unwritten rules."

25 Slavoj Žižek, *Enjoy your Symptom: Jacques Lacan in Hollywood and Out* (London: Routledge, 1992), 43.

26 For a reading of *Double Indemnity* as an example how private enjoyment spoils the network of symbolic relations, see Joan Copjec, "The Phenomenal Nonphenomenal," in *Shades of Noir,* 167–95.

27 Wilder's presentation of the bond between Keyes and Neff must be seen within the context of the Hays Production Code, which forbade an explicit presentation of homosexuality; see Leonard J. Leff and Jerold L. Simmons, *The Dame in the Kimono:*

Hollywood, Censorship, and the Production Code from the 1920s to the 1960s (New York: Doubleday, 1990). For a discussion of the presence of homoeroticism in film noir, see Leighton Grist, "Out of the Past," in Cameron, *Film Noir*.

28 As Peter William Evans in Cameron, *Film Noir*, notes, Phyllis Dietrichson "seems beyond sexuality, an idol of limitless self-engrossed and cruel fatality, rather than of illicit passion." Paradoxically, he adds, "Stanwyck's portrayal of ice-cool, self-conscious and calculating evil creates an image of such compelling egocentricity that it all but destroys the viewer's sympathy for Neff, Mr. Dietrichson, or any of the other men who may have been her victims" (169).

29 Fink, *The Lacanian Subject*, 60.

30 See Sigmund Freud, *Beyond the Pleasure Principle*, in *The Standard Edition*, ed. James Strachey, vol. 18 (London: Hogarth Press, 1955), 3–66.

9

The Thing from

Slavoj Žižek   **Inner Space**

Jacques Lacan defines art itself with regard to the Thing: in his seminar entitled *The Ethics of Psychoanalysis,* he claims that art as such is always organized around the central void of the impossible-real Thing— a statement which, perhaps, should be read as a variation on Rilke's old thesis that beauty is the last veil that covers the horrible.[1] Lacan gives some hints about how this surrounding of the void functions in the visual arts and in architecture; here we shall not provide an account of how, in cinematic art also, the field of the visible, of representations, involves reference to some central and structural void, to the impossibility attached to it (ultimately, therein resides the point of the notion of suture in cinema theory). What I propose to do is something much more naive and abrupt: to analyze the way the motif of the Thing appears within the diegetic space of cinematic narrative—in short, to speak about films whose narrative deals with some impossible or traumatic Thing, like the alien Thing in science-fiction horror films.[2] What better proof of the fact that this Thing comes from inner space than the very first scene of *Star Wars?* At first, all we see is the void—the infinite dark sky, the ominously silent abyss of the universe, with dispersed twinkling stars which are not so much material objects as abstract points, markers of space coordinates, virtual objects; then, all of a sudden, in Dolby stereo, we hear a thundering sound coming from behind our backs, from our innermost background, later rejoined by the visual object, the source of this sound—the gigantic spaceship, a kind of space version of the *Titanic*— which triumphantly enters the frame of screen reality. The object-Thing is thus clearly rendered as a part of *ourselves* that we eject into reality. This intrusion of the massive Thing seems to bring relief, canceling the *horror vacui* of staring at the infinite void of the universe. However, what if its actual effect is the exact opposite? What if the true horror is that of something—the intrusion of some excessive massive Real—where we expect nothing? This experience of "something (the stain of the Real) instead of nothing" is perhaps at the root of the metaphysical question "Why is there something instead of nothing?"

"There Is No Sexual Relationship"

The exemplary case of the Thing is, of course, the mysterious undead alien object falling from the universe, an object which is inhuman, but nonetheless alive and often even possessing an evil will of its own, from *The Thing* to the more recent *Smilla's Sense of Snow*. However, one should not forget that one of Lacan's examples of *das Ding* in his seminar *The Ethics of Psychoanalysis* is Harpo Marx, the mute Marx brother, identified as the monster apropos of whom we are never sure if he is a witty genius or a total imbecile, in whom childish innocence and goodness overlap with extreme corruption and sexual dissolution, so that one does not know where one stands with him: does he stand for the Edenic, prelapsarian innocence or for the utter egotism which does not know of the difference between good and evil?[3] This absolute undecidability —or, rather, incommensurability—makes him a monstrous Thing, an Other *qua* Thing, not an intersubjective partner, but a thoroughly *inhuman* partner. (As has already been pointed out, the three brothers perfectly fit the Freudian triad of ego [Chico], superego [Groucho], and id [Harpo]. This is why the fourth, Zeppo, had to be excluded: there was no place for him in the triad.) This Thing can also be a montrous animal, from King Kong through Moby-Dick to the gigantic white buffalo—obviously a new version of Moby-Dick, the white whale—in J. Lee Thompson's *The White Buffalo*. In this weird, highly idiosyncratic film, Wild Bill Hickok, now an old man, returns to the Wild West, haunted in his dreams by the apparition of a white buffalo (also a sacred Native American animal); the whole movie points toward the staging and organizing of the scene of the final confrontation, when, on a narrow mountain pass, the buffalo will attack the hero and he will kill it. Significantly, Bronson wears dark glasses, the codified sign of the blinded gaze and of impotence, that is, castration (Bronson's impotence is clearly stated in the film: when he meets his old love, Poker Jenny, he is unable to fulfill her expectations and engage in sexual intercourse with her).[4] It would be easy to propose here the elementary Freudian reading: the white buffalo is the primordial father who is not yet dead and who, as such, blocks the hero's sexual potency—his desperate sound is homologous to that of the shofar in Jewish religion; the scene the hero endeavors to stage is thus that of the parricide. However, a further crucial feature is that the Thing (the white buffalo) is linked not only to the motif of sexual impotence, but also to the destructive nature of American capitalism: when Hickok arrives at the final train station, he sees a mountain of white bones of the thousands of slaughtered buffalo (and, as we know from history, he was responsible for much of this mass killing). The white buffalo is thus clearly a kind of revenge ghost of all the dead buffalos. (Hickok is also presented as the Indian killer; his acts in the film—befriending an Indian warrior who is also tracking down the buffalo—are acts of coming to terms with his murderous past in the service of the American colonization of the West.)

What is of special interest to our psychoanalytic perspective is, of course, the way this Thing—precisely insofar as it is in itself asexual—is inherently related to sexual difference: does not the gigantic volcanic rock north of Melbourne in Peter Weir's *Picnic at Hanging Rock* function as another version of such a Thing, more precisely, as a forbidden domain (zone, to be precise) in which ordinary mores are somehow suspended—where, once we enter it, the obscene secrets of sexual enjoyment become accessible? *Picnic* focuses on the strange events that took place at Appleyard College, an upper-class girls' school north of Melbourne, on Saint Valentine's Day, 14 February 1900, when the girls go on a picnic at Hanging Rock, a natural monument formed of ancient lava. (This introduces the first element of mystery: although a persistent rumor asserts that the movie is based on a real-life mysterious disappearance, there is no basis whatsoever for this claim. Why has this conviction persisted for decades without any foundation in fact?) Before leaving, the angelic blond Miranda tells her orphan friend, Sarah, that she will not be at the school much longer. While having their picnic, four of the girls—Miranda, the rich heiress Irma, the rational Marion, and the ugly Edith—decide to explore the rocks. Edith, fatigued and cranky, does not want to go on as the others do; she becomes frightened of something and runs screaming back to the picnic. The other three girls and Miss McCraw, one of their teachers, disappear in the Rock. Two boys who saw the girls while they were approaching the Rock go looking for them. While looking, one of the boys, the rich Michael, becomes delirious and injures himself on the rocks. He has found Irma, though: Irma is still alive, but she cannot remember anything that happened to her. Mrs. Appleyard, the headmistress with a drinking problem, decides that Sarah will not attend the college anymore because she is not receiving money from her guardian. After she tells Sarah of her fate, to go back to the orphanage, she pushes Sarah off the roof of the building (or did Sarah herself commit suicide?). Some days later, Mrs. Appleyard herself dies trying to climb Hanging Rock. What makes the enigma of Hanging Rock so interesting is the sheer multiplicity of interpretations the story suggests. At the level of "literal" solution to the mystery, there are five possibilities:

—the simple, natural explanation: three girls and one of their mistresses fell into one of the deep crevices in the intricate stone structure of the Rock, or were killed by the spiders and snakes which abound there;

—the criminal-sexual explanation: they were abducted, raped, and killed on the Rock, either by some sinister aborigines lurking there in wait for innocent visitors or by Michael and Albert, the two young male characters who obviously find the girls attractive and later save one of them;

—the sexual-pathological explanation: the girls' erotic repression led them to a violent, self-destructive hysterical outburst;

—the primitive-religion supernatural explanation: the spirit of the mountain abducted these intruders, selecting only those who were attuned to its mode (and for that reason rejecting the fat fourth girl with no feeling for sensual mysteries);

—the alien-abduction explanation: the girls entered a different time and space zone. (Incidentally, Joan Lindsay, the author of the novel on which the film is based, seemed to prefer a combination of these last two explanations in the eighteenth chapter of the novel, titled "The Secret of Hanging Rock" and published only in 1987, after her death.)

On top of these, there are at least two "metaphoric" explanations: the story is based on the opposition between the stiff disciplinary Victorian atmosphere of the boarding school, located in an old, neat house, and natural, thriving, unconstrained life, located in the wild protuberance of the Rock. The stiff school atmosphere resonates with just-beneath-the-surface eroticism (semirepressed lesbian longings of students for students, of students for teachers, and teachers for students). In contrast to this proverbial Victorian stiffness with its repressed longings, the Rock stands for the unbridled thriving of life in all its detailed, often disgusting shapes (Weir gives us close-ups of reptiles and snakes, associated with original sin, crawling around the sleeping girls, not to mention the wild, lush vegetation and flocks of birds).[5] So what could be more obvious than to read the story of the disappearance as a variation on the old topic of Victorian repression exploding into the open? The frigid Miss McCraw, the mathematics teacher, describes the birth of the Rock as the molten lava being "forced up from down below . . . extruded in a highly viscous state," more a description of hormones slowly awakening in the repressed pubescent girls than a natural phenomenon, a volcanic protuberance from the great depths of the earth. The Rock thus obviously stands for the unbridled life passion long controlled by social mores and finally erupting. It is also possible to give this an anticolonialist twist: the Rock's evil act of abduction stands for resistance to English colonization (although, of course, such a sexualized notion of the Rock's revenge tells more about the phantasmatic content that colonialists have projected into the colonized Other than about this Other itself). In this reading, the Rock signals the elementary "passionate attachments" which take their revenge and undermine the disciplined routine of the school: at the end, even Mrs. Appleyard, the authoritarian headmistress, loses control of herself, goes to the mountain, and kills herself there by jumping from a high rock.

While the film does not resolve the enigma, it provides numerous hints which point to all these different directions (the strange red cloud seen when the girls disappeared points to the spirit of the mountain as the agent of abduction; the fact that all watches stopped at noon on the day of the picnic, the total amnesia of the survivors, and identical wounds on their foreheads are standard signs of alien abduction and transposition into a different "time zone"). However, the pervasive atmosphere is that of predestined doom (what happened was somehow ordained to happen, not a series of accidents, and it is as if Miranda, the angelic girl who leads the group to the mountain, had a presentiment of this fate), identified with a nonphallic, nonheterosexual eroticism: although the eroticization of the Rock and its fatal attraction is obvious (Irma, the only surviving girl, is properly dressed when found, but significantly, when they undress her to put her to bed, she is without her corset, the symbol of Victorian constraint; Miss McCraw, the frigid mathematics teacher who also disappears in the Rock, is last seen walking toward it, blind to her surroundings, as if strangely possessed by it, and without her skirt, i.e., only in her underpants), the story emphasizes that the girls were not raped (the doctor examining the surviving Irma reassures everyone that her hymen is "quite intact"). More than the standard phallic sexual experience, the Rock stands for the primordial experience of libido, of life in its unbridled thriving, perhaps for what Lacan had in mind with *jouissance féminine*. (Therein resides the difference between this story and *A Passage to India*, in which an unresolved sexual enigma also occurs in the cave of a gigantic rock: although *A Passage to India* is much more complex in its description of colonialist deadlocks, it deals unambiguously with a sexually frustrated heroine longing for the standard heterosexual experience.)

It is crucial that the only sex in the film is between the school's least refined and therefore least repressed inhabitants, the servants Tom and Minnie, who are totally indifferent to the spell of the Rock. The standard explanation would therefore be that the excessive, suffocating fatal sensuality of the Rock affects only those who are under the spell of the Victorian repression. But what if we turn this account around (repression prevents healthy sexual satisfaction and thus breeds misty, decadently spiritualized, perverted global sexualization) and posit that "straight" heterosexuality itself is based on the repression of some more primordial same-sex "passionate attachments," so that, paradoxically, the Victorian repression of heterosexuality itself is sustained by and enables the return of much more radically repressed attitudes? Freud emphasized that the repression of heterosexual urges can only be sustained if it draws its energy from the reactivation of much more primitive prephallic drives: paradoxically, repression on behalf of culture has to rely on libidinal regression. Here we have libidinal reflexivity at its purest: the very repression of (phallic) sexuality is sexualized and mobilizes forms of prephallic perversity. One is reminded here of Elizabeth Cowie's reading of the famous concluding lines of Bette Davis to her lover in *Now,*

Voyager, explaining why they should renounce further sexual contacts: "Why reach for the moon when we can have the stars?" Why straight heterosexual copulation, when, if we renounce it, I can have the much more intense pleasures of lesbian "primordial attachments"?

This is why poor Miss McCraw, the least sexualized of the teachers, this model of frigidity (measured by heterosexual standards), is the only one who joins the three girls and (in the eighteenth chapter) reappears as a mysterious, obscenely sexualized "Clown-Woman." And if we follow this line of reasoning to the end, do we not have to reinterpret the figure of the headmistress herself? What if, far from being simply its opposite, Mrs. Appleyard in a way *is* the Rock? What if her final suicide on the slopes of the Rock, rather than signaling her defeat in the face of the primordial passions of the Rock, points to their ultimate identity?

And does all this not hold even for *Titanic?* Not only is the *Titanic* a Thing par excellence, as the mysterious object dwelling in the deep of the ocean, so that when humans approached it and made photos of it, this disturbing of the wreck's peace was experienced as the transgressive entry into a forbidden domain; perhaps the key to James Cameron's *Titanic* success is the way this film implicitly relates the Thing to the deadlocks of sexual relationship. In contrast to the standard story of a catastrophe, in which the outburst of catastrophe (earthquake, floods, etc.) allows people to overcome their narrow conflicts and generates new global social solidarity, the catastrophe in *Titanic* renders visible the subterranean social tensions between higher and lower classes; it is after the catastrophe that these tensions fully explode. But again, we see how this is framed by the topic of the production of a couple. The moment of the accident is crucial here: it occurs directly after the sexual act, as if the crash were a punishment for the (sexually and socially) transgressive act. More precisely, the crash occurs when Rose proclaims that in New York she will abandon her old life and join Jack. Of course, this would have been the true catastrophe, the ultimate disappointment—could she in fact live happily ever after with him, a vagabond without a proper home and financial means?—so it is as if the iceberg hits the ship, the catastrophe occurs, in order to prevent or occlude the much stronger libidinal catastrophe and disappointment of two lovers who are happy together but then see their union degenerate. This is Hollywood at its purest: the catastrophe (the iceberg hitting the ship) is reinterpreted as an answer of the Real to the deadlock of the creation of the couple. The creation of the heterosexual love couple is the ultimate hermeneutic frame of reference of the meaning of the film.

From the Lacanian perspective, the ideological mystification is thus here double. First, the catastrophe of the iceberg striking in order to prevent the true libidinal catastrophe (i.e., the fact that in America their union will probably fall apart soon enough, that this transgression of class barriers will end in failure): the iceberg catastrophe helps us to sustain the illusion that if the iceberg had not hit the ship, the couple would have lived happily ever after. However, on a deeper level, the very idea that it is the class distinction which is to be blamed for the failure of their relationship obfuscates the fact that this relationship was doomed to fail for a priori structural reasons ("there is no sexual relationship"). Putting the blame on class distinctions is also a lure, a decoy enabling us to avoid the acknowledgment of the inherent impossibility of sexual relationship, that is, it enables us to sustain the fantasy that, in a classless society, a full sexual relationship will finally be within reach.

Against this background one can also properly locate one of the surprisingly refined moments in *Titanic*, which occurs when Jack passes away in the freezing water, with Rose safe on a floating piece of wood, desperately clutching his hands. Upon noticing that she is holding a corpse, Rose exclaims, "Nothing can take us apart! I'll never let you go!" However, the act that accompanies these pathetic words is exactly that gesture of *letting him go*, of gently pushing him away, so that he is sucked into the dark water.

Rather than a full lover, then, Jack is a kind of vanishing mediator for Kate: when her ego is shattered, he restores her mirror image to her (by literally drawing her idealized image) and then, after sacrificing himself fully for her and giving her final instructions ("You will have a lot of children, lead a long life"), graciously disappears into the abyss of the ocean and so erases himself from the picture. So, more than a story of the constitution of the couple, *Titanic* is a film about the restoration of the full narcissistic self-image of a woman. Rose identifies herself after her survival to the officer as "Rose Dawson," taking Jack's name. However, the problem with this is not so much that her liberation is identified with the assumption of the male name, but in the fact that *he* had to die in order for this to be possible. So there is a limit to Cameron's Hollywood Marxism: although one is tempted to admire the simple beauty and cinematic efficiency of the film's very last shot, which repeats the earlier scene in which Jack approaches Rose on the luxurious staircase to attend the first-class dinner to which he was invited for saving her, but this time as a classless dream (passengers from all classes, from the Captain to the third-class immigrants, watch the couple unite and applaud them, with Jack dressed in his normal working-class attire), we learn that after the catastrophe Rose continued to lead an upper-class life—Jack, a vanishing mediator, was to be rejected after he fulfilled his mission of liberating her from the suffocating constraints of her class prejudices. At the film's end, the old Rose throws the big diamond into the sea: throughout the film, the problem has been accepting the loss of some precious object as the price of becoming mature. Ultimately, this object is Jack himself, whose disappearance in the depths is correlative with the diamond's disappearance. This also accounts for the fact that when the ship sinks, the couple jumps into the sea from the very place (the extreme stern of the ship) from which Rose wanted to jump when Jack approached her for the first time and pretended to be ready to join her in her jump in order to dissuade her from doing it: her first jump would have been the suicidal attempt of an immature, spoiled, and disappointed brat, while her second jump, together with Jack, involves a mature person's decision to embrace life.[6]

Cameron's *The Abyss* (1989), his neglected masterpiece, is a kind of *Titanic* in reverse. That is to say, it is interesting to note to what extent the general dispositif of *The Abyss* and (the beginning of) *Titanic* are the same: a group of researchers on the ocean surface trying to penetrate the depths and contact the Thing at the bottom. However, in *Titanic,* the Thing—the ship—goes down, disappears into the ocean, while at the end of *The Abyss,* the Thing from the bottom of the ocean—the alien spaceship—triumphantly (re)appears on the ocean's surface. In both cases, this (dis)appearance is linked to the creation of the couple: in *Titanic,* the Thing sinks to maintain the illusion of a possible happy outcome of the love couple's decision to live together; in *The Abyss,* the Thing appears to restore the failed marriage of the scientist and the deep-sea diver, played by Ed Harris and Mary Elizabeth Mastrantonio, by compelling them to rediscover their love. *The Abyss* is thus distinguished by two interconnected features: the Alien Thing at the bottom of the ocean is fundamentally benevolent, not destructive, and its emergence is inscribed into the Hollywood matrix of the creation of the couple.

However, the climax of *The Abyss*, on account of which the film is nonetheless superior to the standard version of its formula, is the magic scene of communication between the couple of the scientist wife and her deep-sea-diver ex-husband: the ex-husband, after submerging his head in a strange pink liquid (allegedly fluorocarbon) that will enable him to breathe directly through water, without air, as in the prenatal state, dives quickly to the bottom of the ocean, where the alien Thing is located. Crucial here is the material dispositif of their communication: since his head floats in the liquid, he cannot speak, so, while he can hear his wife talking to him through the microphone, he has to type his messages back to her on a small computerlike board attached to his left hand. This dispositif nicely renders the fact that they now inhabit different ontological levels: she remains in the normal surface reality of spoken word, while he "regresses" to another zone, to the incestuous, intrauterine, prenatal state of floating in liquid (when his head is submerged in the breathing liquid, he first reacts to it with traumatic convulsions, but his colleague calms him down: "Don't you worry, it will take just a couple of seconds! The body knows how to do it, it was doing it for nine months—it just has to remember again!"). Direct communication or interaction is thus no longer feasible: she can be heard by him, while his presence is reduced to typed signs that appear on the computer screen. Of course, the old pathetic family-drama scenario is now played out: it is only now, when they inhabit different ontological domains, that they can openly act out their drama. She soon becomes emotional, pouring her heart out to him, staging a true hysterical performance, slowly losing contact with him because of his immersion in the self-enclosed prenatal sphere. At a different level, this scene is comparable to the famous scene in Wim Wenders's *Paris, Texas*, where Harry Dean Stanton communicates through the peep-show mirror with Nastassja Kinski. The underlying idea here is that something akin to authentic communication can only take place when the barrier separating the couple is insurmountable, when each of them inhabits a different ontological space. It is crucial that while she speaks, he writes, emitting signs from a domain which is no longer that of the signifier: women are constrained to the hysterical symbolic outburst of desire, while men are allowed to enter and float in the bliss of the zone's drive.[7]

In the latest in the series of cosmic catastrophe films, Mimi Leder's *Deep Impact* (1998), the Thing is a gigantic comet threatening to hit the earth and extinguish all life for two years. At the film's end, the earth is saved due to the heroic, suicidal action of a group of astronauts with atomic weapons: only a small fragment of the comet falls into the ocean east of New York. Still, it causes a colossal, hundreds-of-yards-high wave that flushes the entire northeast coast of the United States, including New York and Washington. This comet-Thing also creates a couple, but an unexpected one: the incestuous couple of the young, obviously neurotic, sexually inactive television reporter (Téa Leoni) and her promiscuous father (Maximilian Schell), who has divorced her mother and just married a young woman the same age as his daughter. It is clear that the film is effectively a drama about this unresolved proto-incestuous father-daughter relationship: the threatening comet obviously gives body to the self-destructive rage of the heroine, without a boyfriend, with an obvious traumatic fixation on her father, flabbergasted by her father's remarriage, and unable to come to terms with the fact that he has abandoned her for her peer. The president (played by Morgan Freeman, in a politically correct vein), who, in a broadcast to the nation, announces the looming catastrophe, acts as the ideal counterpoint to the obscene real father, as a caring paternal figure (without a noticeable wife!) who, significantly, gives her a privileged role at the press conference, allowing her to ask the first questions. The comet's link with the dark, obscene underside of paternal authority is made clear in the way the heroine gets in touch with the president: in her investigation, she discovers an impending financial scandal (large illegal government spending) connected with "ELLE." Her first idea, of course, is that the president himself is involved in a sex scandal and that "Elle" refers to his mistress. She then discovers the truth: "E.L.E" is a code name for the emergency measures to be taken when an accident that could lead to total extinction of life threatens Earth, and the government has secretly been spending funds to build a gigantic underground shelter in which one million Americans would be able to survive the catastrophe. The approaching comet is thus clearly a metaphoric substitute for paternal infidelity, for the libidinal catastrophe of a daughter facing the fact that her obscene father has chosen another young woman over her. The entire machinery of the global catastrophe is thus set in motion so that the father's young wife will abandon him, and the father will return— not to his wife, the heroine's mother, but to her daughter. The culmina- tion of the film is the scene in which the heroine rejoins her father, who, alone in his luxurious seaside house, awaits the impending wave. She finds him walking along the shoreline; they make peace with each other and embrace, silently awaiting the wave. The wave approaches, and as it casts its large shadow over them, she draws herself closer to her father, gently crying "Daddy!," as if to search for protection in him, reconsti- tuting the childhood scene of a small girl safeguarded by the father's loving embrace; a second later they are both swept away by the gigantic wave. The heroine's helplessness and vulnerability in this scene should not deceive us: she is the evil spirit who, in the underlying libidinal ma- chinery of the film's narrative, pulls the strings, and this scene of finding death in the protective father's embrace is the realization of her ultimate wish.[8] Here we are at the opposite extreme from *Forbidden Planet:* in both cases we are dealing with an incestuous father-daughter relation- ship, yet while in *Forbidden Planet* the destructive monster materializes the father's incestuous death wish, in *Deep Impact* it materializes the daughter's. The scene on the waterfront with the gigantic wave sweep- ing away the embraced daughter and father is to be read against the background of the standard Hollywood motif (rendered famous in Fred Zinnemann's *From Here to Eternity*) of the couple (Burt Lancaster and Deborah Kerr) making love on the beach, brushed by waves. In *Deep Impact,* the couple is the truly deadly, incestuous one, not the straight one, so the wave is the gigantic killing wave, not the modest shake of small beach breakers.

The Id Machine

Furthermore, I want to focus on the specific version of this Thing: the Thing as the space (the sacred or forbidden zone) in which the gap be- tween the symbolic and the Real is closed, that is, in which, to put it somewhat bluntly, our desires are directly materialized (or, to put it in the precise terms of Kant's transcendental idealism, the zone in which our intuition becomes directly productive—the state of things which, according to Kant, characterizes only the infinite divine reason).

This notion of the Thing as the id machine, a mechanism that directly materializes our unacknowledged fantasies, possesses a long if not always respectable pedigree. In cinema, it all began with Fred Wilcox's *Forbidden Planet* (1956), which transposed onto a distant planet the story skeleton of Shakespeare's *The Tempest*: a father living alone with his daughter (who had never met another man) on an island, their peace suddenly disturbed by the intrusion of an expedition. In *Forbidden Planet*, the mad-genius scientist (Walter Pidgeon) lives alone on a distant planet with his daughter (Anne Francis), when their peace is disturbed by the arrival of a group of space travelers. Strange attacks by an invisible monster soon begin, and at the film's end, it becomes clear that this monster is nothing but the materialization of the father's destructive impulses against the intruders who disturbed his incestuous peace. (Retroactively, we can thus read the tempest itself from Shakespeare's play as the materialization of the raging of the paternal superego.) The id machine that, unbeknownst to the father, generates the destructive monster is a gigantic mechanism beneath the surface of the planet, the mysterious remnants of some past civilization that had succeeded in developing such a machine for the direct materialization of one's thoughts and thus destroyed itself. Here, the id machine is firmly set in a Freudian libidinal context: the monsters it generates are the realizations of the primordial father's incestuous destructive impulses against other men threatening his symbiosis with the daughter.

The ultimate variation of this motif of the id machine is arguably Andrei Tarkovsky's *Solaris,* based on Stanislaw Lem's novel, in which this Thing is also related to the deadlocks of sexual relationship. *Solaris* is the story of a space-agency psychologist, Kelvin, sent to a half-abandoned spaceship above a newly discovered planet, Solaris, where recently strange things have been taking place (scientists going mad, hallucinating, and killing themselves). Solaris is a planet with an oceanic fluid surface that moves incessantly and, from time to time, imitates recognizable forms—not only elaborate geometric structures, but also gigantic children's bodies or human buildings. Although all attempts to communicate with the planet fail, scientists entertain the hypothesis that Solaris is a gigantic brain which somehow reads our minds. Soon after his arrival, Kelvin finds at his side in his bed his dead wife, Harey, who, years ago on Earth, killed herself after he abandoned her. He is unable to shake Harey off, and all attempts to get rid of her fail miserably (after

he sends her into space with a rocket, she rematerializes the next day).
Analysis of her tissue demonstrates that she is not composed of atoms
like normal human beings—beneath a certain microlevel, there is nothing, just void. Finally, Kelvin grasps that Harey is a materialization of
his own innermost traumatic fantasies. This accounts for the enigma of
strange gaps in Harey's memory—of course she does not know everything a real person is supposed to know, because she is not such a person, but a mere materialization of his phantasmatic image of her in all its
inconsistency. The problem is that precisely because Harey has no substantial identity of her own, she acquires the status of the Real that forever insists and returns to its place: like fire in David Lynch's films, she
forever "walks with the hero," sticks to him, never lets him go. Harey,
this fragile specter, pure semblance, *cannot ever be erased*—she is "undead," eternally recurring in the space between the two deaths. Are we
thus not back at the standard Weiningerian antifeminist notion of the
woman as a symptom of man, a materialization of his guilt, his fall into
sin, who can only deliver him (and herself) by her suicide? *Solaris* thus
relies on science-fiction rules to enact in reality itself, to present as a material fact, the notion that woman merely materializes a male fantasy:
the tragic position of Harey is that she becomes aware that she is deprived of all substantial identity, that she is Nothing in herself, since she
only exists as the Other's dream, insofar as the Other's fantasies turn
around her. It is this predicament that imposes suicide as her ultimate
ethical act: becoming aware of how he suffers on account of her permanent presence, Harey finally destroys herself by swallowing chemical
stuff that will prevent her recomposition. (The ultimate horror scene of
the movie takes place when the spectral Harey reawakens from her first
failed suicide attempt on Solaris: after ingesting liquid oxygen, she lies
on the floor, deeply frozen; then, all of a sudden, she starts to move, her
body twitching in a mixture of erotic beauty and abject horror, sustaining unbearable pain. Is there anything more tragic than such a scene of
the failed self-erasure, when we are reduced to the obscene slime which,
against our will, persists in the picture?) At the novel's end, we find
Kelvin alone on the spaceship, staring into the mysterious surface of the
Solaris ocean.

In her reading of the Hegelian dialectics of lord and bondsman, Judith
Butler focuses on the hidden contract between the two: "the imperative

to the bondsman consists in the following formulation: you be my body for me, but do not let me know that the body that you are is my body." [10] The disavowal on the part of the lord is thus double: first, the lord disavows his own body, posturing as a disembodied desire and compelling the bondsman to act as his body; second, the bondsman has to disavow acting merely as the lord's body and must act as an autonomous agent, as if the bondsman's bodily laboring for the lord is not imposed on him but is autonomous.[11] This structure of double (and thereby self-effacing) disavowal also renders the patriarchal matrix of the relationship between man and woman: in a first move, woman is posited as a mere projection or reflection of man, his insubstantial shadow, hysterically imitating but never able really to acquire the moral stature of a fully constituted self-identical subjectivity; however, this status of a mere reflection itself has to be disavowed and the woman provided with a false autonomy, as if she acts the ways she does within the logic of patriarchy on account of her own autonomous logic (women are "by nature" submissive, compassionate, self-sacrificing, etc.). The paradox not to be missed here is that the bondsman (servant) is all the more the servant, the more he (mis)perceives his position as that of an autonomous agent. The same goes for woman: the ultimate form of her servitude is to (mis)perceive herself, when she acts in a "feminine" submissive-compassionate way, as an autonomous agent. For that reason, the Weiningerian ontological denigration of woman as a mere "symptom" of man—as the embodiment of male fantasy, the hysterical imitation of the true male subjectivity—is, when openly admitted and fully assumed, far more subversive than the false direct assertion of feminine autonomy. Perhaps the ultimate feminist statement is to proclaim openly, "I do not exist in myself, I am merely the Other's fantasy embodied." [12]

What we have in *Solaris* are thus Harey's *two* suicides: the first in her earlier, earthly, "real" existence, as Kelvin's wife, and her second as the heroic act of self-erasure of her very spectral undead existence. While the first suicide was a simple escape from the burden of life, the second is a proper ethical act. In other words, if the first Harey, before her suicide on Earth, was a "normal human being," the second one is a Subject in the most radical sense of the term, precisely insofar as she is deprived of the last vestiges of her substantial identity (as she says in the film: "No, it's not me . . . It's not me . . . I'm not Harey . . . Tell me . . . tell me . . .

Do you find me disgusting because of what I am?"). The difference between Harey, who appears to Kelvin, and the "monstrous Aphrodite," who appears to Gibarian, one of Kelvin's colleagues on the spaceship (in the novel, not in the film: in the film, Tarkovsky replaces her with a small innocent blonde girl), is that Gibarian's apparition does not come from "real-life" memory, but from pure fantasy: "A giant Negress was coming silently towards me with a smooth, rolling gait. I caught a gleam from the whites of her eyes and heard the soft slapping of her bare feet. She was wearing nothing but a yellow skirt of plaited straw; her enormous breasts swung freely and her black arms were as thick as thighs."[13] Unable to sustain confrontation with his primordial maternal phantasmatic apparition, Gibarian dies of shame.

Is the planet around which the story turns, composed of the mysterious matter which seems to think, that is, which in a way is the direct materialization of Thought itself, not again an exemplary case of the Lacanian Thing as the "obscene jelly,"[14] the traumatic Real, the point at which symbolic distance collapses, the point at which there is no need for speech, for signs, since in it thought directly intervenes in the Real? This gigantic Brain, this Other-Thing, involves a kind of psychotic short circuit: in short-circuiting the dialectic of question and answer, of demand and its satisfaction, it provides—or, rather, imposes on us—the answer before we even raise the question, directly materializing our innermost fantasies which support our desire. Solaris is a machine that generates and materializes in reality itself my ultimate phantasmatic objectal supplement or partner, which I would never be ready to accept in reality, although my entire psychic life turns around it.

Jacques-Alain Miller[15] draws the distinction between the woman who assumes her nonexistence, her constitutive lack ("castration"), that is, the void of subjectivity in her very heart, and what he calls *la femme à postiche*, the fake, phony woman. This *femme à postiche* is not what commonsense conservative wisdom would tell us (a woman who distrusts her natural charm and abandons her vocation of rearing children, serving her husband, taking care of the household, etc., and indulges in the extravaganzas of fashionable dressing and make-up, of decadent promiscuity, of career, etc.), but almost its exact opposite: the woman who takes refuge from the void in the very heart of her subjectivity, from the "not-having-it" which marks her being, in the phony certitude of "having it" (of serving as the stable support of family life, of rearing children, her true possession, etc.)—this woman gives the impression (and has the false satisfaction) of a firmly anchored being, of a self-enclosed life, a satisfied circuit of everyday life: her man has to run around wildly while she leads a calm life and serves as the safe protective rock or safe haven to which her man can always return. (The most elementary form of "having it" for a woman is, of course, having a child, which is why, for Lacan, there is an ultimate antagonism between Woman and Mother: in contrast to woman, who *n'existe pas,* mother definitely *does* exist.) The interesting feature to be noted here is that contrary to the commonsensical expectation, it is the woman who "has it," the self-satisfied *femme à postiche* disavowing her lack, who not only does not pose any threat to the patriarchal male identity, but even serves as its protective shield and support, while, in contrast to her, it is the woman who flaunts her lack ("castration"), posing as a hysterical composite of semblances covering a void, who poses the serious threat to male identity. In other words, the paradox is that the more the woman is denigrated, reduced to an inconsistent and insubstantial composite of semblances around a void, the more she threatens the firm male substantial self-identity (Otto Weininger's entire work centers on this paradox); and, on the other hand, the more the woman is a firm, self-enclosed substance, the more she supports male identity.

This opposition, a key constituent of Tarkovsky's universe, finds its clearest expression in his *Nostalgia,* whose hero, the Russian writer wandering around northern Italy in search of manuscripts of a nineteenth-century Russian composer who lived there, is split between Eugenia, the hysterical woman, a being-of-lack trying desperately to seduce him in order to get sexual satisfaction, and his memory of the maternal figure of the Russian wife he has left behind. Tarkovsky's universe is intensely male centered, oriented on the opposition woman-mother: the sexually active, provocative woman (whose attraction is communicated by a series of coded signals, like the long, loose hair of Eugenia in *Nostalgia*) is rejected as an inauthentic hysterical creature and contrasted to the maternal figure (with her closely bound and secured hair). For Tarkovsky, the moment a woman accepts the role of being sexually desirable, she sacrifices what is most precious in her, the spiritual essence of her being, and thus devalues herself and embraces a sterile mode of existence. Tarkovsky's universe is permeated by a barely concealed disgust for a provocative woman; to this figure, prone to hysterical incertitudes, he prefers the mother's assuring and stable presence. This disgust is clearly discernible in the hero's (and director's) attitude toward Eugenia's long, hysterical outburst of accusations against him which precedes her abandonment of him.

It is against this background that one should account for Tarkovsky's recourse to static long shots (or shots which allow only a slow panning or tracking movement). These shots can work in two opposite ways, both of them exemplarily at work in *Nostalgia*: they rely either on a harmonious relationship with their content, signaling the longed-for spiritual reconciliation found not in elevation from the gravitational force of the earth but in a full surrender to its inertia (like the longest shot in his entire opus, the extremely slow passage of the Russian hero through the empty cracked pool with a lit candle, the meaningless test the dead Domenico ordains him to accomplish as the path to his salvation; significantly, at the end, when, after a failed attempt, the hero does reach the other border of the pool, he collapses in death, fully satisfied and reconciled), or, even more interestingly, on a contrast between form and content, like the long shot of Eugenia's hysterical outburst against the hero, a mixture of sexually provocative, seductive gestures with contemptous, dismissive remarks. In this shot, it is as if Eugenia protests not only against the hero's tired indifference, but also, in a way, against the calm indifference of the static long shot itself, which does not let itself be disturbed by her outburst. Tarkovsky is here at the very opposite extreme from John Cassavetes, in whose masterpieces the (feminine) hysterical outbursts are shot by a hand-held camera in extreme close-up, as if the camera itself were drawn into the dynamic hysterical outburst, strangely deforming the enraged faces and thereby losing the stability of its own point of view.

Solaris nonetheless supplements this standard, although disavowed, male scenario with a key feature: this structure of woman as a symptom of man can be operative only insofar as the man is confronted with his Other Thing, a decentered opaque machine which "reads" his deepest dreams and returns them to him as his symptom, as his own message in its true form, which the subject is not ready to acknowledge. It is here that one should reject the Jungian reading of *Solaris*. The point

of Solaris is not simply projection, materialization of the (male) subject's disavowed inner impetuses; what is much more crucial is that if
this "projection" is to take place, the impenetrable Other Thing must
already be here—the true enigma is the presence of this Thing. The problem with Tarkovsky is that he himself obviously opts for the Jungian
reading, according to which the external journey is merely the external-
ization and/or projection of the inner initiating journey into the depth
of one's psyche. Apropos of *Solaris,* he stated in an interview: "Maybe,
effectively, the mission of Kelvin on Solaris has only one goal: to show
that love of the other is indispensable to all life. A man without love is no
longer a man. The aim of the entire 'solaristic' is to show that humanity
must be love." [16] In clear contrast to this, Lem's novel focuses on the inert
external presence of the planet Solaris, of this "Thing which thinks" (to
use Kant's expression, which fully fits here): the point of the novel is
precisely that Solaris remains an impenetrable Other with no possible
communication with us. True, it returns to us our innermost disavowed
fantasies, but the "Che vuoi?" beneath this act remains thoroughly impenetrable. (Why does It do it? As a purely mechanical response? To
play demonic games with us? To help us—or compel us—to confront
our disavowed truth?) It would thus be interesting to put Tarkovsky in
the series of Hollywood's commercial rewritings of novels which have
served as the basis for a movie: he does exactly the same as the lowest
Hollywood producer, reinscribing the enigmatic encounter with Otherness into the framework of the production of the couple.

   Nowhere is this gap between the novel and the film more perceptible
than in their different endings: at the novel's end, we see Kelvin alone on
the spaceship, staring into the mysterious surface of the Solaris ocean,
while the film ends with the archetypal Tarkovskian fantasy of combining within the same shot the Otherness into which the hero is thrown
(the chaotic surface of Solaris) and the object of his nostalgic longing,
the home *dacha* [Russian wooden countryhouse] to which he longs to
return, the house whose contours are encircled by the malleable slime of
Solaris's surface—within the radical Otherness, we discover the lost object of our innermost longing. More precisely, the sequence is shot in an
ambiguous way: just prior to this vision, one of his surviving colleagues
on the space station tells Kelvin (the hero) that it is perhaps time for him
to return home. After a couple of Tarkovskian shots of green weeds in

water, we then see Kelvin at his dacha, reconciled with his father. However, the camera then pulls slowly back and upward, and gradually it becomes clear that what we have just witnessed was probably not the actual return home but a vision manufactured by Solaris: the dacha and the grass surrounding it appear as a lone island in the midst of the chaotic Solaris surface, yet another materialized vision produced by it.

The same phantasmatic staging concludes Tarkovsky's *Nostalgia:* in the midst of the Italian countryside, encircled by the fragments of a cathedral in ruins, that is, of the place in which the hero is adrift, cut from his roots, there stands an element totally out of place: the Russian dacha, the stuff of the hero's dreams. Here, also, the shot begins with a close-up of only the recumbent hero in front of his dacha, so that, for a moment, it may seem that he has effectively returned home. The camera then slowly pulls back to divulge the properly phantasmatic setting of the dacha in the midst of the Italian countryside. Since this scene follows the hero's successful accomplishment of the sacrificial-compulsive gesture of carrying the burning candle across the pool, after which he collapses and drops dead—or so we are led to believe—one is tempted to take the last shot of *Nostalgia* not simply as the hero's dream, but as the uncanny scene that follows his decease and thus stands for his death: the moment of the impossible combination of the Italian countryside in which the hero is adrift and the object of his longing is the moment of death. (This deadly, impossible synthesis is announced in a previous dream sequence, in which Eugenia appears in a solid embrace with the hero's Russian maternal wife figure.) What we have here is a phenomenon, a scene, a dream experience, which can no longer be subjectivized—that is, a kind of nonsubjectivizable phenomenon, a dream which is no longer a dream of anyone, a dream which can emerge only after its subject ceases to be. This concluding fantasy is thus an artificial condensation of opposed, incompatible perspectives, somewhat like the standard optician's test in which we see through one eye a cage, through the other eye a parrot; if both our eyes are well coordinated in their axes, when we open them, we should see the parrot in the cage. (When I recently failed the test, I suggested to the nurse that perhaps I would be more successful if my motivation were stronger—if, say, instead of the parrot and the cage, the two images would be of an erect penis and a spread vagina, so that, when you open both eyes, the penis is in the vagina. The poor old lady threw me out. And incidentally, my modest proposal was justified insofar as, according to Lacan, all phantasmatic harmonious coordinations in which one element finally fully fits the other are ultimately based on the model of the successful sexual relationship, where the male virile organ fits the feminine opening "like a key into the opening of a lock.") [17]

Tarkovsky added not only this final scene, but also a new beginning: while the novel starts with Kelvin's space travel to Solaris, the movie's first half hour takes place in the standard Tarkovskian Russian countryside with a dacha, in which Kelvin takes a stroll, gets soaked by rain, and is immersed in the humid earth. As we have already emphasized, in clear contrast to the film's phantasmatic resolution, the novel ends with the lone Kelvin contemplating the surface of Solaris, aware more than ever that he has encountered here an Otherness with which no contact is possible. The planet Solaris has thus to be conceived in strict Kantian terms, as the impossible apparition of the thought (the thinking substance) as a Thing-in-itself, a noumenal object. Crucial for the Solaris-Thing is thus the coincidence of utter Otherness with excessive, absolute proximity: the Solaris-Thing is even more "ourselves," our own inaccessible kernel, than the Unconscious, since it is an Otherness which directly "is" ourselves, staging the "objectively subjective" phantasmatic core of our being. Communication with the Solaris-Thing thus fails not because Solaris is too alien, the harbinger of an intellect infinitely surpassing our limited abilities, playing some perverse games with us whose rationale remains forever outside our grasp, but because it brings us too close to what in ourselves must remain at a distance if we are to sustain the consistency of our symbolic universe. In its very Otherness, Solaris generates spectral phenomena that obey our innermost idiosyncratic whims, that is, if there is a stage master who pulls the strings of what goes on on the surface of Solaris, it is ourselves, "the Thing that thinks" in our heart. The fundamental lesson here is the opposition, antagonism even, between the big Other (the symbolic Order) and the Other *qua* Thing. The big Other is barred, it is the virtual order of symbolic rules that provides the frame for communication, while in the Solaris-Thing, the big Other is no longer barred, purely virtual; in it, the symbolic collapses into the Real, and language comes to exist as a Real Thing.

The Fake of the Sacrifice

Tarkovsky's other science-fiction masterpiece, *Stalker,* provides the counterpoint to this all-too-present Thing: the void of a forbidden zone. In an anonymous bleak country, an area known as "the Zone" was visited twenty years ago by some mysterious foreign entity (a meteorite, aliens) that left behind debris. People supposedly disappear in this deadly zone, which is isolated and guarded by army personnel. "Stalkers" are adventurous individuals who, for an appropriate fee, lead people to the zone and to the mysterious room at its heart where their deepest wishes are allegedly granted. The film tells the story of a stalker, an ordinary man with a wife and a crippled daughter with the magical ability to move objects, who takes to the zone two intellectuals, a writer and a scientist. When they finally reach the room, they fail to pronounce their wishes because of their lack of faith, while the stalker himself seems to get an answer to his wish that his daughter get better.

As in the case of *Solaris,* Tarkovsky turned around the point of the novel: in the Strugatsky brothers' novel *The Roadside Picnic,* on which the film is based, the zones—there are six of them—are the debris of a "roadside picnic," that is, of a short stay on our planet by some alien visitors who quickly left it, finding us uninteresting; stalkers themselves are also presented in a more adventurous way, not as dedicated individuals on a tormenting spiritual search, but as deft scavengers organizing robbing expeditions, somewhat like the proverbial Arabs organizing raiding expeditions into the pyramids—another "zone"—for wealthy Westerners. And, effectively, are the pyramids not, according to popular-science literature, traces of an alien wisdom? The zone is thus not a purely mental phantasmatic space in which one encounters (or onto which one projects) the truth about oneself, but (like Solaris in Lem's novel) the *material presence,* the Real of an absolute Otherness incompatible with the rules and laws of our universe. (Because of this, at the novel's end, the hero himself, when confronted with the "Golden Sphere"—as the film's room in which desires are realized is called in the novel—does undergo a kind of spiritual conversion, but this experience is much closer to what Lacan called "subjective destitution," a sudden awareness of the utter meaningless of our social links, the dissolution of our attachment to reality itself; all of a sudden, other people are de-realized, reality itself is experienced as a confused whirlpool of shapes and sounds, so that we are no longer able to formulate our desire.) In *Stalker* as well as in *Solaris,* Tarkovsky's "idealist mystification" is that he shrinks from confronting this radical Otherness of the meaningless Thing, reducing and retranslating the encounter with the Thing to the "inner journey" toward one's Truth.

It is to this incompatibility between our own and the alien universe that the novel's title refers: the strange objects found in the zone that fascinate humans are in all probability simply the debris, the garbage, left behind after aliens have briefly stayed on our planet, comparable to the rubbish a group of people leaves behind after a picnic in a forest near a main road. So the typical Tarkovskian landscape (of decaying human debris half reclaimed by nature) is in the novel precisely *what characterizes the zone itself from the (impossible) standpoint of the visiting aliens:* what is to us a miracle, an encounter with a wondrous universe beyond our grasp, is just everyday debris to the aliens. Is it then perhaps possible to draw the Brechtian conclusion that the typical Tarkovskian landscape (the human environment in decay reclaimed by nature) involves the view of our universe from an imagined alien standpoint? The picnic is thus here at the opposite extreme from that at the Hanging Rock: it is not us who encroach upon the zone while on a Sunday picnic, it is the zone itself which results from the alien's picnic.

For a citizen of the defunct Soviet Union, the notion of a forbidden zone gives rise to at least five associations: a zone is (1) a gulag, a separate prison territory; (2) a territory poisoned or otherwise rendered uninhabitable by some technological (biochemical, nuclear) catastrophe, like Chernobyl; (3) the secluded domain in which the *nomenklatura* lives; (4) foreign territory to which access is prohibited (like the enclosed West Berlin in the midst of the German Democratic Republic); or (5) a territory where a meteorite has struck (like Tunguska in Siberia). The point, of course, is that the question "So which is the true meaning of the zone?" is false and misleading: the very indeterminacy of what lies beyond the limit is primary, and different positive contents fill in this preceding gap.

Stalker perfectly exemplifies this paradoxical logic of the limit which separates our everyday reality from the phantasmatic space. In *Stalker,* this phantasmatic space is the mysterious zone, the forbidden territory in which the impossible occurs, in which secret desires are realized, in which one can find technological gadgets not yet invented in our everyday reality, and so on. Only criminals and adventurers are ready to take the risk and enter this domain of the phantasmatic Otherness. What one should insist on in a materialist reading of Tarkovsky is the constitutive role of the limit itself: this mysterious zone is effectively the same as our common reality, and what confers on it the aura of mystery is the limit itself, that is, the fact that the zone is designated as inaccessible, prohibited. (No wonder that when the heroes finally enter the mysterious room, they become aware that there is nothing special or outstanding in it. The stalker implores them not to impart this news to the people outside the zone so that they do not lose their gratifying illusions.) In short, the obscurantist mystification consists here in the act of inverting the true order of causality: the zone is not prohibited because it has certain properties which are "too strong" for our everyday sense of reality, it displays these properties because it is posited as prohibited. What comes first is the formal gesture of excluding a part of the real from our everyday reality and of proclaiming it the prohibited zone.[18] Or, to quote Tarkovsky himself: "I am often asked what does this zone stand for. There is only one possible answer: the zone doesn't exist. Stalker himself invented his zone. He created it, so that he was able to bring there some very unhappy persons and impose on them the idea of hope. The room of desires is equally Stalker's creation, yet another provocation in the face of the material world. This provocation, formed in Stalker's mind, corresponds to an act of faith."[19] Hegel emphasized that, in the suprasensible realm beyond the veil of appearances, there is nothing, just what the subject itself puts there when he takes a look at it.

In what, then, does the opposition between the zone (in *Stalker*) and the planet Solaris consist? In Lacanian terms, of course, their opposition is easy to specify: it is the opposition between the two excesses, the excess of stuff over symbolic network (the Thing for which there is no place in this network, which eludes its grasp), and the excess of an (empty) place over stuff, over the elements which fill it in (the zone is a pure structural void constituted and defined by a symbolic barrier: beyond this barrier, in the zone, there is nothing and/or exactly the same things as outside it). This opposition stands for the opposition between drive and desire: Solaris is the Thing, the blind libido embodied, while the zone is the void which sustains desire. This opposition also accounts for the different ways the zone and Solaris relate to the subject's libidinal economy: in the midst of the zone is the "chamber of desires," the place in which, if the subject penetrates it, his desire or wish is fulfilled, while what the Thing-Solaris returns to subjects who approach it is not their desire but the traumatic kernel of their fantasy, the sinthome which encapsulates their relation to *jouissance* and which they resist in their daily lives.

The blockage in *Stalker* is thus the opposite of the blockage in *Solaris*: in *Stalker*, the blockage concerns the impossibility (for us, corrupted, re-flected, nonbelieving modern men) of achieving the state of pure belief, of desiring directly. The room in the midst of the zone has to remain empty; when you enter it, you are not able to formulate your wish. In contrast to it, the problem of *Solaris* is oversatisfaction: your wishes are realized and materialized before you even think of them. In *Stalker*, you never arrive at the level of pure, innocent wish-belief, while in *Solaris*, your dreams and fantasies are realized in advance in the psychotic struc-ture of the answer which precedes the question. For this reason, *Stalker* focuses on the problem of belief or faith: the chamber does fulfill desires, but only those of people who believe with direct immediacy—which is why, when the three adventurers finally reach the threshold of the room, they are afraid to enter it, since they are not sure what their true desires and wishes are (as one of them says, the problem with the room is that it fulfills not what you think you wish, but the true wish of which you may be unaware). As such, *Stalker* points toward the basic problem of Tarkovsky's last two films, *Nostalgia* and *Sacrifice*: the problem of how, through what ordeal or sacrifice, it is possible today to attain the inno-cence of pure belief. The hero of *Sacrifice*, Alexander, lives with his large family in a remote cottage in the Swedish countryside (another version of the very Russian dacha which obsesses Tarkovsky's heroes). The cele-brations of his birthday are marred by the terrifying news that low-flying jet planes have signaled the start of a nuclear war between the super-powers. In his despair, Alexander turns in prayer to God, offering him everything that is most precious to him to have the war not have hap-pened at all. The war is "undone," and at the film's end, Alexander, in a sacrificial gesture, burns his beloved cottage and is taken to a lunatic asylum.

This motif of a pure, senseless act that restores meaning to our terres-trial life is the focus of Tarkovsky's last two films, both of which were shot abroad; the act is both times accomplished by the same actor (Erland Josephson), who as the old fool Domenico burns himself publicly in *Nostalgia*, and as the hero of *Sacrifice* burns his house—his most precious belonging, what is "in him more than himself." [20] To this gesture of senseless sacrifice, one should give all the weight of an obsessional-neurotic compulsive act: if I accomplish *this* (sacrifical gesture), the catastrophe (in *Sacrifice,* literally the end of the world in an atomic war) will not occur or will be undone—the well-known compulsive gesture of "if I do not do this (jump two times over that stone, cross my hands in this way, etc., etc.) something bad will occur." (The childish nature of this compulsion to sacrifice is clear in *Nostalgia*, where the hero, following the injunction of the dead Domenico, crosses the half-dry pool with the burning candle in order to save the world.) As we know from psychoanalysis, this catastrophic X whose outbreak we fear is none other than *jouissance* itself.

Tarkovsky is well aware that a sacrifice, in order to work and to be efficient, must be in a way "meaningless," a gesture of "irrational," useless expenditure or ritual (like traversing the empty pool with a lit candle or burning one's own house). The idea is that only such a gesture of just "doing it" spontaneously, a gesture not covered by any rational consideration, can restore the immediate faith that will deliver us and heal us from our modern spiritual malaise. The Tarkovskian subject here literally offers his own castration (renunciation of reason and domination, voluntary reduction to childish "idiocy," submission to a senseless ritual) as the instrument to deliver the big Other: it is as if only by accomplishing an act which is totally senseless and "irrational" that the subject can save the deeper global meaning of the universe as such.

The crucial point here is that the object sacrificed (burned) at the end of *Sacrifice* is the ultimate object of Tarkovskian phantasmatic space, the wooden dacha standing for the safety and authentic rural roots of the home. For this reason alone, it is appropriate that *Sacrifice* is Tarkovsky's last film.[21] Does this mean that we nonetheless encounter here a kind of Tarkovskian "traversing of the fantasy," renunciation of the central element whose magical appearance in the midst of the strange countryside (the planet's surface, Italy) at the end of *Solaris* and *Nostalgia* provided the very formula of the final phantasmatic unity? No, because this renunciation is functionalized in the service of the big Other, as the redemptive act destined to restore spiritual meaning to life.

What elevates Tarkovsky above cheap religious obscurantism is the fact that he deprives this sacrificial act of any pathetic and solemn "greatness," rendering it as a bungled, ridiculous act (in *Nostalgia,* Domenico has difficulty lighting the fire which will kill him, and the passersby ignore his burning body; *Sacrifice* ends with a comic ballet of men from the infirmary running after the hero to take him to the asylum—the scene is shot as a child's game of catch. It would be all too simple to read this bumbling, ludicrous aspect of the sacrifice as an indication of how it must appear to everyday people immersed in their own run of things and unable to appreciate the tragic greatness of the act. Rather, Tarkovsky follows here the long Russian tradition whose exemplar is Dostoyevsky's idiot, from the novel of the same name: it is typical that Tarkovsky, whose films are otherwise totally devoid of humor and jokes, reserves mockery and satire precisely for scenes depicting the most sacred gesture of supreme sacrifice (the famous scene of crucifixion in *Andrei Roublev* is shot in such a way: transposed into the Russian winter countryside, with bad actors playing it with ridiculous pathos, with tears flowing).[22] So, again, does this indicate that, to use Althusserian terms, there is a dimension in which Tarkovsky's cinematic texture undermines his own explicit ideological project, or at least introduces a distance toward it, renders visible its inherent impossibility and failure?

There is a scene in *Nostalgia* that contains a Pascalian reference: in a church, Eugenia witnesses a procession of simple peasant women in honor of the Madonna del Parto. They are addressing to the saint their plea to become mothers—that is, their prayer concerns their fertility. When the perplexed Eugenia, who admits that she is unable to comprehend the attraction of motherhood, asks the priest who also observes the procession how one becomes a believer, he answers, "You should begin by kneeling down"—a clear reference to Pascal's famous "Kneel down and that act will render you feeble-minded" (i.e., it will deprive you of false intellectual pride). Interestingly, Eugenia tries, but she stops halfway: she is unable even to perform the external gesture of kneeling. Here we encounter the deadlock of the Tarkovskian hero: is it possible for today's intellectual (exemplified by Gortchakov, the hero of *Nostalgia*), this man separated from naive spiritual certainty by the gap of nostalgia, by an asphyxiating existential despair—is it possible for him to return to immediate religious immersion, to recapture its certainty? In other words, does the need for unconditional faith, its redemptive power, not lead to a typically *modern* result, to the decisionist act of formal faith indifferent toward its particular content—that is, to a kind of religious counterpoint of Schmittean political decisionism in which the fact *that* we believe takes precedence over *what* we believe in? Or, even worse, does not this logic of unconditional faith ultimately lead to the paradox of love exploited by the notorious Reverend Sun Myung Moon? As is well known, Reverend Moon arbitrarily chooses the conjugal partners for the unmarried members of his sect: legitimizing his decision by means of his privileged insight into the working of the divine cosmic order, he claims to be able to identify the mate who was predestined for one in the eternal order of things and simply informs a member of his sect by letter who the unknown person (as a rule someone from another part of the globe) is that he is to marry. Slovenes are thus marrying Koreans, Americans are marrying Indians, and so on. The true miracle, of course, is that this bluff *works:* if there is unconditional trust and faith, the contingent decision of an external authority can produce a couple connected by the most intimate passionate link. Why? Since love is "blind," contingent, grounded in no clearly observable properties, that unfathomable *je ne sais quoi* which decides when I am to fall in love can also be totally externalized in the decision of an unfathomable authority.

So what is false in the Tarkovskian sacrifice? More fundamentally, what is sacrifice? The most elementary notion of sacrifice relies on the notion of exchange: I offer to the Other something precious to me in order to get back from the Other something even more vital to me (the "primitive" tribes sacrifice animals or even humans so that gods will repay them with rainfall, military victory, etc.). The next, even more intricate level is to conceive of sacrifice as a gesture which does not directly aim at some profitable exchange with the Other to whom we sacrifice: its more basic aim is rather to ascertain that there *is* some Other out there who is able to reply (or not) to our sacrificial entreaties. Even if the Other does not grant my wish, I can at least be assured that there is an Other who—maybe—next time will respond differently: the world out there, inclusive of all catastrophes that may befall me, is not a meaningless piece of blind machinery, but a partner in a possible dialogue, so that even a catastrophic outcome is to be read as a meaningful response; we do not live in a kingdom of blind chance. Here Lacan goes a step further: the notion of sacrifice usually associated with Lacanian psychoanalysis is that of a gesture that enacts the disavowal of the impotence of the big Other. At its most elementary, the subject does not offer his sacrifice to profit from it himself, but to fill in the lack *in the Other,* to sustain the appearance of the Other's omnipotence or, at least, consistency. Let us recall *Beau Geste,* the classic Hollywood adventure melodrama from 1938, in which the eldest (Gary Cooper) of the three brothers who live with their benevolent aunt, in what seems to be a gesture of excessive ingratitude and cruelty, steals the enormously expensive diamond necklace that is the pride of the aunt's family and disappears with it, knowing that his reputation is ruined, that he will be forever known as the ungracious robber of his benefactress. So why did he do it? At the end of the film, we learn that he did it in order to prevent the embarrassing disclosure that the necklace was a fake: of the entire family, he was the only one who knew that, some time ago, the aunt had had to sell the necklace to a rich maharaja in order to save the family from bankruptcy and had replaced it with a worthless imitation. Just prior to the theft, he had learned that a distant uncle who co-owned the necklace wanted it sold for financial gain; if the necklace were to be sold, the fact that it was a fake would undoubtedly be discovered, so the only way to retain the aunt's and thus the family's honor was to stage its theft. This is the proper deception of the crime of stealing: to occlude the fact that, ultimately, there is nothing to steal. This way, the constitutive lack of the Other is concealed, that is, the illusion is maintained that the Other possessed what was stolen from it. If, in love, one gives what one does not possess, then in a crime of love, one steals from the beloved Other what the Other does not possess. It is this to which the "beau geste" of the film's title alludes. And therein resides the meaning of sacrifice: one sacrifices oneself (one's honor and future in respectful society) to maintain the appearance of the Other's honor, to save the beloved Other from shame.

However, Lacan's rejection of sacrifice as inauthentic locates the falsity of the sacrificial gesture also in another, much more uncanny dimension. Let us take the example of Jeannot Szwarc's *Enigma* (1981), one of the better variations on what is arguably the basic theme of cold war spy thrillers with artistic pretensions à la John le Carré (an agent is sent into the cold to accomplish a mission; when, in enemy territory, he is betrayed and captured, it dawns on him that he was sacrificed, i.e., that the failure of his mission was from the very beginning planned by his superiors in order to achieve the true goal of the operation—say, to keep secret the identity of the West's real mole in the KGB apparatus). *Enigma* tells the story of a dissident-journalist-turned-spy who emigrates to the West and is then recruited by the CIA and sent to East Germany to get hold of a scrambling-descrambling computer chip that enables the owner to read all communications between KGB headquarters and its outposts. However, small signs tell the spy that there is something wrong with his mission—for instance, that the East Germans and Russians were already informed in advance about his arrival—so what is going on? Is it that the Communists have a mole in the CIA headquarters who informed them of this secret mission? As we learn toward the film's end, the solution is much more ingenious: the CIA *already possesses* the scrambling chip, but, unfortunately, the Russians suspect this, so they have temporarily stopped using this computer network for their secret communications. The true aim of the operation was for the CIA to convince the Russians that they did not possess the chip by sending an agent to get it and, at the same time, deliberately letting the Russians know that there was an operation going on to get the chip. Of course, the CIA counts on the fact that the Russians will arrest the agent. The ultimate result will thus be that, by successfully preventing the mission, the Russians will be convinced that the Americans do not possess the chip and that it is therefore safe to use this communication link. The tragic aspect of the story, of course, is that the mission's failure is taken into account: the CIA *wants* the mission to fail. The poor dissident agent is sacrificed in advance for the higher goal of convincing the opponent that one does not possess the opponent's secret. The strategy here is to stage a search operation in order to convince the Other (the enemy) that one does not already possess what one is looking for—in short, one feigns a lack, a want, in order to conceal from the Other that one already possesses the *agalma*, the Other's innermost secret. Is this structure not somehow connected with the basic paradox of symbolic castration as constitutive of desire, in which the object has to be lost in order to be regained on the inverse ladder of desire regulated by the Law? Symbolic castration is usually defined as the loss of something that one never possessed—that is, the object-cause of desire is an object which emerges through the very gesture of its loss or withdrawal. However, what we encounter here, in the case of *Enigma,* is the obverse structure of feigning a loss. Insofar as the Other of the symbolic Law prohibits *jouissance,* the only way for the subject to enjoy is to feign that he lacks the object that provides *jouissance,* that is, to conceal its possession from the Other's gaze by staging the spectacle of the desperate search for it. This also casts a new light on the problematic of sacrifice: one sacrifices not in order to get something from the Other, but in order to dupe the Other, in order to convince him or it that one is still missing something—that is, *jouissance.* This is why obsessionals experience the compulsion repeatedly to perform their rituals of sacrifice: in order to disavow their *jouissance* in the eyes of the Other. And, at a different level, does the same not hold for the so-called woman's sacrifice, for the woman adopting the role of remaining in shadow and sacrificing herself for her husband or family? Is this sacrifice not also false in the sense of serving to dupe the Other, of convincing it that, through the sacrifice, the woman is in fact desperately craving something that she lacks? In this precise sense, sacrifice and castration are opposites: far from involving the voluntary acceptance of castration, sacrifice is the most refined way of disavowing it, of acting as if one effectively possesses the hidden treasure that makes one a worthy object of love.[23]

In his unpublished "Seminar on Anxiety" (1962–63, lesson of 5 December 1962), Lacan emphasizes the way the hysteric's anxiety relates to the fundamental lack in the Other which makes the Other inconsistent or barred: a hysteric perceives the lack in the Other, its impotence, its inconsistency, its falsity, but he is not ready to sacrifice the part of himself that would complete the Other, that would fill in its lack. This refusal to sacrifice sustains the hysteric's eternal complaint that the Other will somehow manipulate and exploit him, use him, deprive him of his most precious possession. More precisely, this does not mean that the hysteric disavows his castration: the hysteric (neurotic) does not hold back from his castration (he is not a psychotic or a pervert; he fully accepts his castration); he merely does not want to "functionalize" it, to put it in the service of the Other. In other words, what he holds back from is "making his castration into what the Other is lacking, that is to say, into something positive that is the guarantee of this function of the Other."

(In contrast to the hysteric, the pervert readily assumes this role of sacrificing himself, i.e., of serving as the object-instrument that fills in the Other's lack; as Lacan puts it, the pervert "offers himself loyally to the Other's *jouissance*.") The falsity of sacrifice resides in its underlying presupposition, which is that I effectively possess, hold in me, the precious ingredient coveted by the Other and promise to fill in its lack. On closer inspection, of course, the hysteric's refusal appears in all its ambiguity: I refuse to sacrifice the *agalma* in me *because there is nothing to sacrifice*, because I am unable to fill in your lack.

One should always bear in mind that for Lacan, the ultimate aim of psychoanalysis is not to enable the subject to assume the necessary sacrifice (to "accept symbolic castration," to renounce immature narcissistic attachments, etc.), but to *resist* the terrible attraction of sacrifice — an attraction which, of course, is none other than that of the superego. Sacrifice is ultimately the gesture by means of which we aim at compensating the guilt imposed by the impossible superego injunction (the "obscure gods" evoked by Lacan are another name for the superego). Against this background, one can see in what precise sense the problematic of Tarkovsky's last two films, both focused on sacrifice, is false and misleading: although no doubt Tarkovsky himself would passionately reject such a designation, the compulsion felt by the late Tarkovskian heroes to accomplish a meaningless sacrificial gesture is that of superego at its purest. The ultimate proof of it resides in the very "irrational," meaningless character of this gesture: superego is an injunction to enjoy, and, as Lacan puts it in the first lecture of his *Encore*, *jouissance* is ultimately that which serves nothing.[24]

Cinematic Materialism, or, Tarkovsky Through Marx

How, then, are sacrifice and the Thing related? The very title of Claude Lefort's essay on Orwell's *1984*, "The Interposed Corpse,"[25] provides the clue to this link. Lefort focuses on the famous scene in which Winston is subjected to the rat torture. Why are rats so traumatic for poor Winston? The point is that they are clearly *a phantasmatic stand-in for Winston himself* (as a small child, Winston behaved like a rat, ransacking refuse dumps for remainders of food). So when he desperately shouts "Do it to Julia!" he interposes a corpse between himself and his phantasmatic kernel and thus avoids being swallowed by the traumatic *Ding*. Therein consists the primordial sense of sacrifice: to interpose an object between ourselves and the Thing. Sacrifice is a stratagem enabling us to maintain a minimal distance from the Thing. We can see now why the motif of the id machine has to lead to the motif of sacrifice: insofar as the paradigmatic case of this Thing is the id machine, which directly materializes our desires, the ultimate aim of the sacrifice is, paradoxically, precisely to *prevent* the realization of our desires.

In other words, the aim of the sacrificial gesture is not to bring us close to the Thing, but to maintain and guarantee a proper distance from it; in this sense, the notion of sacrifice is inherently ideological. Ideology is the narrative of "why things went wrong"; it objectivizes the primordial loss or impossibility. In other words, ideology translates the inherent impossibility into an external obstacle which can in principle be overcome (in contrast to the standard Marxist notion, according to which ideology "eternalizes" and "absolutizes" contingent historical obstacles). So the key element of ideology is not only the image of the full unity to be achieved, but, even more, the elaboration of the obstacle (Jew, class enemy, devil) that prevents its achievement—ideology sets in motion our social activity by giving rise to the illusion that if only we were to get rid of Them (Jews, the class enemy, etc.), everything would be all right. Against this background, one can measure the ideologico-critical impact of Kafka's *The Trial* or *The Castle*. The standard ideological procedure transposes an inherent impossibility into an external obstacle or prohibition (say, the fascist dream of a harmonious social body is not inherently false—it will become reality once one eliminates Jews, who plot against it; or, in sexuality, I will be able fully to enjoy once the paternal prohibition is suspended). What Kafka achieves is the traversal of the same path in the opposite direction—that is, the retranslation of external obstacle or prohibition into inherent impossibility. In short, Kafka's achievement resides precisely in what the standard ideologicocritical gaze perceives as his ideological limitation and mystification: in his elevation of (the state bureaucracy as) a positive social institution that prevents us, as concrete individuals, from becoming free to a metaphysical limit that cannot ever be overcome.

What nonetheless redeems Tarkovsky is his cinematic materialism, the direct physical impact of the texture of his films: this texture renders a stance of *Gelassenheit*, of pacified disengagement that suspends the very urgency of any kind of quest. Pervading Tarkovsky's films is the heavy gravity of the earth, which seems to exert its pressure on time itself, generating an effect of temporal anamorphosis, extending the dragging of time well beyond what we perceive as justified by the requirements of narrative movement (one should confer here on the term "earth" all the resonance it acquired in late Heidegger). Perhaps Tarkovsky's films are the clearest example of what Deleuze called the time-image replacing the movement-image. This time of the Real is neither the symbolic time of the diegetic space nor the time of the reality of our (spectator's) viewing the film, but an intermediate domain whose visual equivalent is, perhaps, the protracted stains which "are" the yellow sky in late van Gogh, or the water or grass in Munch. This uncanny "massiveness" pertains neither to the direct materiality of the color stains nor to the materiality of the depicted objects; it dwells in a kind of intermediate spectral domain of what Schelling called *geistige Körperlichkeit,* spiritual corporeality. From the Lacanian perspective, it is easy to identify this "spiritual corporeality" as materialized *jouissance, "jouissance* turned into flesh."

This inert insistence of time as Real, rendered paradigmatically in Tarkovsky's famous five-minute slow tracking or crane shots, is what makes him so interesting for a materialist reading: without this inert texture, he would be just another Russian religious obscurantist. That is to say, in our standard ideological tradition, the approach to spirit is perceived as elevation, as getting rid of the burden of weight, of the gravitating force which binds us to the earth, as cutting links with material inertia and starting to "float freely"; in contrast to this, in Tarkovsky's universe, we enter the spiritual dimension only via intense direct physical contact with the humid heaviness of earth (or still water). The ultimate Tarkovskian spiritual experience takes place when a subject is lying stretched on the earth's surface, half submerged in still water; Tarkovsky's heroes do not pray on their knees, with the head turned up toward heaven, but while intensely listening to the silent palpitation of the humid earth. One can see now why Lem's novel had to exert such an attraction on Tarkovsky: the planet Solaris seems to provide the ultimate embodiment of the Tarkovskian notion of a heavy, humid stuff (earth), which, far from functioning as the opposite of spirituality, serves as its very medium; this gigantic "material Thing which thinks" literally gives body to the direct coincidence of matter and spirit. In a homologous way, Tarkovsky displaces the common notion of dreaming, of entering a dream: in Tarkovsky's universe, the subject enters the domain of dreams not when he loses contact with sensual material reality around him, but, on the contrary, when he abandons the hold on his intellect and engages in an intense relationship to material reality. The typical stance of the Tarkovskian hero on the threshold of a dream is to be on the lookout for something, with the attention of his senses fully focused; then, all of a sudden, as if through a magic transubstantiation, this most intense contact with material reality changes it into a dreamscape.[26] One is thus tempted to claim that Tarkovsky stands for the attempt, perhaps unique in the history of cinema, to develop the attitude of *materialist theology,* of a deep spiritual stance which draws its strength from its very abandonment of intellect and immersion in material reality. In order to locate properly this feature, one should read it against the background of capitalist dynamics as deployed by Marx. On the one hand, capitalism entails the radical secularization of the social life; it mercilessly tears apart any aura of authentic nobility, sacredness, honor, and so on: "It has drowned the most heavenly ecstasies of religious fervour, of chivalrous enthusiasm, of philistine sentimentalism, in the icy water of egotistical calculation. It has resolved personal worth into exchange value, and in place of the numberless indefeasible chartered freedoms, has set up that single, unconscionable freedom—Free Trade. In one word, for exploitation, veiled by religious and political illusions, it has substituted naked, shameless, direct, brutal exploitation."[27]

However, the fundamental lesson of the "critique of political economy" elaborated by the mature Marx in the years after *The Communist Manifesto* is that *this reduction of all heavenly chimeras to the brutal economic reality generates a spectrality of its own.* When Marx describes the mad self-enhancing circulation of capital, whose solipsistic path of self-fecundation reaches its apogee in today's metareflexive speculations on futures, it is far too simplistic to claim that the specter of this self-engendering monster that pursues its path disregarding any human or environmental concern is an ideological abstraction, and that one should never forget that behind this abstraction there are real people and natural objects on whose productive capacities and resources capital's circulation is based and on which it feeds like a gigantic parasite. The problem is not only that this "abstraction" is in our (financial speculator's) misperception of social reality, but that it is "real" in the precise sense of determining the structure of the very material of social processes: the fate of whole strata of the population and sometimes of whole countries can be decided by the solipsistic speculative dance of capital, which pursues its goal of profitability in blessed indifference to how its movement will affect social reality. Here we encounter the Lacanian difference between reality and the Real: "reality" is the social reality of actual people involved in interaction and in productive processes, while the Real is the inexorable, "abstract," spectral logic of capital that determines what goes on in social reality. And, again, is this not more true today than ever? Do phenomena usually designated as those of "virtual capitalism" (future trades and similar abstract financial speculations) not point toward the rule of "real abstraction" at its purest (and much more radical than in Marx's time)? This material spectrality of capital also allows us to locate properly the logic of Tarkovsky's spiritualism, that is, of how his return to spiritual values in a properly dialectical way simultaneously involves the return to the heavy material inertia of the earth.

Along the same lines, it is also crucial to supplement the standard Marxist procedure of recognizing the particular content behind the appearance of an ideological universal with its dialectical opposite. Let us take the classic example of human rights. The Marxist reading can convincingly demonstrate the particular content that gives the specific bourgeois ideological spin to the notion of human rights: "universal human rights are effectively the right of the white male private owners to exchange freely on the market, exploit workers and women, as well as exert political domination." This identification of the particular content that hegemonizes the universal form is, however, only half of the story; its crucial other half consists in asking a much more difficult supplementary question concerning the *emergence of the very form of universality*: how and in what specific historical conditions does the abstract universality itself become a "fact of (social) life"? Therein resides the point of Marx's analysis of commodity fetishism: in a society in which commodity exchange predominates, individuals themselves, in their daily lives, relate to themselves, as well as to the objects they encounter, as contingent embodiments of abstract universal notions. What I am, my concrete social or cultural background, is experienced as contingent, since what ultimately defines me is the abstract universal capacity to think and/or to work. Or, any object that can satisfy my desire is experienced as contingent, since my desire is conceived as an abstract formal capacity, indifferent to the multitude of particular objects that may—but never fully do—satisfy it. Or take the example of "profession": the modern notion of profession implies that I experience myself as an individual who is not directly "born into" his social role—what I will become depends on the interplay between the contingent social circumstances and my free choice; in this sense, today's individual has a profession as an electrician or professor or waiter, while it is meaningless to claim that a medieval serf was a peasant by profession. The crucial point here is again that in certain specific social conditions (of commodity exchange and global market economy), abstraction becomes a direct feature of the actual social life, the way concrete individuals behave and relate to their fate and to their social surroundings. Marx shares here Hegel's insight into how universality becomes "for itself" only insofar as individuals no longer fully identify the kernel of their being with their particular social situation, only insofar as they experience themselves as forever "out of joint" with regard to this situation: the concrete, effective existence of universality is the individual without a proper place in the global edifice. In a given social structure, universality becomes "for itself" only in those individuals who lack a proper place in it. The mode of appearance of an abstract universality, its entering into actual existence, is thus an extremely violent move of disrupting the preceding organic poise. In this precise sense, capitalism, in its very utilitarian, despiritualized stance, stands for the reign of abstract universality. And we can catch a glimpse of the hidden truth of this reign of abstract universality when we cast a glance at its material remainder, at the relics of outdated technology: piled mountains of used cars and computers, the famous airplane "resting place" in the Mojave Desert—in these ever-growing piles of inert, dysfunctional "stuff," which cannot but strike us with its useless, inert presence, one can, as it were, perceive the capitalist drive at rest.

So, back to Tarkovsky: if *Stalker* is Tarkovsky's masterpiece, it is above all because of the direct physical impact of its texture: the physical background (what T. S. Eliot would have called the objective correlative) to its metaphysical quest, the landscape of the zone, is the postindustrial wasteland, with wild vegetation growing over abandoned factories, concrete tunnels and railroad tracks submerged in water, and wild overgrowth in which stray cats and dogs wander. Nature and industrial civilization are here again overlapping, but through a common decay: civilization in decay is in the process of again being reclaimed, not by idealized harmonious nature, but by nature in decomposition. The ultimate Tarkovskian landscape is of a humid nature, a river or pool close to some forest, full of the debris of human artifice (old concrete blocks or pieces of rotten metal). The actors' faces themselves, especially the stalker's, are unique in their blend of ordinary ruggedness, small wounds, dark or white spots, and other signs of decay, as if they had all been exposed to some poisonous chemical or radioactive substance, but at the same time radiating a fundamental naive goodness and trust.[28]

Here we can see the different effects of censorship: although censorship in the Soviet Union was no less stringent than the infamous Hayes Production Code in Hollywood, it nonetheless allowed the production of a movie so bleak in its visual material that it would never pass the Production Code test. Recall, as an example of Hollywood material censorship, the representation of dying of illness in *Dark Victory*, with Bette Davis: upper-middle-class surroundings, painless death—the process is deprived of its material inertia and transubstantiated in an ethereal reality free of bad smells and tastes. It was the same with slums; recall Goldwyn's famous quip, when a reviewer complained that the slums in one of his films looked too nice, without real dirt: "They better look nice, since they costed us so much!" The Hayes Office was extremely sensitive on this point: when slums were depicted, the office explicitly demanded that the set be constructed in such a way that it did not evoke real dirt and bad smells. At the most elementary level of the sensuous materiality of the real, censorship in Hollywood was thus much stronger than in the Soviet Union.

Tarkovsky must be contrasted here with the ultimate American paranoiac fantasy: that of an individual living in a small, idyllic California city, a consumer's paradise, who suddenly starts to suspect that the world he lives in is a fake, a spectacle staged to convince him that it is real, while all the people around him are in fact actors and extras in a gigantic show. The most recent example of this is Peter Weir's *The Truman Show* (1998), with Jim Carrey playing the small-town clerk who gradually discovers that he is the hero of a permanent, twenty-four-hour-a-day television show: his hometown is constructed on a gigantic studio set, with cameras following him constantly. Among its predecessors, it is worth mentioning Philip K. Dick's *Time out of Joint* (1959), in which a hero living a modest daily life in a small, idyllic California city of the late 1950s gradually discovers that the whole town is a fake staged to keep him satisfied. The underlying experience of both *Time out of Joint* and *The Truman Show* is that the late-capitalist, consumerist California paradise is, in its very hyperreality, in a way irreal, substanceless, deprived of material inertia. So it is not only that Hollywood stages a semblance of real life, deprived of the weight and inertia of materiality—in late-capitalist consumerist society, "real social life" itself somehow acquires the features of a staged fake, with our neighbors behaving in "real" life as stage actors and extras. Again, the ultimate truth of the capitalist, utilitarian, despiritualized universe is the dematerialization of "real life" itself, its reversal into a spectral show.

It is only now that we confront the crucial dilemma of any interpretation of Tarkovsky's films: is there a distance between his ideological project (of sustaining meaning, of generating new spirituality, through an act of meaningless sacrifice) and his cinematic materialism? Does his cinematic materialism effectively provide the adequate "objective correlative" for his narrative of spiritual quest and sacrifice, or does it secretly subvert this narrative? There are, of course, good arguments for the first option. In the long obscurantist-spiritualist tradition reaching up to the figure of Yoda in Lucas's *The Empire Strikes Back,* this wise dwarf who lives in a dark swamp, rotting nature is posited as the "objective correlative" of spiritual wisdom: the wise man accepts nature the way it is and renounces any attempt at aggressive domination and exploitation, any imposition of artificial order on it. On the other hand, what happens if we read Tarkovsky's cinematic materialism, as it were, in the opposite direction? What if we interpret the Tarkovskian sacrificial gesture as the elementary ideological operation, as the desperate strategy of defying the meaninglessness of existence with its own instrument, that is, of engendering meaning—of overcoming the unbearable Otherness of the meaningless cosmic contingency—through a gesture that is itself excessively meaningless? This dilemma is discernible in the ambiguous way Tarkovsky uses natural sounds of the environs.[29] Their status is ontologically undecidable, as if they are still part of the "spontaneous" texture of nonintentional natural sounds, and at the same time "musical," displaying a deeper spiritual structuring principle. It seems as if Nature itself miraculously starts to speak, the confused and chaotic symphony of its murmurs imperceptibly passing over into music proper. These magical moments, in which nature itself seems to coincide with art, lend themselves, of course, to the obscurantist reading (the mystical art of spirit discernible in nature itself), but also to the opposite, materialist reading (the genesis of meaning out of the natural contingency).[30]

Notes

1   See Jacques Lacan, *The Ethics of Psychoanalysis* (London: Routledge 1992), chap. 18.

2   Are the heroes of Wagner's first three great operas—*The Flying Dutchman, Tannhäuser, Lohengrin*—in a way also not split between their respective fatal zone (the ghost ship on which the Dutchman is condemned to wander eternally, the Venusberg of continual sexual orgies, the serene and for that reason infinitely boring kingdom of the Grail)? Is their problem not the same: how to escape suffocating existence in the zone (the endless lonely years on a wandering ghost ship; the excessive pleasure in Venusberg; and, probably worst and most boring of all, the eternal spiritual bliss of the Grail) through the trustful love of a mortal woman?

3   "Is there anything that poses a question which is more present, more pressing, more absorbing, more disruptive, more nauseating, more calculated to thrust everything that takes place before us into the abyss or void than that face of Harpo Marx, that face with its smile which leaves us unclear as to whether it signifies the most extreme perversity or complete simplicity? This dumb man alone is sufficient to sustain the atmosphere of doubt and of radical annihilation which is the stuff of the Marx brothers' extraordinary farce and the uninterrupted play of jokes that makes their activity so valuable" (Lacan, *The Ethics of Psychoanalysis*, 55).

4   The same goes for Max Ophuls's early German masterpiece *Liebelei*, in which we encounter the standard oedipal constellation: the tragic hero's older mistress (the Baroness) is a mother substitute whom he wants to abandon for the lower-class younger woman; the ensuing duel with the Baron, of course, is the duel with the paternal double-rival. However, the cliché to be avoided here is the notion that the paternal substitute's act is "castrating" (killing the hero in the duel): the exact opposite holds. It is the paternal figure who is "impotent," "castrated," and the duel with him stands for a ridiculous regression to the imaginary rivalry with the father (whose impotence is signaled by his strange gaze and monocles). Often, the figure who prevents the realization of sexual intercourse is a ridiculous castrato, his outrage a mask, an index of his impotence. *Liebelei* thus tells the story of the hero's failure to break out from the incestuous closure into "normal" exchange, i.e., to accomplish the shift from the incestuous object to a foreign woman. We are thus opposed here to the standard

reading of the severe military or parental figure in Ophuls's films as that of "castrating father" (see, for example, for the Baron in *Liebelei*, Susan White, *The Cinema of Max Ophuls* [New York: Columbia University Press, 1995], 95): this spectacled and stiff paternal figure who obstructs the love relationship is the exact opposite, i.e., not castra*ting*, but castra*ted*; his stiffness masks a ridiculous lifelessness and impotence (the reason the Baroness needs a younger lover!). The general point to be made here is how, effectively, deconstructionist film theory often resorts to terms like "phallic" or "castration" with a rather crude insensitivity.

5   It is interesting to note how today the notion of evil seems again to exceed in both directions the boundaries of "mid-level" human affairs as its proper locus. Not only is the notion of some trans-human, global evil again operative (say, in the guise of the sense of the looming global ecological catastrophe for which humanity as such is responsible, although it cannot be attributed to the intention of any specific individual), but we also increasingly experience evil as a threat looming at the level of the invisible small, of microorganisms (such as the new viruses resistant to all antibiotics). The impact of films like *Picnic at Hanging Rock* relies on this new sensibility for the dimensions of evil which are simultaneously more global, impersonal, and looming at the microlevel, such as the bursting forms of minuscule life on the Rock.

6   What is symptomatic about *Titanic* is the multitude of disavowals, of denials of the threatening attraction of the film, in intellectual circles. The excuses to which intellectuals refer to justify their seeing the film range from "I did it because I have to accompany my children" through "I was only interested by the spectacular technical effects" up to "it's bad, but not as bad as it might have been"; all this, of course, is supplemented by the rejection of seeing the film ("I do not want to spend time seeing such trash!"), in which it is easy to discern the fear that one might be seduced into actually liking the film.

7   For *Stalker*, Tarkovsky was compelled to use the low-quality domestically made stock that tends to lower contrast and give the image a murky greenish-blue cast; he ingeniously used this deficiency to his advantage, so that, when the three characters approach the room in the center of the zone, the action seems almost to be taking place underwater because of the monochromatic color design. We can see that this obsession of Tarkovsky with oceanic shape, and with water in general as characteristic of the Thing, is part of a large, well-established pattern.

8   Interestingly enough, the other big 1998 blockbuster-variation on the theme of a gigantic comet threatening Earth, *Armageddon,* also focuses on the incestuous father-daughter relation. Here, however, it is the father (Bruce Willis) who is excessively attached to his daughter: the comet's destructive force gives body to *his* fury at his daughter's love affairs with other men of her age. Significantly, the dénouement is also more "positive," not self-destructive: the father sacrifices himself in order to save Earth, i.e., effectively—at the level of the underlying libidinal economy—erasing himself out of the picture in order to bless the marriage of his daughter to her young lover.

9   However, apropos of this Hollywood ideological inscription of the global catastro-

phe into the framework of the motif of the "production of a couple," we should not forget that not every link of this kind is *eo ipso* ideological. When we are dealing with what Alain Badiou would have called the declaration of love as a truth-event, as the flash of the dimension of immortal truth within the process of generation and corruption, the only way to render visible, to represent, this dimension of an unconditional insistence is through the "nonsensical," "miraculous" notion of the *stasis* of time: it is as if, in the flash of the truth-event, the very course of time is temporarily halted. There is something of this miracle even in such a common melodrama as Claude Lelouch's *Viva la lie* (Long Live Life, 1984), in which the rotation of the earth around its axis suddenly stops: in the middle of Paris, morning never arrives, there is constant night; fascinated people gather in public places and just stare at the dark sky. At the film's end, this miracle/catastrophe is nicely accounted for as the dream of the hero who wanted to "stop the flow of time" in order not to miss the encounter with his beloved.

10 Judith Butler, *The Psychic Life of Power* (Stanford: Stanford University Press, 1997), 47.

11 Do we not encounter here the same double disavowal as in Marxian commodity fetishism? First, commodity is deprived of its bodily autonomy and reduced to a medium which embodies social relations; then, this network of social relations is projected into a commodity as its direct material property, as if a commodity had by itself a certain value or as if money were by itself an universal equivalent.

12 And perhaps this paradoxical double disavowal enables us to discern the subversive potential of the masochist contract: in it, the second-level disavowal is cancelled, i.e., the servant *openly assumes the position of the servant,* and—since he is all the more the servant, the more he (mis)perceives his position as that of an autonomous agent—he thereby (at the level of the "subject of enunciation") *effectively* asserts himself as an autonomous agent. In short, what we in obtain in masochism, instead of servitude masked as autonomous agency, is autonomous agency masked as servitude.

13 Stanislaw Lem, *Solaris* (New York: Harcourt, Brace, 1978), 30.

14 The formula of Tonya Howe (University of Michigan, Ann Arbor), on whose excellent seminar paper "*Solaris* and the Obscenity of Presence" I rely here.

15 See Jacques-Alain Miller, "Des semblants dans la relation entre les sexes," *La cause freudienne* 36 (1997): 7–15.

16 Quoted from Antoine de Vaecque, *Andrei Tarkovski* (Paris: Cahiers du Cinéma, 1989), 108.

17 Is not the exemplary case of such a phantasmatic formation combining heterogeneous and inconsistent elements the mythical kingdom (or dukedom) of Ruritania, situated in an imaginary Eastern European space combining Catholic central Europe and the Balkans, the Central European noble feudal conservative tradition with the Balkan wilderness, modernity (trains) with primitive peasantry, the "primitive" wilderness of Montenegro with the "civilized" Czech space (examples abound, from the notorious *Prisoner of Zenda* onward)?

18 Is the logic here not the same as that of the false imitation of business class in econ-

omy class on British Airways? Some years ago, I was served simple paper napkins as if they were humid towels, arrayed on a tray and delivered with tweezers. Also, on smaller planes, the separation between business and economy class is often purely symbolic, i.e., a barrier holding a curtain is shifted backward or forward, depending on how many business-class tickets are sold.

19 de Vaecque, *Andrei Tarkovski*, 110.

20 This opens up a possible connection with Lars von Trier's *Breaking the Waves*, which also culminates in an act of sacrifice of the heroine: if she goes to the boat with the violent sailor and lets herself be beaten, probably to death, this sacrifice will revive her crippled husband.

21 Interestingly, although it is difficult to imagine two more different universes than Tarkovsky's and David Lynch's, it is possible and productive to establish links between them at the level of particular visual, etc., *sinthomes:* a wooden house burns at the end of *Sacrifice* as well as at the end of *Lost Highway!* The acts have opposite meanings, of course: for Tarkovsky, the house stands for the authentic safety of the home, while the Lynchean house is the ultimate site of obscene crime and *jouissance.*

22 See de Vaecque, *Andrei Tarkovski*, 98.

23 The mention of le Carré is far from accidental here, because, in his great spy novels, he repeatedly stages the same fundamental scenario of the interconnection of love and betrayal, i.e., of how, far from the two terms being simply opposed, betraying someone serves as the ultimate proof of loving him or her. Is betrayal for the sake of love not the ultimate form of sacrifice?

24 To avoid a crucial misunderstanding: the point of our rejection of the sacrificial gesture as false is not to reduce it to some hidden "pathological" motivation. Psychoanalysis proper involves the very opposite of "spoiling" an act's ethical grandeur by unearthing its common causes (explanations like "the hero's suicidal sacrifice was merely the result of his unresolved oedipal guilt feeling"); for Lacan, an act proper is precisely a gesture that cannot be explained, accounted for, through the reference to its "historical (or social or psychological) context," since it stands for an intervention which, "out of nothing," retroactively redefines the very contours of what counts as a "context." So, when we encounter a gesture like that of Mary Kay Letourneau (the thirty-six-year-old schoolteacher imprisoned for a passionate love affair with her fourteen-year-old pupil, one of the great recent love stories in which sex is still linked to authentic social transgression), the business of psychoanalysis is not to "explain" this act as the outcome of some underlying unconscious mechanisms for which the subject is ultimately not responsible, but, on the contrary, to save the dignity of the act.

25 See Claude Lefort, *Écrire: A l'épreuve du politique* (Paris: Calmann-Levy, 1992), 32–33.

26 See de Vaecque, *Andrei Tarkovski*, 81.

27 Karl Marx and Frederick Engels, *The Communist Manifesto* (Harmondsworth: Penguin, 1985), 82.

28 Among recent English writers, Ruth Rendell did the same for the decaying London

suburbs, discerning the poetic potential of abandoned backyards full of debris and half-reclaimed by nature.

29 I rely here on Michel Chion, *Le son* (Paris: Éditions Nathan, 1998), 191.

30 Therein resides also the ambiguity of the role of chance in Kieslowski's universe: does it point toward a deeper fate secretly regulating our lives, or is the notion of fate itself a desperate stratagem to cope with the utter contingency of life?

PART IV | **love**

10

Alain Badiou | **What Is Love?**

It is commonly alleged that philosophy as a systematic willing erects itself on the foreclosure of sexual difference. True, it is not in the most consistent parts of this willing that the word "woman," from Plato to Nietzsche, tends to arrive at a concept. Is this not perhaps the vocation of the word? But is the word "man," stripped of its generic freighting and returned to sexuation, any better treated? And is it necessary to conclude that sexual difference is, in effect, what philosophy undifferentiates? I do not think so. Too many signs attest to the contrary, if one is aware that the ruses of such a difference (certainly more subtle than those of reason) adapt themselves well to what has not been put forward by either the word "woman" or the word "man." This is only the case because it is philosophically admissible to transpose to the sexes what Jean Genet declared of race. Asking what a black is, he added: "And above all, what color is it?" If it is asked what a man or a woman is, it would be the height of a legitimate philosophical prudence to add: "And above all, what sex is it?" Thus, it will be admitted that the question of sex is the primary obscurity, a difference thinkable only at the cost of a laborious determination of identity that it puts to work. Let us add that contemporary philosophy addresses itself at all times to women. It might even be suspected that it is, as discourse, partly a strategy of seduction. Besides, it is from the bias of love that philosophy touches upon the sexes, to the extent that it is to Plato that Lacan must look for what hold thought has over the love of transference.

Nevertheless, it is at this point that a serious objection arises: what has been said of the true reality of love, precisely outside of its Platonic inauguration—and before psychoanalysis unsettled the notion—has been in the order of art, and most singularly in novelistic prose. This coupling of love and the novel is essential, and it will be further remarked that women have not only excelled in this art but provided its decisive impetus: Madame De La Fayette, Jane Austen, Virginia Woolf, and Katherine Mansfield, among many others. And before all these, in an eleventh century unimaginable for Western barbarians, Murasaki Shikibu composed *The Tale of Genji,* the greatest text in which what is sayable about love in its masculine dimension is deployed.

Let it not be alleged that this is a classical confinement of women to the effects of sublimated passion and the dimension of narrative. First of all, I want to show that the signifying bond between "woman" and "love" concerns humanity in its entirety and even legitimates its concept. Following this, I obviously maintain that women can and will continue to excel in every domain and thereby refound the field. The only problem, as for a man, is to know under what conditions, and at what cost. Finally, I consider the novel an art of redoubtable and abstract complexity and the masterpieces of this art as one of the highest testimonies of which a subject is capable when a truth traverses and constitutes it.

Philosophy and the Sexes

From where can the coupling of the truth-procedures be observed, such as those I noted between passion and the novel? From a place where it is shown that love and art are crossed, or "compossible" in time. That place is philosophy. The word "love" will function here as a philosophical category, a legitimate construction as it is seen in the status of eros in Platonism: the relation of this category to the love that is at play in psychoanalysis, for example in transference, will undoubtedly remain problematic. The latent rule is a rule of external coherence: "Make sure that your philosophical category, however specific, remains compatible with the analytic concept." I will not verify this compatibility in detail.

The relation of this category to the revelations of the art of the novel will remain indirect. Let us say that the general logic of love, as grasped in the rift between (universal) truth and (sexuated) knowledge, ought to be put to the test in singular fictions. This time the rule will be subsumption: "Make sure that your category admits the great love stories like a syntax made from its semantic fields."

Finally, the relation of this category to common beliefs will be that of juxtaposition (since love, compared to art, science, or politics, is not necessarily the most frequent truth-procedure, but the most proposed upon). In this case, there is a common sense from which one cannot depart without various comic effects. The rule might be: "Make sure that your category, if paradoxical in its consequences, remains in line with socially acceptable amorous intuition."

Of Several Definitions of Love that Will Not Be Retained

Philosophy, or a philosophy, founds its place of thought on rejections and on declarations—in general, the rejection of the Sophists and the declaration that there are truths. In this case, there will be:

1. The rejection of the fusional conception of love. Love is not that which makes a One in ecstasy through a Two supposedly structurally given. This rejection is in its foundation identical to that which dismisses being-for-death. This is because an ecstatic One can only be supposed beyond the Two as a suppression of the multiple. Hence the metaphor of night, the stubborn sacralizing of the encounter, the terror practiced by the world, Wagner's *Tristan und Isolde*. In my categories, this is a figure of disaster and as such is related to the generic procedure of love. This disaster is not that of love itself but is the remembrance of a philosopheme, the philosopheme of the One.

2. The rejection of the ablative conception of love. Love is not the prostration of the Same on the altar of the Other. I will maintain below that love is not even an experience of the Other. It is an experience of the world, or of the situation, under the post-eventual condition that there were Two. I wish to subtract eros from the entire dialectic of eteros.

3. The rejection of the "superstructural" or illusory conception of love, dear to a pessimistic tradition of French moralists. I understand by this the conception that love is merely an ornamental semblance through which passes the real of sex, or that desire and sexual jealousy are the foundation of love. Lacan occasionally skirts this idea, for example, when he says that love is what fills in [*supplée*] the failure of the sexual relation. But he also says the opposite when he accords to love an onto-

logical vocation, that of the "edge [*abord*] of being." But love, I believe, does not take the place of anything [*supplée*]. It supplements, which is completely different. It is only messed up under the fallacious supposition that it is a relation. But it is not. It is a production of truth. The truth of what? That the Two, and not only the One, are at work in the situation.

The Disjunction

I come now to the declarations. It is a question here of an axiomatics of love. Why proceed in this way? By right of an essential conviction, argued, moreover, by Plato: love is by no means given in the immediate consciousness of the loving subject. The relative poverty of all that philosophers have declared of love derives, I am convinced, from their starting from the angle of psychology or a theory of the passions. If love, however, implies the follies and torments of those in love, it does not thereby deliver its own identity through these experiences. On the contrary, it is this identity on which their becoming [*adviennent*] subjects of love depends. Let us say that love is a process which arranges such immediate experiences, without the law which arranges them being decipherable from within these experiences. This can also be said: the experience of the loving subject, which is the matter of love, does not constitute any knowledge [*savoir*] of love. This is even a distinctive feature of the amorous procedure (in relation to science, art or politics): the thought that it is, is not the thought of its thought. Love, as an experience of thought, does not think itself [*s'impense*]. A familiarity [*connaissance*] with love certainly demands a test of strength, especially the strength of thought. But it is also even intransitive to this strength.

It is thus necessary to keep the pathos of passion, error, jealousy, sex, and death at a distance. No theme requires more pure logic than love.

My first thesis is the following:

1. There are two positions of experience.

"Experience" here is to be taken in its most general sense, presentation as such, the situation. There are two presentative positions: the two positions are sexuated, and one is named "woman," the other "man." For the moment, the approach is strictly nominalist: there is no question here of an empirical, biological, or social distribution.

That there have been two positions can only be established retro-actively. It is effectively love alone that authorizes us to formally pronounce the existence of two positions. Why? Because of the truly fundamental second thesis, which states:

2. The two positions are absolutely disjunct.

"Absolutely" must be taken literally: nothing in experience is the same for the positions of man and woman. Nothing. That is to say: the positions do not divide up experience, and there is no presentation affecting "woman" and "man" such that there are zones of coincidence or intersection. Everything is presented in such a way that no coincidence can be attested to between what affects one position and what affects the other.

We will call this state of affairs "disjunction." The sexuated positions are disjointed with regards to experience in general. The disjunction is not observable and cannot itself be made the object of an experience or of a direct knowledge [savoir]. All such experiences or knowledges are themselves positioned within the disjunction and will never encounter anything that attests to the other position.

To have knowledge of this disjunction—structural knowledge—there must be a third position. This is prohibited by the third thesis:

3. There is no third position.

The idea of a third position engages an imaginary function: the angel. The discussion regarding the sex of angels is so important because its stakes are to pronounce on the disjunction. But this cannot be done from the point of experience alone, or from the situation.

What is it, then, which makes it possible for me, here, to pronounce on the disjunction without recourse to, or without fabricating, an angel? Since the situation alone is insufficient, it requires supplementation. Not by a third structural position, but by a singular event. This event initiates the amorous procedure: we will call it an encounter.

The Conditions of Humanity's Existence

Before proceeding further, it is necessary to turn to the other extreme of the problem. This is the fourth thesis:

4. There is only one humanity.

What does "humanity" signify in a nonhumanist sense? The term cannot be based on any objective predicative feature, which would be idealist or biologistic (and, in any case, irrelevant). By "humanity," I understand that which provides the support for generic procedures, or truth-procedures. There are four types of these procedures: science, art, politics, and — precisely — love. Humanity is thus attested to if and only if there is (emancipatory) politics, (conceptual) science, (creative) art, or love (not reduced to a mixture of sentimentality and sexuality). Humanity is what sustains [*soutient*] the infinite singularity of truths that inscribe themselves in these types. Humanity is the historial[1] body of truths.

Let us agree to call H(x) the humanity function. This abbreviation indicates that the presented term x, whatever it is, is supported by at least one generic procedure. One axiom of humanity indicates this: if a term x (let us say, with respect to the Kantian atmosphere, a noumenal humanity = x) is active, or more precisely activated as a subject in a generic procedure, then it is attested to that the humanity function exists, insofar as it admits this term x as an argument.

We insist on the point that the existence of humanity, the effectivity of its function, arises at a point x which is activated by a truth in process as this "local verification" [*avérer local*] that is a subject. In this sense, the terms of any [*quelconques*] x are the domain, or the virtuality, of the humanity function. Insofar as a truth-procedure traverses the x's, the humanity function localizes them in its turn. It remains in the balance whether the term x permits the existence of the function that takes it as argument or is rather the function that "humanizes" the term x. This balance is suspended by the initiatory events of truth, in which the term x is an operator of fidelity which endures the coarse duration that an encounter initiates as love. It returns to it through being localized, in which the famous solitude of lovers is a metonymy, as a proof that humanity exists.

The term H as such (let us say, the substantive "humanity") appears as a potential (virtual) mixture of four types: politics (x militant), science (x scientist), art (x poet, painter, etc.), love (x, "elevated" [*relevée*] in disjunction by the Two, male and female lovers). The term H knots the four. The presentation of this knot, one notes, is at the heart of the disjunction between the positions "man" and "woman" — in their relation to truth.

Now our fourth thesis, which affirms that there is only a single humanity, comes to signify this: all truth holds for all its historical body. A truth, whatever it is, is indifferent to all predicative partition of its support.

This clarifies simply how the terms x, the noumenal variables for the humanity function, constitute a homogeneous class, susceptible to no other partition than that which induces the subjective activations initiated by an event, and thought according to a fidelity procedure.

In particular, a truth as such is subtracted from every position. A truth is transpositional. It is, moreover, the only thing which is, and this is why a truth will be called generic. I have attempted, in Being and the Event, an ontology of this adjective.

Love as the Treatment of a Paradox

If the effects of thesis 4 are related to the three preceding theses, we can formulate precisely the problem that will occupy us: how is it possible that a truth is transpositional, or a truth for all, if there exist at least two positions, man and woman, that are radically disjunct in regard to experience in general?

One would expect that the first three theses would entail the following statement: truths are sexuated. There would be a masculine and a feminine science, just as it was thought at one time that there was a proletarian science and a science of the bourgeoisie. There would be a feminine art and a masculine art, a feminine political vision and a masculine political vision, a feminine love (strategically homosexual, as certain feminist orientations have rigorously affirmed) and a masculine love. It could obviously be added that, even if this is so, it is impossible to know it.

But this is not the case in the space of thought that I wish to establish. We hold simultaneously that the disjunction is radical, that there is no third position, and also that the occurrence [qui advient] of truth is generic, subtracted from every positional disjunction. Love is exactly the place where this paradox is negotiated [traité].

Let us take the measure of this statement [énoncé]. It signifies above all that love is an operation articulated with a paradox. Love does not relieve [relève] this paradox but treats it. More precisely, it makes truth of the paradox itself.

The famous curse "the two sexes die in their own way" is in reality the nonparadoxical or apparent law of things. To stick to the situation (if one economizes the eventual supplement and therefore pure chance), the two sexes never cease to die in their own way. Furthermore, under the injunction of Capital, which could not care less for sexual difference, the social roles are not discriminated between. The more the disjunctive law is stripped away, without protocol or mediation, the more the sexes (practically undifferentiated) nevertheless continue to die in their own way. This "way" is all the more compelling for having become invisible and having thereby returned to the total character of the disjunction. The staging of the sexual roles, the enrollment of the term x in two apparent classes, which we will call mx and wx, is not the expression of the disjunction but its cover-up, the obscure mediation administered by all sorts of distributive rites and access protocols. But nothing is better for Capital than if there are only x's. Thus our societies uncover-up the disjunction, which again becomes invisible, and without any mediating display. Whence the apparent indiscernibility of the sexuated positions, which allows the disjunction to pass as such. This is a situation whereby each experiences that it murders possible humanity within itself, grasping it by means of this x that it is through a veracious fidelity.

Love is thus itself stripped bare in its function of resistance to the law of being. One begins to understand how, far from "naturally" governing the supposed relation of the sexes, it is what makes the truth of their dis-conjunction.

Love, as the Stage of the Two, Makes the Truth of the Disjunction and Guarantees the One of Humanity

To understand this determination of love, and thus establish it as a constant transformation in thought—as the poet Alberto Caeiro puts it, "to love is to think"—it is necessary to return to the disjunction. To say that it is total is not to speak from a neutral observation point or third position, but to say that the two positions cannot be counted as two. How could such a count be made? The two are not presented as something which, in the three, would be an element of the three.

One must carefully distinguish love and the couple. The couple is that which, in love, is visible to a third party [*un tiers*]. This two is thus calculated on the basis of a situation where there are at least three. But the third party in question, whoever it is, does not incarnate a disjunct or third position. The two that the third party counts are thus an indifferent two, a two completely exterior to the Two of the disjunction. The phenomenal appearance of the couple, submitted to an exterior law of calculation, says nothing about love. The couple does not name love, but the state (even the State) of love: not the amorous presentation, but its representation. It is not for love's sake that this two is calculated from the point of the three. For love, there are not three, and its Two remains subtracted from all calculation.

If there are not three, it is necessary to modify the statement of thesis 1, because it is more rigorous to say:

1 (a). There is one position and another position.

There is "one" and "one," who are not two, the one of each "one" being indiscernible, although totally disjointed, from the other. Specifically, no position-one includes an experience of the other, which would be an interiorization of the two.

This is the point that has always blocked phenomenological approaches to love: if love is the "consciousness of the other as other," this means that the other is identifiable in consciousness as the same. Otherwise, how to understand how consciousness, that is, the place of identification of self as the-same-as-self, could welcome or experience the other as such?

Phenomenology then has only two options:

—the weakening of alterity. In my vocabulary, this means that it detotalizes the disjunction and in fact returns the schism man/woman to a division of the human, where sexuation as such disappears;

—the annihilation of identity. This is the Sartrean route: consciousness is nothingness, and it has no position by itself, being self-consciousness or non-thetic consciousness of self. But, to put this pure transparence to the test, it is well known what becomes of love for Sartre: an impotent oscillation between sadism (making the other into an in-itself) and masochism (turning oneself into an in-itself for the other). Which means that the Two are only a machination of the One.

To maintain at the same time the disjunction and that there is a truth, it is necessary to depart from on the basis of love as a process, and not from an amorous consciousness.

We can thus say that love is precisely this: the advent [*l'avènement*] of the Two as such, the stage of the Two.

But wait: this stage of the Two is not a being of the Two, which would suppose three. This stage of the Two is a work, a process. It only exists as a track through the situation, under the supposition that there are Two. The Two is the hypothetical operator, the operator of an aleatory inquiry, of such a work or such a track.

This to-come [*ad-venue*] of the supposition of a Two is originally evental. The event is this perilous supplement to the situation that we call an encounter. Properly understood, the event-encounter occurs only in the form of its disappearance or eclipse. It is fixed only by a nomination, and this nomination is a declaration, the declaration of love. The name which declares is drawn from the void of the site from which the encounter draws the bit-of-being [*peu d'être*] of its supplementation.

What is the void invoked here by the declaration of love? It is the void, the unknown [*in-su*] of the disjunction. The declaration of love puts into circulation in the situation a vocable drawn from the null interval that disjoins the positions man and woman. "I love you" brings together [*accole*] two pronouns "I" and "you," that cannot be brought together [*in-accoler*] as soon as they are returned to the disjunction. The declaration nominally fixes the encounter as having for its being the void of the disjunction. The Two who amorously operate is properly the name of the disjunct apprehended in its disjunction.

Love is interminable fidelity to the first nomination. It is a material procedure which reevaluates the totality of experience, traversing the entire situation bit by bit, according to its connection or disconnection to the nominal supposition of the Two.

There is here a numerical schema proper to the amorous procedure. This schema states that the Two fractures the One and tests the infinity of the situation. One, Two, infinity: such is the numericity of the amorous procedure. It structures the becoming of a generic truth. What truth? The truth of the situation insofar as there exist two disjunct positions. Love is nothing other than a trying sequence of investigations on the disjunction and the Two, such that in the retroactivity of the encounter it verifies that it has always been one of the laws of the situation.

From the moment that a truth of the situation occurs as disjunct, it also becomes clear that any [*toute*] truth is addressed to everyone [*tous*], and guarantees the uniqueness of the humanity function H(*x*) in its effects. Because here this point is reestablished that there is only one situation, from the moment that it is truly grasped. One situation, and not two. The situation that is the disjunction is not a form of being, but a law. And truths are all, without exception, truths of this situation.

Love is this place which proceeds when the disjunction does not separate the situation in its being. The disjunction is only a law, not a substantial delimitation. This is the scientific aspect of the amorous procedure. Love fractures the One according to the Two. And it is in virtue of this that it can be thought that, although worked by this disjunction, the situation is exactly as if there has been a One, and it is through this One-multiple that all truth is assured. In our world, love is the guardian of the universality of the true. It elucidates virtuality, because it makes truth of the disjunction. But at what price?

Love and Desire

The Two as post-eventual supposition must be marked materially. It must have the primary referents of its name. These referents, everyone knows, are bodies insofar as they are marked by sexuation. The differential trait which bodies bear inscribes the Two in its nomination. The sexual is tied to the amorous procedure as the advent [*l'avènement*] of the Two, in the double occurrence of a name of the void (the declaration of love) and a material disposition restricted to bodies as such. A name drawn from the void of the disjunction and a differential marking of bodies thus compose together the amorous operator.

This question of the becoming [*advenue*] of bodies in love must be carefully delimited, because it engages [*oblige*] the enforced dis-relation [*dé-rapport*] between desire and love.

Desire is the captive of its cause, which is not the body as such and still less "the other" as a subject, but an object which the body bears— an object before which the subject, in a phantasmatic centering, comes [*advient*] into its own disappearance. Love obviously enters into this defile of desire, but love does not have the object of desire as a cause. Thus love, which marks on bodies, as matter, the supposition of the Two that it activates, can neither elude the object cause of desire, nor can it arrange itself there any longer. This is because love treats bodies from the bias of a disjunctive nomination, whereas desire is related to bodies as the principle of the being of the divided subject.

Thus love is always a predicament, if not with regard to the sexual, then at least with regard to the object that wanders there. Love passes through desire like a camel through the eye of a needle. It must pass through it, but only insofar as the living body restitutes the material marking of the disjunction by which the declaration of love has realized the interior void.

Let us say that it is not the same body that love and desire treat, even though it is, exactly, "the same."

In the night of bodies, love attempts to expand, to the extent of the disjunction, the always partial character of the object of desire. It attempts to cross the barrier of stubborn narcissism, by establishing (but it can only do this by being limited to the object) that this body-subject is in the descent of an event, and that before the unveiling of the brilliancy of the object of desire it was (this body, the supernumerary emblem of a truth to come) encountered.

Furthermore, it is only in love that bodies have the job of marking the Two. The body of desire is the body of offense [*délit*], of the offense of self. It makes sure of the One in the guise of the object. Love alone marks the Two in a sort of unleashing [*déprise*] of an object that operates only by being leashed [*prise*].

It is firstly at the point of desire that love fractures the One in order that the supposition of the Two might occur [*advienne*].

Even if there is something ridiculous about it—like the early church fathers' *Credo quia absurdum*—it is necessary to assume that the differential sexual traits only attest to the disjunction under the condition of the declaration of love. Outside this condition, there are not Two, and the sexual marking is held entirely within the disjunction, without being able to attest to it. To speak a little brutally: all sexual unveiling of bodies that is nonamorous is masturbatory in the strict sense; there is only the interiority of a position. This is not at all a judgment, but a simple delimitation, because masturbatory "sexual" activity is an activity completely reasonable for each of the disjointed sexual positions.

Love alone exhibits the sexual as a figure of the Two. It is thus also the place where it is stated that there are two sexuated bodies, and not one. The amorous unveiling of bodies is the proof that, under the unique name of the void of the disjunction, the marking of the disjunction itself occurs [*vient*]. This, which is in its own name a faithful position of truth, informs itself by having always been radically disjunct.

But this sexuated attestation of the disjunction under the post-evental name of its void does not abolish the disjunction. It is only a question of making it true. It is thus very true that there is no sexual relation, because love founds the Two, not the relation of Ones in the Two. The two bodies do not present the Two (for which there must be three—the beyond-sex), they only mark it.

The Unity of Amorous Truth and the Sexuated
Conflict of Knowledges

This point is very delicate. It is not only necessary to understand that love makes truth of the disjunction under the emblem of the Two, but that it makes it in the indestructible element of the disjunction.

The Two, not being presented, operate in the situation as a complex of a name and a corporeal marking. It seeks to evaluate the situation by laborious inquiries, understood here as inquiries regarding its accomplice, which is also its mistake: desire. Sexuality, but also cohabitation, social representation, sorties, speech, work, travels, conflicts, children: all this is the materiality of the procedure, its track of truth through the situation. But these operations do not unify the partners. The Two operate as disjunct. There will have been a single truth of love in the situation, but the procedure of this unicity stirs in the disjunction by which it makes the truth. The effects of this tension can be observed on two levels.

1. There are in the amorous procedure certain functions whose grouping redefines the positions.

2. What the future of the one truth authorizes by anticipation in knowledge is sexuated. Foreclosed from truth, the positions return in knowledge.

On the first point, in the work of Samuel Beckett (I thus come here to what in the prose novel has the function of thinking the thought of love), the becoming of the amorous procedure requires that there be:

—a wandering function, of *alea*, of a perilous voyage through the situation, that supports the articulation of the Two and infinity. A function that exposes the supposition of the Two to the infinite presentation of the world;

—an immobility function that protects, that withholds the primary nomination, that ensures that this nomination of the event-encounter is not engulfed by the event itself;

—an imperative function, continuing always, even in separation, and which holds that absence is itself a mode of continuation; and

—a story function, which, as the work proceeds, inscribes by a sort of archivage the becoming-truth of the wandering.

We can establish that the disjunction reinscribes itself in the table of functions. Because "man" will be axiomatically defined as the amorous position that couples the imperative and immobility, while "woman" is that which couples wandering and storytelling. These axioms do not hesitate to blend both coarse and refined commonplaces: "man" is he (or she) who does nothing, I mean nothing apparent for and in the name of love, because he holds that what he has valued once can continue to be valued without having to reattest to it. "Woman" is she (or he) who makes love travel and who desires that her speech constantly reiterate and renovate itself. Or, in the lexicon of conflict: "man" is mute and violent, while "woman" gossips and complains. Empirical materials are required for the work of the inquiries of love, in order that there be truth.

My second point is more complex.

What I will first reject is that, in love, each sex can learn about the other sex. I do not think so. Love is an inquiry of the world from the point of view of the Two, and not an inquiry of each term of the Two about the other. There is a real of the disjunction, which is exactly that no subject is able to occupy the two positions at the same time and under the same relation. This impossibility lies in the place of love itself. It entails the question of love as a place of knowledge: what is it, on the basis of love, that is known?

We must carefully distinguish knowledge and truth. Love produces a truth of the situation just as the disjunction is a law of the situation. This truth composes, it compounds itself to infinity. It is thus never presented integrally. All knowledge relative to this truth thus disposes itself as an anticipation: if this never-ending truth will have taken place, are judgments about it then not true but veridical? Such is the general form of knowledge under the condition of a generic procedure, or a truth-procedure. For technical reasons, I call this *forçage*.[2] We can force a knowledge through a hypothesis regarding the having-taken-place of a truth that is in process. In the case of love, the in-process of truth bears upon the disjunction. Each person can force a knowledge of the sexuated disjunction on the basis of love, on the hypothesis of its having-taken-place.

But the *forçage* is in the situation where love is proceeding. If the truth is one, *forçage*, then knowledge is submitted to the disjunction of positions. What "man" knows and what "woman" knows about love on the basis of love remain disjunct. Further: the veridical judgments that bear upon the Two on the basis of its evental opening cannot coincide. In particular, knowledges of sex are themselves irremediably sexuated. The two sexes do not not-know each other, but know each other veridically in a disjunct fashion.

Love is this stage where a truth about the sexuated positions proceeds, across a conflict of inexpiable knowledges. This is truth from the point of the unknown. Knowledges are veridical and anticipatory, but disjunct. Formally, this disjunction is representable in the insistence of the Two. The position "man" sustains the split of the Two, this gap between [*l'entre-deux*] where the void of the disjunction fixes itself. The position "woman" holds that the Two are lost in wandering. I have had occasion to advance the following formula: man's knowledge organizes its judgments with the nothing of the Two, woman's knowledge with the nothing that is the Two. We can also say that the sexuation of knowledges of love disjoints:

1. the veridical masculine statement, "What will have been true is that we were two and not at all one"; and

2. the feminine statement, no less veridical, that holds, "What will have been true is that we were two, and otherwise we were not."

The feminine statement aims at being as such. Such is its destination in love, which is ontological. The masculine statement aims at the change in number, the painful effraction of the One through the supposition of the Two. It is essentially logical.

The conflict of knowledges in love shows that the One of a truth always exposes itself logically and ontologically. Which returns us to the third book of Aristotle's metaphysics and to the admirable recent commentary published by Vrin under the title *The Decision of Sense*. The enigma of this Aristotelian text derives from the passage between the ontological position of a science of being (insofar as it is), and the crucial position of the principle of identity as a pure logical principle. This passage, in general, is no more frequented than the one which goes from the female position to the male position. The authors of the commentary show that Aristotle passes "by force," in the ardor of an intermediary style, that of the refutation of the Sophists. Between the ontological and logical positions, there is only the medium of refutation. Thus, for each position engaged in love, the other position only allows itself to be attained as if it were a sophistics to be refuted. Who is not familiar with the tiresome exhaustion of such refutations, which can be summed up by the deplorable syntagm, "You do not understand men"? An enervated form, we might say, of the declaration of love. Who loves well understands poorly.

I do not know if it was accidental that this commentary on Aristotle, which I am augmenting here in my own way, was written by a woman, Barbara Cassin, and by a man, Michel Narcy.

The Feminine Position and Humanity

This will be the final word. But I will add a postscript that will return to my beginning.

The existence of love makes it appear retroactively that, in the disjunction, the female position is oddly the bearer of love's relation to humanity as I conceive it: humanity, the function $H(x)$ that makes an implicative knot with the truth-procedures, is science, art, politics, and love. It will be said that this is a trivial commonplace. It is said that "woman" is that which thinks only of love, and "woman" is being-for-love. Let us courageously cross the commonplace. We will axiomatically posit that the female position is such that the subtraction of love affects it with inhumanity for itself. Or rather that the function $H(x)$ is only able to have a value insofar as the amorous generic procedure exists. This axiom signifies that, for this position, the prescription of humanity is only a value insofar as the existence of love is attested to.

Let us note in passing that this attestation does not necessarily take the form of an experience of love. One can be "seized" by the existence of a truth-procedure from an entirely other basis than experience. Once again, we must avoid all psychologism: what matters is not the consciousness of love but the fact that it administers, for the term x, the proof of its existence. A term x, the noumenal virtuality of the human, whatever its empirical sex, only activates the humanity function on the condition of such a proof, and we propose that this proof is woman. Thus "woman" is she (or he) for whom the subtraction of love devalorizes $H(x)$ in its other types, science, politics, and art. *A contrario*, the existence of love deploys $H(x)$ in virtually all its types, and above all in the most connected or crossed. This undoubtedly explains the excellence of women in the novel—if it is admitted that it is a "feminized" x that is in question in the writing of the prose novel, which is to be explored further. For the male position, it is not at all the same: each type of the procedure itself gives value to the function $H(x)$, without taking account of the existence of the others.

I have thus come to define the words "man" and "woman" from the point where love cuts into the knotting of the four types of truth-procedure. Again, in relation to the humanity function, sexual difference is only thinkable by using love as a differentiating criterion. But how could it be otherwise if love, and it alone, makes the truth of the disjunction? Desire cannot found the thought of the Two, since it is the captive of the proof of being-One which the object imposes on it. We will also say that, however it is sexuated, desire is homosexual, whereas love, even if it can be gay, is principally heterosexual. It could also be said that the passing of love in desire, whose difficult dialectic I have gestured toward above, makes heterosexual love pass in homosexual desire. Finally, and without considering the sexes of those that a love encounter destines to a truth, it is only in the field of love that there are "woman" and "man."

But let us return to Humanity. If it is admitted that H is the virtual [*virtuelle*] composition of four types of truth, we can advance that, for the female position, the type "love" knots the four, and that it is only on its condition that H, humanity, exists as a general configuration. And that, for the male position, each type metaphorizes the others, this metaphor willing the immanent affirmation in each type, of humanity H.

We have the two schemes illustrated in figures 1 and 2. These schemes show that the feminine representation of humanity is at the same time conditional and knotting, which authorizes a more total perception and

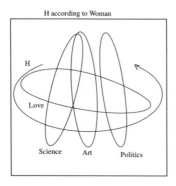

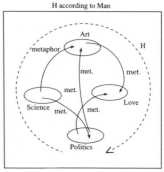

I   2

in that case a more abrupt right to inhumanity. However, the masculine representation is at the same time symbolic and separative, which can entail not only indifference but also a greater ability to conclude.

Is it a question of a restricted conception of femininity? Does this commonplace, even if elaborated, rediscover a scheme of domination which summarily states: access to the symbolic and the universal is more immediate for man? Or that man is less the mere tributary of an encounter? We could object that the encounter is everywhere: all generic procedures are post-evental. But this is not essential. What is essential is that love is the guarantor of the universal, since it alone elucidates the disjunction as the simple law of a situation. That the value of the humanity function H(x) is dependent, for the female position, on the existence of love, can just as well be put: the female position demands for H(x) a guarantee of universality. It only knots the components of H on this condition. The female position sustains itself, in its singular relation to love, so that it can be clear that "for all x, [there is an] H(x), whatever the effects of the disjunction, or of the disjunctions (for the sexual is perhaps not the only one)."

I make here a supplementary turn of the screw with regard to the Lacanian formulas of sexuation. Very schematically: Lacan divides the phallic function f(x). He assigns the universal quantifier to the male position (for-every-man) and defines the female position by a combination of the existential and of negation, which means to say that woman is not-all. This position is to an extent very classical. Hegel, saying that woman is the irony of community, pointed to this effect of the existential border by which woman breaches the all that men strive to consolidate.

But this is the strict effect of the exercise of the function $f(x)$. The clearest result of what I have been saying is that the humanity function $H(x)$ does not coincide with the function $f(x)$. With regard to the function $H(x)$, it is in effect woman who sustains the universal totality, and it is the male position that metaphorically disseminates the virtualities of the composition—one of the H. Love is that which, splitting the $H(x)$ from the $f(x)$, restores to women, across the entire extent of the truth-procedures, the universal quantifier.

Translated by Justin Clemens

Notes

English translation first published in *Umbra* 1 (1996).

1   The distinction is made here between the French "historique" and "historial" deriving from the French reception of Heidegger. Historial implies a nonempirical concept. [Translators]

2   *Forçage:* a term from mathematical set theory which designates the practice of "forcing" an indiscernible. [Translators]

11

The Case of the

Alenka Zupančič | **Perforated Sheet**

Lacan depicts what he calls the "metaphor of love" with this poignant image: a hand reaches out toward a fruit, a flower, or lips which suddenly blaze; its attempt to attain, to draw near, to make the fire burn, is closely connected with the ripening of the fruit, the beauty of the flower, the blazing of the lips. But when, in this attempt to attain, to draw near, to make the fire burn, the hand has moved far enough toward the object, another hand springs up from the fruit, from the flower, from the lips, and reaches out to meet our hand, and at this moment our hand freezes in the closed fullness of the fruit, in the open fullness of the flower, in the explosion of the blazing hand. That which occurs at this moment is love.[1]

The sublime colors of this description must not blind us to the fact that the effect of this kind of configuration is always somehow comical. "Love is a comic feeling," states Lacan,[2] and this is particularly true of what is called "falling in love."

The hand that, much to our surprise and embarrassment, reaches out from the desired object can be, for example, a bottom that blushes. I am referring to the most archetypal scene from Salman Rushdie's *Midnight's Children*. Aadam Aziz has just come back to India from Germany, where he studied to be a doctor. He is called upon to examine a landowner's daughter. When he arrives at the house and asks to see the daughter, her father explains to him that she is a decent girl who does not flaunt her body under the noses of strange men. The young doctor is led to a room where two women, built like professional wrestlers, stand stiffly, each holding one corner of an enormous white sheet. In the very center of the sheet there is a hole cut, a circle about seven inches in diameter. The doctor is told that he can examine the patient only through this perforated sheet, and he is asked kindly to specify which portion of the girl he wants to inspect. Thus begins a three-year process designed to make the doctor fall in love with his patient. During this time, the landowner's daughter contracts an extraordinary number of minor illnesses, and Doctor Aziz's visits become almost weekly events. On each occasion, he is vouchsafed a glimpse, through the perforated sheet, of a different seven-inch circle of the young woman's body. There is probably no need to stress that the landowner's plan works marvelously and that Doctor Aziz develops a very strong desire for the daughter whom he only knows *partes extra partes*. Also, the parts he is asked, or rather allowed, to examine become more and more delicate. So, the desire is clearly there, but what about love? The last part Doctor Aziz was asked to inspect (under the pretense of a pulled muscle in the back of her thigh) was the daughter's bottom. And when he reaches out to feel it, he sees the bottom "reddening in a shy, but compliant blush." Her bottom blushes! At this moment he falls in love. What else to do, if, so to speak, a bottom winks at you? What else to do if the *object* you look at suddenly looks back at you, thus producing an undeniable effect of subjectivation? You either run away or fall, that is, resubjectivize accordingly.[3]

The image, or rather the emblem, of the perforated sheet also contains several other interesting features which can throw some light on Lacan's formulas of sexuation, especially their left or "male" side. It illustrates perfectly the constitution of the subject of desire via the dialectics of the "all" [*tout*] and the exception. The "paradox" of this side of the formulas is well known. They state, first, that there exists one x which does not come under the function of castration (Φx) and, second, that all x's come under the function of castration. Lacan also stresses that "all" is constituted precisely in reference to the exception.

What these formulas imply is not the existence of a totalized set (the "all") plus an exception (i.e., something apart). The exception is not something which has to be added to the set of "all," but rather something which has to be subtracted from an indefinite set in order for this set to become a set. The exception is not One on top of all; it is not a "plus One," but a "minus One," a "One-less." In other words, the exception is nothing else but the hole in the sheet, the hole through which one can now see something. This is to say that the exception is contemporary with the set of "all," and not something previously excluded from it. But what is the relation between this hole and the quantifier "all," since it appears that what we can see through a hole is precisely not all but just some fragments of reality? The point is that the all that we encounter in Lacan's formulas is not the all of some all-embracing totality. It is not as if the father of the bride were to wrap his daughter in a sheet and give her "all" to Aziz. On the contrary, he organizes the whole setting in a way which enables us to translate Lacan's formulas as follows: *all that appears through the hole, which opens up with the One-less of the exception, is worthy of desire*. This means, first, that we have to read the two levels of the formulas (the level of the exception and the level of the all) together; second, that the all is specified by its falling under a certain function (Φx or, in our case, the function of desirability); and third, that the totality at stake is not an all-embracing or "simultaneous" totality but a form of successiveness (the all in question is, to use Lacan's term, *serial*). This latter point is perhaps the most crucial. It accounts for Lacan's insisting that a man can only approach the other sex "one by one," *une par une* (or part by part).[4] And it is important to acknowledge that this serial approach is not linked to the fact that "Woman (with capital W) does not exist" or that she is *pas toute* ("not-all," "not whole"), but is instead inherent in the logic of desire which governs man's position. One must resist the temptation to explain the serial character of the all by the supposedly open set of not-all that characterizes the other side of the formulas of sexuation. In other words, the notion of a never-ending, open series is not foreign to or incompatible with the notion of all. It is, on the contrary, essential to the logic of metonymy which generates the all on the left side of the formulas.

Thus, it seems that we are dealing with a kind of "open totality": although *all* that appears through the hole of exception is desirable, it is precisely never "all," since the series can always be continued. Yet, just as the infinity which springs from the possibility of always going one step further is a "bad infinity," the apparent openness of this set is false. The openness of the series is of the same order as the openness of a capitalist saying to his workers, "I am open to all suggestions on how to improve your working conditions, provided that I will not lose a cent." In other words, the openness at stake is always a *conditional* openness, an openness which operates through the exclusion. Aziz will find all parts of his future wife desirable, *provided that* he sees them through the hole in the sheet. The back or hidden side of the all that we encounter on the left side of the formulas is always some form of "*provided that*." The reason for this lies in the fact that the all is constituted (or is in process of being endlessly constituted) through the hole of the exception. It is also important not to confound the notion of exception with that of exclusion. The exception *is not* that which is excluded from the series, but that which sets off the mechanism of exclusion (or differentiation), thus creating a set of all that comes under a certain condition.

The other important point, which explains the desirability of all the objects that appear in the "hole" or in the frame constituted by the exception, is the following: the institution of the exception (which is the operation of the law) "*exceptionalizes*" *the set of all*. All that appears through the hole in the sheet seems exceptional or, to use another expression, very special indeed. Which is exactly why, although "they are all the same" (they all satisfy a certain condition), each one is special. Except that one should not say "although," but rather "to the extent": to the extent that they all satisfy the same condition, each one is very special. This means that women should probably feel less enthusiastic about the famous "you are very special" line. For it usually means nothing but "you qualify for the series."

Above, we pointed out that the all or the universal linked to the left side of the formulas of sexuation is a conditional universal, which means that only the elements that satisfy a certain condition can enter the set of "all." This brings us to Alain Badiou's discussion of the universal in his book *Saint Paul: The Foundation of Universalism*. Badiou shows how this very feature is an essential characteristic of the law, which always hinges on some particularity and/or exclusion. The universal of the law is always a particular (or particularized) universal. To this notion of the universal Badiou opposes what he calls *singularité universelle,* universal singularity. The distinction between these two kinds of universal (which is also the distinction between two quite different kinds of law) is crucial to our discussion here, so let us examine it more in detail.

Badiou[5] starts from Saint Paul's distinction between the flesh and the spirit and proposes a theory of the way in which this distinction articulates the configuration of law, desire, sin, and love. First of all, he extracts the couple flesh-spirit from the conceptual field constituted by the couple body-soul (with all its connotations) and links it to the couple death-life. Of course, the couple life-death does not refer to any biological facts; it refers to or rather it accounts for the fundamental division of the (living) subject in which the path of life and the path of death always coexist.

Let us first suppose—as Saint Paul does—a state "before the law," the somewhat mythical stage of a subject's innocence in which he does not yet know the law. At this stage, the subject's life is not (yet) the life which constitutes the real of the path of life in the divided subject. It is the life of a supposedly full subject. This innocent life thus remains foreign to the question of salvation. On the other hand, and according to Paul, sin is dead without the law. This means that "before the law" the path of death is itself dead.

Now, what happens with the intervention of the law (interdiction, commandment)? The law appoints to desire its object, and desire finds its determination and autonomy as transgressive desire. The law fixes the object of desire and chains the desire to it, regardless of the subject's "will." With autonomy, desire also finds its automatism. The law is that which gives life to desire, but in so doing, it also coerces the subject into taking the path of death. In other words: "With the law, the path of death, which was itself dead, becomes alive. The law makes death live and the subject, as life according to spirit, falls on the side of death. The law distributes life on the side of the path of death, and death on the side of the path of life."[6]

The life of desire as autonomy, as automatism, is what Saint Paul calls sin: "If I do what I do not want, it is no longer I that do it, but sin which dwells within me" (Rom. 7:20). One could say that the law creates the center of gravity of the subject and places this center beyond the subject's reach (see figure 1). What especially interests us in this account is the fact that the figure of desire that it suggests is not simply that of a divided subject: the intervention of the law (and of desire) produces an "excenterment" of the subject. The "rule of desire" is the rule of alienation which constitutes the subject and, at the same time, subjects him to the automatism of desire. The subject of desire (or the subject of law)

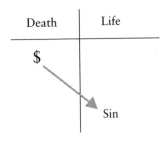

is not, strictly speaking, a divided subject (divided between the path of life and the path of death); he is "all" on the side of death, yet the cause of his desire is something which transcends him and is situated somewhere else, leading an autonomous life. Thus, the subject is not divided between two paths, but rather excentered. The "center" of the subject presents itself as the inaccessible, which gives rise to the infinite metonymy of desire. Life has the status of an exception (which is to say that it remains a fiction of the law) and is always "elsewhere."

The universal attached to this configuration is the universal of a totality which sustains itself as such in relation to a limit or an exception: the exceptional status of the missing object of desire constitutes the limit toward which the subject moves in an infinite, never-ending process. Yet this "bad infinity" is only the expression of the finite, and the apparent openness of the series (there is always still one step possible) the effect of its closure or limit.

Now let us move on to what Badiou, in his reading of Saint Paul, develops as the other figure of the law and of subjectivation. This new law, which bears the name of love [agape], breaks with the law in the ordinary sense of the word and makes the subject "fall over" onto the side of life. However, if the incidence of the law distributes life on the side of the path of death and death on the side of the path of life, then love (which names the other figure of the law) does not imply that life and death now find their "proper" place and simply coincide with themselves. In other words, it is not that the subject now (re)appropriates life. For if Paul says, "If I do what I do not want, it is no longer I that do it, but sin which dwells within me," he also says, "It is no longer I who live, but Christ who lives in me." This is to say that in this new configuration we will not be dealing with a con-centration of the subject as op-

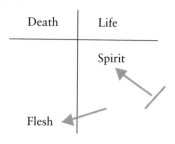

2

posed to the excenterment of the subject of desire. On the contrary—
and this is the most important point—one rather has to say that in love,
the subject is doubly excentered, that she passes onto the side of love by
being excentered for a second time—that is, by being excentered also in
relation to death. The subject is excentered in relation to life *and* in relation to death. It is only with this double excenterment that we arrive
at the divided subject in the strict sense of the term. The subject is no
longer the "mortal shell" which has its life somewhere outside itself and
"lives elsewhere" (in the autonomous-automatic movement of desire).
The subject is no longer an empty envelope but also loses this envelope.
The subject is now nothing but that which is constituted by the nonrela-
tionship between the two subjective paths (the path of spirit or life and
the path of flesh or death). The subject is now on the side of life—yet
not as something which coincides with life itself ("it is no longer I who
live"), but only as that which articulates together the two paths of the
division. One could say that if the law performs the operation of alienation, then love (as the name of the "new law") performs what Lacan
calls separation (see figure 2). Let us now look at that which makes this
new subjectivation possible. In the thought of Saint Paul, this is of course
the event carried by this declaration: "Christ is dead on the cross and
has risen from the dead." As Badiou points out, the death as such plays
no role in the operation of salvation; it acts as the *condition of immanence*. This means that what dies on the cross is *life as exception*. One
could also say that what dies on the cross is death itself, as the feature
which separated the "all" of men from God. Life (or spirit) thus becomes an immanent exception, and it is to be found here and now. We
thus come to some other type of universality which, according to Ba-

diou, sustains itself from a "without exception," and which gives access to no "whole" or totality. "The universal is only that which is in immanent exception."[7] Here we encounter the figure of universal singularity, the figure which combines the dimension of One with the dimension of "for all" [*pour tous*]. We are dealing with the One, the sign of which is "for all" or "without exception." It is not the One of some particularity: "the only possible correlate of One is the universal."[8]

In relation to our previous discussion we could define the two types of universal as follows. The particularized universal is a set of all which coincides or is constituted with the operation of the subtraction of One. The first operation of the law (the operation which coincides with the institution of the law) is to cut a hole in the sheet that it raises between subject and object. The One-less of the exception then supplies the condition sine qua non (the "provided that") which particularizes the universal, the set of all that appears through the hole of the subtracted One. The universal singularity, on the other hand, operates through the inclusion of One. This does not mean that One is added on top of all; rather, it coincides with the all, one is (for) all. We no longer have the situation in which all x satisfy one particular condition. Instead, we have One for all: there is no x for which One is not valid. Now, we know that for Lacan the implication of this is a set that he qualifies as not-all, and we will see later on how and why this is linked to the fact that the inclusion of the exception infinitizes the set.

With universal singularity we are no longer dealing with the infinite of desire, sustained by the inaccessibility of an exception. We are dealing with the infinite which distinguishes itself by immanence, the immanence of the exception or limit. This does not mean that the infinite is immanent to the finite (which is rather the case in the previously discussed configuration, where we had an infinite movement of the desire within a finite, delimited frame). It is the exception which becomes immanent to the all of the finite and thus introduces an opening in this finite, makes it not-all, makes it infinite. Here, we are in the infinite.

All this brings us back to the core of Lacan's formulas of sexuation (figure 3). The lower part of the formulas shows at least a structural homology with the two figures of the subject which Badiou develops in his reading of Saint Paul: the excentered and the divided subject, the subject that still hangs on some pretense of substantiality and the pure sub-

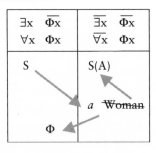

3

ject. One could actually say that if "Woman does not exist" (which, as we know, follows from these formulas), it is because "she" is a subject, in the strict sense of the word; and that if Man exists, it is because he is not yet altogether a subject. The fundamental statement of these formulas would thus be: there are men and there are subjects. One could go even further and deduce from there a kind of practical imperative of universalism: "Let the men become subjects!"

Things get even more interesting when we include in our consideration the upper part of the formulas as well and thus again raise questions of the finite and the infinite, the all and the not-all, desire and *jouissance*. To get to the heart of these questions we will take the path of another text of Badiou, in which he raises a very interesting objection to Lacan and to his conception of feminine *jouissance*.

According to Badiou, feminine *jouissance* has for Lacan the status of the inaccessible. The infinite of feminine *jouissance* is defined as the inaccessible infinity within which the process of determination of the castrated *jouissance* takes place. The other *jouissance* is the undetermined silence in which proceeds, in the finite, the articulation of the phallic *jouissance*. For his purpose, Lacan does not need the existence of an infinite set. It is enough that there operates some inaccessible point for the finite. The infinite is not a set but a virtual point excluded from the action of the finite. This is why, according to Badiou, feminine *jouissance* has for Lacan the structure of a fiction. In order to clarify what is at stake, Badiou takes the example of a cardinal set ω, the smallest infinite set possible from the viewpoint of whole natural numbers. Starting from whole numbers, one cannot construct an infinite set; ω is thus inaccessible from the viewpoint of the entire domain of whole finite numbers.

Although whole numbers indefinitely tend toward ω as their limit, the infinite remains the inaccessible proper to the successive insistence of numbers. "Since the existence of ω cannot be constructed or operationally established, this existence can only be decided upon, by means of that form of decision proper to mathematics which is an axiom." [9] This was the gesture of Cantor, who, with his famous "aleph zero," secularized the infinite. From there follows the main objection that Badiou addresses to Lacan: if feminine *jouissance* were of the order of the infinite, it would have the structure of an axiom and not that of a fiction. Lacan refuses to admit the axiomatic existence of a second *jouissance*. To put it even more bluntly, although Lacan speaks of the infinite (feminine) *jouissance*, he fails, or rather he explicitly refuses, to conceptualize it as such (i.e., as infinite). This is the feature which puts him in the line with the great twentieth-century thinkers of the finite.

Before attempting to answer Badiou (whose long and subtle argument we have been forced to summarize in a few lines), one remark is necessary: the point of this answer is not to prove that Badiou's criticism is groundless. On the contrary, it does actually point to a real problem in the Lacanian theory. However, our argument is that this problem can be answered from within this theory, which, we firmly believe, does not allow itself be reduced to the tradition of "thought of the finite" and "being-toward-death" (Heidegger).

First of all, one should point out that Badiou's conceptual description is entirely accurate; the catch is that what it describes (the functioning of the bad infinity, endless approaching of the limit, the infinite as a virtual point excluded from the action of the finite) could actually be said to take place on the left (male) side of the formulas of sexuation. The inaccessible is the mode of enjoyment of the phallic *jouissance* and does not refer to the question of feminine *jouissance*. This is clear enough from the following passage from *Encore*: "Achilles and the tortoise, such is the schema of coming [*le schème du jouir*] for one pole [*côté*] of sexed beings. A number has a limit and it is to that extent that it is infinite. It is quite clear that Achilles can only pass the tortoise—he cannot catch up with her. He only catches up with her at infinity [*infinitude*]." [10] Here we are dealing with the infinite, the image of which is that of an infinite asymptotic approaching a limit. In other words, we are dealing with a problem homologous to that which Badiou presents by means of the example of the set ω. To the extent that the tortoise functions for Achilles as this limit toward which he moves with his finite steps, it remains (forever) inaccessible to him. What is of crucial importance in this case can be summarized in two points.

1. It is not the feminine *jouissance* which is inaccessible to Achilles, but his own *jouissance* as noncastrated. It is essential not to take the case of Achilles and the tortoise simply as a kind of parable of the (non)relationship between a man and a woman. Tortoise is not (a representation of) a woman. It is a representation of the consequence of the point of exception constitutive of the subjectivation on this (male) side of the formulas of sexuation. It is the incarnated consequence of "$\exists x \, \Phi x$," that is, of the exception to the function of castration. The tortoise is not Woman but *a*. Tortoise is the excentered center of the subject of desire. It is the effect of the operation of alienation executed by the law (of castration).

Lacan says, "Phallic jouissance is the obstacle owing to which man does not come, I would say, to enjoy woman's body, precisely because what he enjoys is the jouissance of the organ."[11] Paraphrasing Saint Paul, one could reformulate this by stating, "If I enjoy, it is not I that enjoy, but the organ which enjoys for me." And I would even venture to say that this organ enjoys for both sexes and that it is because of this (and not because of the absence of the organ) that women also are subjected to castration.

Thus, the inaccessibility of enjoyment is the very *mode of enjoyment* of the subject of desire. From this it follows that:

2. The paradox or the problem of Achilles is not an expression of the nonexistence of the sexual relationship but a way of surmounting, of making do with the nonexistence of the sexual relationship. The story of Achilles and the tortoise is an answer to the nonexistence of the sexual relationship—maybe a paradoxical answer, but nevertheless one that functions. It consists in putting the Other (to whom we cannot relate) out of play and relating oneself to a part of oneself which is situated, by the intervention of the Law, on the side of the Other (or on the other side of the bar). Now, a man can approach a woman. But, as Lacan remarks, "what he approaches is the cause of his desire that I have designated as *objet a*. . . . The act of love is the male's polymorphous perversion, in the case of speaking beings."[12] One could borrow here a formula of Slavoj Žižek: if masturbating is defined as an act in which bodily contact with a partner is only imagined, than a "proper" act of love could be defined

as "masturbation with a real partner." [13] And Lacan was right in stressing that even by repeating this operation ad infinitum, we will never get to the Other, that is, to the infinite. At this level, $1 + 1$ is never 2 but remains 2 times 1. This is, I believe, the rational kernel of Lacan's paradoxical statement from "Ou pire," where he claims that (the number) 2 is unattainable from smaller numbers (0 and 1), linking this inaccessibility to the concept of aleph zero. As Badiou points out, Lacan seems to ignore the equation $2 = 1 + 1$ and to claim that 2 is infinite. According to Badiou, this error is due to the fact that Lacan wants to establish (the number) 2 as inaccessible in order to link it to the question of the second or feminine *jouissance,* which he conceptualizes as inaccessible. Yet, once again, the inaccessibility of 2 (or of the Other) is strictly confined to the male side of the formulas of sexuation. "When one is a man," states Lacan, "one sees in one's partner what one props oneself up on, what one is propped up by narcissistically." [14] This is why, on this side, $1 + 1$ does not amount to 2 (or attain the Other), whereas on the other (female) side of the formulas of sexuation there is no question of the inaccessibility of 2 (or of the Other). On the contrary, here number 2 is the starting point: "Being the Other, in the most radical sense, in the sexual relationship, . . . , woman is that which has a relationship to that Other." [15] In other words, woman's position is characterized by its immanent relationship to the Other, which is precisely why she is *pas toute,* not all or not whole. If she had only a relationship to phallus ($\rightarrow$), that is, if she took only the path of desire, she would be as whole as a man is in his relationship to *objet a*. But she has, in the first place, a relationship to the Other ($\rightarrow S(\cancel{A})$). It is the inclusion of the dimension of the Other that abolishes the Other as that limit toward which one can only approach ad infinitum and which, at the same time, delimits the space of "all." Paradoxically, woman *is One with the Other,* and this is exactly what makes her not-all.

To sum up: even though that which embodies the inaccessible *jouissance* is situated on the other side of the bar, it does not concern the *jouissance* of the other or feminine *jouissance* but represents the originally alienated (and now inaccessible) part of the subject of desire.

However, it can also happen that Achilles does not try to catch up with the tortoise but passes it, that is, passes onto the side of love. Here we are in the infinite. It is important to point out that in the quoted passage in which he speaks of Achilles and the tortoise, Lacan points out that Achilles *can pass* the tortoise. One can see in this the affirmation of a logic different from that which governs desire and which is marked by the predicate of its limit or by the predicate of the inaccessible. "Achilles can pass the tortoise" is a thesis which evokes the axiomatic existence of the infinite. However, one should add that "Achilles who passes the tortoise" is one of the possible definitions of Woman.

This brings us to the other side of the formulas, where, in fact, we are confronted with the question of the other *jouissance*. As to the question of not-all and of the ontological status of the feminine *jouissance*, the following passage from *Encore* is crucial: "Now, as soon as you are dealing with an infinite set, you cannot posit that the not-all implies the existence of something that is produced on the basis of negation or contradiction. You can, at a pinch, posit it as an indeterminate existence." [16] Badiou comments on this passage by saying, "One sees how Lacan still fights desperately against any existential consequence of the not-all." [17] However, although one can actually find several passages in Lacan that speak in favor of Badiou's reading (and give ground to his consequent criticism), it is precisely the above passage which tends to the opposite direction and represents Lacan's most direct acknowledgment of Cantor's notion of actual infinity. In the first step, Lacan takes the existence of an infinite set for his starting point ("as soon as you are dealing with an infinite set . . .") and identifies it with his notion of the not-all. But it is the second step which is crucial. In it, Lacan does not deny every existential consequence (or implication) of the not-all; what he denies is the existential consequence of an *exception* at the level of this set that he calls the not-all. It is not the existence of the not-all that is at stake, but the existence of an exception to the not-all. What Lacan is saying is that from the moment we start dealing with an infinite set (the not-all), we can subtract or add one part *without arriving at some other set than the one from which we started*. In other words, Lacan is referring here precisely to the Cantorian formula $No + 1 = No - 1 = No$. The not-all is impervious to any addition or subtraction. In reference to the upper part of the right side of the formulas this can be expressed as follows: "Not all x are Φx" does not imply that there is an x which is not Φx. And this is precisely what Lacan means when he says that "you cannot posit that the not-all implies the existence of something that is produced on the basis of negation or contradiction." One cannot posit the existence of an exception (which would be a result of negation or contradiction) to the function x, because we are dealing with an infinite set. This also explains why, on this side of the formulas, the difference does not freeze into exception but rather allows for what Badiou calls "the deposition of differences as the material sign of the universal." It is in fact possible to show that Badiou's notion of the universal as universal singularity is very close to Lacan's notion of not-all. They both include a certain "for all" [*pour tous*] (in Lacan's case, in the negative form of: "there is no x which would be exempt from the function Φx") and, at the same time, they exclude any notion of totality.

All this has an important consequence for the explanation of the passage from a first (finite) *jouissance* to a second (infinite) *jouissance*. First of all, one does not get to the other *jouissance* by the negation of the first, since the negation (i.e., the exception) is precisely that which, far from giving access to some other *jouissance*, sustains the phallic *jouissance* and maintains it within the frame of the finite. In other words, the other *jouissance* can never be deduced or derived from the first *jouissance* (not even by negation). In the passage from one to the other, the fundamental presuppositions change.

Instead of negating the first *jouissance* and positing the existence of a second, noncastrated *jouissance*, one takes away from the first *jouissance* its exception (the noncastrated *jouissance*) which maintained it within the finite frame. This is what opens up the space of the other *jouissance*. And this is precisely what strikes the eye in Lacan's formulas: it is only on the right (female) side of the formulas that the function of castration becomes universal, while losing at the same time every reference to totality, to all. In becoming universal, the function of castration becomes not-all. It takes on and endures (the possibility of) some supplementary *jouissance*; it tolerates addition and subtraction.

One often associates feminine *jouissance* with some kind of mystical trance that words fail to express, and Lacan's own developments seem to point in this direction. However, one must be very careful not to confuse two quite different things. Whatever this supplementary enjoyment might be (mystical trance or some other form of enjoyment), it is not what defines feminine *jouissance*. What defines feminine *jouissance* is not simply some supplement of enjoyment, but the fact that it can take on a supplement (or a deficit, for that matter) of enjoyment *without losing its reference to castration*, whereas phallic enjoyment perpetually has to ensure its reference to castration—that is, it has to refer to the inaccessible. For the inaccessible is not some full, uncastrated enjoyment, but precisely the reminder of the function of castration. It is crucial to take the term "infinite *jouissance*" in a mathematical and not in a metaphorical sense. Infinite *jouissance* is not a *jouissance* so great or intense that words fail to express it. To use Jean-Claude Milner's formula, "the infinite is that which says no to the exception to the finite."[18] "Infinite" refers to the structure or topology of enjoyment and not to its quantity (or quality). Infinite *jouissance* is that which puts an end to "exceptional enjoyment" in all meanings of the words.

Notes

1 See Jacques Lacan, *Le séminaire*, book 8: *Le trasfert* (Paris: Éditions du Seuil, 1991), 67.
2 Ibid., 46.
3 This can also help us understand what Lacan is aiming at when, in the seminar *Encore*, he claims that "love is the sign that one is changing discourses." Each of the four discourses articulates a singular subjective figure or subjective position, and love (including the "transference love" which inevitably springs up with the analyst's discourse), in which the subject consents to confine his or her destiny to the hands of the other, makes the passage from one to another subjective position bearable. Love is a reply, an answer to that something in our encounter with the other which makes our universe shake.
4 See *The Seminar of Jacques Lacan,* book 20: *Encore,* ed. Jacques-Alain Miller, trans. Bruce Fink (New York: W. W. Norton, 1998), 10.
5 See Alain Badiou, *Saint Paul: La fondation de l'universalisme* (Paris: Presses universitaires de France, 1997).
6 Ibid., 86.
7 Ibid., 119.
8 Ibid., 80.
9 Alain Badiou, *Conditions* (Paris: Éditions du Seuil, 1992), 297.
10 Lacan, *Encore,* 8.
11 Ibid., 7.
12 Ibid., 72.
13 See Slavoj Žižek, *Tarrying with the Negative* (Durham, N.C.: Duke University Press, 1993), 43.
14 Lacan, *Encore,* 87.
15 Ibid., 81.
16 Ibid., 103 (translation modified).
17 Badiou, *Conditions,* 194.
18 Jean-Claude Milner, *L'oeuvre claire* (Paris: Éditions du Seuil, 1995), 66.

12

Love and Sexual

Difference: Doubled

Partners in Men

Renata Salecl | **and Women**

Why do men and women often double their partners into two figures, one a stable partner and the other an inaccessible lover? People prone to such doubling usually complain about the oppressiveness of their marriages and dream about escaping the constraints that their partners supposedly impose on them. But when their unhappy marriages actually come to an end, the complainers often lose the grounds of their existence and confine themselves to a passionless, solitary life. Most of these cases present hysterical theaters: the suffering partner finds all the enjoyment precisely in suffering, thus a real change in the situation brings a catastrophe for the hysteric. But if it is easy to understand the theater of the hysteric, the question still remains: what kind of roles do the two partners (for example, the oppressive husband and the unattainable lover) play in this drama? Do women and men redouble their partners in the same way? Specifically, how does sexual difference affect such redoubling? And how does the redoubling of the partners relate to the fact that the subject who tries to incite the love of another often presents himself or herself as someone else, that is, redoubles himself or herself, in order to attract the attention of the loved one?

The problems of redoubled partners are well exemplified in many of the novels of Anita Brookner. *Altered States* and *A Private View* focus on how men redouble their partners, while *Incidents in the Rue Laugier*, *A Closed Eye*, and *Hotel du Lac*[1] offer three different scenarios of how women reject their life partners and dream about some inaccessible lovers. These examples will help to illustrate sexual difference as presented in Lacan's formulas of sexuation and the way this difference affects male and female love relationships.

Men in Love

In *Altered States,* the main character, Alan, is a cautious, solitary solicitor whose life was meticulously organized until he had a brief fling with his glamorous cousin Sarah. After this affair, Sarah moves to another country and shows no interest in keeping in touch with Alan. Desolate, Alan marries Sarah's friend, Angela, but secretly goes on dreaming about Sarah. Once he even escapes to Paris in hopes of finding Sarah there, but he fails to achieve his imagined rendezvous. During Alan's short absence, catastrophe happens at home: Angela gives birth to a stillborn baby and falls into a deep depression, which ultimately drives her to suicide. Alan is guilt ridden over Angela's death, but he continues dreaming about Sarah. When they are both middle-aged, Sarah and Alan finally meet again. Alan notices that Sarah has lost her beauty; he feels less attracted to her, and he also observes no feelings for him on her part. Knowing that no future exists for them, Alan nonetheless remains in love with her. Even when he meets a woman friend whom he likes a lot, he decides not to have an affair with her, since he does not want to change the structure of his life—his orderly, solitary existence and the memory of his past passionate encounter.

This novel gives us a clue about the difference between the secret longings of men and women in Alan's description of how he and his wife relate to the structure of their loveless marriage: "Both of us were preoccupied by secrets. For Angela a tense kind of emotional bargaining took place: if she consented to do such and such a thing then she might claim a reward, the reward of freedom and respectability. My own thought processes were not essentially different: if I surrendered all my anarchic longings I could successfully engineer my emergence as a prime example of conformist man, housed, fed, cared for, my continued existence successfully guaranteed." [2] For Angela, settling into the routine of marriage and complying with the demands of its oppressive structure opened the possibility of finding a well-defined place in society: as a married woman she felt equal to others and thus obtained a desired social status. On the side of her partner, Angela searched for the phallus, the signifier that would secure her place in the symbolic network. But then she becomes utterly disappointed. First, she quickly recognizes that the phallus she was searching for is just a fraud: her husband is revealed to her as a boring bureaucrat, and her married life turns into a lonely existence. Second, she also needs to face the fact that she is not Alan's object of desire. Alan is a decent husband who respects his wife and even shows sexual interest in her; however, Angela knows that she did not succeed in replacing his old love, Sarah, as the object of his desire. Although it was Angela who instigated this marriage of convenience, it is she who eventually detests it the most. Even the prospect of having a child does not bring happiness into Angela's life. But when the child is born dead, Angela paradoxically finds a special *jouissance* in a self-enclosed state, a state of pure nothingness and emptiness. At the end, she needs her husband and the oppressiveness of her marriage only as a structure to provide her with total seclusion from the world. Before further analyzing the nature of such self-imposed female isolation, let us first focus on the male protagonist of this story, since this case can offer us a clue about the nature of redoubled partners in male love life.

How does Alan perceive their marriage? His approach to it is different from Angela's: if Angela at first takes marriage as something she must endure in order to get the reward of respectability and afterward sees it as something that allows her to withdraw from the world, Alan reverses the situation. For Alan, it is not that he must endure the oppressiveness of marriage in order to attain freedom or respect, that is, to seek some repayment for his submission to the institution. In his case, the reward is the institution itself. He thus must first renounce an attachment to a threatening object in order to be able to get the security of the institution. This is clear when he says, "If I surrendered all my anarchic longings I could successfully engineer my emergence as a prime example of a conformist man." For Alan, the boredom of marriage appears as a solution—as something that might keep the object of his desire at bay.

At the end, it is clear to Alan that Sarah was a stand-in for this desired but dreaded object. He muses, "Whatever love I had had for her I was now able to decipher as that primeval anxiety that I had always known, as if her very presence could invoke this feeling of loss. To gain her would be to lose the world I knew; to lose her might threaten a loss

of which I so far had no knowledge."[3] Alan thus fixates on Sarah because she becomes a replacement for some primal anxiety. What is the
nature of this anxiety? Why does the subject need to redouble his object
of love, for example, into a wife he barely endures and an unattainable
lover?

Such redoubling is especially common with obsessional neurotics.
When analyzing this neurosis, Lacan took the case of the Ratman, where
one finds a whole series of redoubled figures: the poor woman and the
rich woman in the life of the Ratman's father as well as in his own; the
good friend who pays the father's debt and the good friend who con-
soles the Ratman; the two officers to whom the Ratman is supposedly
indebted. Whenever the Ratman rationally tries to resolve some situation (for example, to pay off his debt), suddenly the officer to whom
he supposedly owes the money redoubles—there appears to be another
officer to whom he actually owes money. Since the Ratman had already
made a plan to pay the first officer, he cannot change it, and so he tries
to find a way to make the first officer give the money to the second one.
Things get even more complicated when the Ratman rationalizes that
behind these two officers there might actually be a third person to whom
he really owes money—the poor girl from the Post Office. And this girl
is also a double of the rich girl he is supposed to marry.

Lacan links this redoubling to the male problem of assuming his role
in life, that is, how he is to recognize himself in his function as a man
and in his work. First, the man has to take upon himself the fruits of
his deeds without claiming that it is someone else who actually deserves
them or that he possesses them only by chance. And second, the man
has to deal with the way his *jouissance* is linked to a sexual object. The
problem of the neurotic is that he cannot simultaneously take on the
two roles linked to his symbolic status and his *jouissance*. Whenever the
neurotic comes close to success, the object of his love interest redoubles
itself.

The redoubling often happens also on the side of the subject. When
a male subject tries to take on his social function and his function as a
man, a male figure might appear next to him with whom he develops a
narcissistic and deadly relation at the same time. The subject puts onto
this other figure the whole burden of representing him in the world and
living for him, which enables the subject to claim that it is not really

he himself who is in charge of the situation—that he is in fact excluded from the world or cannot find his place in it.

To exemplify this redoubling at the side of the subject, Lacan takes a story from Goethe's youth.[4] When Goethe intended to visit Pastor Bion, he dressed himself like a young student of theology, but when he remembered that Bion had an attractive daughter, Friederike, he decided to return home and put on his best clothes. On the way home, Goethe, however, started thinking that it would be unjust to present himself to the Bion family in fancy clothes, so he borrowed a simple outfit from the boy in the village tavern. But then Goethe also put on lots of make-up and finally made himself even less presentable. Lacan takes Goethe's obsession with the right clothes as an avoidance of the encounter with the desired woman: before achieving the desired goal of seducing Friederike, Goethe redoubles himself—he tries to create a substitute toward whom the deadly threats linked to the object of his desire will be directed.[5] Goethe is horrified by the object of his desire—as an obsessional, he is afraid that this object will engulf him—so he tries to create a double to prevent his own annihilation.

In the case of the Ratman, Lacan speaks about the redoubling of the object of love, and in the case of Goethe, he points out that it is actually the subject who redoubles himself and thus again prevents himself from acquiring the desired goal. To complicate things even further, Lacan places this problem of the redoubling in the context of the oedipal structure, claiming that this structure needs to be understood not as a triangle but as a quartet.[6]

The oedipal structure is usually understood as a triangle in which we have the child's sexual desire for the mother and the paternal prohibition. Lacan points out that most of the neurotic symptoms emerge because the actual father is never up to his symbolic function. As the bearer of the symbolic prohibition, the father necessarily fails to actually embody the law in his person and is often perceived as bereft or humiliated. The neurotic typically re-enacts various forms of redoubling (either by redoubling himself or the object of his love) so that he then forms a quartet with the two other figures in the oedipal structure—the mother and the father.

Even at the mirror stage, the subject looks upon his own image as an alien figure, which appears as a coherent whole, while the child perceives himself as incoherent and fragmented. As a result, the subject sees himself in his mirror image as someone else, someone who is more advanced than he actually is. This relation with the image brings utter despair to the subject, since it shows how unformed and split the subject actually is. In his misery, the subject takes the double as a threatening, deadly figure. In the final analysis, the fourth figure in the quartet is none other than death itself. This death necessarily remains only an imagined death. The double comes to incarnate death, and the subject then constantly engages in a struggle with this deadly figure.

For the male obsessional, this deadly double is someone who knows how to enjoy and thus at the same time becomes a figure of admiration and fear. An example of how a man struggles with such an enjoying other is depicted in Brookner's *A Private View,* a story about a retired accountant, George Bland, who lives a meticulously organized life but who mourns the loss of his best friend, with whom he used to plan how they would soon start enjoying the life of wealthy pensioners traveling around the world, living in expensive hotels, and so on. When George has to face the solitude of his old age, the structure and perfection of his life appears more and more oppressive and boring. A radical change happens in George's daily routine when an abrasive young woman, Katy, moves into the neighbor's apartment. The woman appears to be a nuisance; she constantly disturbs George, asking him for small favors and cynically commenting on his lifestyle. When Katy reveals her plan to open a New Age business venture, George becomes utterly afraid that she might want to extract a large sum of money from him to realize this plan. Rationally, George feels nothing but contempt for Katy's behavior; however, he also becomes very attracted to her. Although George desperately tries to retain the well-structured routine of his life, he begins to entertain the idea that Katy might be willing to go on a journey with him. Knowing that such a journey will cost him dearly, since Katy might treat him badly by lavishly spending his money and abandoning him sooner or later, George nonetheless invites her on the trip, but she quickly rejects his proposal. When Katy can no longer stay in the neighbor's apartment, she informs George that she has two options: either to move into his place or to find the money for a ticket to America. George is still attracted to Katy, but he nevertheless realizes that he very much wants to retain his orderly lifestyle; he thus gives Katy a large sum of

money, and she disappears. After her departure, George tries to reestab-
lish his old routines, but he finds no pleasure in them. Finally, George
decides to invite an old friend, Luise, who has been fond of him for many
years, on a journey.

Here again we have a man who is perturbed by a woman but then
tries to find a rescue in the self-imposed rules which govern his daily
routine. However, after indulging in fantasies of a journey with Katy,
George cannot easily go back to his orderly life: "Through envisioning
a future so different from his own undoubted and authentic past he had
given way to the charm of an idyll, one which could hardly stand up
to the light of day. That balcony, that cigar, that red sun sinking. . . .
There was no rule which would say that he could not still enjoy these
things, but he knew that it would be useless to try. It was only the fantasy
that his life might be shared, and shared by someone so alien to himself, that had enabled his imagination to open up these vistas."[7] With
Katy's departure, George's fantasy turned sour: "He would be left with
his dry memories and his small routines, obliged to make his peace with
what remained to him, rather with what he had promised himself. In
that way he would no doubt salvage a little outward dignity, even though
his thoughts, which must be kept secret, might disclose another truth."[8]
Although George indulges in these pessimistic thoughts, he surprisingly
decides to make plans to take the trip (which symbolizes access to some
prohibited *jouissance*) and even invites his woman friend, Luise, to join
him.

In this novel two sets of characters are redoubled. First, we have
George and his male friend. While George lived a meticulously organized life and had no girlfriends, his friend was a lively person with lots
of female lovers. The figure of the dead friend thus functioned as an enjoying double of the rigid George: with his help, George hoped to find
an access to *jouissance* via excessive spending on the planned trips. Later
the figure of the enjoying friend is replaced by Katy. However, Katy also
functions as a double of George's longtime friend Luise, with whom he
had established a close but sexless relationship. (For example, George
had always called Luise at exactly the same hour every Sunday to discuss the routines of their daily life, but he did not show much feeling for
her.) Paradoxically, after Katy's departure, George becomes concerned
that Luise not find out about his passion for Katy. He thus reasons: "If

anyone has been wronged it was Luise, to whom he had denied the offerings he had been ready to make to that almost unknown girl, and for whom he now felt pity."[9] Although George's decision to finally take the trip can be understood as his attempt to gain access to the *jouissance* he first perceived to be denied him by the death of his friend and Katy's departure, one can speculate that this trip will in no way undermine his obsessional lifestyle. It can even be said that George's invitation to Luise to join him on a trip will actually enable him to retain his equilibrium, since Luise does not pose any threat to his well-ordered life.

Why are men so obsessed with retaining the order in their lives? And are women, in contrast to men, more prone to give up this order? Before dealing with these questions, let us try to understand the difference between male and female love troubles with the help of Lacan's theory of sexual difference, articulated in his formulas of sexuation.

Anxiety in Sexuality

In order to understand figure 1, the subject's love relationships, it is crucial to focus on the lower part of the formulas, where one finds on the male side a split subject and the phallus. There is no direct link between the phallus and the split subject: the subject has a relation only to *objet a* on the female side of the formulas. And on the female side, one finds three elements: a barred Woman, who has a relation to the phallus on the side of man and to a barred Other, while she has no relation to *objet a,* which is on her side of the formulas.

The major problem of the male and the female subjects is that they do not relate to what their partner relates to in them. The phallus that one finds on the side of the man is nothing a man can be happy about. Although a woman relates precisely to this phallus, the man is not at all in control of it. A man thus constantly tries to take on his symbolic function, since he knows that the symbolic function is what the woman sees in him. However, he necessarily fails in this attempt, which causes his anxiety and inhibition. As Lacan points out, "The fact that the phallus is not found where it is expected, where it is required, namely on the plane of genital mediation, is what explains that anxiety is the truth of sexuality . . . The phallus, where it is expected as sexual, never appears except as lack, and this is its link with anxiety."[10] For men, the

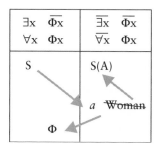

way they desire (which is crucial also for the relation that they form with *objet a* on the side of their partner) is conditioned by the fact that castration marked them by a lack, which also means that their phallic function has been negated. As a result of this negation, men are constantly anxious that they might not be able to "do it," that their organ might deceive them at the time they need it most, that others might find them powerless, and so forth. Lacan points out that it is because of this anxiety that men created the myth of Eve being made out of Adam's rib. This myth allows a man to think that if it was just a rib that was taken out of him, then he is essentially not missing anything—that there is no lost object, and therefore the woman is just an object made of the man. Although this myth tries to assure men of their wholeness, it nonetheless does not alleviate their anxiety. This often happens precisely when a man encounters a woman who becomes an object of his desire.

For Lacan it is crucial that a man give up as lost the hope of finding in his partner his own lack (ϕ) that is, his fundamental castration. If this happens, everything works out well for a man: he enters into the oedipal comedy, thinking that it was Daddy who took the phallus from him, that he is castrated because of the law. This comedy helps a man in his relationships; otherwise, the man takes all guilt onto himself and thinks that he is "the sinner beyond all measure." [11]

What about a woman's problem with castration? A woman is also a split subject and is thus concerned with finding the object she does not have; she is also caught in the mechanism of desire. However, for Lacan the fundamental dissatisfaction that is involved in the structure of desire in case of a woman is precastrational: a woman "knows that in the Oedipus complex what is involved is not to be stronger, more desirable than

mother, but to have the object."[12] Thus the *objet a* is for a woman constituted in her relationship with the mother. Lacan also claims that if a
woman becomes interested in castration (ϕ), it is insofar as she enters
into men's problems, which means that castration is a secondary thing
for a woman. As a result, "For a woman it is initially what she doesn't
have as such which is going to become the object of her desire, while at
the beginning, for the man it is what he is not, it is where he fails."[13] A
woman is concerned that she does not possess the object that a man sees
in her. Thus, she constantly wonders what is in her more than herself;
and because of this uncertainty, she endlessly questions the desire of the
Other.

In short, a man is traumatized by not being able to assume his symbolic role and a woman by not possessing the object of the Other's
desire. This gives us an answer as to why some men are so concerned
with keeping their well-organized lives intact and dread encountering
the woman who incites their desire. Clinging to self-imposed rules gives
a man at least temporary assurance that the symbolic order is whole and
that it might have endowed him with phallic power. But coming close
to the object of desire opens the possibility that this fantasy will collapse and the man will then be stripped naked, exposed in his essential
impotence and powerlessness.

When a man redoubles his partner, for example, by encountering a
secret lover, his primal question becomes: how can I maintain order in
my life? This order does not simply concern the comfort and wealth his
marriage may be providing for him. What a man fears is that by losing
the routine structure of his life, he will be not only deprived of his symbolic power, he will also be devoured by the object of his desire. Even
if a man actually abandons his old partner for the new one, he will be
quick to form another structure in his life, which might further keep his
desire impossible to satisfy.

What about women who redouble their partners? Is their strategy different from men's?

Women in Love

In Brookner's novels *Incidents in the Rue Laugier*, *A Closed Eye*, and
Hotel du Lac, the heroines are ordinary women who are nothing special

in regard to their looks, charm, or achievement and who acknowledge that, "objectively" speaking, they have not done so badly in life in terms of marriage or social status, since they just did not have the "assets" to do much better. But behind this rational acceptance of the situation exists a fantasy life: a burning passion to experience life in full, which is primarily linked to the desire to unite with an inaccessible lover. However, this desire for a different life remains only a desire, since the woman prevents its realization.

The three novels present different scenarios of women's attachments to the figure of a secret lover. In *Incidents in the Rue Laugier*, Maude had a brief, passionate love affair in her youth with the beautiful and charming Tyler, but later, for convenience, married Tyler's friend Edward. Maude takes her married life as something she simply has to endure, while she keeps on dreaming about Tyler. But when, once in her mature life, Maude has a chance to repeat her affair with Tyler, she refuses to do so. The reason for this refusal is not simply that Maude wants to go on fantasizing about Tyler as an inaccessible love object—Maude primarily wants to keep her image alive in Tyler's memory. As we read in the novel: "In that moment she knew she would deny herself her dearest wish, and in that way keep her image distinct in his mind, so that if possible it might stay that way through all the receding summers of his life." [14] Although Maude had loved Tyler her whole life and had created her whole fantasy life around him, she decides to deprive herself of the enjoyment of another encounter with Tyler so that she might stay an inaccessible object in Tyler's desire.

This story exemplifies how a woman wonders about the precious *objet a* that she is supposed to be for her partner. Since she knows that this object concerns the partner's lack, she does everything to keep this lack open. Maude's refusal to repeat her affair with Tyler is thus her desperate attempt to keep herself a precious object that might have aroused his desire in the past; however, to keep this desire alive, Maude has to remain elusive and unavailable. Although Maude's ultimate desire seems to be to unite with her past lover, she actually does not want to fulfill this desire by gaining her precious object, since her desire is to be the object of Tyler's desire. Here we thus have an example of Lacan's well-known formula that the subject's desire is desire of the Other, that the subject desires most to be the object of someone else's desire.

Maude is certain that Tyler has been in some way touched by their past love affair, but she is not certain that he has contemplated her as much as she has dwelled on her memories of him. Being unsure of what kind of an object she was for him, Maude compares her situation with the well-known literary examples of women who gave up everything for love and wonders if the male heroes were worth these sacrifices:

> How could the conformist Vronsky take on a woman who left her husband and child, or the seedy Rodolphe, who had never read a book in his life, understand Emma Bovary, whose notions of chivalry proceeded from a mind stuffed with romantic novels? The appalling lack of suitability in these pairings oppressed Maude, who wondered if all women suffered from this imbalance between their hopes and the reality they were forced to endure. . . . she knew, as if she had been unalterably programmed to do so, that it was her destiny to live the reality of her situation and to keep a closely guarded secret the fact that she had once defied reality, that she knew the difference between acceptance and danger, and that even as she went about her ordinary everyday tasks she would be filled from time to time with the incandescence of a certain memory, and the momentary conviction—or was it merely hope?—that that memory was shared.[15]

When Maude compares herself with Anna Karenina and Emma Bovary, her concern is not that these two women loved men who were not worthy of them; what bothers Maude is the fact that these two women lost their aura of being precious love objects once they fully gave in to their affairs. Maude's concern about the imbalance between a woman's hopes and the reality she must endure thus has to do with the fear that a woman's hopes (or better desires) turn sour when she ceases to be the object of a man's desire.

Although Maude fears that the reality of uniting with the desired lover might not be up to her hopes, she nonetheless persists in staying married to a man she does not love. But after her husband passes away, Maude's life starts looking like a living death: she encloses herself in a solitary existence, as if being drained of any desire to go on living. Maude's married life provided the necessary structure (which she rationally hated) in which she was able to be "alive" and to keep her desire in motion; with the loss of this structure, she falls into a melancholic state in which she stops complaining about the unhappiness of her life and also stops wishing to unite with her beloved Tyler.

In *A Closed Eye,* Brookner offers another scenario of how a woman redoubles her partner. Here, however, we do not have a real past-love encounter, but only a fantasy of a possible one. The heroine, Hettie, makes a marriage of convenience with the much older Frank. She quickly realizes that she will have a comfortable but boring life with him and starts dreaming about a passionate encounter with a gorgeous young lover. This imagined lover suddenly gets a face and body when she encounters Jack, the husband of her friend Tessa. Hettie knows that Jack is a dangerous man, extremely handsome but unreliable, and she also predicts that he will ruin Tessa's life. Nonetheless, Hettie would be willing, at any time, to trade her secure life with Frank for a brief affair with Jack. Although Hettie constantly fantasizes about Jack and barely endures her old husband, she does nothing to pursue Jack. After Tessa's tragic death, Hettie meets Jack once, briefly, and they passionately kiss—but then Hettie quickly runs away from him, thinking that she cannot have an affair, since this might be too painful for her beloved daughter. Hettie then keeps on dreaming about Jack and hopes that, once her daughter grows up, she will resume contact with him. But when the daughter dies in a car accident, Hettie loses all desire to leave her husband and unite with Jack. She moves with her ailing husband to a secluded place in the Swiss mountains, where she remains all alone after her husband's death. Once Jack's daughter sends Hettie a message of her father's love, but Hettie's response is passive: Jack might have had a place in another lifetime, but now all she wishes for is peace in order to be able to grieve for her dead daughter.

In this novel, it is clear that Jack was not particularly interested in Hettie. One can speculate that he was mildly intrigued by her, but he did nothing to pursue her. However, when his daughter sends Hettie his regards, this message opens the possibility for Hettie to resume contact with him. Why did she refuse to do so? It is clear that Hettie "invented" Jack as the object of her attraction in order to keep her desire alive. Jack thus took the place of *objet a*—the nonexistent object, around which she structured her life. This object temporarily assumed the form of the inaccessible love but was later replaced by the dead daughter. In this scenario, the ailing husband is perceived as a companion with whom Hettie is simply stuck, but she does not regard him as the ultimate obstacle to her happiness. The obstacle for her is simply the very nature of the *objet a*. Hettie's refusal to pursue Jack shows that she knew very well that Jack was just a stand-in for the empty object—the object cause of desire. And when she later chooses to live a reclusive life in order to be able to contemplate the loss of her daughter, it is again clear that Hettie's desire targets this very lack, the emptiness of the object. In contrast to Maude, who falls into a melancholic state when she recognizes that she is not the phallus that will complement the Other, Hettie is less concerned with the question of whether she is loved by the Other or not. In her seclusion, she comes closer to the other problem of love: that the subject loves from her lack alone. Her solitude thus appears to be an immersion in a state where the subject comes closest to the lack that marks her being.

If both *Incidents in the Rue Laugier* and *A Closed Eye* deal with the problem of the oppressive institution of marriage being the condition of the subject's desires, Brookner makes another turn in this scenario in *Hotel du Lac*. Here, the heroine, Edith, is again an ordinary middle-aged woman, a semisuccessful writer of romantic novels, who has a passionate affair with a married man, David. Edith knows that David has no intention of leaving his wife and publicly acknowledging their relationship. Being aware that she does not have much of a chance to fall in love with another man with whom she will be able to settle down and get married, Edith accepts a marriage proposal from a man she respects but does not love. But on her wedding day, she changes her mind and runs away. After this embarrassing scene, Edith escapes to a secluded hotel in the Swiss mountains, where she contemplates her desperate love for David and wonders if she can ever return to her old town. In the hotel, she then meets a charming, rich gentleman, Mr. Nelville, who proposes to her a marriage of convenience, in which the partners will not even pretend that they love each other but will simply join forces to create for themselves a more comfortable life. Mr. Nelville has recently been abandoned by his wife and now wants to get married again, on condition that the partnership be based on mutual respect and that each partner be able to discreetly have other lovers. Predicting that Edith does not have many chances to marry in the near future and that she can expect a lonely life, being a woman of low social importance, Mr. Nelville thus offers her a chance to structure her life in a way that will allow her to pursue her actual desires. Being married to a wealthy man and living in a beautiful house will bring Edith social recognition and the time to truly focus on her writing. And at the same time, she will be free to have a secret love life, if she wishes.

Edith is first shocked by this proposal, but on second thought she realizes that she is being offered a good scenario of how to escape the strictures of her old life. Thus, she decides to accept the offer. But before telling Mr. Nelville, she writes a farewell letter to David, in which she informs him about her future plans and urges him not to contact her again. When she is about to post the letter, Edith sees Mr. Nelville, dressed in his nightgown, discreetly escaping from the room of a young woman in the hotel. Edith knows that this encounter was an unimportant fling for him and that he would not object to her having similar encounters. However, she decides not to post the letter to David, but rather telegraphs him that she is returning; she then flees from the hotel.

In this novel we have first the woman's attachment to an inaccessible love object and then an attempt to find a structure which will keep this object at bay. Here it is thus not a rigid structure of marriage that supposedly prevents the woman from pursuing her love interest. The situation is reversed, and redoubling goes in a different direction than in the other novels: now it is the "boring" husband who is invented as the second figure. If Maude and Hettie complained about their passionless marriages, Edith tries to create such a marriage artificially. But why does she twice refuse to realize this plan? Does not Mr. Nelville's proposal give her an opportunity to have it all—a decent husband *and* a lover? This arrangement is similar to the one Maude and Hettie had; however, if, with Maude and Hettie, the marriage appeared to be a trap somehow imposed on them and the unavailable lovers remained unrealizable objects of desire, Edith is offered a chance not only to deliberately create a marriage of convenience, but also to actively pursue her illicit love affair. It is easy to see that such an arrangement leaves no place for her desire: the lack of prohibition makes an extramarital affair much less desirable. However, the problem of the novel is, why is she so shocked when she realizes that Mr. Nelville has been carrying on an affair with another hotel guest? It is not that Edith is in love with him or that she is actually concerned with his love life; her reaction to Mr. Nelville's affair needs to be analyzed in the context of the aforementioned difference in the way men and women relate to desire.

Edith very much desires another man, David. However, when she agrees to marry Mr. Nelville, she becomes concerned with the question of how Mr. Nelville desires. His proposition that they should not bother themselves with passions and just form a marriage of convenience is deeply shocking to Edith: instead of giving her freedom to pursue her own desire, it actually gives her a signal that she is not at all an object of Mr. Nelville's desire. Although at first Edith clearly has no feelings for Mr. Nelville, she nonetheless wants to be respected by him. Thus, it can even be said that Mr. Nelville's strange proposition incites desire on Edith's side. This is why she decides never to see David again, which is a surprising move, since being married to Mr. Nelville would in no way prevent her from keeping David as a secret lover. Edith thus makes a paradoxical decision to accept a loveless marriage and to deprive herself of seeing her past lover again. One can speculate that such a scenario will allow her to go on fantasizing about David; however, one can also predict that she will question Mr. Nelville's desire for her. Accepting such a marriage of convenience thus allows a woman a special form of withdrawal, which sometimes keeps her desire alive. Since this desire is linked to the question of the desire of the Other, one needs to avoid encountering this Other, so that one is not disappointed by recognizing that one is actually not desired by him (or is desired in a way one does not want to be).[16]

Giving Up on Love

With the exception of Edith, all the other female characters at some point give up on love and immerse themselves in a melancholic indifference, while the leading male characters at the end regain "peace" by continuing to obey the self-imposed rules and prohibitions that have governed their obsessional lifestyle. How can we understand such gestures of resignation?

When the subject "gives up" and becomes indifferent to the outside world, it is not that he or she reaches "the zero level of desire, but its reduction more or less accomplished to the foundation of Φ of castration. The subject in this state definitely takes pleasure in something. . . . In effect, doesn't it let the subject take pleasure in the a-corporal consistency of castration as formulated ($\phi = a$)."[17] The subject thus takes pleasure precisely in the lack introduced by castration; however, this symbolic lack (Φ) often gets an imaginary inscription in terms of ϕ. Colette Soler points out that there are various ways in which the subject rejects the gifts of life and detaches himself or herself from the world: "From the conquering desire to the abolished desire of melancholy, passing through the problematic of dubious desire of neurosis, love of the object, self-hatred, and the narcissistic investment of the self arranged themselves in this order. The joint shared with *jouissance* obviously imposes itself: since desire is a defense, *jouissance* raises where desire drops. It may be precisely stated therefore that the depressive state is also a mode of *jouissance*, but the formula will be operative only if we manage in each case to give it the particular coordinates."[18]

In the case of a woman, melancholy is especially linked to feminine *jouissance*. When Lacan tries to decipher this *jouissance,* he usually invokes the example of the mystics—women (and men) who find enjoyment in a total devotion to God, who immerse themselves in an ascetic stance and detach themselves from the world. This feminine *jouissance*, which language cannot decipher, is thus usually perceived as the highest "happiness" that the subject can experience. However, because this *jouissance* is foreclosed from language, it is also something that the unconscious does not know and thus cannot assimilate. If we invoke Lacan's thesis that the remedy for sadness is for the subject to find oneself in the unconscious, then the question becomes, how does the indecipherable feminine *jouissance* relate to female melancholy?

One possible answer might be that the enjoyment a woman finds in a melancholic seclusion from the world is precisely a form of feminine *jouissance*. In this case, an ecstatic mystic and a melancholic woman would not be very different in their *jouissance*. However, feminine melancholy can also be a result of the fact that the woman does not find herself in feminine *jouissance*. Since this *jouissance* does not pass through the unconscious, it passes beyond the woman, which is why in women one often finds "a plus of sadness": "The delirium of melancholic indignity . . . is revealing here: moving to extremes it shows that the fall of the foreclosed *jouissance* into self-insult is the ultimate verbal rampart before the expulsion of that same *jouissance* through the passage to the act of suicide. More commonly, I mean outside of psychosis, the throwback into injury is like the first degree of paradoxical sublimation, having come to this place from *jouissance* 'where it is vociferated that "the universe is a defect in the purity of Non-Being" '."[19] This immersion into sadness or even self-injury often happens when the woman loses love. But why would this loss incite such desperate reactions in women? Following Lacan, Colette Soler claims that it is because of the nature of feminine *jouissance* that one finds in women a specific call to an elective love, which cannot resolve the discord between the phallic and the feminine *jouissance*. In the love relationship that she establishes, a woman will be always Other, that is, Other for herself: "Love will leave her, then, alone with her otherness, but at least the Other that love erects could label her with her lover's name, as Juliet is eternalized by Romeo, Isolde by Tristan . . . or Beatrice by Dante. Deduced from that is the fact that for a woman, the loss of love exceeds the phallic dimension to which Freud has reduced it. For that which she loses in losing love, is herself but as an Other."[20]

If feminine *jouissance* brings women much closer to the real—specifically, to the lack in the symbolic, which might result in either their mystical or their depressive states, women nonetheless are also concerned with the question of what their place is in the desire of the Other. And it is in order to assure themselves of this desire that women engage in redoubling the partners. But such women often seek out men who themselves cannot commit to one woman only. Why does this happen?

A woman who constantly questions if she is the object of a man's love also tries to present herself as the phallus that the man lacks. Paradoxically, a woman finds an answer to her concerns in regard to men's desire and their phallic power in the fantasy of Don Juan, which, as Lacan points out, is essentially a feminine fantasy.[21] For women, this fantasy proves that there is at least one man who has it, from the beginning, who always has it and cannot lose it, which also means that no woman can take it from him. Since women are often concerned that a man completely loses himself when he is with another woman, the fantasy of Don Juan reassures women that there is at least one man who never loses himself in a relationship. The fantasy of Don Juan thus assures women that the object of male desire is what essentially belongs to them and cannot be lost. But women and Don Juan have something in common here: no one can take the object away from women or from Don Juan, since neither one of them ever had it in the first place.

Obsessional men redouble their partners because the object of their desire is something they are essentially horrified by. That is why men cling so to the self-imposed prohibitions and rituals that govern their daily lives. Women redouble their partners because they can never be sure what kind of an object they are in the desire of the Other. Thus, for a woman it is better to fantasize that there is more than one man who is emotionally interested in her. But, paradoxically, a woman often gets the most reassurance about her value as *objet a* in fantasizing about a man (Don Juan, for example) who never actually desired her in the first place.

Notes

1 Anita Brookner, *Altered States* (London: Penguin Books, 1997); *A Private View* (New York: Vintage Books, 1996); *Incidents in the Rue Laugier* (London: Penguin Books, 1993); *A Closed Eye* (London: Penguin Books, 1992); *Hotel du Lac* (London: Penguin Books, 1993).

2 Brookner, *Altered States*, 89.

3 Ibid., 189.

4 See Jacques Lacan, "Le mythe individuel du névrosé," *Ornicar?* 17–18 (1979): 25–39. See also Theodor Reik, *Warum verliess Goethe Friederike? Eine psychoanalytische Monographie* (Vienna: Internationaler Psychoanalytischer Verlag, 1930).

5 To further explain this redoubling, we must take into account another event when Goethe played with his identity. In his late thirties Goethe lived for two years in Italy, where he presented himself as a German painter, Müller. (Later the name was changed to Filipo Miller. And sometimes Goethe even gave a Russian touch to his name and altered it to Milleroff.) In Rome, when Goethe fell in love with a young woman, Faustina, he presented himself as a priest. (Goethe recounts this episode in his *Dichtung und Wahrheit*.) It is well known that in late-eighteenth-century Rome, the church imposed strict moral codes for the masses, while their priests and cardinals enjoyed a very promiscuous life. Thus, when Goethe appeared dressed like a priest, this signaled a respectable social position, while it also implied the hidden underside of his erotic desires. See Roberto Zapperi, *Goethe in Rome* (Munich: Beck Verlag, 1999).

6 Lacan, "Le mythe individuel." See also Michèle Lapeyre, *Au-delà du complexe d'Oedipe* (Paris: Anthropos and Editio Economica, 1997).

7   Brookner, *A Private View,* 230.

8   Ibid., 231, 232.

9   Ibid., 230.

10   Jacques Lacan, "Angoise" (unpublished seminar), 5 June 1963.

11   Ibid., 26 Mar. 1963.

12   Ibid.

13   Ibid.

14   Brookner, *A Closed Eye,* 195.

15   Ibid., 207.

16   Especially traumatic is the recognition that the other desires a woman in a perverse way and is for example attracted only to a fetish object associated with her.

17   See Colette Soler, " 'A Plus' of Melancholy," in *Almanac of Psychoanalysis: Psychoanalytic Stories After Freud and Lacan,* ed. Ruth Golan et al. (Jaffa: G.I.E.P., 1998), 101.

18   Ibid.

19   Ibid., 107. Soler quotes here from Jacques Lacan, "The Subversion of the Subject and the Dialectic of Desire in the Freudian Unconscious," in *Écrits: A Selection,* trans. Alan Sheridan (New York: W. W. Norton, 1985), 317.

20   Ibid.

21   Ibid.

Notes on Contributors

Alain Badiou is Professor of Philosophy at the University of Paris VIII, Saint Denis. His numerous publications include *L'être et l'evenement* (1988), *L'éthique* (1993), and *St Paul ou la naissance de l'universalisme* (1998).

Elisabeth Bronfen is Professor of English and American Studies at the University of Zurich. She is the author of *Over Her Dead Body* (1992) and *The Knotted Subject* (1998).

Darian Leader is a practicing psychoanalyst and Senior Lecturer in Psychoanalytic Studies at Leeds Metropolitan University. He is the author of *Lacan for Beginners* (illustrated by Judy Groves, 1996), *Why Do Women Write More Letters than They Post?* (1996) and *Promises Lovers Make When It Gets Late* (1997).

Jacques-Alain Miller is a practicing psychoanalyst, a founding member of the École de la cause freudienne, and the editor of Lacan's seminars.

Geneviève Morel is a practicing psychoanalyst in Paris and Lille, a member of the École de la cause freudienne, and author of numerous articles on psychoanalytic clinic.

Renata Salecl is Senior Researcher at the Institute of Criminology, Faculty of Law, Ljubljana, and Centennial Professor at the London School of Economics. She is the author of *Spoils of Freedom* (1994), *(Per)versions of Love and Hate* (1998), and *Gaze and Voice as Love Objects* (coedited with Slavoj Žižek, 1996).

Eric L. Santner is Professor of German at the University of Chicago. He is the author of *Stranded Objects* (1992) and *My Own Private Germany* (1997).

Colette Soler is a practicing psychoanalyst in Paris and the author of numerous articles on different aspects of the Lacanian theory.

Paul Verhaeghe is a practicing psychoanalyst and Professor at the University of Ghent. He is the author of *Does the Woman Exist?* (1997).

Slavoj Žižek is Senior Researcher at the Department of Philosophy, University of Ljubljana. His publications include *Tarrying with the Negative* (1993), *Plague of Fantasies* (1997), *The Indivisible Remainder* (1996), and *The Ticklish Subject* (1999).

Alenka Zupančič is a researcher at the Institute of Philosophy, Slovene Academy of Science. She is the author of *Ethics of the Real: Kant, Lacan* (2000).

Index

Library of Congress Cataloging-in-Publication Data
Sexuation / Renata Salecl, editor.
Includes index.
ISBN 0-8223-2437-7 (cloth : acid-free paper)
ISBN 0-8223-2473-3 (paper : acid-free paper)
1. Sex role.   2. Sex differences.   3. Sex differences
(Psychology)   I. Salecl, Renata, 1962–
II. SIC (Durham, N.C.); 3.
HQ1075 .S4975 2000   305.3—dc21   99-050130